VESCO

Other books by Arthur Herzog

Fiction

L*S*I*T*T (TAKEOVER)

THE CRAVING

ARIES RISING

GLAD TO BE HERE

MAKE US HAPPY

IQ 83

HEAT

ORCA

EARTHSOUND

THE SWARM

Nonfiction

THE B.S. FACTOR

THE CHURCH TRAP

MCCARTHY FOR PRESIDENT

THE WAR/PEACE ESTABLISHMENT

VESCO

From Wall Street to Castro's Cuba
The Rise, Fall, and Exile of
the King of White Collar Crime

by Arthur Herzog

Doubleday
New York
1987

Library of Congress Cataloging in Publication Data
Herzog, Arthur.
Vesco: his rise, fall, and flight.
1. Vesco, Robert. 2. Commercial criminals—United States—Biography. 3. White collar crimes—United States. I. Title.
HV6766.V48H47 1987 364.1'68'0924 [B] 87-7423
ISBN 0-385-24176-3

PRINTED IN THE UNITED STATES OF AMERICA
FIRST EDITION

Acknowledgments

José Alfaro
Fred Alger
Carl Anderson
Capt. Paul Aranha
Lilyana Arguello
Jack Auspitz
Shirley Bailey
Everette Bannister
Frank Beatty
Tomás Borge
Captain Ulis Brown
Nigel Bowe
Dr. Luis Burstin
Jessica Burstin
Henry Buhl
Allan Butler
David Butowsky
California Pellet Mill Company
Sheldon Camhy
Rodrigo Carazo
Enrique Carreras
Ken Cartwright
Oleg Cassini
Howard Cerny
George Cihra
Martha Clapp
Paul F. Clarke
Robert Collins
Allan Conwill
Bernard Cornfeld
Richard Coulson
Dr. Arnold Cooper
Betty Cowett
Harvey Dale
Dr. Lev Dobiansky
Ralph Dodd
Paul Drake
Warren Dunn
Roberto Durán
Juan José Echeverría
David Evertt
Philip Farrington
Justin Feldman
Roberto Fernández
José Figueres
Martí Figueres
Garrett Finlayson

Robert Foglia
Ivy French
Raoul Gersten
Peter Gettinger
Gregory Glynn
Milton Gould
Peter Graham
Stanley Graze
Dr. Jaime Gutiérrez
George Haestie
Arthur Hanna, Jr.
Tim Hector
Andrew Heine
Roger Hendrickson
James Herring
Fred Higgs
Anthony L. M. In der Rieden
Kendall Isaacs
Tony Jones
Harvey Karp
John King
Arthur Kramer
Robert Kushner
Ascher Lans
Norman LeBlanc
Melvin Lechner
Bruno Lederer
Arthur Liman
Arthur Lipper, III
John Love
Leslie Mandel
Tex McCrary
Benson McDermott
John McLaughlin
Milton Meissner
Martin Mensch
Raymond Merritt
Emanuel Mosko
George Mosko
Fred Murray
Robert Nagler
Donald Nixon
Daniel Oduber
John Orr
Mike Parnell
Dr. Benjamin Payn
Richard Pershing
Ileana Pinto
José María Pla
David Rea
Laurence Richardson, Jr.
Dawson Roberts
Capt. John Roberts
Thomas Robinson
Donald Rolle
Romano Romani
Henry Rosten
Bill Schacter
Morton Schiowitz
Scott Schmedel
Bud Schlieffer
Horatio Scotland
Stedman Scotland
Ralph Seligman
Paul Shesby
George and Isabel
Patrick Shields
Howard Singer
Fergus Sloan
Martin Solomon
Norman Solomon
Wilbert Snipes
Harvey Spear
Frank Stanton
Mark Strand
Striker Yachts

Julio Suñol
Robert Sutner
Brent Symonette
Tico Times
Tribune (of Nassau)
Patrick Toothe
Said Toub
María Ermida Ulate
Frances Urbina
Robert Vesco
Thomson von Stein
Gerald Walpin
Paul Warnke
Robert Wasson
Norbert Weissberg
Edward Whitcraft

Contents

The Players

(a partial list)

BEATTY, FRANK G.	International Controls Corp.
BIRD, VERN C.	Prime Minister of Antigua
BORGE, TOMÁS	Secretary of the Interior, Nicaragua
BUHL, HENRY	Investors Overseas Services
BUTLER, ALLAN	Butlers Bank, Ltd.
CARRERAS, ENRIQUE	Associate and confidant of José Figueres
CONWILL, ALLAN	Willkie Farr & Gallagher
CORNFELD, BERNARD	IOS
COWETT, EDWARD	IOS
DODD, RALPH	ICC
FIGUERES, JOSÉ	Former President of Costa Rica
FIGUERES, MARTÍ	Businessman and José's son
HOGAN & HARTSON	Washington attorneys
KING, JOHN	Oil fund magnate

KUSHNER, ROBERT	Securities and Exchange Commission
LeBLANC, NORMAN	IOS and Bahamas Commonwealth Bank
LIMAN, ARTHUR	Paul, Weiss, Rifkind
MERRITT, RAYMOND	WF&G
MEISSNER, MILTON	IOS
ODUBER, DANIEL	Former President of Costa Rica
PAYN, DR. BENJAMIN ROBERT	Venture capitalist
PINDLING, LYNDEN O.	Prime Minister of The Bahamas
RICHARDSON, LAURENCE	ICC
SPORKIN, STANLEY	SEC
VESCO, PATRICIA	Wife of Robert, mother of their five children
VESCO, ROBERT LEE	ICC, IOS, fugitive financier

Prologue

Robert Vesco is a historic figure, though not the type who appears on postage stamps. The quarter billion dollars ($425 million in 1986) the U.S. government accused him and others of looting from Bernard Cornfeld's Investors Overseas Services put him at the pinnacle of white collar thieves. That he had simply walked off with all this money was an article of popular faith and it made him a legend despite his comparative youth—Vesco was born on December 4, 1935—as well as the object of probably the most extensive effort on record to bag an alleged white collar crook. He was, if nothing else, durable, and proceeded to hype his way through several small countries on the basis of wealth the Securities and Exchange Commission seemed to have claimed he took, until finally, in Cuba, the strange game ran out, at least for a while.

So notorious did Vesco become, so sullied his reputation, that a man who had worked with him, having most reluctantly admitted me to his office, demanded whether I carried a gun; he was concerned that Vesco had sent me to kill him. I put my hand in my pocket and deliberately pulled it out with a pointed forefinger. "Bang," I said. "You're dead." He nearly jumped out of his skin.

An oddity in the Vesco saga—and there were many, especially after he began to leapfrog around the Caribbean in terror, perhaps demented by then—was that with even a fraction of what he was supposed to have stolen he could have disappeared.

Plastic surgery, a new identity, would have sufficed, or merely a low profile in Costa Rica, for instance, where other purported pirates and brigands have been able to live peacefully. Sooner or later the United States would have lost interest and Costa Rica would have been disposed to let Vesco and his family stay. The fugitive—because Vesco wouldn't return to stand trial—did nothing of the sort. He called attention to himself repeatedly and had the familiar compulsion of the accused to declare his innocence—though not from jail, of which Vesco had a horror.

His protestations went unheard for several reasons. First, though much of the SEC's claims went unproved—defense lawyers attacked them effectively—the news media treated them as established fact, whether they were or weren't, and the case against him seemed overwhelming. The SEC refused Vesco a forum even when he asked for one, albeit on his own terms, and his attempts to clear himself were feeble from a public relations point of view. Second, neither Vesco nor his closest lieutenant, Norman LeBlanc, would or could account for missing money. More than a dozen years later the receivers remained in the dark. Nor did Vesco explain the sources of his at least once abundant cash. Third, the same qualities that had worked for Vesco when he was on the rise—games playing, secretiveness, manipulation, bravado, a slippery streak—worked against him when he was down.

Vesco, intelligent if not articulate, lacked insight into himself. His massive ego and pride led to a self-defeating flair for trouble. Arrayed against him was a savvy, self-righteous government agency that not only detested Vesco for what it called lying but had motives of its own. Lost sight of almost entirely, in the forest of headlines, was that Vesco's supposed crimes had little or no bearing on American investors, normally the SEC's protectorate.

Vesco did not function alone. Assisting him at almost every step in the early days were accountants and attorneys (more than a dozen law firms earned high fees because of Vesco), the cream of their profession, well-tailored, handsomely paid, experienced. Did they knowingly and deliberately participate in a superscam? Were they in their naïveté deceived? Were they objects of SEC overkill? Conceivably, could Vesco not have been guilty except of wolfish ambition, minor league gyps, and influence peddling? Or did he in spite and revenge make the SEC charges realities?

Vesco was a child of the roaring sixties, the "wildest and looniest since the 1920s," in Tom Wolfe's opinion. The period tolerated excesses to a greater extent than we do today, maybe even encouraged them. It encapsulated all manner of high hopes —military (Bay of Pigs, Vietnam), revolutionary (student movement, black riots, the women's movement), monetary (the stock market go-go years), and festooned ambitions. Nobody doubted the sixties would burn still brighter even as the giddy decade skittered toward the fall.

Memory lies, of course—accents the vivid colors, ignores the darker ones, shapes jagged ravines into pretty valleys, deserts into gardens. That house which to childhood's eye appeared so ample is, when revisited, less so. Thus it may be with the past if we remember it as bigger and better than it was. And yet there *was* a special quality about those years—charming, euphoric, insular, greedy, overconfident, comic, extravagant, maybe immature and unfair, as President Kennedy claimed life was. A sense of invincibility abounded. Americans thought they could accomplish (or get away with) just about anything and often did, heedless of the consequences.

The high flying, big new money people, of whom Vesco was one, had a permissive attitude toward the get-rich-quick clause in the American dream. The SEC frequently disagreed with their methods and sought to impose its yoke, sometimes by making examples. Many of the upstart superwealthy, poor to start with, had a contemptuous attitude toward the "establishment" that, for them, the SEC served. Their ambitious intransigence caused the agency to react. Since the American securities industry was increasingly international, the Vesco case related to the expansion of U.S. power over securities markets abroad as well as at home, just as the *pax Americana* of the period sought to impose an American vision of peace upon the world.

Almost like an expression of that superior attitude, an NBC team with a long distance lens sneaked a shot of Vesco, who was prevented by the Cubans from granting interviews, outside his Havana house. If the picture is fuzzy, the mood of the subject is not. A morose man stares across a gap of not just yards but years. He had taken a tortuous road of defiance that had led him and members of his family from New Jersey to the Bahamas, Costa Rica, back to the Bahamas, Antigua, back to Costa Rica, Nicaragua, and Cuba from which he wanted out. His hosts would be happy to have him leave, but Vesco, thus far, has nowhere safe to go.

If Vesco is guilty as charged, he should be understood and learned from. If he is a victim of narrow justice and his own character, the same holds true.

Part One

ENTREPRENEUR

1

AN AMBITIOUS ADOLESCENT

In the late 1960s, as the result of a takeover battle, Robert Vesco's image required a little polishing, and a public relations man named Munro Schwebel suggested that the fledgling financier talk to a tape recorder about his rags-to-riches career which, to the publicist, had all the ingredients of the American dream. As an adolescent, Vesco told the machine, he had three ambitions—to "get the hell out of Detroit," to be the president of a corporation, and to become a millionaire. By then, though, these objectives had been accomplished and superseded by others—to head a major conglomerate; to have his face on the cover of *Fortune* magazine, where Schwebel hoped to put it; to be appointed a U.S. ambassador; and to be among the richest men in the world. Vesco was still less than thirty-five years old.

Vesco's photo was indeed widely published, not as the business hero he fully expected to be but as the perpetrator of the "largest securities fraud of modern times." How his good parents, Barbara and Donald Vesco, must have groaned to read about his historically evil accomplishments, not that they believed him guilty—a looter who had pilfered nearly a quarter-billion dollars of other people's money, and a fugitive who had evaded all attempts of the mighty U.S. government to apprehend him. Over the years, as he popped up here and there, the "Bootstrap Kid," as a Washington columnist dubbed him, became a news magnet and the list of what he was allegedly implicated in lengthened. He was supposed to be the fomenter of a revolution on one southerly island and the would-be king of another, the briber of governments, a trafficker in arms, high-tech equipment, and narcotics. He was even accused of attempted murder.

Vesco was listed in the Encyclopedia Britannica, sandwiched between Liv Ullmann and Kurt Vonnegut, Jr. *Forbes* magazine, even after it raised the bottom limit to $200 million, continued to include Vesco among the four hundred richest Americans, presenting his wealth classification as "Thief." By 1985, though, Vesco had vanished from the magazine's list of plutocrats. Said *Forbes,* October 28, 1985:

> REMOVED:
>
> Vesco, Robert Lee. Havana, Cuba. 50. Estimated $150 million fortune 1984 (fugitive, looted European mutual fund empire). Recent press reports of poverty and house arrest by Castro create doubts about previous wealth estimates.

He was the subject of more than one Doonesbury cartoon—"Robert Vesco . . . In prideful recognition of all you've gotten away with, the Baby Doc college of physicians takes great pleasure in conferring on you the degree of Doctor of Arts and Leisure."

The magnitude of the charges against Vesco, the publicity he received and the embarrassment his successful defiance caused American authorities led to an unparalleled effort by the U.S. government to prosecute the "Kingfish." ("Operation Kingfish" was the government plan to bring him back, by force if necessary, to the country he denied he was any longer a citizen of. Involved were the CIA, FBI, U.S. marshals, Securities and Exchange Commission, Department of Justice, IRS, Customs Service, Department of State, Coast Guard, and congressional committees.) Vesco became Public Enemy Number 1. Nothing in his gung-ho America background or attitudes suggested such a denouement.

Catholics, Vesco's parents lived in a working class, multiethnic neighborhood on Detroit's near east side, close to good schools and relatively safe. Years later, in Costa Rica, Vesco would demonstrate his street smarts with a piece of paper dipped in ink to leave a mark on his opponent as though the paper were a switchblade. It is symptomatic of the transient, decaying nature of many U.S. inner cities that nobody now in the neighborhood remembers the Vescos, and the address on Hastings Street where Bob supposedly grew up is a vacant lot. Then, though, the Vescos were upwardly striving, if not for themselves, for their son, of whom they were greatly proud. Robert's mother, born Barbara Sassek and of Slovenian heritage, had an office job. Donald, whose parents had been northern Italian immigrants, worked for Chrysler as a supervisor on an assembly line, and, in the 1960s, for the company's Redstone rocket project in Alabama. Vesco often spoke about the poverty he and his elder sister, who became a professor of psychology at a Midwestern university, were reared in, and one reason he adduced for his consuming love of pizza was that it was about the only food the family could afford to order when eating out, hence a luxury. Still, he was born in 1935, and was thus a child during World War II, when unemployment barely existed and pay was good. Typically, Vesco may have made too much of the family's financial straits.

When Bob was seventeen, the Vescos rented a nice, five-room brick-and-shingle house, planting a European vegetable garden in the backyard. A then-neighbor called them "a nice family, friendly when you saw them in the yard or on the porch, but hard workers, with little time for socializing." Donald Vesco must have puzzled over what he, a stern disciplinarian, had taught his offspring. "He and his father would hit the books every night at a table in their kitchen. Sometimes they'd still be poring over them, his father helping the boy, at two or three in the morning." Another neighbor, who lived across Hastings Street from the Vescos for nine years, reported, "You couldn't have asked for nicer neighbors than the Vescos. Bob was always a good, clean-cut boy. Polite. Respectful of his elders. He couldn't get enough education. He was always studying." That Vesco was a quick learner was noted then as well as later. "He was a thinker."

The thinker went to Cass Tech, one of the best technical schools in the city, dropping out for economic reasons, he said. He first sold newspapers and then laid brick. He worked at a body shop and later remembered, "We took in cars that were wrecks and we put new fenders on, painted them—that was during the day. At night and on weekends I worked as a driver. Including the moonlighting, I made fifty dollars a week." He may have been arrested once or twice, but Michigan authorities have no such records and perhaps the cases were dropped. Vesco started his junior year at Pershing High but quit again. In early 1953, he tried high school still a third time, at Denby, also considered first-rate, but dropped out once more. In 1983, the Denby class Vesco would have graduated with held its thirtieth reunion but only three recalled, or admitted to recalling, young Bob. One described him as the "class bully. He was kind of a chubby kid." Another said he was "pretty much of a loner. I don't remember him as having any friends." The third said, "He was very quiet, very quiet."

Vesco had a grown-up reason for leaving school, a wife. Patricia Melzer was plain, short, round-faced, sweet, and dependent. Of German descent, one of her parents was Catholic, the other Baptist. She was the only female among four children and the youngest. Her father was so proud to have sired a female that he walked several miles to tell his neighbors. The Melzers were farmers and poor, yet had Pat possessed an operable crystal ball, she would have seen a Boeing 707 with her husband's initials on the tail and *Patricia* emblazoned on the sterns of luxury yachts. The Melzers had recently moved to Detroit from Bad Axe, in what the locals call the "thumb" area of northern Michigan. The couple married in June 1953—both were seventeen, with Pat a few weeks older than Bob—and later that year Daniel William was born. Vesco's thoughtful (though in private sometimes bad-tempered) behavior toward his wife invariably impressed people, and he seems to have been a dutiful son-in-law as well. A relative said about Pat's mother, Anna, "From what she used to tell me, she liked him a whole lot. He took care of her, she being old and such."

The Vescos lived in a studio apartment in a simple four-room brick-and-fieldstone house not far from where he had been raised. "He was the only educated man I ever had as a tenant," the landlord said. "And they left the place scrupulously clean—I'll never forget that, either." Vesco continued to study diligently at night. He attended, he told the tape recorder, evening courses at Wayne State University three times a week as "part of my own internal improvement program to get an engineering background," but the school has no record of his having been there—perhaps he sat in. He took correspondence courses at the American School, in Chicago, for nearly three years, through 1957, for a high school diploma, completing only half the courses. "He did excellent work, I must say," a school official observed. "He must've had something on the ball or he wouldn't have gotten the grades he did here. It's amazing he didn't go on and finish, but he didn't need to, in my opinion. He had enough without it."

Throughout his career, Vesco was guilty of exaggerations—hyperbole seemed an essential part of his makeup. He told a friend two different stories about military service—that he had served briefly in the U.S. Navy, but had been discharged for flat feet, and that he had been rejected for military service for the same deficiency. The friend, curious enough to glance at Vesco's feet on the beach, didn't think they looked especially flat. More likely, he thought, Vesco was draft-exempt because he had a wife and young child, but he wanted to embellish.

In the early 1950s, leaving the body shop, Vesco was able to convince the Packard Motor Company to hire him as a blueprint operator and trainee draftsman. Years later, in Cuba, he blamed problems with his sight on long hours he spent in his youth squinting at a drafting board. He read a want ad for a job at a Detroit aluminum-and-brass company. He had grown a mustache to look older and lied about his age; though underqualified, he was hired as an "extrusion engineer," a metal shaper. (Later, he was always searching for an aluminum extrusion company to acquire.) He was well aware of his "questionable lack of background" but believed, along with countless others facing the Chinese puzzle of how to start the job experience part of a résumé, that if he were hired he would perform. As always, he put in long hours and began "physically designing tools" and "estimating costs." He still earned only $50 a week and received no overtime.

The adolescent Vesco emerges as an unusual young man. His motivation was intense. He had no spring breaks during which to beer it up at Fort Lauderdale or the Bahamas. Not a student, he was a stripling careerist, extraordinarily ambitious, cannily appraising his prospects for success. He was a youth determined to break out of the lower middle class, and quickly or not at all. He would have no help except for what he himself could provide. And he already had a wife and child. He wanted to be in business and decided that although company presidents were "typically engineering- or manufacturing-type people" the keys to the kingdom were in "marketing and sales."

Vesco quit the aluminum company for a sales job at Reynolds Metal at a salary of $505.50 a month. He wore a sports jacket and slacks—he couldn't afford a suit—and his shoes were described as "zipped up in front, with a tongue over the zipper." During his year and a half at Reynolds, he was credited with helping to design the first one-piece pressure-produced aluminum grille for, he said, the 1958 Oldsmobile. Since, according to what reporters were told by Oldsmobile, aluminum grilles were introduced on its production cars only in 1966, the discrepancy, after Vesco became a villain, was employed by journalists as one more proof of his propensity to fabricate, which, in this instance at least, wasn't the case. He probably worked on an experimental model and received a letter of congratulations and a check for $500, not small for those days.

Soon after, following his impatient and precocious game plan, Vesco quit Reynolds. He had acquired the "sales-engineering background. The next thing was to get into something like a staff function . . . so that I could get experience as a general manager running something and being directly responsible for it and [at the same time] getting exposed to the financial community as such," thought he, who could scarcely complete a sentence without "get." At age twenty-one or so, he was hired by Olin-Mathieson (later the Olin Corp.) as an extrusion engineer starting at $750 a month. He was soon promoted to administrative assistant in the engineering division and transferred to the head office in New York City. To "get the hell out of Detroit" had been accomplished.

2

CAPTIVE SEAL

In 1986, in Cuba, Vesco was thin but not gaunt, good-looking and youthful for his fifty years. In 1974, he was described as a "colorless person with a tendency toward spreading flaccidity. He stood six-foot-one, weighed about two hundred pounds, and had dark, greased-down hair, heavy eyebrows and small avaricious eyes that conveyed the impression of eternal wariness. He did not stare at people but coldly peered through them, and his speech was often brutally direct."* Vesco would squint and his eyes wavered in social situations when he wasn't comfortable; his eyes didn't strike me as especially small, and, in any case, eyeballs don't convey avariciousness or anything else, although the pupil may dilate if the individual is sexually aroused or on drugs. The writer strained for a cliché about a master crook. (If white collar crime usually involves lying, the accomplished liar, to be good at it, must of necessity avoid the eye stereotype—shifty, cunning, deceitful—so as not to be detected.)

Despite his lack of a matching business suit, Vesco did well at Olin, but he wasn't considered a standout although he made a specialist rating and worked as an engineer and a designer. The "180 lb. six-footer with pale intense eyes and a long upper lip bisected [sic] by a thin 1950s mustache," as the New York *Post* put it (after Vesco became notorious, the mustache was termed "Hitlerian"), lived in a modest frame house in Rowayton, Connecti-

* Robert Hutchison, *Vesco*, Praeger, 1974, pp. 13–14.

cut, commuting by train. His salary was $10,500 annually, about $28,000 in 1986 dollars, not bad for a high school dropout in his early twenties. Olin paid higher than usual wages to attract capable people.

He remained with Olin for three years, his longest employment and his last as a salaried worker. His departure was slightly acrimonious because his bosses thought Vesco owed more loyalty, while he regarded himself as underpaid and trapped within a seniority system that didn't properly reward his self-proclaimed talents. "After a while," he said, "I became involved in cost accounting and finance and decided I no longer wanted to be just an employee. I left Olin and formed a small company of my own, selling merchandise to manufacturing firms on a commission basis. It was a struggle, but I was my own boss."

A neighbor with whom the Vescos had backyard barbecues and drinks, and with whom Bob played poker, recalled that Vesco came over and announced boldly, "I quit. I'm going off on my own. I'll be a millionaire in five years." For the neighbor, "It was the damnedest thing. He didn't have a cent." Vesco had an active fantasy life.

Borrowing several thousand dollars from a bank, twenty-four-year-old Vesco moved with his family to Denville, New Jersey, their belongings filling the car and piled on the roof. "I had a 1957 Plymouth. I used to hop in the car Monday morning and come back Saturday night after trying to sell and buy things." He discovered an outfit called Eagle Aluminum Products, in Dover, New Jersey, with an idle press in its plant. Vesco proposed that if Eagle would hire a crew he would merchandise the output and split the profits. He had a card printed up that said "Aluminum Services Incorporated," and, adding several men who moonlighted for him, he sold aluminum garage doors, sidings, awnings, and so on. He also formed his own company, Primawin. "I had this terrible problem of accounts receivable . . . in the course of this, some of my receivables went bad. So I took stock instead in the companies that couldn't pay. It was my first taste as an equity owner—generally in losing concerns." He made "quite a few dollars," but he was twenty-six, with three children to support.

"Eventually, Vesco obtained financing from somewhere—but the sources have remained a mystery. Federal investigators told me, however, that they traced some of the money to organized crime figures."† This was the sort of unsubstantiated allegation that would crop up continually in the Vesco case in which unnamed "Federal investigators" were quoted. Far from being a Mafioso, Vesco's first serious investor was a slight, aristocratic, European independent entrepreneur and financial adviser named Dr. Benjamin Robert Payn. An author and specialist in international relations, Payn held the French Legion of Honor for his contributions to Franco-American relations. He lived in New York, where, on March 30, 1961, his diary recorded, a stockbroker phoned and, knowing Payn was interested in technological companies, suggested he talk to a Robert Vesco, who had one to offer. Payn managed to find a half hour in his schedule toward the end of the day, and Vesco told him that he was a consultant for a tiny company in Fairfield, New Jersey, that owned the rights to, and assembled, two engineering devices, a valve and a pressure switch containing a small access hole sealed by an O-ring, hence Captive Seal, formerly Bergen Research & Engineering, which had developed the valve. The devices were primarily used in aerospace and defense industries and had been accepted for the Pershing, Gemini, and Titan rocket booster systems. Among the customers, said the young man, were such companies as Martin Marietta. Vesco showed Captive Seal's profit and loss statement to Payn and was candid in saying that unless the company got an instant infusion of $125,000, it would go under.

Payn, although impressed by the products, said that under no circumstances would he be involved or involve his friends without the opportunity to investigate Captive Seal from top to bottom, for which there didn't seem time, given the emergency. Vesco, who struck Payn as financially sophisticated, seemed prepared. If he could have $25,000 within a matter of days, "I can get by for a month until you decide whether to invest more money." (Payn noticed the first-person singular.)

The independent entrepreneur then went from his office to

† Michael Dorman, *Vesco, the Infernal Money Making Machine,* Berkley Medallion Books, 1975, p. 210.

the nearby Harmonie Club, where a dinner was being given in honor of Baron Edmond de Rothschild. Also attending were such friends and associates as General David Sarnoff, of RCA, and Frank and Arthur Stanton, brothers who had the Volkswagen import license for New York and distributorship on Long Island. Over brandy after dinner, Payn learned that the Stantons had just become partners with Rothschild in a venture capital outfit called HH Industries and were interested in small technological companies. Frank Stanton wondered if Payn knew about any. "As a matter of fact," said Payn, "there was this young man this afternoon . . ."

The result was a lunch with Payn, Vesco, and Frank Stanton. Payn and Stanton visited the Fairfield, New Jersey, company, which had about a dozen employees and did $100,000 a year in business. "I like the kid," Stanton said tentatively. "He has a lot on the ball." Payn sized up Vesco as a man of high intelligence with a computerlike mind—"He could put together a financial edifice it would have taken three or four Wall Street guys to accomplish." Payn advanced the $25,000 on his own, but later had a private reservation that tells a little about how smart investors use clues. "It was his car, a late-model Lincoln with air-conditioning and a telephone. In those days, only tycoons had telephones in their cars. I said to myself, 'Air-conditioning! A phone! This is a boy who knows how to spend.' A warning flag went up." Payn didn't realize the Lincoln was leased by Captive Seal for Vesco.

HH Industries—the Rothschild, Stanton group—partly because of Payn, invested $100,000 in Captive Seal and that was the start of Vesco's remarkable career. Still, Frank Stanton had doubts. Vesco made him uncomfortable. The New Jersey kid came to see him at his apartment in the Dakota on a hot summer day wearing a double-breasted suit, a homburg, and gloves, saying, "If my chauffeur calls, tell him to circle the block if he has to." Stanton was reasonably sure Vesco did not have a chauffeur, unless Ralph Dodd, the plant manager, could be considered one. (In the early days, Dodd and Vesco would flip a coin to decide whose heap they would drive to the city.) Bob's tendency to be careless with information led Stanton to have him investigated by a detective agency which turned up the fact that Vesco was not a graduate of Wayne State, as he claimed. He also said so later in his listing in Who's Who in Finance and Industry. Nor, as time passed, was Stanton impressed with Vesco's business methods. "Instead of talking about building a sound engineering company, he was always dropping names of people he knew," observed Stanton, who also especially didn't like Vesco's "bandying the Rothschild name." How Vesco learned of Rothschild's investment was a mystery to Payn. The supermillionaire Rothschilds, of course, are legendary in world finance, and Payn, who was both Edmond's friend and, on occasion, a financial advisor, went out of his way to conceal the connection, but somehow Vesco found out and bragged about it constantly to his New Jersey pals. Still, Rothschild backing or not, Captive Seal was sometimes so broke that Vesco pitched pennies with the garbageman for the bill, and won.

As a result of the HH investment, Payn, Stanton, and a senior partner of a New York law firm went on the Captive Seal board, with Payn becoming unpaid treasurer. Vesco as operating head of the company earned $15,000 a year. He was later raised to $18,000 but never asked for it—in Payn's opinion, Bob regarded the money as chicken feed. Payn sometimes lunched with Vesco at Fairfield and Bob spoke about his background. "He would show the well-born rich that he could play the money game as well as they. He was obsessed with success and little else mattered except his family."

To the European, Vesco was a brilliant engineer despite his lack of formal training, with "an uncanny ability to grasp a problem no matter how intricate," and tireless, too. Once, when a Captive Seal device failed to function properly, which might have jeopardized a vital contract, Vesco, along with Dodd, flew to Martin Marietta in Denver, worked there all day and half the night, flew back, went directly to Captive Seal, showered, spent the day, flew back to Denver and returned to Captive Seal. He had been without sleep for thirty-six hours but showed no sign of fatigue. "He had energy and stamina that I'd never witnessed," Payn observed.

An important board meeting was scheduled by Vesco, who

lay in a hospital with a urinary complaint. A half hour after the meeting started, a car drew up outside the building, and Vesco, helped by Dodd, emerged, sickly white and wearing padding around the middle of his body that Payn correctly suspected housed a catheter in his penis and a bottle. That sort of courage and tenacity—Vesco, Dodd, and their wives would assemble valves on weekends, and the men worked twelve hours a day, seven days a week; Vesco and Dodd won the New Jersey Small Business Award—had to be weighed against negative factors that, over the years, would appear again and again in Vesco's behavior. A potentially profitable sale of the company fell through because of Vesco's overly aggressive bargaining. There was Vesco's treatment of the company's founder and president, Peter Palen, to consider. Palen, a martinis-at-lunch man, found himself slowly stripped of his functions by the capable, forceful Vesco, the executive vice president. It reached the yelling, pushing, and shoving stage, until Palen appeared at Frank Stanton's home nearly in tears over the humiliation. Palen then resigned. It was not unusual for an inventor to be supplanted by people superior at business, but the board found young Vesco harsh.

Vesco had a flair for the dramatic, as when, due to fly out of Kennedy Airport with Payn, and late, he phoned from a chartered aircraft to leave word he'd meet him at the plane. Small companies didn't normally have a telex and sophisticated switchboard equipment such as Vesco had installed. He was always thinking ahead to larger endeavors, and ever more money was needed. The HH partners complied until they had put $400,000 in Captive Seal, some in bank loans they guaranteed. Vesco had his sights set on a big business.

Although the investors by then held 52 percent of the company, they found Vesco impossible to control. An idea approved by them would be changed and the change executed by the time they met again. Vesco would bid for even larger contracts, neglecting smaller ones the company already had. Captive Seal swelled to thirty employees, and the profit-and-loss statement looked good because it included work in progress, but the figures made no provision for jobs being rejected, as happened frequently in the precision-components business. The partners didn't know where they stood.

Vesco wanted to go public. The partners refused because they weren't certain the company would succeed. In the summer of 1965, Vesco called a directors meeting at which he presented a detailed plan, several inches thick and replete with charts and diagrams, for growth and acquisitions. They found the proposal good, and might have gone along except for the fear that the $1 million they would have to put up could become $2 million before long. Where would it stop? Bob was too much to handle and they asked to be bought out, accepting Vesco's offer. "I have a good thing going," he announced, "and I don't want you to come back and say I didn't tell you."

Vesco paid only $12,500 in cash and notes. Payn took the cash, as he subsequently regretted, in settlement and he lost money as a result. Rothschild held on. Later, when the price of his International Controls Corporation stock had soared, Vesco offered to exchange the notes for ICC letter shares, that is, unregistered stock. "We came out all right with Vesco," Rothschild remarked. On an investment of $250,000, he emerged with a profit of between $1 million and $1.25 million in less than eighteen months.

Payn said, "Bob never lied to us. He gave us the news as it came, good or bad, and he ran the company well. He was an excellent manager, though extravagant. He had only a slender hope for money and power, and once he got them, greed—hubris —may have overtaken him and led him into exile. But if the goal of capitalism is making money, Bob did the right things. I might have thought that Vesco suffered from what the Germans call *Grossenwahnsinn*—grandiosity syndrome—except that he achieved what he set out to do. He was too intelligent to have been dishonest, at least then."

3

A BRASH GUY

In Denville, where the family lived in a $27,000, ranch-style development house, paying by installments, Vesco wasn't taken seriously at first. He was regarded as somewhat eccentric, a show-off without much substance. He wished to be accepted, serving on a town board and joining two country clubs, but he struck people as a hustler in search of a break and always hungry for money. Nobody could have been more surprised than those to whom Vesco had bragged he would become a millionaire when he suddenly was one.

Howard Milligan, a millionaire-to-be road builder, bought a parcel of land, setting aside an acre for recreation on which he put a tennis court. He also installed a baseball diamond, and Vesco and other neighbors worked with bare hands to construct it. Though not a good athlete, Vesco was a decent hardball pitcher and coached a Little League team on which a son played. With Milligan and another partner, Vesco bought a bar on a highway, the Powder Mill Inn, at little cost, and they fixed it up, with Vesco sometimes running the cash register. His name went on the liquor license application, which meant he had to undergo an investigation that included fingerprints. Milligan was slightly relieved that Vesco didn't have a criminal record.

Vesco was on the flashy side. When Milligan was elected mayor of Denville (population 14,000), Vesco playfully presented him with a top hat. To celebrate a wedding anniversary, he had

Pat fetched by chauffeured limousine, amusing the neighbors who knew he couldn't afford the gesture. He wasn't believed when he claimed that a Rothschild was his backer or that he had placed the first overseas telephone call from a car. (He had phoned Payn who was in London.) He would order the most expensive wines on the menu, and, at the Englewood Country Club, some of whose members were Buddy Hackett, Joey Bishop, Dick Shawn, and assorted Mafiosi (one of whom, later murdered, played golf accompanied by three bodyguards in business suits), Vesco had the best equipment though he was a poor golfer and something of a cheat. At the other club, Rockaway River, whose members included New Jersey politicians and judges, his handicap was thirty, the limit, and after he became a fugitive, a member amused himself by putting other people's scores in Vesco's name so that his handicap quickly fell to one or two, making him perhaps the most improved golfer in the land. The FBI made an excited visit, believing Vesco had returned.

Some thought that Vesco liked to imagine himself as a swashbuckling Errol Flynn. He would later call himself the "Che Guevara" of international finance. But Pal Joey, or Sky Masterson in *Guys and Dolls,* would have been more accurate. People recall him as having had a strong resemblance to Richard Gere in *Cotton Club.* He wore what he considered sharp clothes, like a black mohair suit, a red velvet smoking jacket, and ascot. He put clear polish on his fingernails. Always more than a bit of an actor, he could talk out of the side of his mouth when with a gambling crowd. He partied, drank too much sometimes, and played around when away from home. Once, in Las Vegas, he woke up late. Quickly leaving the woman in bed, he raced to the airport, wearing only shoes, pants, and an overcoat. For such reasons, perhaps, his wife, a "sweet, friendly, long-suffering dumpling," as she was described, occasionally blew up, and when she did, where didn't seem to matter. "Go fuck yourself, you son of a bitch," she'd rage in public and, throwing up her hands, add apologetically to someone who had overheard, "You know Bob." One of her outbursts occurred at the fashionable New York restaurant Lutèce.

The couple drank—Vesco once ostentatiously left a hundred

dollar tip for one round, which Pat snatched off the table; a little scuffle between them ensued—and ate out, but almost never entertained at home. They didn't have a chauffeur—an employee sometimes drove Vesco—a maid, a summer house, or a boat, even when rich. (Vesco's yachting tendencies came later.) An associate related that Vesco showed him a large oil painting he had on consignment, and, when the man returned some weeks later, Vesco had copied it, returning the original. He was proud of his creation. "Culture," however, wasn't for the Vescos—no museums, ballet, theater, opera, or even many movies. Pat liked soap operas on TV, but Bob generally ignored television. Two of his 1960s favorites, though, are interesting in retrospect: the movie *The Thomas Crown Affair* with Steve McQueen, about a swindler, and "Mission Impossible." Overweight, he didn't exercise a great deal. He did play a fine game of chess, but what he enjoyed most was gambling—of almost any sort—and he knew gamblers. He hung out at race tracks ("Bob could figure out the odds on the tote board before the track people," said one companion), and, for a while, he and Dodd ran a string of bingo parlors in Pennsylvania. Vesco won $1,000 in a chess game with a well-known comic. The comedian delayed paying, and when Vesco finally collected he sold the check in a roomful of people for $200 to embarrass the man, who was present.

Serious poker players believe card style is the best reflection of personality. Vesco had rented a small office in Denville to house a stock market ticker, he said, but as far as anybody could see the only use for the place was to keep gifts for the kids at Christmas time and for poker games that sometimes ran from Saturday evening until Monday morning nonstop. Once, Vesco staked a card shark in a game without telling his friends. He asked someone almost plaintively why he always called his bets and was told, "Because I know you're trying to steal the pot." Vesco's bluffs were sometimes foolish. During a table-stakes session on a Sunday morning, a little guy the others considered a lightweight hood, a term used liberally in those parts, stood pat. "Honest John," who had an auction house on the highway and lent money at high interest, took one card in five-card draw, as did Vesco. Raises were limited; he took the last allowed, though to raise into a pat hand *plus* a one-card draw means you almost have to have a high hand yourself. The others called as Vesco had gambled they wouldn't, thinking they bluffed. The little guy showed teeth and aces full, but Honest John laid down, card by card, a king-high straight flush. Vesco couldn't afford the loss—$9,000 or $10,000—and had to ask for time to pay. "However sleazy Bob could be, he was always scrupulous about personal obligations," remarked a gambling buddy. "But if he won he'd tell you what a great gambler he was, and if he lost he'd pretend he didn't care, which, given his finances, of course he did. Vesco was tremendously proud. The worst thing you could do was to humiliate him."

The gambling became bigger as Vesco got richer. Once his secretary had to lend him $10,000 because shylocks were after him, but later he won $130,000 at the Paradise Island (Bahamas) casino in a single night. At Las Vegas, Vesco and Dodd had a rented Cadillac convertible, and instead of waiting to be parked, Dodd drove the car into a hotel lobby and up the steps, leaving the keys. When they emerged from the casino, the convertible was ready in front. On an airline, the two replaced the flight attendants and served drinks, touting their company. Snowbound in a bowling alley, they persuaded the bowlers to dance and turned the place into a disco. "Vesco was a sweetheart," Dodd recalled.

Still, "Rapid Robert," as someone nicknamed him, hated to part with his own money and used it as little as possible. He charged gambling losses to the company, and, though repaying them, "acted as though he had a private printing press for company stock," said a former ICC employee. In 1967, the Vescos sold the Denville house for $35,000, buying, for $52,000, a four-and-a-half-acre property in nearby Boonton Township (population 3,000), thirty miles west of New York City. The Vescos rebuilt the split-level house and two-car garage into a fairly modest U-shaped house.

Included in the acreage were three other houses. One ". . . a small bungalow situated on one and a half acres along the western boundary of the estate, had been owned by an International Controls employee named Scott, whom Vesco had transferred to California. As part of the transfer package, Vesco had

International Controls buy the property, which he then incorporated into his expanding estate, installing his parents in the Scott bungalow rent-free. Vesco's intention was to transfer ownership at cost to one of his family holding companies, but he never got round to it. It was an eminent example of his using corporate assets to finance his personal deals."* Vesco's rationale was that he was the company and vice versa.

He then began to add eighty or so acres to the original property. Vesco built a kidney-shaped swimming pool, a man-made lake stocked with fish, and, for his daughter Dawn, an indoor stable they called the "barn." Nearly the length of a football field, it had eighteen stalls, two indoor riding rinks, and a manager. Vesco installed a landing pad for helicopters to which neighbors, who rarely saw Vesco, violently objected. The estate cost about $500,000 without the $75,000 stable. Patricia seemed to understand her husband's business but displayed a poor perception of his wealth though Bob gave her a $65,000 ring. (He tried to hand himself a bonus to pay for it, but company lawyers stopped him, pointing out that summer was not the time for bonuses.) "I never asked for anything," Pat said. "I rarely used charge accounts at New York stores." She mostly shopped instead at medium-priced New Jersey dress shops. "I don't know if we owned stocks. I know he earned more than $10,000 a year. We spent more than $10,000 a year." Pat's faulty mathematics led her to bounce checks, so Vesco's secretary since Captive Seal, Shirley Bailey, paid the family bills. "I was busy raising a family," Pat explained. "I had a hyperactive kid. It took all my time."

In 1964, when she was six or so months pregnant, Pat gave birth to twins weighing only a few pounds. Paige (of all the six kids, Robert Jr. and Paige were the only ones baptized) died shortly after birth—the Vescos bought a plaque for her at Riverside Hospital, for which Pat gave teas and lunches to raise funds. Robert Jr. was born with coordination difficulties and a learning disability that stemmed from hyperkinesia. He was excitable and easily distracted. The Wilson School at Mountain Lake, where the the Vesco children went, had a special department for children

* Hutchison, *Vesco,* p. 38.

with such problems, and Vesco equipped a wing for them. He also bought a building across the street for the headmaster's use as a residence—these were charitable contributions in Vesco's International Controls warrants, which he couldn't sell because of short-term profits. (Under federal securities laws, short-swing profits by insiders are recoverable by the company.) Robert Jr.'s condition caused his father anguish, even guilt, and that may have been a reason for the gifts he heaped on the kids, like two Snowmobiles and a basement filled with pinball machines. (Later, Vesco flew home from Europe at the expense of one of the companies he controlled to watch his sons play baseball; for effect, his associates thought.) He kissed the kids goodnight and took time out from business to watch them play sports. Still, he was all work and they may have resented it. Danny, who emulated his father although his schoolmates told him Bob was a Sicilian hood, ran away twice and had to be retrieved.

Vesco was a creature of his own images. If he had his secretary, Shirley Bailey, take notes during dinner at a restaurant, and then work half the night with her, it was almost as though he imitated the Hollywood version of a big business executive. If he could be tough to deal with, that was the American way, and Vesco was a patriotic, Republican American. If he name-dropped to show his influence, that was part of the game. Vesco was a man who tried to turn everything to his own advantage, even illness. About his chronic urinary problem, he muttered, "It isn't your run-of-the-mill ulcer. You must have the pressures important leaders are exposed to, to have the disease." (Once, sick with it, he didn't want a one- or two-day absence known because he thought the price of ICC's stock might fall.)

A photograph taken at the Alfred E. Smith Memorial Dinner in December 1968, shows President Johnson and President-elect Nixon, both in evening clothes, with Vesco, similarly attired, just behind them. The proximity was a distortion caused by the tiered seating, and Vesco was there only because his new friend Henry Buhl had invited him after Vesco had made a contribution to the dinner, largely funded by Buhl's mother. Vesco was introduced to Nixon when he came by to say hello to James Roosevelt, Buhl's other guest.

In London, in late 1968, Vesco said he had to give money away because of income tax problems. Buhl suggested charitable donations and had three ideas, the London Symphony Orchestra—Buhl was on the board; his alma mater, the Brooks School—Vesco wanted to send his children there; and the Smith dinner. The three contributions came to $65–$70 thousand, Buhl thought. Vesco also attended, with Buhl, the Smith event in 1969.

There was no indication that Vesco was ever a Nixon friend, much less a confidant—though later he did know the President's brothers, Edgar and Donald—but he proudly gave copies of the picture to close associates, inscribed, "Would you believe the U.S. government the next ICC acquisition? Bob."

4

A NEW TYCOON

The about-to-be tycoon—from the Japanese *taikun* (shogun), derived from the Chinese for "great ruler"—immersed himself in literature on acquisitions, mergers, proxy fights, accounting, and other techniques for corporate aggression. Spotting a relevant law book in his attorney's office, he borrowed it and returned it a few days later with the contents memorized. "I woke up with a substantial interest in various small companies, and I decided to put them all together into one company and run it like a business. That, I suppose, was the birth of an idea which materialized into the company called International Controls," said Vesco. The only substantial asset Vesco had was Captive Seal, heavily in debt, and his notion of running a business was to increase its size.

But his instincts were unerring. What was to be the go-go decade on Wall Street had begun badly, with the Dow Jones industrial average dropping from its previous high of 734, in mid-November 1961—the Bay of Pigs occurred during this period—to 524 by May 1962, a decline of about a third. On one day alone the market dropped almost 35 points—read more than 100 points in today's terms—and many feared the Big Bear, a 1929-type collapse. Starting then, though, the market turned buoyant, breaking 1,000 in 1965, which, if subsequent inflation is weighed in, would be 2,500 now. Conditions were ideal for the rise in price of the stocks of conglomerates.

Far-sighted people understood that serious inflation was in

the wings—that "A dollar was a deposit on ten." Borrowed dollars could be repaid with inflated dollars that would cost far less. Acquisitions made sense *if* you borrowed to pay for them. And interest in what we call today "high technology" was increasingly intense, especially if the technology concerned missiles and military equipment needed by the U.S. government for the Vietnam war.

In 1965, Vesco incorporated International Controls. The name meant little unless as an unconscious expression of his intense need to control every aspect of his environment. Another dwarf, Cryogenics, headquartered in Virginia, manufactured ultracold devices. Though its esoteric technology had promise, Vesco wanted it for a different reason. Also in debt, Cryogenics was a public company, listed over the counter, and Vesco saw it as a vehicle to list International Controls without having to undergo SEC filing and registration proceedings. He got in touch with Richard Pershing, vice-president of Western Business Associates, the majority owner of Broadway-Hale Stores, and bought with ICC stock 51 percent of Cryogenics' outstanding shares. Vesco appointed himself president and, with stockholder approval, merged International Controls into Cryogenics, which changed its name back to International Controls, the corporate survivor, legally domiciled in Florida. ". . . we became a public company through the back door," Vesco said.

The new company issued additional stock that could be used to acquire other companies. "Vesco had an uncanny ability to find people who were weak," said a former associate, and pointed to the 1965 example of a New Jersey machine shop Bob learned was in financial trouble. He had the machinery appraised, took the appraisal to a leasing company and borrowed money on it. Paying the company's debts, he issued preferred stock in the same company and gave it to the owner as payment. "The thing is, the owner could have done the same himself." But Bob insisted that the stock, convertible into ICC shares, would gain in value, and the profits far exceeded what the original owners might have earned by running their own business. And, as long as the ICC stock price rose, everybody was happy.

Vesco was always on the trail in search of money. Warren

Dunn, his personal lawyer, kept a briefcase in his office with socks, underwear, a toothbrush, and a razor in case Vesco called at the last minute, as he did, for instance, from an airplane, wanting Dunn in Houston by 11 P.M. that night. After a bargaining session that lasted until dawn, Vesco wrangled another loan. He was talented at raising funds and making acquisitions, and he had to engender trust or people wouldn't have lent to, or merged with, him. By the end of 1966, tiny ICC showed a paltry net income of $229,000 on sales of about $4.5 million from the manufacture and assembly of precision parts for computers, airplanes, cryosumps, rocket casings, wheel hubs, and so on, but the company consisted of only two machine shops employing about forty people each. The business was mostly military. Like hundreds of small companies, ICC had qualified as a government contractor. The General Services Administration issued letters as to its needs, and the contractors bid. ICC's performance was not unusual.

The company, however, was public and that made the difference. In 1966, with ICC trading over the counter in the $2 to $4 range, Vesco, at thirty-one, had achieved his final adolescent objective. With about 26 percent of ICC stock, he was a paper millionaire. He was gathering a small, loyal, youthful, and bright management group—for instance, Dodd, vice president of production and planning, was a former assembly line worker who earned a BS and MBA in night school—attracted by Vesco's nerve, imagination and energy and who thought the company was going places. Morale was high. The executives would often be at their desks until ten or eleven at night and be back in at eight or eight-thirty. "You didn't want to miss a workday. They were too exciting," said one. "We were on a rocket headed up." Every Saturday, the team met to talk about the next step down acquisition road.

Importantly, Vesco had found backing: American Bank and Trust in Morristown, New Jersey, lent ICC $50,000, which "sort of broke the ice," Vesco said, because it gave ICC a credit rating. (The loan officer, Wilbert Snipes, became an ICC director and Vesco confidant.) Vesco charmed Ruth Axe, a graduate economist in her sixties, who, he claimed, tried to hire him. Axe shrewdly invested in acquisition whiz-kids like Vesco (and Charles Bluhdorn, of Gulf & Western), and the $25 million Axe Science Corporation, a mutual fund, put $200,000 into ICC as a private placement. He persuaded respected people to join his board—Malcolm E. McAlpin, a brokerage company executive and a director of various corporations, including International Telephone & Telegraph (Vesco would frequently repeat McAlpin's advice: "Don't drink at lunch. Let others do it.") and Pershing, by then president of Hale Brothers, a San Francisco investment company. Hale had two partners on the board of the Bank of America, which would contribute mightily to Vesco's rise.

In 1967, Vesco acquired a number of other glorified machine shops, one of them—the largest—Century Special Corporation, having double the volume of ICC. An inducement to sell in exchange for stock was the jump in ICC, from 4¼ bid early in the year to 23 in the fourth quarter. (Every point was worth more than a million dollars to Vesco.) Century Special provided the manufacturing facilities for what Vesco believed would be "our money tree"—it didn't prove to be—exclusive U.S. and Canadian rights to manufacture and merchandise German-developed valves. In the fall, a 600-acre airport with a rundown hangar and various facilities was added to the organization chart. Vesco, who had to know everything and reviewed everything (unlike most chief executives) from registration statements to press releases, prodded relentlessly for still more acquisitions—precision instruments, plastics, savings and loan associations. On one such deal, Empire, Vesco, because of regulatory problems, bought the stock himself with $6.5 million borrowed from the Bank of America. The stock price went up and he personally made $1.6 million, over the objections of a minority of his board. (The transaction appeared entirely legal, though at least one board member began to distrust Vesco at that point, feeling he hadn't kept his word.) ICC was an active, almost hyperactive, company, and its stock was increasingly well thought of for speculative purposes. Vesco was proud of himself—he had, after all, founded what looked to be, and ultimately was, a successful business. (By 1987, ICC, long without Vesco, regularly hit new highs on the New York Stock Exchange.)

With more than 4,000 acquisitions and mergers, double the number of the preceding one, 1968 was called the "Year of the Conglomerate," and, as Vesco put it, ICC "jumped on the bandwagon of extreme diversification," including Intercontinental Manufacturing, which made casings for 2,000-pound bombs to be dropped in Vietnam. The restless Vesco wanted to start a commuter airline that would feed into metropolitan airports and become a national system, and ICC acquired Golden West Airlines, Van Nuys (Calif.) Skyways, Pacific Learjet Sales, and was negotiating for a lease on the Princeton, N.J., airport.

A Vesco objective was to reduce dependence on military suppliers by acquiring businesses with new technologies about which the company might know little—computerized billing, gamma ray shielding for nuclear reactors, irradiated wood flooring that spotted—a fact apparently well known in the industry. The companies he went after—International Controls had come to have five operating units, with thirteen subsidiaries and 5,000 employees—were often broke, eager to sell, and subject to bargaining in which Vesco could be tough. In one instance, a lawyer for the president of a company received an offer from ICC that seemed so favorable he advised his client to accept, although he made small changes, as lawyers will, to prove he was on the ball. From Vesco's side came adjournment after adjournment—delay, after all, can be psychological warfare designed to make the opponent in a negotiation apprehensive and more willing to scale down his demands, the sort of maneuver divorce lawyers, for instance, engage in. Sensing that, the attorney became suspicious, while the president was more and more nervous about the outcome of the sale. Finally, a call came telling him to be at ICC headquarters at Fairfield at 7 P.M. The president and his lawyer went. Seven became eight became eleven—tardiness can be another style of harassment, for he who wants something, and is kept waiting, is all too likely to assume that he (or what he's selling or offering) is hardly worth the other fellow's time, much less respect. Better take it while you can.

At last, the doors to the conference room burst open, and in charged Vesco at the head of a small parade of lawyers and accountants. He threw papers on the table and commanded they be signed in five minutes, insisting the contract had not been changed. But, while Vesco fumed, the lawyer turned pages and noticed that favorable provisions had become options subject to the wiles of ICC. "Don't sign it. You'll be screwed," the lawyer counseled, but the president signed anyway. Six months later the man was ruined. To the lawyer, it had been a deliberate plot. To Vesco, who had been known to spit at a contract he didn't approve of, good business.

Almost the only ideas Vesco liked were his own, but he had topflight advisers, with whom he checked every step, to lead him safely between the Scylla of the SEC and the Charybdis of the IRS. Lybrand, Ross Brothers, Montgomery (later, Coopers & Lybrand) was one of the "Big Eight" accounting firms, and Hogan & Hartson was among the largest legal firms with SEC expertise in Washington. While Vesco would claim to know more than the lawyers and accountants did, and sometimes seemed to, he was insistent on staying within the limits of legality. On one occasion, he refused to go through with a merger because he thought he was dealing with crooks. Still, as if oblivious to the Mafia image, or maybe because of it, Vesco would order pizza at meetings, even though he had mostly stopped eating the dish, and when he said "Italian," the emphasis was on "eye." He could come on with a tough street manner and was not above using words like "motherfucker" in staid corporate settings. The intensity of his anger sometimes took people aback.

Moeller Tool, a subsidiary of Century Special, which Vesco acquired, had valuable assets in Swiss machinery. Malcolm McAlpin, who sat on ICC's board, was a director of a parent company of another called Equalease. McAlpin phoned an Equalease executive, Norbert Weissberg, and suggested he meet with Vesco on the Moeller acquisition, and after several meetings Equalease agreed to lend ICC $2.5 million. Vesco, whom the Equalease people referred to as "checkered vest" because he always seemed to wear one, repaid the loan ahead of schedule, but what stuck in the minds of the executives was that Vesco brought a woman to one of the meetings, and her function, so far as they could determine, being a little drunk, was to offer herself, to sweeten the deal, as they say.

Despite a mercurial hard-boiled charm he was able to muster almost at will, the generally humorless Vesco was hard-driving and exacting. If any Captive Seal employees failed to come in when it snowed, they could be fired. If you arrived for work at Lowden Tool after 7 A.M., and Vesco was present, you were canned on the spot. He had frequent fallings-out with his own management and could be vengeful, especially if anyone in the organization attempted to sell ICC stock, a cause for dismissal. He personally checked sales with the brokers and would yell at them for not trying to arrange private placements that wouldn't affect the price of the stock. He was capable of reneging on deals to register privately held shares because he feared they might be sold, thus lowering the price about which he had almost an obsession. (Vesco talked people into ICC stock options instead of high salaries, but when they wanted to unload, he wouldn't let them. Nobody seems to have quit as a result.) Vesco's ethics, remarked Howard Singer, ICC's then general counsel, were "coming out ahead. He wouldn't steal but he'd mess people up. It wasn't exactly true, as he claimed, that everything was done for the stockholders and he was only one of them. Bobby always had perks, like the company credit cards for his kids. He could borrow from banks on his shares, which the small stockholders couldn't. Still, all things considered, Vesco was honest, at least then, though he'd use people and forget them. He lacked personal loyalty and he didn't care about others." With that appraisal, many then close to Vesco would agree.

By mid-1968, ICC shares, registered by then on the American Stock Exchange (Vesco cut a red ribbon), reached 50⅞, and Bob's holdings, zero a scant three years before, exceeded $50 million—over $100 million today. That was real wealth, as he was fond of pointing out, but though Vesco had shown skill in creating his junior conglomerate, the stock, like others of its kind, was extremely speculative and could easily tumble, not only because of general market conditions but because ICC accounting (the company was not alone) was weighted heavily toward future growth. Circumstances, objective in terms of the company, subjective in terms of the founder's ego, demanded that ICC plunge on. Vesco was obsessed with business dreams, like others who were written about on the financial pages. Occasionally though, he seemed to lose touch with reality. He testified he'd been in Venezuela in the early sixties on a job for the World Bank. Milton Meissner, who was supposed to be working with him, had no knowledge of any such event. Neither did Ralph Dodd. Vesco would sometimes make things up.

INTERNATIONAL CONTROLS CORP.
CORPORATE ORGANIZATION
DECEMBER 31, 1967

International Controls Corp.
(Parent Company)

Fairfield Aviation Corporation (100%)	ICC Manufacturing, Inc. (Formerly Lowden Machine Company) (100%)	The Special Corporation (100%)	Silber Products, Inc. (100%)	Moeller Tool Corporation (100%)

5

BOB'S NEW FRIEND HENRY BUHL

At the beginning of 1968, Vesco met Christian Henry Buhl III, who would be a significant element in Vesco's destiny, being the right man in the right place at the right time. It's more than conceivable that without him the Vesco case would never have happened. Buhl's father's side was old Detroit, his mother's Jewish and very rich—Henry's maternal grandfather had bought 51 percent of Fischer Body and sold it to General Motors. Henry went to the Brooks School in Massachusetts and Trinity College in Hartford, Connecticut—two of the tonier educational institutions. He didn't finish Trinity, partly because of his atrocious, perhaps dyslexic, spelling. He served in the Naval Air Corps and attended business school at Fordham, also taking night courses at New York University. Again, he failed to graduate.

Buhl worked on Wall Street for a decade. He became vice-president of McDonnell & Co., members of the New York Stock Exchange, but he wanted to live in Europe. In 1961, he took a job with a Geneva bank to manage its American portfolio. On a visit there the year before, he'd given two girls a lift in his white convertible and, on this trip, struck up a conversation at a café with a pretty girl who recognized him as the driver of the car, but she wouldn't go out with him because she lived with Bert Cantor, personnel director of a company Buhl had never heard of, Investors Overseas Services. The woman told Cantor about the new blade in town, and before long Henry met Bernard Cornfeld, an excitable man with a stutter who was impressed with Buhl's pedigree. An early one-minute manager, "Cornflakes," as they called him, hired Buhl in fifteen minutes. "I'll m-make you a millionaire," Bernie promised, as he promised everyone else. Buhl's starting salary was $100 a week, the lowest of the six executives. (When Buhl joined, the IOS staff numbered thirteen.)

Henry, who sensed opportunity, had a pleasing, low-key personality and was boyishly handsome, with a square, stubborn face, though sharp-tongued Cornfeld told him his chin was weak and he ought to grow a beard like Bernie, and Ed Cowett, the second in command, and Buhl complied briefly. Henry stood out in the seething IOS atmosphere. He wasn't from a New York City outer borough, and he wasn't Jewish enough to count (he had, in fact, been raised a Catholic). (He later quipped that he'd considered changing his name to "Buhlfeld.") Buhl wasn't rich but everyone assumed, mistakenly, he'd have a vast inheritance. (His mother chose to adopt Spanish twins and favor them.) He wasn't a salesman like most of the rest. Although Cornfeld always claimed he hired Henry not for his investment expertise but because of his business and social connections, within a year Buhl was president of IIT, International Investors Trust, the then-major IOS fund, small as it was. Later, he was appointed manager of fifteen IOS funds and briefly ran Fund of Funds after Bernard Cornfeld was out of IOS in 1970.

Henry introduced the fox to the chicken coop. In Geneva, on the high society circuit, Henry dined with Baron Edmond de Rothschild, who glowed about a fabulous New Jersey monsieur on whom he'd made money in his Captive Seal investment, which became ICC stock. "He'll be here soon. He has great promise," the Baron said.

Georges Karlweiss, who had been around the Captive Seal premises without revealing whom he worked for (he ran the Rothschild Banque Privée), called Buhl on behalf of Vesco. The two met first in Geneva, after Bob phoned and asked to see him. Buhl understood what that meant. To his small office—IOS had taken over an apartment building at 111 Rue de Lausanne, floor by floor, and another building down the street; Henry's office had been a bedroom, while Cornfeld's had been two—came a constant stream of business people seeking investments in their companies. Buhl was in a fine position to help since IIT had $600 million in its coffers by then.

Vesco seemed to know more about Buhl than Buhl knew about him—characteristically he had asked questions. Vesco was methodical. "You're from Detroit—Grosse Pointe," Bob offered.

"Fat Pointe, the Kennedys called it," Henry said nervously. He never announced he was from Grosse Pointe, where the automotive rich lived, because he feared that sounded snobbish. The Buhl Building in Detroit was named for his family.

"I'm from Detroit, too," Bob said, and went on to talk about starting a business and thriving on hard work. Vesco, with his odd mustache, struck Buhl as a bit "hoody," his name like a company's, but he had big plans for his little operation—little, that was, in Buhl's view.

Often absentminded Henry began to listen carefully. Vesco was straight out of Horatio Alger—in fact, he'd been a runner-up for the Horatio Alger Award. Buhl liked hearing that Vesco was a family man (little did he know that Bob was a high-stakes gambler and skirt chaser) with four children to whom he was devoted. The seeming simplicity of Vesco's style appealed to Henry, who in his Catholic way had begun to worry about the self-indulgence of the IOS brass, Cornflakes especially but also Henry himself. Bernie had a castle in France with a moat he had had dug ("When the guys buy castles, they become polygamous too," Cornfeld remarked), a Paris apartment, two uptown New York apartments and a penthouse downtown, five aircraft, including a BAC-111 on order and the twenty-odd-room Villa Elma, in Geneva, for which he paid $700,000. Cornfeld hadn't felt sincerely rich before then. That the villa had belonged to the Bonapartes appealed to Bernie's sense of history. Buhl had recently married, and Francis Cardinal Spellman of New York had flown from Rome to officiate —the bride was from an influential French Catholic family. He also had a lovely place with a $900,000 mortgage on nine acres on Lake Geneva, a house in the south of France and another in Antigua, which Vesco later visited, part of a Bordeaux vineyard, and, in the wings, a Learjet with three pilots. Henry planned to rent the plane as Bernie did his, but still . . . Bob made Henry remember reality. He hardly imagined that Vesco would soon be flying in a private Boeing 707 and sailing on a superluxurious yacht.

No, the only excess Vesco displayed to Buhl was his ego. He struck Henry as almost *too* confident—he was certainly not a man who would be easily discouraged. He had just turned thirty-three, five years younger than Buhl, and, for one so young, he had an awful lot of money. Bob let on he'd soon have much more.

Buhl, as others had, checked on Bob and found him highly recommended. ICC seemed to burst with good financial health and the Bank of America intended to become his backer—good credentials indeed. After several meetings Buhl decided to buy, for IIT, 50,000 shares, for over $750,000, registered ICC stock at a 40 percent discount and an additional 50,000 ICC shares on the open market. Henry also agreed, as a personal favor, to help Bob find an investment banker. He would require one to take over Electronic Specialty, his prime acquisition candidate.

Vesco thought about the Buhl Building. He reminded himself that the only way to compete with serious old money was to do exactly what it had, to acquire other businesses. That the major manufacturers had taken over minor car enterprises and emerged as giants was sharp in his mind—one day, for sure, ICC would be as prominent as Gulf & Western or Ling-Temco-Vought. Henry Buhl could be a major step toward that objective. And humble-background Bob had social aspirations as well. He was already exploring ways to guarantee his sons admission to Princeton.

The two met again in February 1968, a month later, where a covey of jets had brought IOSers for a meeting in the Bahamas, which was convenient to both Geneva and New York. Convenience wasn't the only reason, however. IOS had recently agreed to a decree with the SEC guaranteeing the company wouldn't do business in the United States. Vesco had come to sign the papers for the stock placement with IIT. As he sometimes did, Henry stayed with a chic couple named Butler, who occupied an entire block in downtown Nassau and had a gorgeous, multiservanted home, Jacaranda House, along with a bank they owned. Buhl wasn't entirely enjoying himself because when Shirley Butler drank too much she got sharp with Allan, who endured it stoically. Henry, who had lived with Shirley in the fifties—the two remained close friends—invited Vesco over, and they all went to a black-tie Washington's Birthday dance at the rich-Americans-only Porcupine Club on Paradise, *née* Hog, Island. Allan wanted to leave around midnight, but Henry was talking to a short man with a balding head. Henry seemed mesmerized, like a mouse before a snake, and, finally, in exasperation, Allan, somewhat tipsy and holding a bottle of champagne, poured it on the bald pate. Fists up, the man jumped to his feet but couldn't find a target because of the champagne in his eyes. "What are you doing?" Henry cried. "That's Bernie Cornfeld!" which Butler knew. Henry took poor Bernie off to wash up—they went to the ladies' room by mistake.

6

BOB'S NEW FRIEND ALLAN BUTLER

Another fateful figure in Vesco's future career was Allan Churchill Butler. Bright and ambitious as was Vesco, Butler, then in his late thirties, had a striking John Barrymore profile and impeccable credentials. His father had been a professor of medicine in Boston. Allan graduated from the Fountain Valley School in Colorado Springs, and, in 1946, from Harvard as an ensign in the Naval Reserve, in which he served briefly. He had been captain of Harvard's ski team. He had a certificate in international economics and Russian language from the University of Geneva, and a master's degree in international economics from the Johns Hopkins School of Advanced International Studies. He had founded a newspaper in New Hampshire that still exists, worked for the First National Bank of Boston in London and had been financial vice president of Fairbanks, Morse & Co. of Chicago. He was a descendant of Benjamin Franklin Butler who, among other things, was Attorney General of the United States from 1833 to 1837, Secretary of War in 1837, and founder of New York University Law School. Butler's maternal grandfather was the turn-of-the-century author Winston Churchill, a distant cousin of the English Churchill, and the first golf course in the United States was built on the Butler family farm at Yonkers, New York, in the 1880s. "There was always enough money to go around," Butler said.

Butler had married for the second time. His bride was Shirley Lewis Oakes, who made her debut in Philadelphia in 1947 and

London in 1950. She had been a classmate of Jacqueline Bouvier and was one of her bridesmaids when she married John F. Kennedy. Her curriculum vitae, as she termed it, was as long as her husband's—". . . Institut d'Études Politiques, University of Paris, 1949–1950; School of Law, Yale University, New Haven, Conn., U.S.A., J.D. 1954; School of Law, Columbia University, N.Y., U.S.A., Phi Beta Kappa; Virginia Swinburne Brownell Prize for History, Vassar College. French (fluency in all aspects). Spanish (general reading and conversational ability)."

Shirley, a Bahamian citizen, was the daughter of Lady and Sir Harry Oakes, a tough little American gold prospector who, after fruitless solitary years all over the world, finally hit pay dirt in Canada and became one of the globe's richest men. Moving first to England and then to the Bahamas, a tax haven, he had been active in local affairs and had bought a title by making a generous contribution to an English hospital, which was not unusual. Allan kidded his wife for taking Oakes's title seriously, but she did.

Oakes predicted he'd die violently, with his boots on, and in 1943 he was murdered. The famous case was never solved, but a popular theory had it that Meyer Lansky sent men to rough up Oakes because of his off-again, on-again opposition to Lansky's first attempt to obtain a Bahamian gaming permit, but they went too far and killed him. The trouble with this view was that Oakes, even teamed up with his friend, Sir Harold Christie, an important Bahamian, would not have been able to obtain for Lansky a Certificate of Exemption from Bahamas law forbidding gaming, so deep was the opposition to casinos then. Another notion, which Butler shared, was that the real culprit was a Swedish industrialist named Axel Wenner-Gren, the motive being millions of dollars Oakes had provided him during World War II. Wenner-Gren had a Mexican banking operation and persuaded Oakes to capitalize it, the story went. The Oakes trustees could never locate the money, about $9 million, it was thought, and Wenner-Gren, who seemed broke during the war, suddenly reemerged as a wealthy man. Who will ever know the truth?

Immediately after her husband's death, Lady Oakes sent her daughter and son on a trip with their governess, and Shirley read about the murder in the newspaper. The experience was traumatic and Shirley's relationship with her mother was turbulent. Beautiful in a patrician way, Shirley was tall and thin, and the couple stood out at the black-tie dinners that seemed to take place in Nassau almost every night.

Shirley and Allan had married in 1961. She would have preferred living in the United States, but Allan talked her into returning to the Bahamas. He felt that Shirley, a tense person, would do better in the relaxed atmosphere of the islands. Allan had no clear idea what he'd do in Nassau, but the two decided to start a bank, the original capital being $100,000 of Shirley's money and much more later on. Butlers Bank began in 1962 as a vehicle for investing Shirley's money, but the couple quickly saw that there was a shortage of capital for local enterprises. There had been only one Bahamian bank fifteen years before—the others were foreign—audited by its owner by kicking the cash box. When the empty box flew across the room, the bank closed. So the Butlers lent money to black businesses and brought black shareholders into operating companies, and theirs became a merchant bank with investment clients, including rich Greeks like Stavros Niarchos (whom Allan couldn't stand) and the Goulandris family, with whom Vesco dealt. Profits were tax free but the bank didn't produce any.

Among the whites in the Bahamas, the Butlers were unusual—they were not conservative. Allan's father had been a liberal, while Shirley was concerned that the Oakes family had not done enough for the islands. They were open supporters of the black party, and they were adamantly opposed to casinos.

Allan didn't like the man on whose head he'd poured champagne—he found Cornfeld pretentious and hated his posturing statements like "I really don't see why affluence should cause one to surround himself with ugly people and gloomy surroundings. I think that if the affluence didn't exist, I'd also strive to surround myself with amusing, creative, if you like, beautiful people rather than gloomy, dreary people. And I really don't think it's a product of affluence, because I think that all of the same kind of people were around as far back as I can remember." Allan figured that back in Brooklyn, where he was from, Bernie had never imagined he'd dine with Rothschilds, have movie stars like Laurence Harvey and Tony Curtis for friends, or girl it up with *Playboy*'s Hugh Hefner. But Butler did like Vesco, whom Buhl brought to the Butlers on the night of the Porcupine Club party. He saw him, as did many others, as a boy wonder. That Vesco was hardworking and a dutiful husband appealed to him as it had to Buhl. Butler valued discipline, which Vesco had in abundance. To Butler, "life-style" was a telling matter. If bankers lived simply, so, he thought, should businessmen. That Vesco was pyramiding a nothing company into a mini, maybe major, conglomerate seemed admirable by his lights. Allan was aware of Bob's arrogance but that, Butler supposed, was necessary to Vesco's confidence, which was in turn necessary to his deal making. It was a fine line to draw, but Allan drew in Bob's favor.

Besides, and most important, when Vesco came along, Butler's group had lost its momentum, though it controlled 60 percent of the automobile and liquor business in the islands and a chain of drugstores. After the black Progressive Liberal Party took power, in 1967, some black politicians had deserted the party and somehow Allan Butler was thought by the government, which gave him a hard time, to have been responsible. Butlers Bank was looking for new business, which Vesco seemed able to provide.

The first serious contact between Vesco and Butlers Bank was through one of its officers, Anthony Pilaro, also of Italian extraction and intensely ambitious. Pilaro courted Vesco in New Jersey and helped him sell a $25 million bond issue in Europe that summer, to be offered by a Netherland Antilles subsidiary, ICC-NV, so that Europeans could buy the bonds without being subject to U.S. taxation on dividends. Americans wouldn't be allowed to invest. Impressive European houses, N. M. Rothschild, Crédit Suisse, Union Bank of Switzerland, Industrial Bank of Italy, Warburg, Dresdener Bank, the Bank of America in London, were involved, but Bob needed an offshore underwriter and Pilaro led him to Butlers. Allan was as surprised as anyone when Vesco and Pilaro in Europe sold the entire issue in a matter of weeks and could have placed $50 million had the bonds been available. It seemed almost a miracle, though Henry Buhl's IIT fund contributed by taking about a quarter of the total, at a discount as usual.

7

THE WHALE

Tired of minnows, the predators at ICC's Fairfield headquarters decided to harpoon a "whale," their word for a large company. Abex Brakeshoe, Fairchild Aviation, and Electronic Specialty (ELS) were the candidates.

Vesco required greater capitalization for such an undertaking and, in raising it, showed entrepreneurial flair. He had become a limited partner in Orvis Brothers & Co., a stock brokerage house —he invested $500,000 of ICC stock in Orvis, probably unregistered—and was around the Street touting his company. (He was a silent partner in another brokerage house, Blalock Wells.) Orvis underwrote ICC's first public offering, which, fully subscribed, brought almost $7 million into the treasury. When the price of ICC spurted, the company called in part of the units, so that warrant holders bought the stock at one half the market price. ICC thus made $3 million more. At Orvis, the partners regarded Vesco with something like awe, especially when he enabled them to buy INC (ICC trading initials) at less than the market price. They made good profits on 30,000 shares. To become a limited partner, Vesco had to pass an investigation by the New York Stock Exchange, where Orvis had a seat. Nor would Orvis, one hundred years old and respectable, have touched Vesco had it had the slightest suspicion that he was shady.

Still, to Fergus Sloan, Orvis's managing partner, Vesco was cold and all business, a nonentity in social situations. He once had to push Vesco's feet off his desk. Sloan felt that the purpose of Bob's involvement in Orvis was to control underwritings of his own. "When I blocked him, he lost interest except for getting his stock back. In 1969, the company needed additional capitalization—ICC was our most important asset—but Vesco wouldn't return phone calls and we went under along with a lot of other Wall Street firms." To try to improve its position, Orvis declared uncollected revenue as capital, and, as a result, three of its executives served light terms in jail.

ICC was acquiring as fast as it could. "It's as easy to take on a large company as a small one. The steps are the same," Vesco said at one usual Saturday skull session at company headquarters. And certainly acquisitions were preferable to starting businesses from scratch—nobody in his or her right mind did *that,* unfortunately, perhaps, for the American economy. Having considered compatibility, size, and potential legal problems, ICC selected as the whale Electronic Specialty, a California-based maker of electronic components, heating and cooling equipment for aircraft, and major structural parts for Boeing. It had started by manufacturing electric razors and had grown in much the same fashion as Vesco's company. Through Richard Pershing of Hale Brothers, Vesco arranged a $10 million—ultimately $49 million—loan from Bank of America, only two years after the $200,000 Axe transaction he had been flabbergasted to have pulled off. The BOA backing, as he would tell anyone who would listen, made his corporation extremely desirable. BOA, the Eurobond issue success, and the Goulandris deal financed the whale hunt.

Vesco had convinced a group, which included a Greek shipping family named Goulandris, to buy about $4.6 million of ICC shares at a 12 percent discount, the money to be used in a takeover. ($1 million was deposited in Butlers Bank.) Said Toub, who arranged the transaction, found Vesco "personable and really impressive"—he had checked on Vesco's credentials. The only trouble was that Vesco guaranteed that the group wouldn't lose money and it did, about 75 percent of its investment, but there had been no deal, except to Toub maybe a moral one, that Bob make good.

Henry Buhl had come through on his promise to introduce

Vesco to investment bankers. In New York, he brought his protégé to Lazard Frères; Salomon Brothers; Allen & Co.; John Loeb, Sr., of Loeb & Rhoades; Lehman Brothers; Smith Barney; and so on—the top of the profession. Buhl said about Vesco, "He always acted haughtily and never conducted himself humbly with very successful men. I thought he should show a little bit of humility, and they all called to ask me not to bring him back again. At one meeting I attended at Arthur Andersen [a large accounting firm], he told the executive V.P. that he didn't know what he was talking about. I would say it was just bad manners. Bobby had a chip on his shoulder, but he was goddam smart and turned out to be correct about Andersen."

Smith Barney agreed to work for the troublesome tycoon in the still secret Electronic Specialty merger, which Vesco apparently expected to be amicable. He made his intentions known through an intermediary to ascertain how well the ICC embrace —"bear hug" it would be called today—might be received, and instructed Butlers Bank to buy 100,000 shares of ELS for prices less than $40 a share; but Butlers had time to pick up less than half of that, amounting to 2.5 percent of the company, before Vesco met with Electronic Specialty's founder and chairman, William H. Burgess, in Los Angeles. Burgess was shocked at the prospect of becoming junior partner to a pint-sized concern he'd never heard of, especially as he had his own plans to merge with Carpenter Steel (later Carpenter Technology), which, like ELS, manufactured airplane components. (At one point, to stop Vesco, ELS searched desperately for Carpenter's president, who was on a fishing trip in Wyoming.)

The two met at Burgess's large Pasadena house, and the ELS president may have shown his nervousness by reverting constantly to the topic of butterflies, of which he had a magnificent collection. Vesco reported to his board that Burgess had been cooperative and friendly, but he nonetheless suspected that the ELS men stalled and felt the deal must be quickly resolved. (An important motive was that ICC needed a takeover to maintain the price of its stock.) Burgess, for his part, asked Vesco how much ELS stock ICC had bought, and he came away with the impression that Vesco had more than he really did. "These are negotiating tactics and we did not say anything untrue," Vesco insisted to the SEC. "But we didn't answer the question, either."

The misrepresentation issue intensified after Vesco took a call at Smith Barney, talking in private to a *Wall Street Journal* reporter, from which came an item that ICC had 5 percent of ELS. (ICC people were shocked that Bob would talk to a reporter during delicate negotiations.) Vesco maintained he hadn't mentioned such a figure, which made ICC seem more powerful and menacing than it was, but he probably did. Later, a judge, blaming "the frailties inevitable in human communication," wouldn't take sides in the trial but disapproved of Vesco's tactics.

Burgess and Vesco met on a Saturday, August 3, 1969, in New York, after which the men and their wives had dinner. The merger appeared off, with ELS agreeing to buy its shares held by ICC for $42 a share, about what ICC had laid out. But a snag soon developed. ELS, which was to pay ICC's expenses on the deal, wanted a strict accounting, and Vesco, either fearing the purchase would fall through, or trying to provoke a dispute, or both, refused.

On August 5, both sides announced that merger talks had ended, but Vesco still drafted details of a tender offer. After lunch, on Tuesday, he suddenly sold 5,400 ELS shares on the phone—"stupid of him," said one of his officers. "He just did it." Vesco had planned to unload more, at not less than $35 a share, but his investment banker and lawyers stopped him because the transaction would be viewed as manipulation of the market if ICC made a formal offer, and, indeed, Vesco was attempting to lower the price of ELS so the premium ICC would have to pay would be less. That would have been illegal.

Though proxy fights were commonplace then, "hostile" takeovers, in which "raiders" pursued "targets," gobbling them up with stock purchases, were not. So-called white shoe investment bankers wouldn't touch them. If a company didn't wish to be acquired it was generally let alone. Not so Vesco, who in hostile-acquisition terms, was ahead of his time—even his board had been against an unfriendly takeover. He remarked of ELS, "Top management was more interested in playing golf and chasing girls. There was no harm in chasing girls, but you can do that

INTERNATIONAL CONTROLS CORP.
CORPORATE ORGANIZATION
DECEMBER 31, 1968

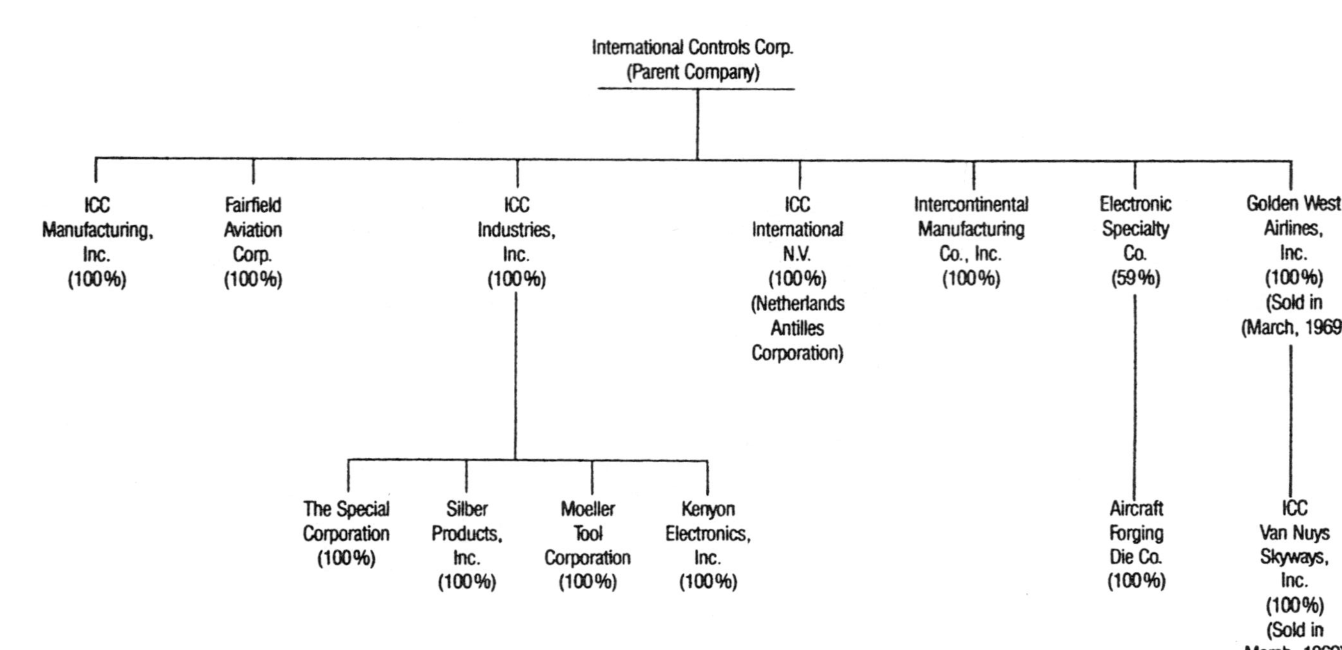

on your own time. And going off on safaris down to Africa. But this was their idea of bigtime management, so to speak." He implied acidly that ELS, whose new headquarters opened on the day Vesco's takeover broke, had moved to Pasadena for Burgess's convenience because he lived there.

The events that followed resembled the hostile acquisitions we read so much about today. On August 14, 1968, ICC sent a telegram to ELS to probe its willingness to go through with the purchase of ICC's ELS shares, but there was no response, and the next day Vesco recommended a tender offer to his board; the black knight from New Jersey intended to fight, and Smith Barney resigned. The irregularities disturbed it. Smith Barney's Hugh Knowlton said that in an unfriendly acquisition they would all be sued and the risks weren't worth the bother. Vesco went straight to Carl W. Anderson, the partner in charge of corporate finance at Orvis Brothers, also respectable, though less rich, which agreed to be the underwriter and which had participated, with Butlers, in the $25 million Eurobond issue. On August 19, hastily prepared advertisements announcing the offer to buy 500,000 shares of ELS on the New York Stock Exchange at $39 appeared, to the horror of the whale's executives.

Burgess, evidently furious, wrote ELS stockholders "DON'T ACT IN HASTE. Electronic Speciality Co. is being raided by a small AMEX Company called International Controls, financed by foreign investors. It is a much smaller company with sales in 1967 of $6.8 million compared to our 1967 sales of $112 million."

Days passed. Vesco offered to return the ELS stock to those who had tendered, if they felt misled, but not much ELS stock had come to ICC depositories. Over a weekend, Vesco convinced his board to tender not just for part of ELS stock, as had been announced, but all of it, even though the Bank of America had not agreed to finance such an amended deal. BOA eventually did, but, as said a participant, "Vesco was playing high-risk poker. If the bank hadn't come through, we might have lost."

The California company sought a temporary restraining order, which a judge denied, although agreeing there was "a reasonable probability" that ELS would be able to substantiate its accusation that ICC made false representations. Burgess had said that if the ruling went against Electronic Specialty he and other key officers would resign and tender their shares, assuming Vesco would gain working control. However, the ICC board thought that Burgess didn't believe ICC had the money and would be forced out. When ELS executives suddenly tendered their shares, ICC, backed by BOA, ended with 59 percent of ELS and a paper loss of $17.4 million in the selling off of ELS stock that followed. From the Eurobond offering and the BOA loan, ICC had to pay $3 million annually in interest charges, and its shaky finances led Vesco to conclude that still other acquisitions were required.

Said its former executive vice president Frank G. Beatty, "ICC had been a collection of dogs and cats. ELS turned it around." The California concern was to be the heart of the business, and Vesco closed its Pasadena office, firing most of the employees, although he brought a few of them East.

After a trial, a judge found, in December, like the one before him, that Vesco had allowed published, misleading reports to go uncorrected and had violated securities laws prohibiting fraud or deceit, but that to force the company to divest itself of ELS stock would be "impractical, inappropriate and punitive" as well as unprecedented. ELS stockholders might want to take advantage of the ICC offer. A month later, an appeals court dismissed ELS's suit.

Vesco was jubilant, though others in his company, touring the West Coast to examine the prize, were a little awed by the size of the conquest. In existence only four years, ICC at one stroke became 688 by sales among Fortune's 1,000 largest American industrial corporations. But the ELS victory had its cost to Vesco, who, meeting Benjamin Payn by accident at a restaurant in December, said lividly, "Why, that goddam judge came close to calling me a crook."

Even during the takeover, which cost ICC $52 million, it picked up two more companies with sales of $15 million. The corporation decided it needed more office space, and Vesco asked for, and received, a raise to $50,000 a year from ICC. (He was paid another $50,000 from ELS.) It was time, he said, to consolidate.

By 1969, when Vesco talked into a tape recorder for Munro

Schwebel, he was successful in every respect, though he'd emerged with the reputation of a raider. He had the admiration of perhaps overly loyal associates, the potential of building a major business, strong political influence in New Jersey, serious money, a family that appeared to love him, and, yes, a long-lasting affair with another woman—in short, the components of what many would consider the good life. He could be mendacious, overbearing, secretive, boastful, and something of a con artist, but no serious scandal had yet been attached to him. "If Bob did all those things he's accused of, and I'm not saying he didn't," observed Carl Anderson—formerly of Orvis and closest in business along with Dodd to Vesco, who had few if any purely social friends —"something happened to him. The question is what. Maybe it was a latent quality that we didn't see, but even so, what is supposed to have gone on is hard for us who knew him well to believe."

Part Two

IOS

8

THE RISE OF IOS

Bernard Cornfeld started Investors Overseas Services in Paris with a capital of $300 in 1956. It was originally aimed at selling Dreyfus Fund shares to GIs in Europe for as little as $25 a month. At one point, Cornfeld's group of salesmen, broke American expatriates, brought in one-third of Dreyfus's new money. In 1960, interested in independence and management fees, Bernie, as everyone called him, formed International Investors Trust (IIT), a mutual fund that was followed by Fund of Funds in 1962. The notion behind Fund of Funds was to invest in American mutual funds, because of their market-guessing skills. The "great money catcher," as they called it, was an enormous success, as was IOS itself.

Fund of Funds caught the attention of the Securities and Exchange Commission in Washington, which argued that it was misleading to imply that a fund containing ten other funds in its portfolio would be ten times better. The SEC (See Everything Crooked, as it had been dubbed) seemed oblivious to the enormous impact the eager IOS sales force had on customers too small for ordinary financial institutions to bother with and began to watch IOS with a cold eye.

Cornfeld, originally named Benno Cornfield, was born in Istanbul, Turkey, in 1927, of European parents. A former social worker, he worked fourteen hours a day, as Vesco did, and his business also grew with astonishing speed as did Bernie's wealth.

At its height, his paper worth was over $200 million, read $400 million plus today. Normally so soft-spoken that people had to strain to hear him, his temper could be violent. He threw ashtrays and was known to scream profanities in restaurants and stalk out. He had stuttered all his life, but, except when he was tired or angry, he had learned to control the difficulty with the aid of therapy. He forced himself to pause, even for long periods, until the hazard passed. About five-foot-five, plump until he entered the jet set with the aid of his friend, the designer, Oleg Cassini, Bernie was a lover of gadgets and elegant clothes. Despite wit, charm, and high intelligence (Cornfeld spoke four or five languages, later perfecting his French in a Swiss prison), Bernie seemed to need to show off and to have constant companionship. Though he neither drank nor smoked, he'd stay up half the night in discotheques, sometimes sleeping in his office. His attention span was notoriously short, and he was always late, sometimes by days. Women preoccupied him. He always had girls around, including Victoria Principal, later of "Dallas," who got a London court order against Cornfeld for roughing her up; they reunited briefly. Bernie believed in "sexual anarchy" and hadn't married, he said, because family responsibilities would detract from his job, to which he was devoted. Cornfeld and the company he created were for him inseparable, and he might have said, in the manner of a French king, "L'IOS, *c'est moi.*" Although he often held others in contempt, Cornfeld was usually loyal to those who had been in the IOS family from the early days. One was Edward Cowett, who, as much as anyone else, was responsible for the crisis in IOS that opened the way to Vesco.

Cornfeld saw Vesco as hardly better than a hood, while Vesco perceived Cornfeld as a business dandy who richly deserved being dumped. To Vesco, Bernie's company had too little will and too much jet set. Allan Butler, knowledgeable about IOS, agreed with Vesco's appraisal. The two "talked quite often about his plans for IOS. He had a fantastic ability to encompass the whole mess, such as IOS then was, and get to the root of the matter. He pointed out that in his opinion IOS was not in need of additional funds, that was not their problem. He felt they were basically in need of discipline. He talked very sensibly, very comprehensibly, about the horrors of the Cornfeld era, about the inadequacy and criminal negligence in the . . . IOS board at that time, and I think we at Butlers Bank felt that [he] was probably the only individual alive who stood a chance of rescuing that operation . . . I don't think at that point he had any firm plans. I mean, it was a day-to-day emergency operation with the Cornfeld people still on the board of the company, with Cornfeld doing insane and crazy things on a daily basis, and with the savings of thousands of small people involved."

Cowett, though a generous man, was an enigmatic, austere figure even for those who knew him well. He had a sense of humor but didn't smile much. Understatedly arrogant, brilliant, egocentric, tense, Cowett had ulcers and had been partially paralyzed for six months, after which he would never allow himself to become agitated, outwardly at least. (Still, the strain after IOS began to collapse in 1970 must have been profound. With no previous history of heart disorders Cowett died on the day before his forty-fourth birthday, after he collapsed on an airplane, following a Denver court hearing in the matter of John King.) He had a powerful belief in his ability to solve problems without consulting anyone. He made enemies and could, like Cornfeld, frighten more timid souls. He functioned best under pressure and waited until the last minute to get things done—a sign, perhaps, of insecurity. He enjoyed complicated deals and shuffling money around and did not always keep written records. "He created unnecessary complexities," said one who worked with him closely. "The challenge for Ed was to find out how far he could pull the string. He would never use words like 'moral,' 'ethical,' 'principles.' They weren't part of his vocabulary. If he didn't have an answer, Ed would make one up. If he didn't want Cornfeld to do something, he'd invent a law against it."

Born in 1930, Cowett graduated from Harvard Law cum laude. He co-authored, with a leading law professor, Louis Loss, a definitive work, *Blue Sky Laws,* so named from a judge's remark that some stocks had about the same value as a patch of blue sky, on government regulations intended to protect investors from being fleeced by con men. From a middle-class Jewish (Springfield, Mass.) family, he worked for a top New York law firm, Strook

& Strook & Lavan, and became the junior partner overseeing Strook's dealings with the Dreyfus Fund, a client. Cornfeld, who sold for Dreyfus, met Cowett in 1956 and the two flashed to each other's intelligence, as bright people will. Bernie admired Ed's legal abilities—"He could dictate a prospectus, make minor changes, and go into final draft. Any other lawyer would have taken weeks," Cornfeld remarked—and Cowett became IOS legal counsel in New York.

If Cowett was superficially steady compared to the volatile Cornfeld, he was also a greater gambler despite a more conservative front. Cowett left Strook & Strook for another firm and then joined a new one that became Feldman, Kramer, Bam, Nasser and Cowett. Nobody there knew much about him, although it was later rumored that he'd been in some kind of trouble with a Boston law office. Eddie, as they called him in the new law firm, was supposed to bring in business. Bernie Cornfeld was around the office, but the fees from the still small IOS were tiny. Cowett's specialty was the legal work for new stock issues, and only later did his partners learn that he was acting as underwriter as well, raising the money to float them. He had formed a network with brokers, and they were able to manipulate the prices of certain stocks, since the number of available shares was small. Cowett was adept in telling people what they wanted to hear, and in the midst of his as yet unknown troubles he was asked at a partners' meeting how things were, and replied nonchalantly, fine. The others noticed that Eddie's hand, holding a cigarette, began to tremble, but thought nothing of it.

"The first event that caused my distrust of Ed Cowett," Buhl reported, "was in 1961, slightly after I joined IOS. Cornfeld, Cowett, and I met with George Moore, president of Citibank (then the First National Bank of New York) and Walter Wriston, executive vice-president of international operations. The purpose was to establish relations with the bank's worldwide branch network. Both Moore and Wriston agreed with our proposal but changed their minds the following day, because they discovered that Cowett had written an unauthorized check on his law firm, Feldman, Kramer, which Citibank used extensively. They even closed our small checking account at their Geneva branch and said they'd sustain that policy as long as Cowett was associated with IOS."

In the '61–'62 debacle on Wall Street, the drop in value in Cowett's highly speculative holdings broke him. He was in debt $800,000 at one point. Trying to shore up his stocks, he diverted funds from a family trust. Each of the law partners could write checks, and at the start of the month Cowett wrote one for $40,000, cleaning out the partnership. When the firm discovered the embezzlement, one of the partners called Eddie, who was lingering in Geneva, hoping the market would turn around, and said, "Don't come back. Just send the money." The next day, his name was scraped from the door.

One of Henry Buhl's first acts after he became president of an IOS fund, International Investors Trust, was to examine its portfolio. Four of the worst dogs, in Buhl's opinion—all were companies that went bankrupt—had been put there by Ed Cowett, who had used his power as an IIT director to stuff the fund with issues in which he had an interest. He confessed with a shrug, and Buhl remained distrustful of him thereafter. Cowett shared an attitude that would be characteristic of the decade—an unflappable faith that the force that drove the green fuse was unceasing, that everything would "work out," as the Bay of Pigs and Vietnam would "work out." Cornfeld covered Cowett's debts but was outraged at his first lieutenant for unloading IOS options he had no right to sell, and Cowett was forced to resign as an IOS director. Cornfeld attributed Cowett's problems to poor luck on the market. He stayed on as legal counsel but was briefly banished from the emperor's court.

Cowett's return from exile in 1963, after Cornfeld forgave him, coincided with the explosive growth of IOS around the world. Among the lures dangled by the sales people (called "investment counselors") were tax avoidance and the company's ability to remove currencies, especially dollars, in violation of local law, with couriers if necessary. (Swiss banks engaged in the same practice.) The existence of this pool of "flight" capital—"hot" or "black" money—was well known at IOS headquarters, though the exact amount was not. For Vesco it would be a major factor.

On the seventh story of 119 Rue de Lausanne, hung a board where sales were posted, and every working day the cash under management grew. Rational organizations usually attempt to simplify, to reduce complexity to a minimum in the interests of controlling operations, but IOS did the opposite. Investment programs that avoided taxes, including death duties, compliance with or avoidance of national laws, management fees and diversification into banking, insurance, real estate, and natural resources led to a jigsaw puzzle of some 180 pieces.

IOSers believed Cornfeld's incessant claim "I'll make you a millionaire," and Cowett peddled the same line. Starting in 1963 or 1964, he delivered reports on IOS's condition to sales managers "in a very low-key fashion, as the figures and statistics were impressive. They required no embellishment or interpolation."* He talked about how shares in the Stock Option Plan would double in value. "The Happy Hour," they called it. "Unfortunately, those who listened to it neither possessed the sophistication to realize that growth cannot continue unabated nor wished to take away from The Happy Hour anything other than confirmation that they were going to be very, very rich." "We'll be managing assets of one hundred billion. We will all become millionaires," predicted Allen Cantor, chieftain of the sales force. Greed was encouraged and few dared to ask hard questions such as whether the sales force, eventually 16,000 strong (though many part-time), might cost more than it brought in.

Cornfeld was often closeted with Cowett and the third "C," Cantor. The trio was gaily referred to as "la kosher nostra" or, as p.r. man Tex McCrary put it when he worked for IOS, "the dreamer" [Cornfeld], "the schemer" [Cowett], and "the reamer" [Cantor]. They had a lot to think about. So much money was pouring in that the possibilities of what to do with it seemed endless. The dreamer spoke of a new world order, "people's capitalism," a phrase also bruited by the New York Stock Exchange in trying to promote investment collectives for the small fry (who lost their money in the collapse of 1970–1971). An-

* Edward M. Cowett, "Preliminary Textual Material and Outline of Proposed Book," 1974. Among Cowett's suggested titles were "The False Religion of IOS" and "We Thought We Were Infallible." I have not cited specific pages.

nounced the sage of Rue de Lausanne, "We're in the business of literally converting the proletariat into the leisured class, painlessly and without violence. It's revolutionary and goddam exciting." The old Norman Thomas socialist believed that if the workers of the world put their shekels, francs, guilders, pesos, lire, and so on into his mutual funds they (and the funds) were bound to prosper.

The reamer's job was to sell, the schemer's to handle tricky legal matters and make the business as profitable as possible. One device was to create multilayered managements with contracts. IOS (Panama) dealt with IOS Overseas Management Services Ltd., of Canada, which paid a fee to the parent company while collecting fees from the management companies of the funds it supervised, which in turn received fees from the funds. Whatever the utility of this arrangement, and whatever extra protection it offered the fundholders (who knew little or nothing about the buffering they paid for), it was top-heavy to start with and the management companies would be a major burden if sales declined.

Still, the funds performed so well that expenses didn't seem to matter, and IOS seemed able to surmount any adversity. When illegal sales in South America were revealed, and the company was expelled from some of its most lucrative markets, it concentrated on Europe instead, until one-third of its customers were West Germans. Cowett was candid about the rationale: "Why not begin a clandestine operation in a country where there was a good market [even if] such an operation would be illegal? Why discontinue operations which became illegal, when they could be camouflaged? Just be careful! Avoid the law. After all, U.S. and other foreign banks do the same thing." The Swiss had become increasingly irked because IOS salesmen and literature, stressing the secrecy of Swiss banking laws, the stability of the Swiss franc, and the tranquillity of Swiss politics, seemed to hint IOS was almost a Swiss company. IOS owned its own bank in Geneva, and therefore IOS salesmen said that investors could buy through a Swiss bank, but the Swiss Bankers' Association didn't enjoy IOS's use of its coattails, and Swiss bankers, after all, were competitive with the Americans for business. Nor did Bernie's tantrums help —he threw a handful of ball-point pens into the face of a Swiss official and called him a son-of-a-bitch. The Swiss began to clamp down, ostensibly on the issue of work permits, which fewer than a hundred IOS employees had. (The others were listed as students.) IOS might have been closed, but an arrangement was made. The headquarters staff at Rue de Lausanne could stay, but the others—over 1,200 by then—had to leave. A deal was made with the French to house the company in a provincial French town a few miles from the airport. It was named Ferney-Voltaire because the famous philosopher had spent the last twenty years of his life there. In a matter of months, the complex of prefabs, blue with plate-glass windows, was finished at a cost of $4 million. After a party, drunks changed the road signs to "Berney-Voltaire."

But the most ominous obstacle to IOS was the SEC, which felt FOF was deceptive in boasting it outperformed the Dow-Jones index without revealing that its growth included the reinvestment of dividends, as the Dow-Jones did not; that the FOF prospectus was changed without shareholder notification; that to get a clear picture of FOF investments, investors had to make a special request, etc. The agency didn't like the double or triple management fees plus the front-end load (original charges for buying into an IOS fund; at the start, at least, IOS had the same commission schedule as Dreyfus and most other mutual funds), and it especially didn't like Ed Cowett. In the early sixties, Cowett, wanting to start a U.S.–IOS fund, went to the SEC in Washington, where he saw Allan F. Conwill, formerly general counsel and later Director of Corporate Regulation. Conwill, who would become one of IOS's main lawyers, was quietly amused by Cowett's arrogance—he had a way of putting others down. Cowett wrote a bombastic letter to the SEC chairman and commissioners accusing the agency of abusing IOS—the "great Cowett letter," SECers called it—and demanded a meeting, which he got. He offended people and was known at the SEC as a bastard.

Once the SEC focused on IOS, it found much to complain

about, too much perhaps. As another example, Fund of Funds was a substantial investor in several mutual funds. Couldn't FOF rig stock prices? The SEC's job was to assure orderly and fair trading to protect American investors, and didn't want them fleeced. IOS-controlled capital might someday reach the point of being able to materially affect U.S. securities markets; on some days, it was said, IOS accounted for 5 percent of trading on the New York Stock Exchange. The SEC maintained that IOS was under its jurisdiction, but IOS declared it wasn't. The last thing Bernie and Ed wanted was to let the U.S. government rule on, and forbid, their overseas activities. The SEC demanded a full list of IOS clients, regardless of their nationality, and IOS refused to comply, saying it had to abide by Swiss bank secrecy laws.

Early in 1965, the commission decided to investigate the effect of IIT and FOF on American securities markets and to learn if IOS, as the SEC was already convinced, had violated U.S. laws. Most of the IOS records were in Geneva, but the company did have Investors Continental Services in New York, used to sell to Americans abroad and service those clients when they returned. IOS at its inception had registered with the SEC as a broker/dealer, which meant that the SEC could inspect at will and demand records.

In May, two SEC investigators appeared at IOS's New York office and uncovered a Cowett letter warning the staff to remove from the files correspondence indicating obvious violations, because the "results could be disastrous" if discovered. What Cowett meant was that an IOS salesman home on a visit might, through ignorance or overzealousness, sell IOS fund shares inside the United States, which was against the rules of the SEC and IOS. Some such sales had in fact been made that, while not on the surface seeming such a serious matter, could provide the SEC with a reason for the sort of massive investigation that had eaten up companies before. The letter was a masterpiece of legalistic ambiguity, so carefully phrased that it could have been interpreted as an attempt to conceal guilt, but was still an instruction to strip the files of possibly incriminating material. That was how the SEC read it and proceeded to release the document. It never formed the basis of any charges, and Cowett seemed to have justice on his side when he denounced the commission for "McCarthyism." But the SEC pressed on, asking jurisdiction over all of IOS and formally requiring the company to produce its records. IOS sued the SEC in Puerto Rico, on the grounds of preserving the secrecy of its records; the SEC countersued, for subpoena enforcement, and won.

Cowett attended a meeting at the elegant IOS offices on Park Avenue with some twenty financial hotshots, from Allen & Co., Morgan Stanley, and the like, to discuss a large offering for a railroad. Among them was Arthur Kramer, a partner in the firm that Eddie had taken $40,000 from. Kramer, who hadn't seen Cowett in some seven years, found himself thinking that the one-time thief and the poor boy from Brooklyn had become the toast of Western Europe, and now, to judge by the assemblage, of the New York financial community as well. As the minutes passed, Kramer wondered if Eddie wasn't out to show them up with his success. He had another thought: was Cowett a real person, or was he, deep down, a pathological personality—Eddie was awfully hard to relate to. The dandyish Cowett, in a black turtleneck sweater and carrying a cigarette holder, arrived an hour and a half late but didn't bother to apologize.

In 1967 a fateful peace was reached between IOS and the SEC, which said, in effect, "Do what you want with foreigners but keep your hands out of American pockets." The SEC wouldn't interfere with the company so long as it didn't sell to Americans anywhere, offered Americans free redemptions, and ceased U.S. operations. IOS could not take a controlling interest in any U.S. company and, importantly, couldn't do anything that would place it under SEC jurisdiction.

> After two years of battle, we've finally made peace with the SEC. What's significant, however, is not simply that we have finally made peace but that we have done so honorably; that we didn't give the SEC any client information without the client's consent; that there were no findings of any wrongdoings in the settlement

> and finally that the settlement not only doesn't hurt our operation but in many ways helps and, as in the case of our FOF proprietary funds' move to Canada, makes more money for our clients . . .
>
> Bernie

The rules could have effectively prevented IOS from trading on American stock exchanges, but the SEC hadn't fully reckoned on the gut smarts of the monster across the ocean. The problem for IOS was to have an entity to place orders with the funds' main broker, who had become Arthur Lipper, a member of the NYSE, from outside the United States, because IOS couldn't do business in the United States under the SEC consent order. The year before, FOF had set up "proprietary" funds, some twenty of them in all, in which the "proprietors," or money managers, were given a free hand to play with the large sums IOS entrusted them to invest. The "prop" funds were domiciled in Canada, but their managers remained in the United States. Although they couldn't legally place an order with Lipper, or Lipper receive one from them, an astonishing "echo" system was devised by Lipper and Cowett. "Suggestions" from the props were collated by Lipper and telexed to London, where Lipper had a firm to receive them. From there they were passed immediately to Geneva for confirmation—sometimes, to make it look good, a transaction would be refused—returned to London as an order that was dropped through an interconnecting window to the Lipper London office next door and telexed to Lipper in New York. A "suggestion" could become a buy order in as little as forty-five seconds, so well did the system work.

The funds flourished, although some assets were illiquid and could not be evaluated on a daily basis. One reason for growth was payment on the installment plan. Buhl's IIT, whose assets had increased 155 percent from 1962—to $474 million in 1967—was in that year and others the top performing fund internationally, while FOF's per share value increased 38 percent, as compared to the Dow Jones index of 18 percent and Standard & Poor's "500" 23 percent for the year. Bearded Bernie smiled angelically from the cover of FOF's annual report.

The day after the deal with the SEC was announced, the IOS charitable foundation sponsored a Geneva conference called Pacem in Terris II, the successor to a similar gathering held in 1962. The theme (as it happened, the meeting coincided with the resumption of American bombing in Vietnam and the outbreak of the Six Day War in the Middle East) was peace and how to achieve it. In attendance were four hundred leading intellectuals, clerics, ambassadors, scientists, and so on from seventy countries, but no movie stars. The "peace" oratorio *El Pesebre,* by Pablo Casals, the famous Spanish cellist and pacifist, was performed for Pacem II by a distinguished group. "Peace is bullish," Bernie said when asked to justify the $500,000 expense by the IOS Foundation (which gave generously to worthy causes), but the literature was marked "IOS presents" and cynics suggested that Cornfeld was exploiting peace.

9

JOHN KING

Cornfeld and Vesco had powerful ego needs. So, too, did John McCandish King whose failure to become the savior of IOS helped break its spirit and opened the way for Robert Vesco. Born in 1927, the same year as Cornfeld, who would be his mortal enemy, King had asthma as a child. From age four to fourteen, he stayed in bed where he became a great knitter, won a Bergdorf-Goodman women's clothes design competition, and, though or because he didn't speak much, he read everything he could set hands on, especially world religion. Possessed with an incredible memory, he was able, he said, to memorize the whole Bible in a matter of hours. (Whether he had to rememorize it was another question.) King had wanted to be a Methodist minister but eventually decided that a pantheistic belief like his, which could see God in an oilwell, couldn't be strapped into conventional denominations.

With hardly any high school, he self-taught himself well enough to enter, at fifteen, the University of Washington, where his parents had sent him in the mistaken notion that the moist climate would be good for his health. In 1945, he got a job as an aide to Harold Stassen at the San Francisco conference to organize the United Nations. From observing prominent figures at close range, he lost his awe of authority, he said.

Studying economics and political science, "Big John" as he was known, went on to the University of California at Berkeley, then to Wheaton College in Illinois, and to Northwestern, where he founded and became chairman of the Young Republican College Federation. Lecturing constantly, he used the organization as a base to support Stassen's first unsuccessful campaign for President. Not having time or inclination for normal pursuits, he didn't graduate. In 1950, having worked eleven months for Sears, Roebuck, he ran for the Illinois State Legislature and served three terms before losing narrowly because of redistricting. In 1952, with $1,500, 40 percent of his capital, he sank an oil well on a friend's farm in Oklahoma. The chances of a wildcat strike are worse than getting the right number on a roulette wheel, but King hit in commercial quantity and continued to hit fifteen or twenty times in a row—twice in one night—an almost unheard of streak. King had a theory that oil prospecting was more art than science. He believed there were perhaps seventy-five "oil finders" in the world, men with photographic memories and three-dimensional minds who could "see" into the earth and he, despite his lack of formal training, was one of them, though the others were introverted as he was decidedly not.

In 1963, after he had moved from Chicago to Denver, an Oklahoma well in which King was heavily invested reached a "bubble point." Instead of propelling the oil, gas emerges. Since gas was not marketable then, King almost went broke. He spent three or four months traveling around the country and talking to experts as he looked for new methods to prospect for oil. He claimed to have come up with a computerized system that could study an entire basin so that a number of wells could be packaged and sold to an oil company. King Resources, of which he owned 73 percent, became a force among the independents, and was active in virtually every phase of the business—drilling, funding, exploring, and pipelines. He employed, directly or indirectly, 5,000 people, and was using, at one point, some 15 percent of the drilling rigs in the world. He made major discoveries off Texas and Louisiana. *Forbes* magazine playing its annual "How much?" game, thought that $300 million would be a low guess for Big John's worth. "It is probable that no man, including Henry Ford or John D. Rockefeller, ever made a fortune faster than John King," opined *Dun's Review,* equally admiring, in the American dream spirit, of great wealth. King looked forward with confidence to personal assets of a billion dollars.

If anyone was "larger than life," as they say, it was King—six-foot-three, weighing in at 250 pounds, and also known as the "gasbag" because of his longwindedness. His cowboy boots and the cowboy hats that covered his bald dome had "K" monogrammed on them. He had six homes, including a 400-acre spread in the Rockies that he called the Little King Ranch, actually owned by King Resources. It had an airstrip, a small auditorium, a beauty parlor, and bunks for 120 guests, and he planned an addition of 70,000 square feet. He or his company had already spent $3 million on the place. He had a stretched-out black Lincoln limousine with a sunroof fixed so that he could hunt from it. John had 3,000 pairs of cufflinks.

He traveled several hundred thousand miles a year and was on the road three-fourths of the time after he went international. On a typical day, he would rise at 5:30 A.M., spend two or three hours on the phone to the Far East, arrive at the office, return home at 7:30, "block out" a couple of hours for his wife and four kids, and get on the phone again until midnight. Often, his scanty sleep was interrupted by phone calls.

There were those who believed that Big John's grasp of the oil business was shallow, that his real strength was as seller of mutual funds. He was the first to create petroleum tax shelters for the common man, and you could invest in a King fund for as little as $150 down and $50 a month. A man named Frank Sweetser, who had been at the Dreyfus Fund and originally hired Cornfeld, had become involved in King's Colorado complex. He wanted to sell oil funds in Europe and traveled there in 1967 on a fact-finding mission, visiting Bernie. King went over after that, spending six weeks exploring the situation, and the djin of Denver met Geneva's guru. Cornfeld was in his office lined with red silk—Cowett's was done in red leather—when the call came from King.

Bernie swooped in for the meeting from his nearby castle in France by helicopter, wearing jodhpurs. Except for their love of entrepreneurialism and material possessions, it would have been hard to imagine a more disparate pair—small, soft-spoken Cornfeld with his women, fancy designer clothes, and discomfort with most non-Jews, facing the outsized, transplanted Western macho with his booming voice and piercing blue eyes. Still, they had uses for each other: the "Dollar-Crested Moneycatcher," FOF, had too much of its assets concentrated in the uncertain stock market and King Resources needed endless infusions of cash to maintain its drilling program. Bernie suggested that John talk to Ed Cowett, the executive vice president, and in December, at the New York offices of Willkie Farr & Gallagher, by then U.S. lawyers for IOS, they met. King had considered building an international sales force, but Cowett talked him out of it. Better, he suggested, that John do business with IOS. Would King add FOF to his customers list? "Do bears shit in the woods?" cornily joked the gasbag.

IOS floated a dollar bond issue in Europe for King Resources and in Acapulco in March 1968, he made an effective presentation to the FOF board. He was interested in "elephant hunting," looking for large oil reserves, the riskier side of the business, but he was also in uranium, gold, silver, copper, and diamonds. There was already talk that IOS would go public, and if John was even half right about the future of oil, the value of IOS would soar because of FOF's investment in King—$10 million for openers, despite the claim in the FOF prospectus that the fund wouldn't make "illiquid" investments—and, since IOS executives would have shares in the issue, they would see their millions (O Lord!) at last. Though King became a seller of properties to IOS, little was on paper, because, King said, of Cowett's apprehension about the 1967 consent decree with the SEC forbidding American dealings, and, anyway, King was accustomed to handshake deals. (The lack of records, which could have been construed as an invitation to steal, went heavily against King in the courts later on.) Soon, Cowett was virtually begging King to present proposals.

IOS became King's most important customer. Whatever the exact relationship between them was—King claimed his role was strictly as a seller, but the U.S. government maintained otherwise—more than $100 million of FOF's money had been invested in King by the end of 1969. In some cases, King quickly upvalued properties he had just bought by 1,000 percent before selling them to FOF, but John said that the properties had been good buys to start with, which was why he acquired them. (John also sold dry holes to FOF. His excuse, he said, was that he'd invested money and he sold the properties as "normal" parts of a deal.) In any case, no one at IOS knew how to read King's reports. Sometimes, King didn't even send a report—just a bill. King was betting heavily on the Arctic, where he had started buying drilling permits in 1968, after the discovery of oil on the Alaska North Slope. In 1969, he bought an interest in millions of acres more and sold half of about 22 million acres, an area greater than the size of New York State, to Fund of Funds for $11 million. (IOS seemed unaware that the purchase carried an exploration obligation for another $10 million the following year.) King's Arctic enthusiasm was contagious. He said he believed there were billions of dollars locked in the King–IOS parcels, if only ways could be found to get it out of the ground and delivered. Gas was discovered; an economical means of retrieving it was not. (Significant oil was found only in the 1980s.) But everybody had blind faith in technology and the Canadian government's participation. Bernie told the IOS sales force that the Arctic lands were the most exciting thing that had ever happened to the company.

"From the moment Cowett had launched the IOS Stock Option Plan, back in 1960, IOS's entire corporate existence was focused on one day achieving a public market for the company stock so that insiders could cash in their paper at a tremendous premium."* In December 1968, the fateful decision was made in Geneva.

Much of the pressure to go public was because of the Stock Option Plan. The concept was that employees could (and were almost forced to) buy stock in various amounts according to their position in the pecking order. The stock price constantly rose as earnings rose, and the stock split according to a formula price. IOS came to face a serious dilemma. To allow retirees to keep their stock and continue to benefit from the efforts of others who may have held far fewer shares seemed unwise. Yet to buy the shares at current levels would impose a crushing burden on the

* Hutchison, *Vesco,* p. 95.

company. The answer seemed to be in a public offering so retirees could sell their stock. Some wondered whether the disintegration of IOS would have occurred without the public offering.

That summer, IOS, in Canada, had floated off 600,000 shares of IOS Management Ltd., the management company for the dollar funds, so-called because their net asset value was quoted daily in U.S. dollars, at $12.50. Investor interest had been intense—trading began at $75. (The stock, split three-for-one, reached $210 a share in pre-split terms in March 1969.) To the IOS directors, a signal had been sent—people displayed the same confidence in the company that they themselves expressed. The directors decided to take the company public in Europe the following fall, which meant that some of their stock options, turned into shares, could be sold on the open market. (Cornfeld later said that issuing voting shares was his greatest error.)

10

INEVITABILITY BECKONS

In January 1969, Vesco became chairman, president, and chief executive officer of Electronic Specialty, whose profits could be used to offset the cost of further acquisitions. Though he made over $1 million for himself in a Van Nuys airways company, he took a loss for ICC in selling Golden West Airlines, describing it as a mistaken investment, but ICC sales had increased "remarkably," he told the board. Earnings in the second quarter of 1969 would be double the first. The BOA, pleased with the financial condition of the company, would maintain its loan, and Prudential Life Insurance Company was coming in with $20 million more, in two installments. (Vesco was proud of the Pru contract, which he had negotiated on terms he thought favorable to ICC.) In May, for the first time, ICC began to pay its directors fees for attending board meetings.

Like Cornfeld, Cowett, and King, Vesco predicted miracles. ICC, he said, would soon be a billion-dollar company, then a $100-billion one. But, for that to happen, Vesco would have to bring into the fold an outfit much larger than ELS, with meteoric growth of its own.

ICC was still an exciting place to work, but the young boss was more aloof. He no longer attended the Saturday skull sessions, closeting himself with financial people and bragging about deals in a mysterious Swiss money fund. (The minuscule fund was called Executive Growth and folded. Vesco had $280,000 in it, and Carl Anderson was a substantial investor too. Both lost. Managing it were Gilbert R. J. Straub and Ulrich J. Strickler. Vesco insisted the fund was unimportant, and it seems to have been, though Straub and Strickler became Vesco stalwarts.) The company had become more complex, and discussions about finances were endless. "One of the problems at ICC," remarked a former executive, "was that people held Bob in awe. They wouldn't stand up to him." The outside accountants had long negotiations with Vesco, whose financial statements had to demonstrate the ability to handle so many subsidiaries. Vesco applied pressure. "All the big accountants were the same. They'd put up a fight and raise their bills but ultimately they'd play the tune they were supposed to play. They'd blow the whistle only on absolute fraud."

To be sure, not everything worked. Vesco's commuter-airline scheme collapsed because he couldn't get the subsidies for U.S. mail. There were serious plans—blueprints were drawn—for a plant of 150,000 square feet to be built in the New Jersey marshlands near the Hudson River. ICC divisions would be brought together in a real manufacturing organization. But Vesco, without whom nothing significant could happen in the company, seemed to lose interest.

ICC stock had steadily declined along with the other conglomerates, but Vesco was still plenty rich. He never had less than several millions in convertible debentures, plus his stock. But money wasn't the only objective. Vesco wanted to become a power to be reckoned with. He flew constantly in the company Gulfstream. He couldn't settle down. He still had to prove himself and coveted a major victory on the corporate battleground, one that would make him a legend in the annals of the big rollers.

In August 1969, in anticipation of the public offering of IOS stock in September, some three hundred IOS managers assembled in Geneva for a meeting, and Allen Cantor said, to applause, that one hundred of them were on the brink of being millionaires.

The offering price, $10 a share, had been agreed on, though not without rancor. The investment bankers had suggested a price of $8.50, then $9.50, but Cornfeld had fought for $10 because that was the price everyone expected, and he even threatened to withdraw the issue. The bankers capitulated, which was in retrospect a grave mistake, because if the stock dropped below $10 it could be in serious trouble; $8.50 provided greater latitude.

But who, certainly not Bernie, could have anticipated a catastrophe? IOS was at its apogee in 1969, with companies over the world (sixty in Nassau alone), fifty-five principal subsidiaries, sixteen open-end funds, banks, commercial and investment insurance, substantial real estate, in Spain and Florida, for instance. More than one million people throughout the world were IOS clients. Fund assets were $2.7 billion. Bernie claimed the stock would go to $25, then $40, then $50. He anticipated $4.5 billion in fund sales the following year. By 1975, IOS would have $15 billion under management. Anything-but-Cassandra Cornfeld predicted 1969 profits for IOS would be $25 million, $30 million for 1970.

The $110 million offering of IOS Ltd.—since 1967 the company had been domiciled in Canada—was the largest in European history and the third largest in all history until recently. Many major financial institutions were in it—Allan Butler, with his distrust of Cornfeld, declined to participate—and the issue was heavily oversubscribed. The advance price went as high as $29. After opening on September 24, it spurted to $19. Into the pockets of the 490 insiders, who converted the allowed portion of the preferred shares they had acquired in the Stock Option Plan into the new class of common for sale at the underwriting, flowed $55.3 million of which Bernie's part was $8.2 million. In all, Cornfeld said, he realized over $10 million from the sale of his IOS stock. Soon, though, in the general market retreat, and for no other discernible reason, the price began to drop.

That fall, there had been a brief but significant conversation between Cowett, in Geneva, and King, who was having a cola for breakfast at the bar at his Colorado ranch. Cowett predicted the stock might drop in the aftermath of the offering, and that, in the $12 range, it would be a good investment. Ed proposed to form a buying pool for a million dollars or so, with Bernie in it for

$300,000, and John, with no particular thought, said he'd come in, too.

Cornfeld had a fighting side. That fall, too, he was in Acapulco with Oleg Cassini to look at a potential project. Oli's columnist brother, Igor (Cholly Knickerbocker) didn't appreciate Bernie. He thought Cornfeld was exploiting Oli for social reasons and women. Bernie needed girls so much because of insecurity, Oli thought. For him, Cornfeld could have made it into top European society if only he seemed to care and he wasn't always late. But Oleg liked Bernie and would always be loyal.

They were in the lobby and a couple of Texas oilmen were insulting women. Though Bernie was not above being rough with females himself, he stoutly told the Texans to apologize. One swung at Cornfeld, who wrestled him to the floor—an IOS lawyer jumped into the fray, kicking the Texan and breaking a toe; he was the only casualty on Cornfeld's team—while Oleg knocked out a tooth of the other. Tex McCrary, who happened to be there though not knowing Cornfeld yet, applauded. All was well the next day when the Texans conveyed regrets. Bernie proceeded to hire McCrary to do his p.r.

Oli Cassini had a secret fear about Cornfeld that stood in the way of making a boutique deal Bernie badly wanted. He worried that Cornfeld's tremendous success had turned him careless.

In December, Bernie went to visit the Pope, since the Pope wouldn't come to him; the Pope's support would be invaluable in Catholic countries, and, at Tex McCrary's urging, Bernie had agreed to build an American hospital in Rome. For the Holy See, Cartier's in Paris was commissioned by IOS to make a gold globe inlaid with ruby chips designating the location of each of the cardinals of the Catholic Church.

Bernie's eighty-odd-year-old mother, Sophie, lived in a tower of Bernie's Geneva villa. Cornfeld had installed an elevator and Sophie had the furniture from her apartment in Brooklyn. She, too, wanted to meet the Pope. McCrary, uncertain of the protocol, feared that the trip might be endangered. Dutiful son Bernie insisted, and all were ushered into the Papal presence.

Sophie and Pope John quickly began conversing earnestly and pointing at the wall. They rose and walked over, and the Pope touched the wall covering. Sophie had asked where the white velvet came from, but the Pope hadn't been aware that it was velvet.

Bernie gave a 1970 New Year's party at the Geneva Intercontinental and passed out 5,000 bottles of his own champagne, Château Pelly de Cornfeld. For Bernie, the new year had to be the best yet. With Cowett as president of IOS, Cornfeld would be free to do what he really liked, to develop new ideas. He envisioned a credit card for IOS investors—no chance of nonpayment would exist. Under construction in Munich was a huge IOS complex that would be the headquarters for the 1972 Olympic Games. Hotel projects were popping up all over. If Cassini would come into the deal, IOS would create three hundred boutiques over the world to be supplied by Cassini-designed products manufactured in Italy. Cornfeld had a special unit developing new lines—prefabricated plastic playgrounds, the importation to the United States of European chocolate and gourmet foods, soups that would appeal to children. Soon, Bernie would present his thoughts to an important New York forum and then fly to Acapulco to meet Hugh Hefner about an IOS-*Playboy* condominium-hotel venture. After that, he'd visit Israel, and after that, maybe, a vacation, which he hadn't taken in ten years. Maybe Oli Cassini, whom Bernie adored, would come along. They'd have fun. IOS stock, he thought, was bound to go up in 1970.

The business magazines loved big numbers, to inspire junior executives. Only those in *Business Week* (January 10, 1970) were raw as sushi. "*Well off.* IOS has plenty of money: $60 million in retained earnings as of the end of 1969 and $52 million raised last September from the first public offering of IOS shares. Beyond that is the money the mutual funds draw in each year. Cornfeld figures the $900 million in net new cash of 1969 will swell to $1.5 billion this year. As one Wall Street investment banker observes 'The richer you get, the more respectable you get.' "

Sophie Cornfeld was proud. She passed the article to her girlfriends.

In February 1970, the witching year for IOS, Cornfeld, having tripped between London and Paris five times in the previous week, mostly for women reasons, winged into New York to be the main speaker at a conference hosted by the magazine *Institutional Investor.* The night before, Bernie had been the untitled guest of honor at the annual party for prestigious folk thrown by the Washington *Post* in New York. Cornfeld's hour had come round at last. Smiled at for his foppery, dismissed as a charlatan or worse, baited by the federal government, the mutual fund Count of Monte Cristo, a mere forty-two, had demonstrated once again the spell cast by *la belle dame sans merci,* big dough. "He is probably the world's greatest conceptual salesman," rhapsodized John King, much of whose prosperity was related to IOS. "He has one of those types of minds that has an instantaneous grasp of any subject he chooses to be interested in."

Good Humphrey liberal that he was, the former socialist talked to his gelt-edged audience of the concerns of the period—the Vietnam war that wouldn't go away; the blacks, who wouldn't go away, either; inner cities; air pollution. He seemed to relate America's social problems to those of the stock market for which he blamed the SEC. Animosity barely concealed, he accused the SEC of "attacking virtually every sector of earnings in the securities business. And a weak, unprofitable securities business means a weak, unprofitable market." He claimed that the public interest was last on the agency's mind, and, largely because of it, he sensed "a malaise within the investment community here." He demanded that the SEC be less meddlesome and more fair-minded. He noted that IOS had a positive cash flow of $100 million a month, and, by 1975, five short years off, the company would have $15 billion to play with. But the money wouldn't necessarily be invested on Wall Street. If Washington didn't let up, Bernie implied, IOS might seek greener pastures. Bernie had been flailing at the SEC in other forums, and the combative commission didn't like threats, especially from IOS whose financial clout concerned it.

His Guy Laroche (he had bought half of Laroche and part of Oleg Cassini lines as well) trousers angling over the backs of his shoes, Cornfeld climbed aboard his Falcon with a gaggle of girls and flew to Acapulco for the meeting with *Playboy*'s Hugh Hefner, coming on *his* plane with *his* harem.

Also in February, more serious matters were under way. Before he left for Japan, Cowett ordered that if IOS stock dropped below $12, shares should be bought. According to Cornfeld, Cowett did not realize that some $14 million worth had been acquired by Overseas Development Bank (Geneva). Cowett proceeded to farm them out with ODB loans—one from Cornfeld's account without his knowledge—to John King, for $6 million, and two of King's friends, for another $2 million. Cowett took $2 million in shares, and the remaining $4 million was acquired by ODB. What had started as a "buying pool" had become a full-scale program to support the stock—of which Cornfeld wasn't aware—and in violation of Canadian law, IOS being a Canadian company. If it had been initially based on an as yet unpublicized $10 million performance fee for IOS, the investment could also have been construed as trading on inside information.

Cowett's cool facade and long hours (once, he almost worked himself through a wedding-anniversary evening) concealed a prankster, as he'd been at Harvard. A friend, a Swiss banker, sent Ed and his wife a bottle of champagne at a restaurant. Cowett responded with two bottles, and champagne escalation was underway. Cowett arranged for a uniformed waiter to arrive at the friend's bank. The banker was told he had to accept a delivery in the lobby and duly arrived, whereupon the waiter opened a bottle of champagne and poured it into a glass he carried.

The banker, embarrassed, schemed back. At a time prearranged with Cowett's secretary—she was to keep him there—the Swiss banker arrived outside 119 Rue de Lausanne with a crane, which deposited him on the balcony to Cowett's office on the sixth or seventh floor. He knocked and entered, champagne bottle in hand.

In November 1969, Cowett wanted to buy more King Resources bonds—IOS had helped float a $15-million European-dollar issue for King Resources and IIT had picked up some of it as well as other IOS funds. Henry Buhl was dispatched to Denver. He took with him an energy expert, and they spent three days in Denver talking to King and his staff and inspecting Big John's oil-discovery computer. Buhl concluded that FOF shouldn't invest any more than it already had in King Resources and called Cowett to say so. Ed informed King by phone. Buhl was at an L.A. hotel by then, and John called, asking Henry to meet him at the Burbank Airport. It was Friday night and raining, and Henry fought traffic on the freeway to meet King, who had flown in on his Lockheed jet. Since King's family was on board, the two talked in Buhl's rented car for two hours, with the big man trying to convince the little man. John said he could produce a 60 percent return on an investment in a year, but his reasoning was hard to follow, and cautious Henry didn't believe in such claims. "Come on, John," he said, and headed back to Los Angeles.

To be chronically short of cash was normal in the speculative oil business and King Resources was, despite (or because of) paper assets of $1.5 billion. King's organizations were pumping 260,000 barrels a day—110,000 out of the Sinai alone.

In December, King had another conversation by telephone with Cowett. John was at his ranch, where he'd gone for Christmas. IOS shares were under pressure and Cowett proposed using King and Cowett family trusts, already in existence in the Bahamas, to buy stock for the buying pool, as had been already discussed. The money would be lent by IOS and wouldn't cost King a dime. Cornfeld would have control of the stock voting rights. King said sure but insisted that Cowett be made the investment adviser, because, if Bernie was, it would look as though nobody supervised the account.

Other calls to King in London, late in 1969, were about a matter over which Cowett had agonized—the value to be placed on the Arctic permits. King had told Allan Conwill, the IOS Willkie Farr & Gallagher lawyer, that the Arctic drilling rights were worth $3 billion, and Conwill was staggered. He'd thought only governments were involved with *billions*, and he believed King was "puffing." But even if King were only half right, FOF had a problem. Those buying in would eventually reap a bonanza and those selling out would be gypped because they wouldn't know the value of the Arctic lands. Arthur Andersen, the accounting firm that had offices in Geneva and represented IOS as well as King, said the only way to revalue was to sell part of the holdings. Cornfeld asked King if he could sell some, and John said yes, provided he received a commission. Little effort, it would seem, went into obtaining an independent appraisal by oil experts.

Cornfeld phoned a week later and said he wanted to sell a piece that King insisted was too small to give the buyer a satisfactory position. The only way to do it, King explained, was to create a leverage structure over a longer period of time. Bernie called back with Cowett on the line again. How about a larger sale in which the buyer had seven years to pay?

As an accommodation to IOS, and because he wanted to continue to sell to FOF, King and a group of oil people he knew agreed to buy 10 percent of the IOS Arctic lands. On December 29, IOS announced, on the basis of the sale to "three independent oil companies" that FOF's value in natural resources had increased by $107 million, which produced for IOS, as the "manager," a performance fee of almost $10 million that was not announced. King later went to jail for representing the revaluation was based on "arms-length" sales, when he had secretly agreed with the "buyers" to repay them if they chose.

March 1970 marked the beginning of the end for IOS under Cornfeld. Geneva board meetings from March 9 to 13 made apparent for the first time that profits might not match prophecies, though it was hard to be sure, given the company's creaky accounting system, and Cowett, who had become president, announced a $44 million expansion program, funds for which weren't allocated. There was curiously little effort to perform a thorough analysis, one reason seeming to have lain in the attitudes of the IOSers toward Bernie and to a lesser extent Ed, though Cowett in the end worked for Bernie, too. Since the salespeople, as most of the leadership was, identified deeply with the company and its founder, they could not and did not peer into him too deeply. If they had, they might have seen that while Cornfeld enjoyed being superrich and receiving outlandish amounts of attention, he had another set of needs revolving around his role as a corporate father figure. He believed in the organization's expectations of himself. Criticisms of IOS were criticisms of Bernie personally. If there were problems, Bernie and Ed would solve them, as they always had.

Cowett told the directors that profits were projected as $19 million, instead of $27 million, with expenses much higher than anticipated, in the $56 million range. Costs had to be cut. Cowett wrote, "Perhaps, I did not convey to Bernard Cornfeld and other top management personnel the depth of my concerns of the seriousness of the potential problem. Or, perhaps, they were incapable of appreciating the situation. More likely, all of us were afraid to upset the equilibrium by appearing to deal with an emergency."

That meeting was difficult enough, Cowett noted, as what he called the IOS "myth of infallibility" had come into question and so had the founder. ". . . Bernard Cornfeld had lost control of himself and of the IOS board. In a twenty-minute tirade, he so demeaned and berated each and every director that the previously unthinkable—an IOS without Bernie—became a possibility. Between sessions of the meeting, directors met in small clusters to debate what should be done about Cornfeld. For the first time, one heard talk of impeachment or resignation."

Cowett had become critical of Cornfeld. He knew Bernie better than anyone else—they sometimes worked all night together, and Cornfeld was a frequent visitor at Ed's house—and, for him, "Bernie's charisma was aimed less and less at IOS and more and more on personal publicity. He had burned out. . . . He was introduced to the jet set and surrounded himself with progressively greater numbers of the beautiful, but vapid, people who make up the set. . . . Ego got the better of Bernie. His lifestyle became outrageous and his personal extravagances became more pronounced. He began to believe his 'press notices.' He was a financial genius, or at least he believed so."

To Cowett, Cornfeld was charming but rude, single-minded,

tasteless and discriminating, disrespectful of authority, socially aware, magnetic, lonely ("he was the loneliest person I ever met"), soft-hearted, and self-destructive.

> He always accused others of being self-destructive. But, he was the most self-destructive person one could imagine. He was like the little boy who chooses to build sand castles directly in the path of the incoming tide because he wants to see them destroyed. In a peculiar sense, he almost enjoyed the destruction of IOS—since he could not distinguish between the Company and himself. IOS was his sand castle.

But "from the outset," Cowett wrote, "IOS was flawed. There was no clear definition of the lines of corporate authority and responsibility. . . . There was growth—at a spectacular rate of 80% a year. Growth without adequate controls can be disastrous. . . . There was no corporate plan. . . . There was no functioning chief executive officer. Cornfeld was the dominant figure, but he did not know how to delegate authority. His was personalized management, best suited for the small business. His withdrawal from day-to-day management left a void. He refused to surrender his authority, and he failed to exercise it. . . . I moved into that void from time to time—but never with the assurance that the decisions I would make would go unquestioned. From the date when IOS stock was first offered to the public [in the fall of 1969] to April 8, 1970, IOS was largely unmanaged. Bernard Cornfeld, following a pattern he had set in late 1967, spent little time in his office and seemed bored with all IOS business other than matters relating to portfolio management. I absented myself from Geneva for vacations and on special business trips. Other top executives followed a similar course. The result was a business which on a day-to-day basis was run by its middle management. There was surface tranquillity. All was going well—at least that was what we preferred to think."

Cowett cited lack of financial controls, an absence of business professionals, excessive fees to sales chiefs who earned as much as $1.5 million a year simply because operations under them grew so fast and because of a snap decision by the IOS Executive Committee not to limit them. In one year the "super general managers," as Cowett called them, were paid $12.5 million. To Cowett the advantage of lack of discipline was that individuals could develop freely, but the disadvantages outweighed the advantages. "In many ways," Cowett said, "IOS and Bernie Cornfeld were mirror images. Its flaws were apt to be his flaws, and its strengths were apt to be his strengths."

And, Cowett said, "The remarkable thing is that the flaws did not become apparent until after the process of disintegration had been set in motion. . . ."

Allan Butler wasn't interested when, in 1970, Vesco told him he wanted to make Butlers Bank the center of a new banking operation. Allan had begun merger talks with Warburg of London and the First National Bank of Miami, which he hoped would provide Butlers Bank with capital, personnel, and a base outside the Bahamas, but the deal fell through. That winter, Allan had been helicopter skiing in Switzerland—the chopper would deliver him to virgin slopes in the mornings, fetching him in the evening —and Butler collapsed, either from a heart attack or too-strenuous exertion at high altitudes: the doctors didn't know. His prospective partners pulled out because, if Allan were incapacitated, they'd have to contend with Shirley, who could be difficult at meetings and drank too much.

The Butlers were constructing a $9 million structure, Charlotte House, on Charlotte Street in Nassau, the largest office building in the Bahamas, which had been intended to house the new banking combination. (Butlers Bank had $6 million equity in the building.) Allan acquired, and became chairman of, a Canadian outfit, Security Capital, which had gold mines, nursing homes, office equipment, savings-and-loan companies, and gross sales of $60 million. He was running lots of businesses, and while he sometimes hit he also erred. He had a running bet with a friend on profits from various transactions, and he owed the friend thirty-two cases of Dom Pérignon champagne. Aboard a North American Sabrejet he'd bought, he sometimes logged 60,000 miles a month and might easily be in three countries a day.

The merger's failure left the Butlers in an overextended position and forced them to consider Vesco again, even as Bob had begun to scout IOS. Vesco was always supportive and seemed to keep his word. The fraud allegations in the ELS takeover hadn't resulted in prosecution, and the Bank of America, which had backed Vesco, hadn't walked out on him. Butler worked on another takeover in Canada, Seaways–Multicorporation, and Vesco promised to help. If Allan succeeded, he would be able to repay Shirley's investment in their company, and a psychic yoke would be lifted that might give their troubled marriage a chance. All things being equal, people with wealth use it, however subtly, as a weapon against those who are without.

11

HENRY BUHL'S DISCOVERY

Henry Buhl was the sort who emptied ashtrays in other people's homes. He was nervously meticulous and uncertainty caused him to tighten his lips.

At a bar in Ferney-Voltaire, not long after the March 1970 board meeting when Cornfeld blew up, a member of the accounting office, having had a drink or two, confided apprehensively to George Hill, an IOS statistician, that the company's cash position was precarious. In the till, he believed, was only $4.5 million, not enough to meet next month's payroll. Hill was astonished. The figure was contrary to everything that had been said about the company's riches. The next day, though dubious, Hill brought the unsettling information to an incredulous Buhl. Hardly six months before, IOS Ltd. had scooped in $52 million—$47.2 million after underwriting costs—and it should have had its $10 million performance fee on the revaluation of the Arctic properties and cash from normal sales as well. Still, Henry decided to investigate, without making his purpose known. He had harbored doubts about Cowett all along. Although he had been with the company almost a decade, he didn't really trust those with whom he was so closely associated. Not that Cowett thought highly of Buhl.

Buhl went to the "junior Pentagon," the IOS complex at Ferney, but the source of the story, apparently frightened, avoided him. Buhl's suspicions deepened, but he was not yet convinced anything was amiss. He dropped in, as though casually, at the office of Melvin Lechner, IOS's treasurer, hoping to peek at the books, but Lechner stopped him and asked why he was there. The bespectacled Lechner's uneasy manner made Henry hesitate even more. He made up a ridiculous excuse, which Lechner seemed to accept. Buhl pretended that he wanted to make sure that Cornfeld's planes weren't rented for IOS business, since that would have been against the rules.

Almost as soon as Henry had returned to his Geneva office, Cowett called to demand, "What were you doing at Ferney?" Buhl was in a sensitive spot. If, as he still hoped, his information was wrong, he'd be inviting trouble with the second most powerful man in the company; if it proved correct, and money was missing, Ed would have to be implicated. Might Cowett try to cook the books? The question intruded itself mercilessly into Henry's mind. So he repeated the fabrication about Cornfeld's planes, adding, as if to justify himself, "I'm a director. I have a right to know." "I'm the president. Why didn't you ask me?" Ed said sharply.

Cowett's defensive tone, and the fact that Lechner had evidently found it imperative to report his visit immediately, added to Buhl's doubts. After a few fretful days, still wishing to avoid a confrontation with Ed, Buhl returned to Lechner's office—the treasurer seemed tired—with direct inquiries as to IOS's financial health. Lechner continued to sound evasive, and the moment Henry was back in Geneva, Ed called again to ask his reason for pestering Mel. This time Henry asked for a complete financial report and Cowett said, "Okay."

But nothing happened. Radar whirling, Buhl convinced Hill to obtain a statement from the accountant who, after a week or so, complied almost tearfully. The figures indicated IOS had tens of millions of dollars less than it was supposed to. Where the money had gone was a mystery.

Lechner himself had misgivings he didn't confide to Buhl. He was concerned that Cornfeld only spent time in areas that interested him—the company's growth and his own projects. It seemed to Lechner that Cowett made a point of keeping him off the board of directors and the executive committee so that Ed would have a free hand. He had confronted Ed about the numbers, and Cowett flew into a rage, telling Mel to mind his own business. Despite an accounting staff of 250, Lechner was unable to get a clear picture, although he finally deduced that Cowett's profit projections were way off base. When Henry Buhl walked into his office, he was preparing the facts and had already urged Cowett to cut spending. He was so concerned that he flew to New York for the weekend (which was why he looked tired) to ask his uncle, an esteemed accountant, whether he was crazy. His uncle, inspecting the figures, assured Lechner that he was, perhaps unfortunately, sane. Mel wanted to resign but feared that if he did, Arthur Andersen, the IOS accountants, would also resign and IOS might collapse then and there. Lechner was scared.

Buhl was scared, too. If there had been a scam, whoever had perpetrated it (Cowett?) might be desperate enough to try to silence him. Not that Henry didn't want to be silenced—under the stock option arrangement his IOS Ltd. shares would be worth over $8 million. Then he girded himself. The panic he experienced had to do with fear of Bernie's wrath and being ostracized from the IOS family, a pariah, an untouchable. It had happened before. But Henry had a responsibility as a top officer. Ed, he noticed, seemed oddly calm, even passive, as if he had already stood trial and been sentenced. Buhl scheduled an ad hoc meeting of the board for Friday, April 10, presumably to discuss the cash flow. He did not alert Cornfeld because Bernie might be involved. Buhl wished the facts put on the table without giving Cornfeld a chance to change them.

But, caught up in the melodrama, Henry phoned people as far away as Hong Kong he thought he could trust. "Do you know we're broke?" he whispered long distance, urging them to attend the Friday meeting. And he arranged a stealthy conclave a day or so earlier with what came to be known in company lore as the "Four Horsemen of the Apocalypse"—himself; Sir Eric Wyndham White, former British treasury official and former General Secretary of the General Agreement on Trade and Tariffs (GATT), who had joined IOS through James Roosevelt who also worked for IOS; Richard Hammerman, longtime IOSer and president of International Life Insurance Ltd., another IOS outfit, whom Henry asked to arrive quietly from his headquarters in London; and Professor George von Peterffy, former professor at the Harvard Business School and former consultant to such firms as Polaroid. They met in an office other than Buhl's because Henry feared that his own might be bugged in the electronic Persian court. Von Peterffy grilled Lechner relentlessly. The reluctant treasurer agreed to talk at the Friday meeting.

In Israel, where he had been in self-exile for a month, Cornfeld was arranging to buy three hotels to be managed by the Hyatt chain—he would lament that IOS would have quadrupled its investment except for the crisis—and was losing at backgammon to a sheik at Eilat when the bad-news telephone rang. From Geneva, sales director Allen Cantor, not privy to Buhl's secrets, warned in a low, unhappy voice of another "bear raid" by German banks to depress the price of IOS stock—an allegation that, though Bernie repeated it, was never proved. Support had to be found quickly or the stock would pierce the black-magic threshold, the $10 offering figure—on Thursday, April 9, it did—and who knew, in the worst securities panic since the Kennedy assassination in 1963, what the bottom might be.

"The story of how the break came is quite remarkable," Cowett said. "It is expected in Europe that public companies will buy back blocks of their own stock in order to maintain an orderly market. A bank in the Italian part of Switzerland had a block of 25,000 shares to sell. The bank's trader fully expected that the Company would be a willing buyer of the stock. He called IOS and found, much to his surprise, that no one at IOS had ever heard of that custom. He learned IOS was not in the business of buying back its own shares.

"The trader became panicky. He proceeded to 'dump' the shares at whatever price he could get on the market. This panic selling, coming at the end of a normal trading day, drove the market price down below $10. But that was all that was needed."

While those at IOS to whom the trader must have talked had

never heard of the custom of buying back your own stock, Ed himself had bought it extensively with IOS money.

"Bernie's on his way!" they cheered at Ferney-Voltaire, those little people who'd hocked their souls to buy the stock, often on 50 percent margin, and who would be sold out if the debacle continued. Airborne in his orange-and-white Jet Commander, Cornfeld gave himself a lecture. He'd been inattentive. He'd been so busy being the cynosure of the staff's envy images that he hadn't paid heed to the company. He would have to act, he decided, because he couldn't let the small fry suffer or the not-cashed-in millionaires, either—they were his family and he loved them—to say nothing of the hundreds of thousands of stockholders.

Miraculously, the stock stabilized, but not for long. At 119 Rue de Lausanne, they were in double-barreled shock. IOS shares dove to just over $8 on Friday. The paper millionaires could have cashed in part of their holdings but many hadn't, believing the price would rise. Still, the nouveaux riches had the first inklings that they might become nouveaux pauvres. On the other hand, they had had it so good for so long that they couldn't really accept that calamity might befall them.

Buhl met Cornfeld, returned from the airport, in the hall at Bella Vista just before the meeting. "What's this about?" Bernie asked, and Henry said grimly, "You'll learn."

The fateful meeting, held in Ambassador Roosevelt's office draped with the Stars and Stripes, began at 5 P.M. on the tenth, and went on for six hours, with Cornfeld in the chair. One of the first items was $10 million transferred from Overseas Development Bank (Geneva) to an IOS Bahamian bank to pay for IOS stock purchased for King and Cowett family trusts there. "On whose instruction?" Lechner was asked; he murmured, "Ed's." "Is this true?" Bernie said, Buhl watching him closely, not yet fully convinced Cornfeld wasn't in on it. The surprise on Bernie's face was too convincing to be feigned, though. Cowett raised his hand like a guilty schoolboy, nodded his head and said, "Yes." He had given an affirmative answer at once. Amid the shouting, Cornfeld closed his eyes and sort of blacked out.

Buhl believed that the $10 million amounted to theft—Cowett had taken pain to conceal the transactions—and said so on TV later. Cornfeld maintained the purchase had been largely accidental (King, though, would claim his signature on the documents had been forged), but that was far from all Cowett had spent supporting the stock. Although the $10 million had been debited against Cornfeld's account, IOS still owed it and when the facts were clear, it turned out that between $15 and $25 millions from other IOS entities (not fund money but money from the IOS underwriting and the Stock Option Plan) had been spent for the same purpose. Some were aware the stock had been supported, but not to that extent, and the buying was a major reason the once-opulent IOS was apparently broke. Despite his brilliance, Cowett's outrageous naïveté shocked Cornfeld. When Bernie had personally gotten involved months before, it was because he thought the stock was a good bet, but Ed's had been a highly dangerous gamble. For Bernie, there was no need to make a market, but Cowett had done funny things with money in the past. When the inside directors had worried about Cowett's becoming president of IOS, Bernie had said, "You guys are crazy. Here's a guy we gave a second chance to. He'll never do anything to hurt us." Yet Ed had hurt them badly, and it was Cornfeld's fault for trusting Ed's judgment. Cowett said that John King, whose King Resources brought in $2 million a day, would probably cover the debts, but Big John didn't play marbles, Bernie reflected. He'd want control and that might mean the end of Cornfeld's reign. Bernie was frantic. "Communication between Ed and me broke down. He was helping King. He'd helped put Willkie Farr people on the board. It was institutionalized madness."

April 10 was Cowett's fortieth birthday, but he didn't smile much when he delivered what would prove his final "Happy Hour." He could sense the skepticism of the sales managers from Germany. Later that day, Allen Cantor and he addressed a hastily called meeting of IOS executives, and one confronted Cantor with the fact that the volume of sales was less than 60 percent of the comparable 1969 period. Cantor hadn't noticed the shift.

"That night was a welcome relief. Most of the senior executives of IOS, together with a dozen or so close friends from outside the IOS family, gathered at my house to celebrate my birthday. It was a marvelous party and lasted well into the morning hours," Cowett wrote. "It was also the last time when there could be a gathering of IOS executives that was free of acrimony, recriminations, and unpleasantness." But Betty, Ed's attractive wife, observed the party was smaller than it might otherwise have been.

The directors met again on Sunday when Mel Lechner answered questions for ten hours, minus a lunch break. That the company had been profligate was known, the extent of the profligacy was not: purchase of a Canadian fund, $7 million; millions invested in a fledgling California conglomerate, Commonwealth United; new offices, $2.5 million; increased bank capitalization, $4 million; and on and on. Then there were numerous loans and guarantees—$5 million for Cornfeld's planes, and millions to John King's NOPIs (Net Operating Profit Investments) that were tax shelters for the would-be IOS executive millionaires—for over $40 million in obligations. Cowett promised a complete report. The best policy, they decided, was to keep the lid on things, countering the inevitable bad publicity and seeking short-term help. Nobody believed the company could collapse; the cumulative value of investment programs already purchased, that is, money pledged to be invested, exceeded $2 billion for the funds.

Vesco, in Geneva to raise $2 million to service ICC's debts, came by Buhl's office. The crisis atmosphere was touchable, and Bob, seeing IOS's vulnerability for the first time and thinking what a great acquisition it would make for ICC, asked if he could help. Henry said no; if a savior were needed, he wanted someone more prestigious. But he did ask Vesco in for assistance with the vexatious Commonwealth United problem that, if solved, would remove a major burden.

The stock was down to five by the following Friday, April 17. Part of the difficulty was that the press—there had been leaks, IOS learned from bugging its own phones—refused to distinguish between the parent company, some of whose troubles had come out, and the funds, which still remained relatively healthy. But some of the worst casualties in their portfolios were the speculative issues on which the funds had made a bundle and whose drop IOS managers contributed to by selling them off in what was proving to be the worst stock market panic since 1929.

Confidence was required, such as a rise in price of the stock might generate; Cornfeld tried to force IIT to buy IOS stock and blew up when the portfolio manager refused. On Monday, April 20—the same week in which he suggested that he might purchase all the IOS stock himself—Bernie sold, owing money on his planes, 450,000 shares to Meshulam Riklis of Rapid-American Corporation, a large conglomerate (apparel to liquor) at $4 a share (the sale, being private, didn't affect the market price), 60,000 of which was for Cowett to cover his debts. A pale and nervous Ed, escorted by a subdued Bernie, went to the Geneva airport and took off for New York.

When Buhl asked him to analyze the Commonwealth United situation, Vesco thought of Milton Meissner, a management consultant who had worked far above him at Olin in Detroit, and, in New York "Bud" Meissner was told to expect a call. CUC was broke but it had a valuable asset, Seeburg, the country's largest manufacturer and distributor of juke boxes, pinball machines, and coin-operated vending machines. Vesco's notion was that, salvaged from the Commonwealth wreck, Seeburg would give value to the Commonwealth paper of which the IOS group had about $10 million worth. A vehicle was required that Vesco proposed to provide. At meetings at the Regency and the Seeburg suite at the Carlyle, which Buhl flew over for, Vesco and Meissner discussed the acquisition of Seeburg if International Controls could bail out Commonwealth as well. Vesco proposed issuing $5 million of "funny preferred" stock in All American, his latest acquisition, to be sold to an IOS fund, which in return would give Commonwealth stocks and bonds that would then be tendered to Commonwealth, controlled by IOS, substantially reducing Commonwealth's debt. ICC would add Seeburg to its organization chart. (Hogan & Hartson, ICC's lawyers, recorded 165 expensive hours on Seeburg/Commonwealth matters.)

Before the "Monopoly"-like exchange fell apart in the ruin of IOS, Meissner flew on ICC's Gulfstream to Chicago with Vesco to discuss the Seeburg deal with a bank. All-business Vesco, never at a loss for grandiose projects, talked of taking over the mammoth Prudential, one of his two main lenders, which showed the direction of his ambitions. He also spoke of acquiring Connecticut General Life Insurance. But IOS represented the golden chance. It was like the sun setting outside the airplane cabin window. With Vesco's help IOS, too, would rise, provided that John King and the European bankers failed. The deal would make a lot of money for ICC and Bob himself.

Vesco, a specialist in analyzing takeovers, deduced that IOS was ripe for plucking. Although it looked huge on an organization chart, the parent, as opposed to the children, which had the major assets, wasn't all that large. The raider figured IOS might prove too much of a headache for all but the most daring, of whom he was one. And he was prepared to bet he could outbluff the SEC.

12

BIG JOHN KING ARRIVES

Solutions to the IOS squeeze might have existed. If the company was cash short, it might somehow have borrowed $20 million or so from itself to tide it over, replacing the money later on after selling off assets. Previously, IOS fund managers and IOS itself had not scrupled at using customers' assets to borrow money, buy on margin, lend assets out, and handle real estate. Such schemes might have required financial mirrors, and IOS had used them in the past. But this time the situation seemed too ominous and the world watched, as did Robert Vesco.

Also, expenses could have been cut and the worldwide sales force drastically reduced or eliminated. Without the sales organization, IOS, as manager of the funds, could have been profitable to the point of doubling its stock price. Morton Schiowitz, a former financial vice president still affiliated with the company, who offered such a plan, was shouted out of a meeting. And there were the valuable properties in life insurance, banking, and real estate that produced revenues. IOS had merely to sit tight, Schiowitz thought. But "Cornfeld," commented Schiowitz, "had pushed the salesmen to the top of the heap. It's unusual for a salesperson to be a good executive—they're *too* aggressive and always active. Ours couldn't stand the idea of dull, plodding, smaller mutual funds. IOS was a convention of Shriners."

Desperate to recover credibility and the lost millions, uncertain as to how serious the situation was, the frenzied board of

IOS, a company that had never had debts, decided to look for outside financial help. In New York, Cowett failed to convince Gulf & Western's Charles Bluhdorn to take Commonwealth paper off IOS's hands. Then Cowett went to Denver and John King, who, interested enough to offer $4 a share, wanted control of IOS while the loan was in effect, terms Bernie had anticipated.

In late April, as the stock markets continued downward, rumors flew that IOS funds were selling large blocks of stock to cover redemptions. It was the scenario the SEC had worried about, an off-the-wall foreign entity breaking the backs of American investors, although IOS funds had almost $500 million in cash.

In the midst of the worst troubles IOS had ever experienced, the April 27, 1970, issue of *New York* magazine carried a cover article unlikely to reassure anyone about Cornfeld's businessmanship. Titled "The Nirvana Conference with Bernie and Hef," the piece portrayed the Acapulco meeting just after Cornfeld's *Institutional Investor* speech in February—the date wasn't specified in order to make the article look timely. Given the two men's predilections for showing off their software, their eccentricities, their conspicuous aircraft consumption, a prudent public relations counselor would have tried to bar the press from this occasion, especially the sensationalist *New York* and most especially the reporter—spiky, acidulous, name-dropping (she could easily put a hundred names in one article)—Julie Baumgold. Hefner arrived in his black DC-9 called the "Big Bunny," Cornfeld in his white Falcon with Swiss markings (two of the female passengers, the article implied, acted romantically toward each other on the flight). But so secure were these pashas, of such a colossal or infantile scale their egos, that not only didn't they care about, but were proud of, and may even have seen some Byzantine business advantage in, the attention their antics garnered. It didn't matter to Hef—his empire was secure from invaders, and maybe he stirred the envy of his subscribers and increased their numbers. Cornfeld's position was different. He sold mutual funds, not bare breasts. In the shockingly short interval between Nirvana and nemesis, IOS had become vulnerable. Bernie was portrayed as a megalomaniac just when his tottering authority was under assault. *New York*'s editor, Clay Felker, who had worked as an IOS consultant in the 1960s, ridiculously insisted the piece wasn't embarrassing, and Cornfeld incautiously agreed since he passed out reprints. Later, he changed his mind: "I called Felker to tell him just what I thought of his story."

On Saturday, May 2, the IOS board, all of whom had read the *New York* article, began an exhausting series of meetings that would help decide the fate of IOS. The banker-underwriters who attended were incredulous to learn that the company lacked a capital budget—IOS was even more helter-skelter than they had thought—and that affected prospects for assistance. Word spread that those responsible for this awful *folie à deux,* Bernie and Ed, would have to be guillotined if IOS was to be saved. Not that European banking circles liked IOS except when money was to be made from it, nor did IOS like them. "There was a persuasive corporate paranoia," Cowett said. "The financial establishment was considered as only slightly less of an enemy than the upstart competitors." It was assumed both groups were constantly plotting against IOS.

Publicity was a major reason for trouble. The story, as reported in the New York *Times,* for instance, was an inch thick in clips for 1970, mostly for the key six months, far more coverage than the newspaper had given IOS since its inception. Cornfeld's flamboyant ways were a natural target. On the lawn outside Bella Vista, the company mansion on Lake Geneva once owned by the Colgate family, reporters mingled with members of the IOS Afrika Korps, routed like Rommel's because of the press, and eager to talk. The world knew by early May that the financial giant staggered, and, said a London paper, "the plain fact is that a more settled mood in world markets is unlikely to emerge until the whole IOS situation is resolved."

No one could enter the building without credentials, partly because threats had been made on Cornfeld's life, and, it was rumored, Palestinian terrorists intended to kidnap the Jew and hold him for ransom. Two armed guards accompanied Bernie wherever he went. Inside, directors and invited guests heard strategy talks from the likes of Lehman Brothers' George Ball (formerly of the State Department), Charles Bluhdorn, and Meshulam Riklis, whose message was "I don't know what your particular problem is. However, whenever I have problems in my business, I just stop paying the bills. The creditors have no alternative but to go along."

Day after day passed without an official announcement while groups of past directors and present executives silently paced the lawn outside Bella Vista. The press scrounged for material. Articles appeared ridiculing twenty-one grown men (one director didn't attend) who played in the corporate "sandbox," and reports came in about wholesale defections from the sales force. The directors feared that one of their number might be planting stories. They adopted elaborate security measures, and "target" directors were subject to round-the-clock surveillance. Without evidence, many directors decided George von Peterffy was the rat, and the professor was ostracized. He cracked, it was said, under the pressure.

More than fifty names had been put before the directors as candidates for assistance, and, of them, the Rothschild Paris interests and John King seemed the logical candidates, each with advantages. Rothschild, IOS's new partner in Rothchild Expansion, had the magic of a name, King the drive to revitalize the flagging sales force. All Rothschild had to do was publicly "adopt" IOS, with some vague assurance of limited aid in the short term. For King, the terms were more specific: pay off personal loans, among them Cowett's, provide $20 million and another $20 million if needed. The loan had to have participants, at least two recognized financial institutions. That way, they hoped, King's image as a promoter would be neutralized.

The Rothschild group didn't seem to offer much encouragement to Allen Cantor, who tried to negotiate with them, but Cowett's talks with King produced a written offer. The board was badly divided. Said Richard Hammerman, leader of the anti-King action, "John King is largely responsible for the problems we have. He is not to be trusted and under no circumstances will I ever do business with him." Wary-of-Rothschild forces wanted a cash infusion and terms that would protect the company from rape by the establishment. Cornfeld agreed to outside help but on the condition that it would be so fractionalized that the participants couldn't exercise control. Bernie said, in one of his outbursts, "I am the captain of this ship. If there is a choice between the ship sinking with me at the helm and the ship being saved with someone else at the helm, there is no choice to make. I am not giving up the helm." To Cowett, "Cornfeld was under the illusion he still ran the company."

The contentious board voted to accept King's proposal, then not to accept it but wait to see what the Rothschilds might do. A delegation went to Paris in total secrecy, but satisfaction was not forthcoming, to Bernie's bitter disappointment, and it became clear the board had no choice to make. The company seemed to be losing $1 million a month.

On Tuesday, May 5, 1970, Cowett resigned, although it had seemed to Buhl he hadn't been around much in the previous few weeks. Cowett had decided his close relationship with King, and his role in the negotiations with him, had rendered him ineffective—"my usefulness to IOS was at an end." With Cowett gone, board attention turned to Bernie. Speaker after speaker implored Bernie to resign for the good of the firm. Ingrates, he called them; only he could be the savior. An impeachment resolution was introduced and carried with only two dissenting votes. Another motion would rescind it if Bernie would resign as chairman, and Cornfeld delivered his signed letter, making him a rank-and-file board member. An hour later he wandered back and asked to look at the letter. He made a defiant gesture when he had it in his hand and tore it up, challenging the board to impeach him. But he was out. Sir Eric Wyndham-White, who had replaced Cornfeld as chairman, ruled that the resignation remained in effect.

Understood by "all but the most irrational of IOS directors," as Cowett put it, King's terms were far more generous to IOS than might have been expected from other bidders, as Big John was keenly aware. His own empire was on the edge of collapse. Even before the IOS crisis, King companies were in deep trouble. IOS had been his major source of investment money, and he eagerly awaited a new, closed-end natural-resources fund, to be entrusted to King management. The money would have bailed him out.

With IOS on the ropes, plans for the new fund were suspended, but if IOS fell into sophisticated, less friendly hands, the results could be disastrous. Embarrassing questions could be asked about previous transactions. The ongoing relationship with IOS would cease and ugly litigation start. So King took the biggest gamble of his life. He would offer terms too generous to be refused. If he succeeded with his rescue effort, and IOS regained momentum, King's profits from IOS could have been enormous. And there was the ego factor—King could emerge with an international reputation as the man who saved IOS.

"Curiously enough," Cowett wrote, "if King had been able to . . . take over . . . the arrangement probably would have been beneficial to all concerned. For, despite his now obvious weakness and motivations, King was probably the only 'outsider' who truly understood the enormous value and sensitivity of the IOS sales force."

Big John's credentials impressed them. King, as he was not shy about letting on, had been an adviser to four U.S. Presidents —Nixon, Johnson, Kennedy, and Herbert Hoover, when he ran the Hoover Commission under Truman. He was the former vice president of the Republican Finance Committee—he had, he said, unwittingly laundered money for the Republicans—and a personal friend of Dick Nixon's, for whom he had given a party at his walled-in mansion in Denver. The President had recently appointed him U.S. Ambassador Extraordinary to the 1970 World's Fair in Osaka, perhaps in return for King's $250,000 contribution to Nixon's 1968 campaign. If John wasn't exactly establishment, he seemed the next thing to it. Rumors were that King had already talked to the President about IOS.

But before King would be allowed to bring his IOS dreams to Geneva, he had to repay the loans wrought by Cowett for the stock purchases. "I'm the mailman. I'm going back tonight," said a weary man arriving from New York, on May 3, with the money. None of the IOSers had seen a check with $10 million written on it, and they passed the paper silently around the conference table. Somebody rubbed it to see if the numbers would come off.

Cornfeld, who'd raised the company from infancy, was more than reluctant to sever his ties, and he hurled accusations about King's mistreatment of IOS. The thoughts of Big John taking charge led him to call Jacob Rothschild of the London, not Paris, Rothschilds, and implore help. He was turned down. Bernie suddenly talked about a truce with the SEC but no deal with the oilman who, he was willing to bet, would be broke within a year. IOS broker Arthur Lipper took him up on a $10,000 wager. Fortunately for Lipper, Bernie wanted his check returned. Cornfeld would have won.

In the fall of 1969, King, whose operations relied heavily on computers, had been asked to introduce a systems team to analyze IOS. His electronics experts hadn't had time to thread their way through the labyrinth, but for him, IOS records were so inadequate that the company didn't know it had been using fictitious earnings, and he had wondered if the confusion wasn't in some sense deliberate, to make it hard for any outside authority to understand what went on.

John would have changed all that. He intended to bring the not-so-innocents-abroad back home, subject to U.S. tax and securities laws. IOS wouldn't need to attract illegal flight capital. It would become a healthy force in the U.S. economy. He wasn't, of course, an altruist. He foresaw that oil prices would double or triple in the next few years—they rose by a factor of ten—if he could put IOS in the oil business, using its sales force, he felt certain, with the help of King Resources, it would become one of the largest companies in the world.

But in Washington lurked the SEC. King had Nixon's private telephone number, and, he said, explained to the President what he had in mind. "Okay with me if it's okay with the Attorney General, the Secretary of Commerce, and the SEC," King said Nixon said. King visited John Mitchell and Maurice Stans and received the green light. The SEC's close-to-the-vest Stanley Sporkin struck King as having almost a fetish about IOS, but he came away convinced that the commission would somehow void the 1967 consent decree, in which IOS agreed not to do business in the United States. For King, See Everything Crooked seemed free to do pretty much as it liked.

A theoretical distinction exists between narrative truth and historical truth, the former being what people say happened and the latter being what actually did, if anyone can find out. In John King's narrative, he flew to Geneva on a commercial flight, with three assumptions. First, he had the U.S. government behind him; second, he had IOS behind him to guarantee the financing for his loans to the company; third, he had Bernard Cornfeld with him—Cowett had given him a guarantee. True, he bargain hunted but as a white knight, not a hostile raider. The emperor Cornfeld, King understood, would abdicate, to let John establish his authority—King's own man, Harding Lawrence, formerly chief of Braniff, would arrive shortly to take charge—and to placate the SEC, in whose throat Bernie's barbs had stuck. King needed Cornfeld for staging purposes and Cowett for his knowledge of the company, and he was prepared to offer positions to both; but the world had to know that power had passed to him.

When King entered the IOS boardroom Wednesday morning, having arrived the evening before, he was shocked by the haggard appearance of these people who had been in almost continuous session for weeks, hearing one disclosure of secret accounts after the next. Nerves were frayed. A man stood up and shouted to no one in particular, "I'm being foreclosed! You did this to me!" John worried about Bernie's opposition, displayed from the start, but ascribed it to petulance, which, he believed, would pass. King made a skillful presentation, and on Saturday the board voted to accept his fifty-four-page offer despite Cornfeld's contention that King planned to use FOF's money to buy IOS. Bernie also insisted angrily that $20 million had been paid to King by FOF since the start of the year, despite claims that the figure was $10 million and had been owed.

Bernie's credibility had been further weakened. One of the Willkie Farr lawyers, Raymond Merritt, brought up IIT's investment in Eon Corp., after which Cornfeld purchased stock at a penny a share when Eon was selling at several dollars. Bernie, said Merritt, "was very upset that I would have characterized his conduct as being anything but in the best interest of the shareholders, and advised me the stock was in fact donated to the Bernard Cornfeld charitable foundation. When I indicated that that didn't change my view, Mr. Cornfeld's anger seemed to be further incensed. From that day on, Mr. Cornfeld . . . had no kind words for me and . . . exhibited a singular hostility." The reason, from Cornfeld's point of view, was that Willkie Farr people occupied the slots of those who had resigned, and they voted against Bernie, who felt stupid about letting them on the board.

The press marveled at King's inaccessibility. But John was oblivious to the journalists. He left his hotel hidden in the back seat of a limousine and vanished into the tightly secured Villa Bella Vista. He made flying visits to IOS enclaves in Germany, Italy, and Spain—building up the morale of the sales force, which he regarded as the world's finest, convincing those people to accept him. Working twenty-two hours a day—he was to lose thirty pounds in the next few weeks—he tried to learn more about the company he was about to buy. In March or April, he claimed to have discovered for the first time the $10-million performance fee IOS had awarded itself on the upward revaluation of the Arctic permits—there had been, though, a similar, smaller fee of that kind the year before, as King should have been aware—and he said he was startled because it might be inferred that he, IOS's second-largest stockholder after Cornfeld, was profiting from what he knew was a sham transaction. Now he saw interoffice correspondence that showed that without the $10 million, far from making a profit, IOS would have lost money in 1969. He was more determined than ever to play Galahad, even though Charlie Bluhdorn told him in Geneva that he would be chewed up by the press. "There's something in the American character that wants to cheer and boost a winner and at the same time look for another champion. They put a guy up, then try to shoot him down," Bluhdorn observed. "I wish I'd listened," said John.

King's payment of $20 million was due on May 15 and he needed help. He telephoned the Rothschilds in Paris but they wouldn't accept the call, and he met with the underwriters in London, who wouldn't aid him, either. In New York, the Willkie Farr lawyers were told to expect a check, and a line to Geneva was kept open so that Henry Buhl could be notified immediately when it came. All day the phones rang, with King on the line or the president of the Marine Midland Bank, across the street, which was trying to structure the deal, saying that the check was about to come. They waited eighteen hours at Willkie Farr and, at last, the money arrived—$8 million, scraped from King's companies, instead of $20 million. King was given time to find the rest.

King sensed difficulty as it became clear that financial institutions were not springing for the deal—the SEC apparently had been warning American banks not to participate. The expected IOS loan guarantees seemed not to have materialized, and, in the high anxiety descending on all of them, John saw Bernie's hand. He knew there was trouble when he could no longer reach Nixon, but he continued to sound confident at an hour-and-a-half press conference he gave in New York on May 21. Then he left for Washington. King would later claim that Rockefeller interests, not wanting IOS domiciled in the United States, and frightened of King Resources' geological inventory, which rivaled that of Exxon—in which the Rockefellers had large holdings from Standard Oil—had influenced the government, but he publicly blamed the SEC for shooting him down. The commission responded by saying King didn't have the money, and it was true—perhaps because of the SEC.

In London, on this occasion, the Willkie Farr lawyers waited thirty-six hours for King's second check, which never arrived. John's IOS misadventure cost him the confidence of American banks, which, strapped for funds themselves, called his loans. His company also owed $8 million to the State of Ohio. Big John King, wishing he had never heard of Investors Overseas Services, was on the road to ruin.

In 1977, after a year in jail, King was hunting on horseback when a bear frightened his horse, which reared, and Big John went down. A stick pierced his neck. He was able to tie himself to the horse and ride home, hours away. But a dozen strokes followed and King's speech, which he regained, was affected along with his memory. Still, he recovered well enough to try to return to the oil business, though by 1986 he couldn't afford hotel rooms and traveled by bus, he said.

13

HELP WANTED

When, on Friday, May 29, 1970, a battered King officially dropped out, another father figure had disappeared, and panic returned to the Villa Bella Vista. The funds' decrease in assets plus a redemption rate that had risen to $3 million a day resulted in smaller management fees. Discussions with an international consortium of rescue banks had came to nothing. Buhl, unable to find help in New York, returned to Geneva. He learned that Peter Flanigan of the White House staff wanted to see him, and he flew back to Washington to assure Flanigan that there was no danger of bankruptcy. Buhl called Vesco. He wanted Bob to analyze IOS to "find out what it was about" and to introduce the company to financial institutions ICC had a relationship with, just as he'd helped Vesco with an investment banker two years before. Though Henry preferred Loeb, Rhoades in combination with Standard & Poors, after what IOS had been through, Bob looked better and better. Vesco lacked an international reputation, and he wasn't an institutional investor, as IOS wanted; but if he were teamed up with the Bank of America or the Prudential, he'd be quite good enough.

Vesco had begun to believe IOS was indeed takeoverable. He contacted the BOA, and, learning it was interested—according to Buhl, who talked with a bank official in San Francisco, it was—arrived in Geneva with Milton Meissner, whose management consultancy lacked clients for the moment. Bud planned to retire to

Mexico the following year. Born in 1914, in New Jersey, over six feet, five inches tall, Meissner was a graduate of Lehigh with two degrees, in chemical engineering and science, and Oxford doctorates in physical chemistry and philosophy. He had been a Rhodes scholar—he was a championship high jumper—and, during World War II, had worked on the atomic bomb with a "Q," or top, clearance. He was an expert in chain reactions, high pressure technology, and superconductivity. He had been employed by U.S. Steel, Westinghouse Electric, and Olin Mathieson, which built nuclear reactors. He had been a bank director, president of a real estate company, and executive vice president of Bell Intercontinental, an investment holding company with assets of $80 million. He'd also been in charge of a company that manufactured electrical equipment in Mexico. He was familiar with the problems of mutual funds, and Vesco asked him to appraise IOS so that he could show the results to the Bank of America. Meissner, though he drank a bit, seemed to be a serious and honest businessman although later the SEC didn't think so.

Meissner prepared a "green book," a loose-leaf folder with a green cover—it graduated to blue, then black, as he went along—in which he compiled copious notes. He decided IOS didn't understand what its assets in insurance, real estate, banking, currencies, and so forth were really worth, or even its outstanding loans. According to his figures, IOS was strangling on commissions—in some cases there were thirteen levels of fees taken out before a dollar reached the company—and services to its clients (not to say its executives). He put overhead at $91 million a year, far too high. The company would indeed be bankrupt unless it could reduce costs and provide itself with a reasonably stable income. He concluded that IOS's assets amounted to $2.8 billion even with the decline in the funds. Vesco was excited. "My God, it's a money tree," he said, as he had before. He regarded IOS as the "challenge of my life."

But Vesco had to wait. On June 9, he told his board in New Jersey that a possible investment in "a European financial institution"—nobody at Fairfield had any doubt about which one—"had been terminated because of apparent arrangements that institution had made with other parties." But, when the discussions between the banking consortium and IOS collapsed, Vesco was informed, by a prominent IOSer, that IOS had abandoned the "illusionary desire" to deal with the "establishment" (it hadn't) and desired an immediate cash infusion to meet the payroll, an investment of $15 million. Vesco was thrilled, though contemptuous of IOS's irresponsible inability to put a hand in its own back pocket, but he played it cool, demanding more and more information until IOS became eager to deal with him.

Attorneys from Hogan & Hartson joined Meissner in Geneva to help update the analysis for Vesco. By mid-June, the corporate Steppenwolf had moved to Geneva with his family for the summer, staying at Hotel La Reserve. Vesco wrote a letter to IOS summarizing the talks so far. It wasn't "our" (ICC's) intent "to assume control of IOS but simply to benefit by what may be an attractive investment opportunity." Cornfeld or his "affiliates" could not be involved. "Our proposal is that $20 million in the form of an irrevocable letter of credit be made available. . . ."

ICCers smirked. Mr. Control had denied any such intention, but what had the company been up to for the past few years except taking control positions? The corporate amoeba had eaten its way into junior-gianthood by aggressive activity, and IOS was by far the biggest game so far, with the funds and other assets. It was a great deal larger than ICC but helpless without a moneyhole. Bobby . . . lied? Was corporate America a bastion of truth? Yes, Vesco wanted some control of IOS, and, if he couldn't obtain it, he'd at least emerge with a bundle of warrants. The "risk-reward ratio," as he liked to say, seemed good.

Nor did the letter specify *who* would make $20 million available. ICC had, or would have, the $20 million loan from Prudential but was forbidden to lend more than $1 million of it. A benefactor had to exist, the Bank of America. Meissner, in fact, believed that Vesco only pretended to act for himself when he was nothing more than a front man for BOA. To dark, dapper Levantine Arthur Lipper, Vesco's intention was to clear out unneeded personnel, establish financial safeguards and turn IOS over to a financial institution (the Bank of America), with ICC receiving millions for Vesco's efforts.

Hogan & Hartson notes of a June 30 ICC board meeting

recorded, "Mr. Vesco explained . . . we are the only horse in the race and do we want to finish the race. We are presently stalling to hear what the Bank of America is going to do. Mr. Vesco stated that if ICC goes forward with the IOS transaction or something similar that it is time for ICC to look around for a new President to relieve Mr. Vesco to do an IOS or Merrill Lynch transaction. Mr. Vesco said we are aggressively looking for the right person."

Merrill Lynch Pierce Fenner & Smith, the largest brokerage house in the United States! Vesco, at thirty-four, having in his mind outgrown ICC, was eager to pursue his ambitions, and IOS could provide the vehicle. But first he had the rescue mission to perform. In July, he wrote Buhl to remind him of BOA's interest but scaling down the loan offer to the $5–$15-million range. To lower offers was a Vesco bargaining specialty, intended to make the opposition aware that its worth might be less than it thought. The tactic worked best with insecure targets, and IOS decidedly qualified.

It wasn't as though IOS didn't continue to look elsewhere. Buhl talked with Howard Stein of the Dreyfus Fund; Lehman Bros.; William Zeckendorf, Jr.; Hugh Knowlton of Smith Barney; William Salomon of Salomon Brothers; Lazard Frères; Charles Allen of Allen & Co.; Thomas Mellon Evans of Pittsburgh, and who knows how many others in New York and Geneva, where they roared in and out in their jets like voyeurs at an exhibition of corporate nudity. At least six seemingly solid-gold deals had fallen through. In one, Loeb, Rhoades, with Standard & Poors, had put in several months' research on an offer. The group fitted IOS's needs perfectly, Buhl thought, and a press release was drafted for a July Friday release, but, on Monday, Henry was hastily recalled to Geneva from Sardinia, where he had just arrived—he and his wife had taken a house there but he'd never had time to go.

He learned that Loeb, Rhoades had called off the deal because the SEC had warned of putting pressure on the firm's underwritings, on the grounds that IOS couldn't do business in the United States. (The SEC denies having done so, but Buhl was told of the pressure by John Loeb and Mark Millard, two senior Loeb, Rhoades partners.) The Loeb, Rhoades backout, on top of

King's, was critical for the IOS board, which, from then on, took ICC's offer seriously. For some, at least, the SEC's intransigent attitude toward potential IOS investors was a major bridge toward what came next. The agency appeared to lack flexibility—as Stanley Sporkin had been accused of—or to display interest in the almost entirely foreign investors in IOS who would be the ones to suffer if the company collapsed. In Geneva, suspicions deepened that See Everything Crooked wanted to put IOS out of business, and the perception helped push the company into the arms of Vesco.

Vesco continued to attract admiration because of his adherence to the work and family ethic—a faithful family man, in that setting, was judged to be stable. If Bob was to be late to dinner, he would always call his wife. Said Cornfeld's assistant on meeting Vesco, "I knew I was in the presence of one of the greatest financial geniuses of the twentieth century." He was not the only one to so respond. Vesco's very tenacity heightened respect for him, and, because he could convey authority, he emerged as a substitute for the father figures that had let them down—Bernie, Ed, John King, the numberless rescuers who had brought only empty promises and disappointments. Vesco perceived their infantile side. "It was pure chaos," he said. "Cornfeld was trying to start a proxy fight. Wyndham White was fighting with someone else. All the kids were in the sandbox waiting for someone to tell them to get out."

Indeed, chaos was profound, and was reflected in sharp animosities among former friends, alcohol, sleeping pills, and nervous disorders. Henry Buhl, who made six trips to the United States in a month, came near to a breakdown, as did Cowett and Richard Hammerman, who became president briefly but quit because of the pressure, unable to make decisions. Wyndham White, chairman and acting chief executive, was frequently ruffled and physically exhausted. He stomped out of meetings complaining, "I can't handle this." Robert Slater, former chairman of the John Hancock Mutual Life Insurance Company, who replaced him, may have suffered a minor stroke. Bernie also acted erratically, but there was nothing new in that.

Cornfeld's influence remained strong. While some would

have gladly killed him, others would have died for him. Bernie was divisive, and as long as he loomed large obtaining the vital outside financing seemed impossible. It was clear that Cornflakes wanted nothing more than to return to the bosom of his family as its leader, which "Sir Eric Windmill"—Bernie's nickname for Wyndham White—was determined to prevent. The former GATT official showed an unexpected talent for corporate infighting belied by his mild manner. Cornfeld had been soliciting proxies for use at the June 30 annual meeting in Toronto; but, in the belief he had made a truce with Sir Eric, Bernie gave his shares to be voted, confident of remaining on the board. Instead, he was thrown off altogether. "That wasn't very knightly of him," Bernie said tartly of Sir Windmill.

There was a conference of IOS directors and managers at the Drake Hotel in New York the following weekend. Bernie, angry at himself for having neglected to go to Toronto, visited meeting after meeting, calling everyone a schmuck. He brought a suit against Sir Eric and everyone else he thought might be involved. He promised a proxy fight for control. "He spouted forth in public and in a series of very bizarre press conferences; venom ran rife," Cowett complained.

In June, the long-delayed IOS 1969 annual report, audited by Arthur Andersen, was finally released, though Anderson said it was incomplete. The figures gave IOS, at the end of the year, a net worth of $100 million, but the report confirmed that without the $10-million performance fee earnings would have been negligible. In a letter to stockholders, Wyndham White said the present management was committed to "elimination of certain of the extraordinary items found in the footnotes," meaning the loans and loan guarantees to and for insiders, who were not named. Trading in IOS shares in London and Canada was suspended until the company provided the list.

As press attention mounted, it was pointed out that the collapse of IOS could have a corollary—the loss of confidence by the small European investor in stocks, and American stocks in particular, which could reduce the inflow of cash to the United States and aggravate the negative American balance of payments. The demoralization of IOS became an international incident when IOS stock dropped to $3. Bernie with "incredibly sad eyes" barricaded himself in his Geneva house, the palatial Villa Elma, though pastrami and salami were flown in for him from New York.

14

THE SAVIOR

"The idea was simple," Vesco said. "ICC was going to come in and do the negotiating because we were a little more agile than other people. Get an agreement, turn around and lay off on some institutions, become white guys, and, with all the banking institutions around the world, pick up a profit or some sort of continuing participation. That was why we got involved in IOS. That was the whole intention. I could use my quick wit, legal knowledge, accounting things, to try to influence the (IOS) board as best I could."

The ICC board, meeting in Geneva, was far from united. Down-to-earth Ralph Dodd opposed the IOS involvement strongly. He barricaded Vesco in a revolving door with his foot to force him to discuss the matter, and they talked all night at Vesco's hotel. Dodd believed ICC was slipping because it needed Bob, and he wanted the company to concentrate on manufacturing as he always had. Vesco finally said, "You don't see the whole picture." Wilbert Snipes, senior vice president of American National Bank and Trust Co., which had lent ICC its start-up money and was on the board, was frightened by IOS's size and financial condition—he would have preferred a smaller target: an acquisition was in the air. (Pat Vesco didn't understand IOS's allure in the first place. "Oh God," she cried, hearing of the possible takeover of IOS, "who needs that?") After Norman LeBlanc, vice president in the Paris office of the ICC accountants Coopers &

Lybrand, explained IOS to the ICC directors, Vesco insisted on a unanimous vote for such a momentous step, and Dodd and Snipes finally voted in favor, though Dodd recorded his objections in the minutes. Typically, Vesco brushed aside questions as to where the money was to come from.

Was the idea to purchase IOS? Vesco said mushily, "Not to purchase IOS. Get a handle on it. The problem with it was mishmosh. Cornfeld was in, Cornfeld was out, you know. When White was in, nobody got a handle on the mush, okay, and you had Marine Midland, the Royal Bank of Canada, Chemical, the Bank of America, and all those funny little people [the would-be rescuers of IOS] all wanting to get a piece of the gravy and get in. They could not get a handle on the deal. They couldn't deal with the IOS board. That was the problem. So I, we, said, okay, we'll go in and use our, you know, skills, whatever they were, to get a handle on IOS. But we got shafted in the process."

Vesco next appeared at an IOS board meeting. The atmosphere was tense, with half the directors hating Cornfeld and the other half detesting Vesco, who was cool and tough, though not so tough as he would be after he won. While aware the ICC loan might not be enough, he said, sounding reasonable, he wouldn't have gone this far without being sure he could obtain additional financing. His company, whose net worth was $42 million, less than half that of IOS, was prepared to wager $10 million on that. Vesco underscored the interest of the Bank of America, and, indeed, Alvin Rice, a vice president, had sent to Geneva a team of a half dozen or so—headed by Samuel H. Armacost (later BOA's president) of the bank's London office—that stayed at La Reserve, though to Buhl the bankers seemed to pretend they weren't there. That was the kind of backing IOS coveted. A committee was formed to negotiate with Vesco, consisting largely of former Cornfeld supporters. Henry asked not to be included because of bias—he was a Vesco man.

Under the so-called "Peace of Paris," if Bernie dropped his lawsuits and proclamations, he could return to the board. Cornfeld had bought, for $1 million, a 10,000-acre tract of land near Palm Springs that he planned to develop as the movie-making capital of the world, to be called Cinema City, and he proposed to raise $50 million by selling participations of $5,000 each, using the redoubtable sales force to give IOS a new lease on life. His presentation struck the board as vague, and Bernie, rejected and having threatened to put the directors in jail, went home with his girls. He'd appeared twice that day, on a boat festooned with them. He was weary of trying to make the directors understand that IOS didn't need Vesco, whom he called a "hoodlum." One of his four Great Danes was dying, and so, Cornfeld feared, was his company.

When Vesco visited Cornfeld at Villa Elma the next day, Saturday, August 8, Bernie's impression of Bob was snobbish. To him, Vesco was a shoe-salesman type in bizarre, undesigner clothes—loud jacket, socks of the wrong color. Earlier, Bob had said, "I've looked at the company, and the only person who's worth anything is you." Secretly, Cornfeld agreed. Bob had gone on, "I want to put the company back on track with you." Bernie had responded crisply, "Sorry. I don't think you can be of help. There are people who can contribute, and you're not one of them."

One of Vesco's methods was to buy friends, and he invested, or caused ICC to invest, $60,000 in a private Bali hotel project of Buhl's almost as a gift. John King had also put in money.

Said Vesco, "Henry wanted to build a hotel because he loved the island, and he and his little jet-setters used to go over there and he was putting together a group. I subsequently found King was involved in the goddam thing, which Henry didn't tell me. It ticked me off a little because John King is not one of my favorite people, to put it mildly."

Neither was unaware that Buhl had clout; Vesco, who held grudges, was still sore at Cornfeld because Bernie had backed out of investing heavily in ICC's recent Eurobond offering—to some at ICC, to get Cornfeld was a primary reason for the IOS takeover. Still, sitting in Bernie's ornate living room, Vesco tried to muzzle his invective and so did Cornfeld. As though IOS were his daughter and Vesco a suitor for her hand, he asked Vesco about ICC's financial situation. Healthy, Bob said, mentioning the BOA. Vesco's intentions? Bernie wondered. Bob replied that he only wanted to be of assistance and earn a fee. He said he'd be out of IOS by the following year.

Cornfeld invited Bob for dinner, prepared by his French chef. The girls and his partially deaf mother, Sophie, were also at the table. ("Bernie's a good boy," she told a journalist.) In the interval, mercurial Cornfeld started to fume again. What assurance was there that Vesco would really get out, once in? Here was this "Wop" hanging around the company as though he already owned it, and Bernie was powerless to get rid of him because of those assholes on the board who didn't realize Vesco was a con artist. Over consommé, Bernie demanded to know where the financing was to come from, and, for once, Bob didn't seem entirely sure of himself, rekindling Cornfeld's suspicion that Vesco intended to buy IOS with its own money. Bernie then asked where he would fit in the reorganization Vesco had in mind, and Vesco, changing his tune from the afternoon, replied bluntly that there was no room for Cornfeld until Bob had finished and left. After that he didn't give a shit who ran the company.

The notion that the founder was unnecessary, even an encumbrance, was the wrong button to push. As Cornfeld viewed himself, suddenly sorry to have entrusted power to weak sisters like Henry Buhl who had turncoated him, he, Bernie, was the only person at IOS strong enough to stand up to Vesco, and that was why Bob wanted to remove him. Bernie became angry. Again he threatened to sue. He had been gathering proxies. He had given $10 bills that he autographed in exchange for "irrevocable" proxies (there was no such animal under Canadian law) and an option to buy the shares at $5 each by July of the following year. He had, he said, 23 million proxies locked in his basement safe, though they were never voted. Bernie said afterward that Bob had lousy table manners.

Though Vesco continued to insist that the only control over IOS sought was financial discipline, it looked to BOA's Sam Armacost as though ICC had a more sweeping plan in mind. Armacost wrote in a memo:

> The basic transaction proposed between ICC and IOS is a $10 million credit package on a short term basis which has attached to

> it stock subscription warrants and other conditions which effectively provide ICC with control of IOS. . . .
>
> The company's (ICC) ultimate aim is to own 49% of a holding company which controls IOS. The other 51% will be syndicated among various international financial institutions. . . .
>
> International Controls has discussed its interest and intent with the SEC and other U.S. governmental agencies concerned with the IOS problems and have apparently received information of full support for its program. . . .

Armacost was misled, for such was not the case. Hogan & Hartson's notes concerning a meeting between the lawyers and Irving Pollack and Stanley Sporkin of the SEC stated:

> Pollack (the deal) would make ICC an affiliate of IOS 1% rule.

Under the 1967 (consent) order, any company that owned more than one percent of IOS was automatically an affiliate.

> Should ICC be concerned about statement that financial condition of IOS is sound and represents "an attractive investment opportunity?" Is this a problem for ICC in representing the good condition of IOS? Are people buying ICC stock on this basis?

To the lawyers, these were "problem areas," but the SEC had given its first warning to ICC not to proceed with the acquisition of IOS. Still, Hogan & Hartson thought the SEC could be circumvented because ICC had not been party to the 1967 order.

"Generally," Vesco said, "we thought the BOA was behind the thing. They were in and we were going to parcel it out. That's why this guy in London, Armacost, kept coming. He didn't float in from out of the blue. Why was he so familiar with IOS? We thought we were going to close the deal but they left us out on a limb."

After negotiating sessions in Paris and Geneva, the final one lasting late into the night, Meissner claimed that Armacost said, " 'This is absolutely bankable, no question.' He got on the phone to San Francisco, and, as far as we were concerned, we had a deal . . . the deal had been signed. The money was due on a closing date. . . ." According to Meissner, Armacost received a late-night call and then phoned Vesco—BOA had rejected the deal. (Rice later testified that the bank had never made any commitment to Vesco and that Vesco had improperly used the bank's name. But Buhl maintained IOS was in touch with the Bank of America until Vesco went to jail in late 1971.)

Vesco had, he said, a "serious case of indigestion. I think the thing I did was, you know, spend a long weekend on the telephone with various people at BOA using a few foul words." The savior had counted on the Bank of America, but he wouldn't quit. The risk-reward ratio was too favorable. ICC would receive warrants to buy 7.5 million shares of IOS stock at $2 a share: for every dollar the stock rose above $2, ICC stood to make a profit of $7.5 million. (Due to Vesco's intervention, the stock rallied from $2.22 to $2.82.) IOS, despite the decline of the funds, was very probably the largest source of capital unregulated by governmental authorities in the *world.* Yes, if Vesco could make IOS profitable again, ICC (and he) deserved to be handsomely rewarded But first he had to gain control of the aging empire, almost no matter how.

Chancy maneuvers designed to replace BOA as the apparent source of funding followed. IOS's bargaining team insisted on a guarantee that ICC had $5 million cash on hand, but BOA wouldn't confirm that—indeed, the bank cast doubt on the reliability of ICC balances—and Vesco was stuck, but not for long. A telex, purportedly from American National Bank and Trust, promptly arrived.

> Pursuant to you [sic] request this will confirm that as ol [sic] the close [sic] business on August 21, 1970 that International Controls Corp. including its subsidiaries had cash deposit on [sic] excess of 5 million de [sic] W. Snipes Senior Vice President.

Snipes was on vacation when this message—artfully worded, Vesco agreed—had been sent, and Snipes would have considered it artful, too, if he hadn't been supposed to have signed it. ANBT wasn't responsible, either—someone else had dispatched the telex, perhaps from ICC headquarters. What did the message say? That ICC, including its subs, had "deposit" in excess of $5 million, but where? Not necessarily at ANBT. In case there were questions from IOS, a telex arrived from Butlers Bank.

> Pursuant to your request, this will confirm that as of the close of business August 21, 1970 a foreign subsidiary of ICC had a time deposit in the amount of US dollars of 5,000,000 and a subsidiary office had a US dollars [illegible] deposit with our bank and trust company.

Vintage Vesco, cooked up by Butlers Bank at Vesco's request, the message failed to explain if the money was available for withdrawal (it was a time deposit; Allan Butler never expected Vesco would withdraw it, though in fact he could have with a penalty) an omission explained by Butler, disliker of Cornfeld and Vesco admirer: "Nobody asked." Vesco had used the time deposit trick —equaling the deposit was a liability—in the ELS takeover to pretend that ICC was richer and more liquid than it was.

The savior had tranquilized the victim. Wyndham White advised the board to accept ICC's offer, telling it that one of the leading banks in the world reported that, although Bobby was tough, he was a person who had "gone against the financial establishment in the United States and won."

Cornfeld, implacably anti-Vesco, produced still another angel, S. G. Warburg & Co. of London. Warburg's Sir Harold Lever, former Labour Chancellor of the Exchequer, strongly advised against accepting ICC's embrace. Lever could almost guarantee that the Bank of England would be favorable to a Warburg offer and would assure support. That wasn't enough for IOS, which had waited so long, and, that same day, September 3, the board voted twelve to ten in favor of ICC.

That same day, Vesco and two associates visited Ed Cowett and asked him to return to IOS as president and chief executive officer. Cowett declined, suggesting Buhl or James Roosevelt as acting CEO. Cowett told Vesco that a "very strong man, unafraid to make decisions, was needed." Cowett, who recognized that the $5 million loan document was tight—its provisions such that IOS would be in default from the start—made a deal with Vesco. "I would hold myself available at any time to provide information and/or to give advice on the condition that he would keep me advised of developments within IOS and provide me with ready access to him for the purpose of bringing troublesome personnel problems to his personal attention. There was to be no fee. Vesco kept his end of the bargain. I kept mine. I seldom met with Vesco, but we spoke often on the telephone. Also, on frequent occasions, particularly in the first few months after his first loan transaction, I met with his key associates. I never quite knew where Vesco was heading with IOS, but I had the distinct feeling he was trying to reestablish order where chaos had prevailed."

The agreement provided that International Controls Investments Ltd. (IIL), a Bahamian subsidiary of ICC, would make available $5 million on September 17, and provide another $5 million if necessary. The loan was repayable in May 1971, with an option to extend. IOS would issue warrants to IIL that could be exercised at discount prices. In a default, if IOS were unable to buy its warrants, it would have to pay a $3 million penalty. A U.S. judge would rule the contract was unusually harsh, but, Vesco said it was the "first draft of the Prudential loan agreement (with ICC) with the names changed. That's the IOS agreement," which wasn't entirely true. The Pru didn't sit on ICC's executive and finance committees as ICC did on the IOS committees. Vesco, as chairman of the finance committee, would supervise expenses and almost no transaction would be small enough to escape his scrutiny. It was as easy, he said, to control a company by means of its debt than by having the voting rights. That was how financial institutions did it, he said.

The $5 million question, though, was who would lend the money. Hale Brothers's Richard Pershing, a member of the ICC board, who had aided Vesco to gain control of Cryogenics which became International Controls, read about the delayed closing, and, knowing Bob, figured he was short of cash. He called Vesco in Rome offering to help and Vesco said, "Thanks for your offer but don't worry. We'll work everything out." Two days later, though, Vesco phoned Pershing, suggesting a meeting at which he asked for a $4-million loan—ICC would provide the other million. Vesco said the purpose of the loan was to have a reputable organization involved. In October, Pershing, grown distrustful, went to Nassau and said he wouldn't leave until he had the check, which came from Butlers Bank. Pershing didn't resign from ICC until the end of 1971, however.

The Butlers loan was not without strings. Having already felt the international recession in the Bahamas, and being uncomfortable in the political climate there, Allan had decided to retrench and move his basic operations to Canada. Above all, he had to protect Butlers's liquidity, and could Vesco guarantee that? Vesco said again he'd make Butlers the main bank of IOS, with an account of perhaps $10 million and a million a year in brokerage commissions from stock sales. He would find deposits to equal the $4 million Butlers lent. Asked why Vesco chose Butlers Bank as his vehicle, Butler said, "It was obvious that we were the last resort. And, though I didn't understand it then, Bob was as desperate to do the transaction, because of his problems with ICC, as we were to have his business."

IOS had previously contracted to sell a majority interest in its Italian mutual fund to the Italian government for $10 million. The transaction had been specifically excluded from the ICC loan agreement, but Vesco claimed he had a right to make sure the money wasn't squandered. Robert E. Slater, who had been appointed president and chief executive officer of IOS on October 1, 1970 seemed to agree, and, in any case, Vesco brandished his weapon, a default on the loan.

Besides, Vesco still claimed major American banks were interested in assuming IOS's debt to ICC. That sounded good to Slater, who wanted IOS to do business in the United States. The "First Amendment" was entered into, under which IOS agreed to deposit $4 million in Butlers Bank. Vesco and Meissner insisted that no connection existed between the Butlers loan and the Italian fund-money deposit, but the numbers were almost identical and Bernie screamed foul. It looked to him, as it had looked to him with John King, that Vesco was buying IOS with its own money. Vesco hadn't; but he *had* provided Butlers with liquidity, and the SEC asked questions.

15

BERNIE'S SHARES

Until then, Vesco had been playing under some sort of rules but suddenly the game turned dangerous.

Cornfeld's six million preferred shares, 16 percent of the total, could mean trouble and even control in a proxy fight. Beleaguered Bernie hurled epithets and challenges from his Geneva palace and his French château: he was determined to "get rid" of Vesco. At one point, Meissner arrived with a $5 million offer to Cornfeld, who was flanked by a Great Dane and a guy with a switchblade knife. "Stuff the five million up your ass," said Bernie.

Bob said he began to look for a buyer for the Cornfeld shares in October, and had approached the Rothschilds. Cornfeld's loans on his airplanes, guaranteed by an IOS entity, were undercollateralized because of the drop in price of IOS stock, Vesco claimed. A purchase of the shares would force Bernie to repay, and Vesco insisted that no financial institution would touch IOS as long as Cornfeld could start a proxy contest. Thus, Bernie's shares were pivotal in ICC's stated goal of finding a backer and withdrawing, although Bob privately had other plans.

High Midnight occurred during a December meeting at Villa Bella Vista. Vesco sought to make a deal with Gramco, an offshore real estate fund, but Bernie was opposed and the resolution failed, 11–10. Over dinner, Vesco said to Meissner, with his usual profanities, "This company is going to be destroyed if we can't get that fucking Cornfeld out," and, when the meeting resumed, he told Cornfeld the neighborhood was too small for both of them. Bernie should put up or shut up, sell his stock or buy out ICC. What, asked Cornfeld, was the price? Vesco would only discuss the matter in private, and, during a recess, the two enemies went to an overdecorated Louis XVI salon next to the boardroom and stared at each other.

"How much do you want?" Vesco said. "A buck a share," said Cornfeld, an outrageous price in terms of what the stock sold for by then—$.33—but little enough, it seemed to Bernie, for an empire. Vesco said nothing. "How much do you want?" Cornfeld repeated. To be rid of *him,* Vesco said, it would cost over $9 million, including the warrants ICC had, or almost double the money ICC was supposed to have lent a few months before. They were at loggerheads because neither could pay the other's price.

The next day, Vesco sent Slater a letter that expressed his rage with Cornfeld. Having consulted his lawyers, Vesco declared still another default on the IOS loan because Bernie, who was back on the IOS board only with ICC's consent, had also been appointed to another, though minor, IOS position, to which Vesco could have objected earlier had he wished. But Bernie had once more threatened a proxy contest, as he'd been forbidden to, and Bob in effect forced IOS to pay a penalty of an additional $1.5 million to be deposited in Butlers Bank as collateral against obligations. Slater agreed, among other reasons because Vesco continued to dangle promises of banking partners who would make possible a ticket for IOS to the United States.

Vesco had critical problems about the buyer of Cornfeld's shares. The buyer could *not* be: IOS Ltd., because a Canadian corporation, as IOS had become, was forbidden to purchase its own shares as treasury stock (what Cowett had done); an IOS fund, because it would have been deemed improper to use assets of investors to purchase the IOS founder's shares; ICC or a subsidiary, for two reasons. ICC was an American company registered with the SEC and might be in violation of the 1967 consent order forbidding IOS to conduct business in the United States. Second, since the price Vesco eventually offered was far above the market value of the shares, ICC would have been open to a lawsuit on the grounds of wasting corporate assets by paying too much.

Cornfeld returned to California and Vesco called to offer $.65 a share, which Bernie refused. Vesco called a week later with an $.85 bid, announcing he had an institutional buyer whose identity he wouldn't reveal, and Bernie agreed to a meeting in New York. Exhausted, Bernie was ready to bow out.

Such was Vesco's secrecy that even his outside counsel, Hogan & Hartson, sounded bewildered.

> Who will real purchaser be? Can't be IOS—economically or legally. Stock worth much less than $5.5 million . . . Who could suffer $3 million loss?

A Willkie Farr lawyer, David Rea, who specialized in "green goods"—high-level financial deals—was briefly involved in the transaction. He had been told to act as though there were a purchaser for Cornfeld's shares, whoever or whatever it was, and though he didn't personally like Bob Vesco, who reminded him of Spiro Agnew, Rea thought the price wasn't excessive for control shares. At a prep session at ICC's suite at the Regency, on New Year's Eve, two days before the Vesco-Cornfeld meeting, Vesco told Rea that Cornfeld could come on in two ways—highly emotional and difficult to deal with or very calm. Bernie, in a chic sports jacket and sweater, was placid. IOS was in his past, he said; he anticipated a career in films.

At last, Vesco told Hogan & Hartson:

> Buyer of [Cornfeld's stock] would be Consulentia, a sub of Bank Cantrade, a sub of UBS, says RLV.

Only at a meeting at the Villa Elma on January 8, 1971, did Vesco reveal to Cornfeld that the purchaser of the shares would be a subsidiary of Union Bank of Switzerland, and, he hoped, the sale would presage Union's backing of IOS. But, Vesco warned sternly, if the bank's presence were divulged, it would withdraw. It didn't want trouble with a rival, Crédit Suisse, the cash depository for IOS, and didn't intend to have its name connected with Cornfeld. Bernie whitened but investigated. He was told that there had, indeed, been high-level discussions between Vesco people and Union Bank though the outcome wasn't known.

Originally, Slater, wanting to end the Vesco-Cornfeld feud, thought IOS could buy Bernie's shares itself. Meissner discussed the matter at Bank Cantrade with an official who agreed to lend the money, but restraints having to do with the IOS charter and mutual funds prevented the deal. Vesco and Meissner looked elsewhere for a bank that would set up a dummy corporation to buy Cornfeld's shares.

In early January, Meissner attempted to have transferred, from one of the dollar funds, $6.2 million to a numbered account in an American bank in Germany, Manufacturers Hanover, but the transfer was stopped by Crédit Suisse. Meissner said he believed the transfer was to a Bank Cantrade account, but, though almost no one knew it, the account turned out to be Butlers Bank. A Butlers Bank official in Switzerland, who later became a highly paid employee of Vesco's, and Vesco attempted to have the bank, with the $6.2 million, issue two large checks in the name of Bernard Cornfeld against the deposit. A portfolio manager who had loudly complained the money was intended to buy Cornfeld's shares was sacked with the unanimous consent of FOF's board, Buhl among them. Henry thought it "improper conduct of an employee not to go through normal channels," though he was strongly opposed to the use of fund monies to buy out Bernie. To Vesco, "If employees did not trust management, they could leave." But in the Bahamas, Allan Butler had also refused to authorize the transaction, which he regarded as devious.

Cornfeld, back at Villa Elma from California and learning of the attempted transfer, hit the roof. "Now *that* was stupid," he screamed at Meissner. He ran through Villa Bella Vista, shouting that he would kill Willkie Farr's Ray Merritt. "I was asked," Merritt said, "if I would exit the office and remain out of the office until Mr. Cornfeld left for London." Merritt fled by way of a balcony. Ken Beaugrand, IOS's general counsel, hid in a closet.

The money to purchase Cornfeld's shares finally came directly from Butlers Bank. The bank also lent Cowett $280,000 he owed on 600,000 IOS shares, in exchange for voting rights and an option to buy. If Allan didn't agree to help, Bob said that he might lose control of IOS, and Butlers Bank, because of its previous loan, could then be in trouble. Butler later said:

> We were extremely sympathetic in terms of the removal of Cornfeld and Cowett, so . . . we thought we were up to the wrists and might as well get in to the elbow, I mean we really had no alternative. So we said, all right, we'll do what we can, but again if we do anything . . . not only do monies have to be provided in order to make this loan, but also the long-range liquidity of the bank has to be protected, because it was then apparent that the Swiss Banking Commission and the SEC and a number of entities had an extremely vindictive and perhaps irrational approach toward the whole IOS empire, and we knew that we were in for a very hard time and that we would have bad publicity, and we heard the Bank of America had turned down any kind of rescue operation because they didn't think they could weather the storm, and, certainly, if the Bank of America didn't think they can weather the storm Butlers Bank was going to have a very difficult time weathering the storm. . . . We gave an indication . . . that we would consider it on the basis of . . . future business, and our bank is protected in terms of present and future liquidity, for our depositors. We anticipated adverse publicity. We anticipated the cancellation of bank lines. There's no Federal Reserve System in the Bahamas. . . . You're all by yourself, so it was a big decision and we decided we would do it, if we possibly could.

Vesco was knee-deep in trickiness; and what followed, after the SEC untangled the transaction, led to its frontal assault. Vesco had bought Linkink Progressive (SA), a shell corporation he pretended was still owned by Bank Cantrade. But the money to back the Linkink loan came from Arthur Lipper, the IOS broker. Lipper deposited with Butlers Bank $6.2 million on a six months' basis with the understanding that Lipper would handle half of IOS's U.S. brokerage or receive a large consulting fee for five years. Butlers's code name for Lipper was "Bunny Rabbit," for Linkink "Rinkidink."

The transaction nearly fell apart when a Union Bank official discovered that the papers for it referred to Cantrade and had them destroyed. At the London closing, Vesco said he'd left the papers in a taxicab and dispatched Gilbert Straub, head of ICC

European Services by then, to Zurich for another set. Egon Lechner and Frederic Weymar, of Butlers Bank, the official lender, had the authority to sign the loan to Linkink without Cornfeld's knowledge, but the two had to be kept out of sight because Bernie would realize Butlers Bank and Vesco were behind the sale and back out, as Bob feared he would anyway. Weymar had some of the papers in his hotel room all night, and, thinking he heard a prowler, drew a gun.

The next day, January 16, Cornfeld was shown documents establishing, it seemed, that the buyer of his shares was Consulentia Verwaltungs A.G., a sub of Cantrade, though his attorney wasn't allowed to keep a copy or place one in the closing binder. (In 1975, a document was found disclosing that on January 15, 1971, Consulentia sold Linkink and its officers resigned.) Bernie was satisfied. "I cannot disclose the terms of the transaction or the purchaser," said his statement. "However, I can say that the purchaser is affiliated with a major international financial institution. I sincerely hope this will prove a valuable new association for the company." He was handed two checks, one of which he endorsed to cover his debts, and he departed. "I enjoyed the work, my success, the excitement, the people. It could have gone on forever as far as I was concerned," Bernie later said.

Once again, Vesco had displayed awesome audacity. Since the price, $5.6 million, was far more than the shares were worth, the purchaser, a "major financial institution," had to understand the true value of IOS better than others did, would pay extra for Cornfeld's controlling shares, and would be willing to invest a fortune in its new partner. So Bernie must have concluded, or convinced himself. The purchaser, of course, was Vesco, who, constrained by regulatory authorities and fear of dissident shareholders, tried to be invisible. Hogan & Hartson arranged the transaction with Butlers Bank, according to Butler. Frank Beatty, ICC's executive vice president, said that H&H didn't feel "all that troubled by Linkink."

Bernie's shares, reregistered in Panama, went to a safe-deposit box in Geneva instead of to Butlers Bank as collateral, but by the time Allan learned of that they were nearly valueless, since the underlying assets were gone. He had been assured that Union

Bank would eventually fund the loan—it didn't—and after his disillusionment with Vesco he strongly doubted Union had ever been in the picture. He had hoped that Lipper would maintain his deposit but the broker, claiming he hadn't received his promised benefits, and under pressure from the SEC, withdrew the money instead. Vesco replaced some of it with funds from ICC subsidiaries, though most of the loan was never repaid. Eventually, ICC's Hemispheres Financial Services emerged as the owner of Cornfeld's stock. The elaborate ploys were intended to assure ICC's control of IOS without offending the SEC's rules on disclosure. If IOS in some form or other emerged as a planetary financial power, who would remember "Rinkidink"? Or so Vesco reasoned.

Cowett warned Vesco "that he was dealing with people who would fight him until there was absolutely no mathematical chance of their winning the vote of the stockholders *and* until they had exhausted their remedies in court. He did not believe me—and he almost lost control at the 1971 meeting of stockholders at Toronto."

On February 25, the frazzled Sir Eric Wyndham White having resigned, Vesco was elected board chairman of IOS. "Absolute Control Now All the Way Around," H&H handwritten notes recorded "RLV" as stating. RLV was wrong.

16

THE DISSIDENTS

Vesco impressed the IOSers in sharply different ways. Charming almost at will, he was for many a rough diamond. To those who liked him, Bob was admirable for the speed of mind, ability to sort out financial issues, determination, and courage. Vesco could be forceful and persuasive, as those willing to give the devil his due would admit. To those who distrusted him, opinions ran along a spectrum—from cunning financial adventurer, to out-and-out thief, to figure of real evil, to corporate Dracula sucking IOS's blood. Vesco contributed to the negative impressions by his coolly manipulative behavior, evasiveness, and verbal game-playing, qualities he'd exhibited since his early New Jersey days and would continue to.

Morton Schiowitz, the former IOS financial vice president, first met Vesco at Cornfeld's house, the Villa Elma. Such was the confusion and despair that, Schiowitz thought, if Bernie stalked to his office and assumed command, everyone would fall into line. Cornfeld wouldn't march. Schiowitz, an amiable, intelligent man with a crackly laugh, regarded Vesco, with his odd mustache and slicked-down hair, not as a serious contender but as a "wise-ass," little dreaming that Vesco would prevail. Schiowitz was distressed when Vesco achieved control over the key finance committee, but what really made him see red was an early 1971 ICC financial statement in which the New Jersey company hyped almost nonexistent earnings by claiming $1.5 million of "warrant income" from IOS. Vesco, as always, tried to show profits in almost any way he could, to maintain the price of ICC stock, but to Schiowitz a clear signal had been sent. ICC shouldn't have been permitted to take the profit unless IOS failed to live up to the agreement to reorganize by a certain date. To Schiowitz, it meant that Vesco had no intention of reorganizing and leaving IOS but planned to hang on.

Joined by others, including Meshulam Riklis, who picked up the legal bills but wanted the money he'd paid for Cornfeld's shares returned, Schiowitz launched a proxy fight, claiming to control 4.4 million of the 40.5 million outstanding preferred shares. (Preferred shareholders elected two-thirds of the IOS directors.) And he sued Vesco, accusing him and ICC of "conspiracy and an unlawful plan to take advantage of the beleaguered position of IOS in order to loot and plunder its assets," a statement Schiowitz repeated to the press. Vesco countersued for libel, demanding $20 million for damage to his reputation for "integrity and honesty."

Vesco claimed, "We did not have a majority. If you look at an IOS [board] meeting, you can see we had all kinds of screaming and yelling and meetings that went on for days. You know, things like that. ICC could not exercise its control over IOS. Never could. That was one of the reasons we got on." But Vesco demanded to be removed from IOS for the $9–$10 million he'd offered to sell to Cornfeld for. IOS, Vesco knew, couldn't pay. He jockeyed for field position at the IOS annual meeting in Toronto on June 30.

Slater complained the cash situation was critical: "The Company is now conducting negotiations with a subsidiary of International Controls Corp. whereby financing can be made immediately available. . . ." A familiar tune! But, said Slater, if the Vesco team wasn't elected at the annual meeting, ICC wanted its money back, which meant, according to what IOS chairman Vesco told the *Wall Street Journal,* the company would need $15 million to survive. ICC chairman Vesco agreed to wait until after the annual meeting before defaulting the other company he was chairman of. Later on, Vesco met with the dissidents in London and agreed to sell ICC's IOS holdings to Riklis for $10 million, a substantial profit to ICC. That was supposed to have been the objective in the first place, but, even though Riklis had issued a press release, Vesco, with his IOS empire dreams, backed out.

In March 1971, to defuse mounting opposition, Vesco unveiled some of his plans to twenty-five or so IOS preferred shareholders who had assembled from all over the world. The meeting was scheduled for the Regency Hotel in New York City, but, at the last minute, because reporters had appeared and fearful perhaps of a subpoena from the SEC, which had just launched an investigation of ICC, Vesco switched the locale to the Holiday Inn at Wayne, N.J. A fleet of black limousines waited outside the Regency. En route to the George Washington Bridge, as the caravan passed through Central Park, an old-line IOSer cried, "It's the Mafia! I don't need this!" and jumped from the car when it stopped.

The motel meeting was held in a long, narrow room with tables covered with green felt. Vesco spotted an attorney for one of the shareholders and said, "I told you! No lawyers. Okay, you can stay, but don't open your mouth." Vesco spoke about recapitalizing IOS and said, "I have a group that will lend to us, but it's off if there's a proxy fight." He also announced semiseriously, "I invited you to show you why my proposal could cost you the stock you now own. My plans are to steal everything I can from the company and you'll never know I'm doing it. When you find out, it'll be too late." To nervous laughter, Vesco began to write on a flip chart.

After the meeting, the shareholders milled around outside. "This guy must be okay. Nobody who would steal would say so," they consoled themselves, but when they got down to it they weren't all that certain.

The dissidents, as Vesco called them, thought he was up to no good and were determined to gain control. Supporters put up $5,000 each and Schiowitz rented an office in New York City. Being mostly from the sales force, the opposition had contacts over the globe. The phone bill was astronomical as proxies were collected and numbers and names posted on a board. Vesco displayed some uncertainty. Several ICC executives were told to obtain passports and be ready to leave the country to buy IOS shares—dissident pressure was forcing ICC to take an ownership position in IOS, as the ICC board voted to do in April. Far from "Absolute Control Now All The Way Round" Vesco was suddenly embattled.

A bundle of shares lay in a vault at Overseas Development Bank (Geneva), collateral for personal loans to former IOSers. Vesco asked whether the shares could be legally sold, and a Swiss counsel believed they could be. Vesco wanted a confirmation of the opinion in writing, but by the time it arrived the bank was closed.

Scheduled to leave for New Jersey, Vesco hurriedly tried to purchase the shares for Hemispheres Financial, ICC's IOS stock-buying arm, on Saturday, but a Swiss director of ODB, Jacques Wittmer, objected, disagreeing with the Swiss counsel's opinion. As heated conversations went on during the day, there was talk of firings. Vesco met that evening with two of the bank's deputy managers and commanded them to produce the shares, because two ODB directors had ordered it.

One of the deputy managers replied in a shaky voice, knowing he could lose his job, "It is not possible. The safe is locked. It could be opened in an emergency, but the certificates are in a lock-box and the key is in another cabinet which cannot be opened since the man with the key is away for the weekend. . . ."

"Get me those goddam securities!" Vesco yelled.

On Sunday morning, the deputy managers, along with three other bank employees, opened the safe, but they didn't have the key to the cabinet that held the key to open the box that held the securities. Ulrich Strickler, an accountant, IOS director, and member of the Vesco inner circle, forced it open with a crowbar and 135,652 preferred shares were handed over against receipt. Transfer work began at once, but Wittmer declared it could not proceed because almost 60,000 shares belonged to one David Tucker, also a dissident, who objected violently to Meissner on the phone from Paris. The Tucker shares, worth all of $13,000, were hurriedly returned, but two weeks later Tucker filed a criminal complaint.

That weekend at the Geneva airport was the first time anyone at IOS had seen the "flying castle," the used Boeing 707 ICC had taken delivery of from Pan Am earlier in June. With ICC's logo and Vesco's personalized registration "N11RV" emblazoned pretentiously on the tail ("N" stood for North America, "11" meant luck, as in craps), it put ICC in the unique position of probably being at that time the only public company in the world not engaged in commercial air transportation to have a 707. The aircraft was the epitome of Vesco, president of, by Fortune "500" standards, a fairly small industrial company, and his insensitivity toward those who believed he took advantage of IOS. After quarrels with airport authorities about noise levels, the plane departed for Toronto, with Vesco and cardboard file cabinets full of stock certificates on board. "The flight back to Newark, as far as Vesco's behavior is concerned, was the grimmest I had ever experienced. He sat by himself covered with papers, ledgers and note pads, all of which he studied with the intensity of someone cramming for a final exam that will make or break him. I don't think he ate a bit of food or had a single drink all the way across. It had become routine for Vesco to visit with me in the cockpit during these long flights. Not this time," reported the pilot, Alwyn "Ike" Eisenhauer, referring to cockpit visits by Vesco, a "white knuckle" passenger, on the previous ICC plane, a Gulfstream. Eisenhauer (who claimed to be a distant relative of President Eisenhower despite the different spelling) tended to be colorful about Vesco: "By the time we landed at Newark Vesco had a snarl on his face that made him look mean as a cornered Doberman. He was ready for a fight—and God help the other guy."*

At an ICC board meeting June 28, Hogan & Hartson again recorded Vesco's expectation of success at Toronto, perhaps by a landslide. Close to three million IOS preferred shares had been bought by Hemispheres Financial at $.22 each, and the ICC board had been asked to increase its loan even if other loans had to be reduced. Vesco had tried to browbeat dissidents by calling their IOS loans if they wouldn't side with him, even if he forced them into bankruptcy, but strong opposition remained and Eisenhauer was told to fuel the plane as though for a long trip and to appear at the meeting in full uniform, he said.

* *The Flying Carpetbagger,* by Captain A. L. ("Ike") Eisenhauer and Robin Moore with Robert J. Flood, Pinnacle Books, 1976, p. 86.

On June 30, the Ontario Room at the Royal York Hotel was packed with nearly 350 shareholders. The atmosphere was chaotic, and tension existed between the dissident IOSers and those who favored Vesco, who stated that IOS had reached the break-even point. With stable management, it would turn a profit by the end of the year and had offered to register with the SEC. (The agency denied receiving such a proposal, and, in any case, would have rejected it.) "It's like the Vietnam war in there," said Vesco. He still believed the chance the dissidents could win was remote, but the vote counter told him privately that his management slate had lost. In shock, Vesco adjourned the meeting before the official tabulation had been finished, and, that afternoon, fourteen people crowded into a room at Zimmerman & Winters, IOS Canadian legal counsel.

Earlier in the day, the opposition had obtained an injunction that prevented management from voting the 3.6 million shares owned by the IOS Stock Option Plan, and the Canadian lawyers advised that the shares couldn't be voted even if they were bought. Without them, Vesco said, he could fail, and the risk-reward ratio heavily favored voting the shares. Someone made the argument that even if an element of illegality existed, wouldn't it be more immoral if management didn't make every effort to protect the company from the old group that had done such harm? The argument seemed to carry the day and a check for $798,542.58 went to the Stock Option Plan.

Vesco told the dissidents, glancing at Eisenhauer in uniform, that he could force a postponement and fly anywhere necessary to obtain more proxies, but the dissidents were unconvinced, believing that they had triumphed. That evening, one approached Meissner and asked him to stay on at IOS after Vesco was kicked out. Meissner said he'd consider the offer.

The tabulation was announced the next day amid cheers and furious cries. In the pandemonium, Vesco ordered a man ejected. Management had elected twenty-four of the twenty-seven directors and the dissidents seemed finished. But they had by no means given up. On July 8, the Schiowitz group filed suit in the

Supreme Court of St. John, New Brunswick, where IOS was registered, charging irregularities in the way proxies were solicited and the vote was counted at the annual meeting. They said the Stock Option Plan shares shouldn't have been voted at all.

17

RAGE

The blow fell. At St. John, a Canadian judge issued an injunction that prohibited Vesco from acting in any capacity for IOS, whose officers and directors were restrained from conducting other than ordinary business before the trial.

The risk-reward ratio had turned sour, especially since the Ontario Securities Commission also ruled against Vesco on the Stock Option shares. Incensed, Vesco, who enjoyed playing tough guy ("It's only a smokescreen," he told Eisenhauer), talked about taking care of Schiowitz, but his response came on the corporate front on July 15. Frank G. Beatty, ICC's executive vice president, sent a letter reminding IOS that it remained in default. The demand had been postponed pending the election of at least two-thirds of management's slate, but since the New Brunswick injunction in effect prevented the directors, and particularly Vesco, from serving, all bets were off. Beatty wanted $10 million, or, in lieu of that, stock in key IOS subsidiaries that could be sold, perhaps to ICC, unless the injunction were vacated, a sort of threat to the dissidents to back off. This time, Slater stood his ground. "It is our present position that such defaults and events thereof do not now exist," he replied in gobbledygook.

The lawyers' notes from a July 21, 1971, ICC board meeting in Geneva sounded grave. It was all very well to talk about the reorganization of IOS, but what if the legal action tied their hands? In the silence, they looked at their young leader who had proved again and again that a strong will and enough stock in a company would prevail, that attorneys and boards of directors could become mere instruments.

> RLV 3 alternatives
> (a) get out of IOS
> (b) get out forcefully—try
> to put IOS in liquidation
> (c) stay in and purchase more
> stock to get majority, about
> 7,000,000 shares more, at
> $2,000,000 approximate cost . . .

Ralph Dodd and Wilbert Snipes preferred the first solution, to "walk away," as a Hogan lawyer put it, reach an accommodation on the loan, and return to the business of ICC. Snipes worried, rightly, that attaining a majority interest in IOS would leave ICC open to the already publicized charges of "looting." The second, to put IOS into bankruptcy and receivership, seemed studded with legal problems. The boldest course was to plunge on until ICC had 51 percent of IOS and could keep some IOS income, estimated at $10 million in 1972, and which would be, Vesco expected, most of ICC's profits that year. Curiously, perhaps, because of Vesco ICC had become dependent on IOS.

Vesco, deeply involved in the IOS reorganization and determined to resist the SEC, anticipated "two months" of problems until International Controls had a majority interest; he could then call another shareholders meeting without real opposition. According to him, after the New Brunswick injunction, "We said, oh shit, you know, we're going to be fighting for the rest of our lives plus some SEC problems." He was trying to "syndicate IOS to banking institutions . . . Because of the SEC, nobody in the world would touch IOS because it would have the same problems ICC had. And that's the bottom line." Vesco claimed he attempted to put IOS in a condition where it could be sold. "The board made a policy decision to approve an increase in the investment of its subsidiaries in IOS. . . ." said the formal minutes. One type of purchase was to buy rights of first refusal at a penny a share, and Henry Buhl, who wasn't alone, received a check for over $4,000, which by then he needed.

Willkie Farr for IOS and Hogan & Hartson for ICC won sweeping victories in the Canadian courts, but the Tucker charges remained. In August, observers appointed by the Swiss Federal Banking Commission issued a report concluding:

> . . . if certain irregularities have been committed by Vesco, Meissner and Strickler, they are substantially less serious than what one could believe from the testimony of the Swiss [ODB] directors . . . on the other hand they are partly due to wrong legal advice which had been given to them and which they have accepted in good faith. . . . In our opinion the real irregularity in the sale of the 135,000 shares consists in the fact that the shares have not been sold in the primary interest of Overseas Development Bank (Geneva) but in the interest of the Vesco Group that was trying to vote those shares . . .

The criminal case, with the Schiowitz forces behind it, persisted, though Vesco's lawyers tried to settle. (In early 1972, Tucker, for $78,358.53 and the sale of his shares, dropped the charges.) The case had been assigned to Judge Robert Pagan, a crusty investigating magistrate who, four months after he commenced a hearing, had not yet heard testimony from the Swiss Banking Commission observers, the Swiss attorneys who had given advice, or from most of the ODB personnel who had participated. On November 30, he summoned Vesco, Meissner, and Strickler to his chambers in St. Antoine prison for conferences that lasted less than five minutes, with the judge not listening, Meissner said. Pagan proceeded to order the arrest of the three for "disloyal conduct" and a bail hearing was set for the following afternoon. To Vesco's American lawyers, what the trio was accused of probably wouldn't have formed the basis for a civil, much less criminal, complaint in the United States.

A block square and visible from anywhere in the ancient part of Geneva from its hill, St. Antoine prison, 150 years old, lacked amenities. Meissner, who had never been jailed, was put in a cell with three other men, deprived of his belt and shoelaces, and spent a sleepless night pondering imponderables. What did the charge amount to, especially since he hadn't known about the Tucker incident until Tucker had phoned him after the fact? When would he be allowed to have a lawyer? How long could he be kept without a hearing? The Napoleonic Code does not guarantee the right to habeas corpus proceedings. What kind of a sentence could he receive? Meissner didn't have his blood pressure medication with him, nor had his pleas for it been heeded. Would he survive the night?

Vesco's thoughts were just as grim. He, too, had never been locked up (nor had Strickler). He had still hoped for institutional backing for his IOS reorganization, like that of the Bank of America, but realized that newspaper headlines would put him in an even more unfavorable position than he was already, with the SEC investigation having begun. He would be what he hated most, humiliated. He couldn't trust the Swiss authorities for certain, and, once out of this mess, wouldn't return to Switzerland. Vesco vowed never to be in prison again.

Through the bars of his cell, Vesco dropped to an associate a matchbook from the 707, with "RLV" initialed on the cover, on which he scribbled "GET IKE AND RALPH." Dodd and Eisenhauer—the 707 was in Texas for modifications—were quickly dispatched on Swissair.

But more powerful intervention was underway. At Fairfield, where it was still morning, the most important of the frenzy of phone calls was to Harry Sears, a prominent, much respected New Jersey politician. Sears had done legal work for ICC and was about to join its board. Through Republican circles, he knew the Attorney General of the United States, John Mitchell, and telephoned him. Mitchell had made previous calls for Vesco, to Lebanon and Hong Kong, where Vesco wanted recommendations. That Vesco had been, and might be again, a contributor to the Republican party, doubtlessly increased his concern, but Mitchell had helped other American businessmen abroad, he stated. The Attorney General telephoned the American Embassy in Berne, and, a few hours later, contacted Sears to say that Vesco would be released on bail. (The American ambassador was reportedly highly irritated at Mitchell's intervention.)

Dodd and Eisenhauer landed in Geneva the following morning. They were met by an IOS security man who carried a gun and taken to an IOS duplex apartment at 147 Rue de Lausanne. "IOS security people were all over the place. . . . I had noticed that there were an unusual number of cars parked in the immediate vicinity of the apartment building. Some of them were even up on the sidewalk and there were a lot of people standing around. Several of them had cameras hanging around their necks. And I realized that an awful lot of people considered Vesco's jailing of major importance."

Pagan set a bail hearing for 2 P.M., though it was by no means certain that the three confederates would be released. ICC's Richard Clay, with Vesco since his Olin days in Detroit, seemed to be running the show. He decided to pack the house, hoping that Pagan would be intimidated, and Eisenhauer estimated that, including the press, some two hundred people—many had come in a motorcade—were jammed into a room meant to accommodate forty or fifty. Vesco, Meissner, and Strickler, who was frightened, appeared in the walkway from the cells, and cameramen began shooting. All appeared "defeated and bedraggled" as they entered the courtroom, Eisenhauer said, though Vesco still had his necktie and shoelaces, which might have meant a bribe.

During the hearing, which lasted about an hour, Pagan heard arguments from attorneys for Vesco and Tucker. The latter urged Vesco's continued incarceration. The judge then retired to decide. He finally ruled the three would be released that evening, on $250,000 bail for Vesco and $25,000 each for Meissner and Strickler. The bail was returned when Vesco settled with Tucker. (Willard Zucker, Tucker's attorney, would later open the Swiss account for the National Security Council's Oliver North in the Iran affair.) Uncertain what to expect, Clay had brought almost $1 million. A new worry was circulated. Suppose, on leaving prison, Vesco was served another complaint? He could be returned to jail. It was arranged for Vesco to walk out the rear exit, to avoid the press, but he came out the front instead, saw Eisenhauer in a Mercedes, who, though followed by a press car, itself followed by a police car, brought the boss to 147 Rue de Lausanne unscathed.

In the party that followed, Vesco regained his cockiness with a glass of Crown Royal Canadian whiskey in one hand and a pepperoni hero in the other. But he unsmilingly told Merritt before he quit Geneva by the first commercial flight the next morning, "If they're going to treat me like a fucking crook, screw them. I'm going to act like a fucking crook."

Vesco also talked with Ed Cowett on December 23, 1971, two days after his release from St. Antoine. They met in Peacock Alley at the Waldorf-Astoria in New York. "Just before parting from each other, Vesco looked squarely at me and said, 'Ed, you know how hard I have tried to play fair with everybody. I have always tried to protect everyone's interests. And look what it has gotten me. You warned me about those dodos [in IOS], and I never took you seriously. I'll tell you one thing: one night in St. Antoine is enough. Now I'm going to steal every dime I can lay my hands on.' "

18

THE BIG SPINOFF

The press accusation against Vesco and his group was that they bilked IOS and the funds of some quarter-billion dollars. It would seem to follow, and the SEC stressed the point, that Vesco lacked a legitimate business purpose. Still, the reorganization of IOS was discussed repeatedly at ICC headquarters in Fairfield, N.J., in January and February 1971. One meeting, on January 27, involved over twenty lawyers and accountants and lasted more than eight hours. The "business purpose" seemed to have been to make money. The question was how and for whom.

"We met in my office," Vesco said, "because I had the largest table. There were three meetings going on at once, and six phones working at the same time." Vesco's style was to present the broad outlines, leaving details to the professionals. Using a flip chart with large blank pages, he wrote his ideas with a Magic Marker, though lawyers spoke too.

They faced diverse problems. IOS was losing, Meissner estimated, $5 million a year and one answer was to cut costs. The staff would be reduced from 2,000 to 200. The sales force, already demoralized and dwindling, would be eliminated. No sales force meant no sales. The answer arrived at was to shut down the funds after the fundholders had a chance to redeem. Everyone agreed at that time the fundholders must have the opportunity, legally and morally. The lawyers punched away at the point again and again.

At the heart of the plan was the old IOS belief that a pot of "hot," "flight," or "black" money wouldn't be reclaimed, because it had been illegally invested in the funds in the first place. The black money records were kept in numbered accounts. The figure of between $100 million and $150 million was mentioned and Meissner had a number of $200–$300 million that came from an unofficial computer run at the IOS data center at Nyon, Switzerland, one of the largest in Europe.

IOS salesmen, who either lived in or visited their areas frequently, would take payments in cash. The hot money, sometimes carried out by suitcase, would be deposited with IOS under false names, and, if a customer wanted a payment, he would contact his salesman. After the sales force evaporated, the customer had no means of reaching his representative. Nor, in a few cases, did IOS know who the customer was.

Vesco, according to Beatty, spoke of making money legitimately from IOS through management fees. "With his tremendous drive for success, he turned himself inside out to accomplish his goals. He could never admit failure. But after St. Antoine, he said, 'I can't do it. I'll move the assets out.' And it can be construed as stealing when legitimate owners lose control."

Vesco aimed as he did later to close-end the funds and put the boodle in an independent company controlled by him. After he was accused of "looting and plundering," Vesco wanted to call the new entity "LPI," for "Looting and Plundering, Inc.," a suggestion he repeated often enough to make the Ivy League lawyers gag. (He also called it "RPL"—for "Rape, Plunder & Loot.") The name that emerged, first recorded in Hogan & Hartson handwritten notes dated January 4, 1971, was "ABC" which, though said to stand for "After Bernie Cornfeld," was standard business nomenclature for as-yet-uncreated corporations and Vesco had used the letters before. (ABC was also known in Willkie Farr files as "FUBAR," for "Fouled [or Fucked] Up Beyond All Recognition.") "Ultimately, it would appear," noted Robert M. Jeffers, of H&H, "that Hogan & Hartson will be counsel for ABC Corp." Louis Lundborg, the Bank of America's board chairman, was listed by H&H as future chairman of ABC.

ABC was to be an offshore company that would "do lots of

deals," Vesco said. IOS stock would be split so as to benefit those who had paid $10 a share, on the open market, with a far lesser return to insiders who had opposed Vesco. IOS stock would be swapped for ABC's. Fundholders electing not to cash in would receive ABC-related shares. The other assets would be sold. The plan called for leaving behind the very name IOS—Vesco wanted to eliminate the "past crap with King and Cornfeld"—and liabilities like losses and lawsuits. That raised questions about fairness to creditors, but they weren't focused on. (Dumping liabilities was a standard Vesco technique.)

Although the details would change continually, the general idea remained the same until the bitter end with the SEC. In essence, Vesco aimed to create, from the "hot" money pool, a new company with investment capital. He, ICC, or both would own one-third of ABC in exchange for reorganization and management. A third of ABC would go to IOS, which would swap its assets. The final portion would be sold, for $11 million at one point, to new investors, and Vesco produced a list, perhaps fabricated, that included a Rockefeller fund, a Rothschild fund, and various banks. ABC would make a public stock offering. It would have its home in an "international business (or maritime) zone" over which the company would have virtual sovereignty. Sites studied and/or visited by Vesco or his people included the Bahamas, Costa Rica, Morocco, the Azores, and islands off Haiti and the Dominican Republic and one in the South Pacific. The scheme was ambitious, complex (Vesco reveled in complexity), and potentially profitable—the "IOS deal could mean *huge* economic benefits for ICC," an H&H lawyer noted.

Vesco, who had been considering such a reorganization since the summer of 1970, pursued his plan to the point of ruthlessness. In January 1971, the Fund of Funds board met at the Castle Harbour Hotel in Bermuda. It had commissioned a law firm, Donovan Leisure, to write a report on John King's relations with FOF that was less than flattering toward King, and it recommended that the fund sue Big John. Vesco became enraged. Not a bit intimidated by illustrious names like Wilson Wyatt, former Lieutenant Governor of Kentucky; Pat Brown, former Governor of California; Dr. Pierre Rinfret, a financier, Vesco yelled profanities, pounded the table, and threatened to take "each and every one of them to court for innumberable years" for having exceeded their "authority in authorizing" the King Arctic investments, said Rinfret, who quit. Wyatt reported that Vesco's statements "made me much more doubtful about [his] judgment." Brown's reaction was "one of suspicion, dislike and distrust. . . ." The Donovan Leisure man called Vesco's performance "extortion in Bermuda," adding that "Vesco was a very bad man and he acted badly." Vesco didn't want FOF to sue John King because his reorganization would be impeded, and, though the directors found Vesco rude, aggressive, arrogant, abrasive, a blackmailer, and just about everything else, the board failed to sue King Resources, and Donovan Leisure resigned. Vesco had won.

Vesco told a reporter that his intention with IOS was "getting the beast by the tail so that we could beat its head against a wall." "Won't you have a dead cat?" "Yes, but it could have nice little kittens." Even before the ICC loan, Vesco and Meissner had spoken of spinning off the banking, real estate, management, and insurance business of IOS to bring down costs but had kept the kittens secret because they feared that IOS would conclude it could do the same without them. In November and December 1971, after the Canadian court victories, the assets were spun off as International Bancorp Ltd., of which ICC received 22 percent of the voting stock, and Value Capital Ltd., of which ICC got 38 percent, again because of its IOS holdings. Said the SEC in a 1978 brief, "Since Vesco controlled both ICC and IOS he was in a position, about [sic] any sense of fiduciary obligation to IOS shareholders, to dole out to ICC any amount of IOS (IBL-VCL) shares."

Although International Controls had received valuable assets, Vesco was more with ABC by then. "I was interested in and infatuated with the offshore financial world. . . . It's intrigue, it's out there, something new, you know, it's a challenge. . . . We (I) are not too good at assembling valves on an assembly line but we (I) can sure spit out agreements. . . ."

Vesco could never confess to bad judgment and easily swayed others. His quick mind, almost total recall of numbers, and, as the corporate world admires, untiring work habits masked for the lawyers and accountants, who seemed deficient in insight, his psychological problems. He was always highly compartmentalized, perhaps even from himself, motivated by whatever grandiose fantasies. Nobody was permitted to know more than a fraction of his internal equations—where this accounting piece or that legal maneuver, or, ultimately, the disposition of the IOS hoard fitted into the schemes he kept to himself. Because he always appeared in complete control, others were discouraged from prying, though they should have. They might have discovered that Vesco's universe was designed almost exclusively to benefit himself. He would pursue his schemes to the point of folly, regardless of the SEC or the growing effect it had on ICC.

The investigation was like a slow-acting poison in the ICC boardroom. Vesco berated H&H for evading responsibility and equivocating with regard to IOS, and he called the company's general counsel, Charles Egan, who didn't like the manner in which Vesco was handling the SEC investigation, "stupid," "ineffectual," a "sissy." Vesco spoke of "deVescoizing" ICC to placate the SEC by selling his stock or placing it in trust for his children, who would then own a Bahamian corporation that would "do" ABC. But he couldn't seem, or didn't want, to resolve the problem of "corporate opportunity," meaning a personal benefit to him from an action by the company. He was unwilling to relinquish IOS despite the growing risk.

Nothing would stop him from building an offshore empire. Never mind the SEC. Never mind that IOS "caused distracting external pressures on our operations," as Vesco said. Never mind that Vesco faced increasing opposition from within IOS, like Buhl's. Henry lacked power—he only worked part-time by then, and his office was changed so often he forgot where it was—but he had been loyal to the Vescoites and could get a hearing. He scolded Meissner about $2 million advanced to former IOSers Martin Solomon and Robert Sutner, who formed Dominion Guaranty (the money was later returned with interest) because, Henry said, the Fund of Funds shouldn't make illiquid investments. Meissner didn't pay particular heed, knowing, as Buhl didn't, the reorganization being a well-guarded secret, that before long the funds would cease to be invested in marketable securities. ("Willkie Farr suspects but doesn't know. Beaugrand, Hoffman, LeBlanc and Meissner know. Howe & Bennett suspect," wrote Hogan & Hartson.)

Buhl criticized the $5 million FOF had placed in Keyser Ullman shares at the same time IOS was negotiating with the British bank for the sale of IOS's International Life Insurance, U.K. Henry said, "You just can't do this." Stanley Graze (stocky and of medium height, a championship wrestler who had been an economics teacher and vice president of a Wall Street brokerage firm and who became IOS's investment adviser in January 1972), told him that Keyser Ullman was the fastest growing merchant bank in London. "I don't care if it's the best in the world—there's a conflict of interest," Buhl said. "It looks very much as if you are giving them the money to buy a division from you."

It later looked like that to the SEC, too, but the facts were different. Vesco and Meissner had been at Keyser Ullman, and overhearing news about its stock, Vesco told Graze to buy it. For Meissner, that was using insider information, and helped him conclude, as did Keyser Ullman, that Vesco wasn't ethical, though because of his IOS responsibilities, he claimed, he stayed on. When Solomon asked him, "Are we doing things honestly?" Vesco said, "Yes." "You're not a crook?" Solomon persisted, and Vesco said, "No."

Buhl and others resigned from the funds, in June 1972, because of such investments, but Henry was still an IOS director. He went to a meeting in Toronto, wasn't admitted, and he was out. If Buhl had been sometimes unhappy over how Bob played the game, Richard Hammerman, president of International Life Insurance, was more than unhappy. Unable to get certain guarantees, he closed his London office door, leaving Vesco, in a Hawaiian sports shirt, outside, shouting that his plane waited. God-fearing, old-line IOSer John Templeton didn't trust people with corporate jets, much less a 707, because it meant they were big spenders. He was furious with Vesco, whom he'd given a party for in his home in the Bahamas, for repeated delays in paying him for his considerable ILI stock. "I had an uneasy feeling about Bob," said Templeton. "I was concerned that there was a lot of cash around. He was one of the few people I've done business with I didn't like. Most businessmen are very direct. Vesco did all that talking and nothing happened. He stalled and stalled."

A proposed $20 million loan to ICC from the Central States Teamsters Pension Fund—Vesco flew union officials, and the fund's Allan Dorfman, who went to jail, cross-country in the 707 —fell through. Part of the loan would have been to help ICC with its financial problems, such as credit ratings, and part to buy IOS shares. Another potential purchaser of IOS was Raymond Mason, president of Charter Corp., and Edward Ball, Chairman of St. Joe, a paper company, and trustee of the A. I. Du Pont estate. Early in 1972, the Charter/Du Pont deal collapsed. Ball is supposed to have told Vesco, "I had a dream. You and I slept together on a cold night. In the morning, you had all the blankets."

19

ABC IS HATCHED

In September 1971, the funds still had $480 million and the IOS-ICC corporate front was relatively quiet by the end of the year, though Vesco was increasingly frustrated by, and obsessed with, the SEC. He then began major maneuvers designed to remove the meaty assets of IOS, leaving only the shell.

The first half of 1972 brought the transactions that would form the main basis for the SEC lawsuit. The objective, according to Vesco, was to remove IOS from ICC to rid him of SEC jurisdiction and to set up shop offshore. The special counsel for ICC appointed by the SEC thought otherwise. For him, Vesco aimed at "misappropriating the assets of the IOS-managed investment companies."*

In January and February 1972, in numerous fatiguing and secret meetings at Fairfield, N.J., the decision was reached to push ABC, the projected offshore company, from planning to action. Raymond Merritt of Willkie Farr prepared a document of which there were ten carefully targeted copies. ("Due to the extremely confidential nature of this memorandum," he wrote each recipient on February 1, 1972, "I would appreciate it being held in strict confidence.") His document entitled "Attorney Work Product" analyzed the mechanics of investing substantial assets of the dollar funds in a single, closed-end corporation. ABC would issue $100 million in bonds to be purchased by IOS entities and would

* "Report of Investigation by Special Counsel [David Butowsky]." U.S. District Court, Southern District of New York, 1977. P. 446.

offer to buy IOS shares with ABC stock or it would tender for them. The directors of all the four funds—IIT, FOF, Venture, and Growth (largely German)—would vote to liquidate. An extremely large transaction was outlined in less than three sparse pages.

But Merritt warned that ABC could be construed as a scheme to "frustrate the redemption rights of the [fund shareholders and violate the] directors' obligation to insure that . . . [fund] assets are invested in reasonably marketable securities." It could be viewed as "repugnant to the concept and policies" of the mutual funds as to "constitute breach of fiduciary duty. . . ." Another Willkie Farr lawyer telexed, "Please advise whether the names Atlantic Financial SA or Financial Equities SA are available as corporate names in the Bahamas" (the domicile of ABC had not yet been settled), but there were serious objections to the plan by others. "Egregiously wrong," thundered Hogan & Hartson about one version. There was constant concern about Vesco's tendency to lie, or, at least, present carefully selected versions of the truth, and the IOS Canadian lawyer, Gilbert Bennett, of Zimmerman & Winters, resigned for himself and his firm, despite a financial sacrifice, because of the proposed transactions. "Gil," an H&H lawyer observed, "was one of the few people who would stand up to Vesco." But, said Bennett emotionally, "I did feel that Vesco in particular had in mind carrying out a transaction which would deprive the Fund shareholders of the ability to obtain redemptions of their shares, and it would also place control of the assets of the Funds in, to a greater degree, the hands of whoever controlled IOS. . . . In the course of my involvement in the discussion of the proposed transactions, I came to the conclusion all the transactions would be done and would be done in a way that I found, at least morally, unacceptable and perhaps in my view, unlawful. . . . I had an opinion that it was not possible for me to control Vesco or to change his determination to proceed." To Bennett, the proposals were "virtual thefts from the shareholders." He failed, though, to notify the SEC, at least not then.

Merritt claimed that Bennett's real reason for resigning concerned the Canadian's private life. However, for a young Willkie Farr lawyer, John D'Alimonte, "Bennett just didn't care for the ABC transaction, I guess."

The well-paid attorneys—Hogan & Hartson pulled in about $2 million a year at one point from ICC—disagreed with Bennett. Willkie Farr's Allan Conwill was loyal to the core. He had risen to his firm's executive committee at least partly because he was the lead lawyer on the profitable IOS account—over $1 million a year in fees. Merritt, Conwill's partner and Vesco's main contact at Willkie Farr, detested Cornfeld and to him Vesco looked good in comparison. They got on well. D'Alimonte, also of Italian extraction, liked and said he trusted Vesco. "Naturally," a Willkie Farr lawyer admitted, "the self-dealing problem remains."

"Self-dealing" meant that you dealt with yourself even if you pretended you didn't. Self-dealing was a no-no with the SEC, whose November 1972 complaint against Vesco was studded with the words: if you dealt with yourself you could set arbitrary values and that could lead to fraud. Still, because the SEC's *cordon sanitaire* left IOS in an isolated position, Vesco acted *as if* independent third parties existed even if they didn't. To accomplish the internal mechanics of the intended ABC deal, a familiar cast of characters was used, and H&H noted, "interrelationship of [Norman] LeBlanc with IOS and Global Holdings; relationships between IOS, Kilmorey, ICC, RLV, and Global . . . someone could develop a pretty good complaint."

The previous September, an exhausted Slater had resigned from IOS, citing "continued harassment by dissident shareholders," but also saying that he "didn't appreciate Vesco's method of operations." (In addition to his other problems, Slater hadn't been given a Swiss work permit and was obliged to operate out of France.) Bud Meissner succeeded him and Norman LeBlanc became financial vice president. A Canadian who'd attended Sunday school, LeBlanc graduated in accounting at McGill University in Toronto with top marks and taught the subject there. He had won an accounting prize. Vesco said, "I only control LeBlanc forty-nine percent," meaning he didn't control him (though he did); Norman held Bob in deep admiration and would do his bidding. Vesco had asked him to leave Coopers & Lybrand's Paris office and he agreed, sensing a brilliant opportunity at IOS. ("Knowing what I knew in 1971," he was to say, "I'd have done it all over again. I had no means of predicting what was to be.")

LeBlanc and Vesco, the same age and blue-collar background, had an affinity that to Norman was almost spiritual. They knew what was in each other's minds sometimes to the point of not needing discussion. Vesco never so much as sent LeBlanc a memo. They specialized in bargaining tactics. The theory was that one of them should be the bad guy and the other fair and reasonable, trying to restrain the bad one. Their strategy was carefully worked out, even as to when the bad guy should take a walk, and for how long—Vesco, having stormed out of a meeting, could be seen laughing in the hall—and who on the other team was the weakest and should be scathingly attacked by the bad guy, over the protests of the good guy. For the two, LeBlanc said, the fun was not in concluding a deal but negotiating and winning. ("Vesco and LeBlanc were awfully smart separately," remarked someone who had seen them in action, "but together they were like Don Quixote and Sancho Panza.")

Vesco and LeBlanc's game-playing would figure importantly in the war with the SEC. The only way to accomplish ABC was to free Vesco from the scrutiny of the SEC; therefore, it was vital to detach ICC from IOS to prove International Controls wasn't an IOS "affiliate" and thus subject to SEC dictates. An IOS "management team" composed of Meissner, LeBlanc, Stanley Graze, and Ulrich Strickler had acquired a corporate shell called Kilmorey to buy ICC's IOS shares, including Cornfeld's, for $6.5 million. Only $200,000 was paid, borrowed from the newly created Bahamas Commonwealth Bank, neither of which ICC's press release disclosed, nor did it reveal that there wasn't even a note between ICC and Kilmorey.

The idea was to put a distance between ICC and Kilmorey in order to convince the SEC they were separate and independent. That establishing Kilmorey, like Linkink before it, was a device was taken for granted by its four "owners." That ICC might not be paid was discussed by its board, but Kilmorey was a means to an end. Vesco asked the Hogan & Hartson lawyers if the sale would make the SEC go away and they said, "No, but it could help." H&H referred to the "damned presence of the SEC."

"I could have painted a picture if I wanted to paint a picture," Vesco said. He maintained he could have decorated Kilmorey with the names of international political figures, of which he was no doubt capable, to make it respectable. But "we were making a legitimate deal. We were trying to give the guys a chance to do their thing and at the same time get a problem out of our hair. Well, it didn't work out so we made a mistake, what can I say, you know . . . give me credit for being a little more sophisticated than [being a con artist]. . . . The first thing we wanted to do was to say, hey, SEC, look what we did." But "everything that's right doesn't always look right. . . ."

To Graze, asked by Vesco to invest $2,000 in Kilmorey and who knew next to nothing about it, Bob insisted the SEC had agreed that the transaction would liberate ICC from the agency's jurisdiction. Again, Vesco had either exaggerated or lied. "Bob," said Graze, "had a way of inventing reality and then making the facts conform."

Kilmorey, which would put another nail in Vesco's IOS coffin, closed in the Bahamas on March 31, 1972, and Vesco resigned his positions in IOS, though he became an "unpaid" consultant to Kilmorey and IOS, among other reasons so that IOS, through Kilmorey, could still be billed for expenses like the 707. (Vesco's expense account mania was one of his fatal flaws.) Despite Vesco's clumsy attempts to explain it, the commission believed his new role was a sham, a means of pretending that Vesco had relinquished power even though he hadn't, and Kilmorey was added to the SEC's list of grievances.

With Kilmorey out of the way, Vesco and his legal beagles turned to further permutations designed to advance the ABC maneuver. ICC, Vesco had said, would retain its interests in Value Capital Ltd. and International Bancorp Ltd.; but to deprive the SEC of a pretext for intervening, he decided to strip ICC of both. LeBlanc, whose bad disposition and nervous laugh during his alcoholic days earned him the nickname "Nasty Norman, the Burble," capitalized the new shells, the Globals, in the Bahamas at $1,000 each. For $7.35 million in notes, ICC sold the Globals its VCL and IBL shares which were destined to become part of ABC.

"And now, having disengaged ourselves from these matters, International Controls will focus its attention on the development of our exhaustive operations for their continued growth," Vesco said. ICC's attention, maybe, but not Vesco's, still focused on the ABC plan. From the start, it envisioned capturing the "hot" money. The open question was what the IOS shareholders would be told, if anything. Vesco now answered that question: nothing. LeBlanc's Globals had no money; Venture Fund had $40 million. The fund was chosen to finance the latest phase of ABC because it had been formed to invest risk capital, albeit in the United States. ("This sure is venturesome," Willkie Farr's D'Alimonte remarked.) Unlike FOF, which had 1,300 residual American investors and which the SEC might claim was in violation of the 1967 order and use to establish its jurisdiction, Venture had none. Merritt having advised the IOSers who strongly objected that the investment was "lawful under the bylaws and regulations" of the fund, the Venture board seemingly approved the transaction on June 20, in Nassau, though there is evidence the meeting never took place. Meissner claimed the vote was a one-and-one-half tie, which he, as chairman, broke by voting yes. For him, $20 million was a small sum, he said, considering the amounts he dealt with, and the money went to the Globals. (The Willkie Farr file word for one of the ABC transactions was *krasis*, "merger" in Greek, a language Merritt had studied. Another definition of *krasis* might have served as well for the SEC: "watering the wine.")

The Venture transaction was Vesco's Rubicon, reaffirming the SEC's conviction that he couldn't be trusted and rekindling its efforts, which had begun to falter. Venture also marked a departure from Vesco's original plan, or so he had informed the lawyers, to close-end the funds with at least a semblance of shareholder approval and give the investors a chance to redeem. Instead, half of the Venture assets went to LeBlanc's Globals, and over $7 million of that to ICC.

Global Holdings printed bonds to exchange for $100 million from the funds, but one more gigantic deal remained before the dollars marched across national frontiers. Vesco "signature" transactions, as the SEC called them, had his style. Typically, Vesco used a two-tier corporate structure, issuing to company A most of the control stock and a large block of nonvoting stock in a second company, B. The investors, IOS investors, would buy stock in company B, which A controlled.*

Property Resources was destined to become part of ABC, the new offshore empire, armed with IOS shareholder money, that Vesco would control. The attorney Merle Thorpe of H&H became so concerned about PRL's possible unfairness that he flew to Fairfield to discuss it with Vesco and apparently threatened to resign from ICC's board. Vesco reassured him the board would review the transaction and he hired one Roger Tamraz, an American partner in Kidder-Peabody's Beirut office, to evaluate PRL. (Vesco had met Tamraz in his unsuccessful efforts to acquire Intra Bank, in Lebanon, which controlled Middle Eastern Airlines and other properties.) The SEC sneered at Tamraz's efforts, and the possibility existed that Vesco had given Tamraz figures in advance, but Kidder-Peabody sent a team to Europe and the United States to evaluate PRL's assets.

PRL was just the sort of fancy deal-making Vesco delighted in, if only to prove he could outsmart the other guys. He told Laurence Richardson, who replaced him as ICC president in late 1970 (Vesco remained board chairman and CEO) and who traveled to Beirut on the Intra Bank deal, "We've handled Wall Street. We've handled Europe. We'll go after the Arabs and then it's Hong Kong." Such snippets of grandiosity registered in people's memories, but didn't mean much at the time.

Another H&H lawyer, James J. Rosenhauer, went further

* Property Resources Ltd. (PRL) was just such a transaction. As originally put forth by Vesco, a newly formed holding company, PRL, would issue its shares in exchange for assets from three sources: (1) IPI (Investment Properties International) with approximately $50 million in questionable real estate values and almost another $50 million in cash; (2) most of the assets of Global Natural Resources (Global), the pre-Vesco spinoff by FOF to its shareholders that included gas and oil properties and other mineral interests, such as King's Arctic permits for exploration under the ocean ice near the North Pole; and (3) various insurance and real estate holdings of Value Capital Ltd. (VCL). The latter was key since ICC owned approximately 38 percent of the VCL shares and no IPI or Global shares. Vesco's objective was to get a minimum of 20 percent of the Property Resources stock for VCL so that ICC could recognize its share of the income VCL expected from PRL. Global was eventually dropped from the transaction on several grounds. The deal was completed in 1972 with IPI and VCL exchanging their assets for PRL shares. IPI got 78 percent of the PRL shares and VCL 22 percent. The court-appointed liquidators for IPI and VCL litigated the transaction for years, and finally it was settled on the basis of an 89–11 split of the PRL shares between IPI and VCL, which, because of Vesco, received too much of the assets.

about PRL: "The fundamental difficulty with the proposed transactions is the inconsistent valuation method applied . . . the disproportionate benefit is received by VCL, in which ICC has an economic interest much greater than its interest in [other affected entities whose shareholders might be gypped in favor of Vesco's ICC]." His comments were expressed on March 26, 1972. A few days later, Merle Thorpe did resign from ICC's board for personal reasons and general H&H policies about having members serve on boards of directors, he said. However, ICC's special counsel David Butowsky concluded that a principal reason for Thorpe's resignation was concern about possible liability from PRL, though Thorpe didn't tell the ICC board that.

One purpose of Property Resources was to buy Resorts International's Paradise Island casino, two hotels, shipyard, and marina plus the independently (mostly the late James L. Crosby) owned toll bridge to Nassau and Resorts stock for almost $100 million, of which $15 million, from an entity called Gulfstream, funded by IIT, was for the bridge and casino. Willkie Farr's file word for the transaction was "Faded," as in craps.

Aided by deal makers like Bert Kleiner, of the Los Angeles brokerage firm Kleiner, Bell, who had helped James Crosby finance the purchase of Paradise Island from Huntington Hartford, Resorts International had tried to take over Pan American World Airways and been stopped because the U.S. Congress, regarding Pan Am as virtually a national monument, passed a law declaring that nobody could buy more than 5 percent of an American airline without prior approval of the Civil Aeronautics Board. After the Pan Am deal collapsed, Crosby, the majority Resorts shareholder, wanted to sell. As he told his childhood pal, Richard Pistell, who had become close to Vesco, he was tired of doing business in the Bahamas.†

Another wheeler-dealer, Pistell had gone through several fortunes and headed companies like Goldfield and General Host Corporation, which tried and failed, only for legal reasons, to take

† In 1987, Donald Trump, the New York developer, was engaged in purchasing stock in Resorts and Pan Am, with the idea of tying the two together for Bahamian gambling flights, much as contemplated by Crosby and Kleiner.

over Armour, the huge meat-packing concern. Called "Mr. Wonderful" because, to "How are you?" he would always respond with "Wonderful," Pistell wanted to start an undersea restaurant and had been known to tear a menu vertically in two and jokingly give half to the waiter as his order.

Pistell told Arthur Lipper, IOS's main broker, of Crosby's interest and Lipper introduced Pistell to Vesco. The three had lunch at the Metropolitan Club in New York and discussed Paradise Island, which had been on the market almost a year.

In February 1972, Vesco, Crosby, Jack Davis (Resorts' second in command), Pistell, and the ubiquitous Henry Buhl, who happened along, sat at lunch in the dining room of the Ocean Club on Paradise Island. The atmosphere was quiet but tense. What had started as a talk about purchasing Chalk Airways from Resorts turned into a full-fledged discussion about an acquisition of Resorts' part of Paradise Island plus purchases of Resorts' stock. "I'll buy it," Vesco said with his show-offy confidence. Investment Properties International (IPI) apparently was destined to put in $50 million but Vesco saw the deal as part of an effort to put IOS into casinos in a big way, though as usual he didn't know where the rest of the money was to come from. Paradise Island might even have become IOS headquarters; the Swiss had applied pressure on the company to leave, and Vesco was exploring other places, but was that how IOS investors wanted their money spent?

With Paradise Island, the Vesco "signature" was somewhat different. A new company would be 50 percent owned by the government and 10 percent by the Bahamian people in exchange for no taxes on gambling profits, with the other 40 percent to be nominally owned by Gilbert Straub, who had joined IOS. Vesco needed someone in charge whom he could both trust and order around; and to his mind there were very few candidates.

The SEC treated IOS's proposed Resorts investment in a contemptuous fashion, as if it were merely another way of lining the Vescoites' pockets, but the participants claimed it was legitimate. Straub explored expanding to Freeport, Grand Bahamas, while Resorts readied cash flow projections; marine, sewage, hotel, and food specialists were brought by IOS to have a look. The negotiations were difficult and broke down completely at one point. Pistell described them as a "shoot-out." Crosby may have been difficult because, according to Pistell, he was proud of what he'd developed and didn't really want to sell.

The Paradise Island transaction dragged on. One problem was Arthur Lipper's finder's fee. Pistell's was to come from Resorts, Lipper's from PRL; and Lipper, if the deal came to $100 million, wanted $15 million, which Merritt considered too large. He phoned Lipper "who became annoyed at me and angered at me for suggesting that he receive a lesser compensation. In that conversation, I pointed out to him that his activity consisted of an attendance at a lunch, unrelated to the transaction, for which he did not pay, and one visit for an hour to the island. It was an unfortunate event, because I always considered him to be a genuinely nice person and a good friend. Our friendship terminated with that conversation," Merritt said.

Had it closed five days before it was supposed to, Vesco's people would have owned Paradise Island, but the deal aborted largely because of the SEC complaint, as the agency proudly announced.

During the "shoot-out," Vesco dined with Crosby at the Brittania Hotel, and a Crosby aide whispered excitedly into his ear. Vesco guessed correctly that Howard Hughes, who had been a potential competitor for Paradise Island, was even then descending on a back elevator and was about to leave the Bahamas. "I wonder if I'll become a second Howard Hughes," Vesco said.

20

MONEY ON THE MOVE

A fatal dance had commenced. To have the cash available for the new IOS, ABC, the funds sold massive amounts of stock (Meissner claimed the funds saved $80 million, Vesco $130 million, because the market declined sharply thereafter) and the SEC had to take notice. Vesco's response was to dance faster. Fearing the agency would block assets or sue ICC and IOS, Vesco responded by "spiriting" money to places the U.S. Government or banking authorities couldn't touch it, and did so before the funds were closed-end and investors had a chance to redeem.

In March and April, 1972, Vesco caused cash and securities to be taken out of a "responsible" bank, Crédit Suisse, as part of the conspiracy, the SEC said. Crédit Suisse was supposed to have resigned in March because Swiss legislation forced it to, and Meissner unsuccessfully tried to find a European successor. (Crédit Suisse puzzlingly denied Swiss legislation was responsible for its decision to leave.) The Swiss bank was replaced by Overseas Development Bank (Luxembourg), a small and thinly staffed IOS bank, and Vesco was warned that it wouldn't look good. "What can I do?" he snapped. "The Europeans won't touch us." According to Meissner, the Luxembourg banking commissioner, then on good terms with Vesco, wanted the dollars in his country, requiring only that ODB's capitalization be increased, and it supposedly was, to $5 million.

By April, the relationship between the Bank of New York and

IOS had deteriorated. BONY, said Meissner, wanted to double its fees and take on Crédit Suisse's functions. It refused to recognize ODB (Lux) as cash custodian, and, instead of transferring the funds to the Luxembourg bank, put them in its London branch on a twenty-four-hour call. The loss of the fund accounts meant about $3 million a year, and BONY seemed reluctant to say goodbye. It also evinced concern over what would happen to the money.

Vesco, Merritt, and Graze had a meeting with BONY officials and told BONY that American National Bank and Trust would succeed it—oddly, BONY and IOS didn't have a written agreement—and when Merritt returned to Willkie Farr, he remarked in apparent surprise, "We just fired the Bank of New York." The SEC referred the choice of ANBT as "curious," but although the New Jersey bank had never seen the kind of money the funds were about to generate, several IOSers were dispatched to teach the locals how to perform custodial duties. Edward A. Stoltenberg, treasurer of various IOS entities, said, "The services we've gotten from these people in New Jersey have been—I think they're excellent, they are fine people, they are a pleasure to work with. . . . They have done an outstanding job." (Wilbert Snipes, credited with bringing the tremendous new account because he acted as the bank's liaison with Vesco, was a local hero until the boom fell on him after the SEC complaint. He was let go.)

In August, two months after the Venture deal with the Globals, the march of dollars resumed as the deposed Bank of New York transferred $60 million, in three payments authorized by WF&G, to, eventually, Bahamas Commonwealth Bank. Enter Bruno Lederer, whom Vesco accused of "going too too far." Lederer, an American lawyer and prime SEC source after the fact, was the "compliance officer" for the IOS funds. His job was to "make sure the system wasn't violated, that the conduit of funds was followed, that restricted securities weren't sold," he said, "and that no significant investments were made in any one stock." Lederer, later assistant general counsel of the New York Stock Exchange, had watched the depletion of IOS personnel, and felt more and more isolated. He was somewhat nervous about the $20 million Venture investment in the Globals because it seemed too large. He worried that it hadn't been at arm's length and Meissner said it wasn't really, but nothing was wrong with that. When he received word of the $60 million in transit to BCB, Lederer sent an anguished telex from the Bahamas, where he was stationed, to Willkie Farr, underscored not by him but during one of the innumerable later lawsuits. "In view of the *enormous and unprecedented transfers of money to Nassau* . . . I am astonished that no one has seen fit to advise me of the *details of the investment being contemplated,* or for that matter of the entire new direction the funds seem to be taking. . . . I will no longer approve any transaction unless and until I am thoroughly satisfied of its legality and propriety, regardless of the pressure exerted on me for immediate action. . . . *In the recent past transactions have been rushed through, which, on additional investigation, may well have been rejected. One of these involved a sizable investment by Venture Fund, of which you are well aware.*" Merritt viewed the telex as being "what may be described as a parting shot," the resignation of Lederer.

The compliance officer was distraught. So much money was on the move and nobody would, or could, tell him why. Stanley Graze, the investment adviser, was supposed to be in London—he was in the Far East—but Lederer couldn't reach him on the phone. He talked to Stoltenberg, but Venture's treasurer didn't know what it was about either. Nobody seemed to. Norman LeBlanc summoned Lederer to Bahamas Commonwealth Bank and said about the telex, "What's all this?"

"You tell me," Bruno said. "The sixty million . . ."

"Oh that," said LeBlanc offhandedly. "It's called Inter-American."

"What is it?"

LeBlanc waffled. Lederer said he wasn't happy about Venture. Norman said Bruno was being too picky.

Lederer's mind went back to a party for IOS big shots at the Nassau home of Gilbert Straub, whom Lederer had never trusted. Straub took him aside and made some curious remarks. Some people thought Vesco was Mafia, Straub said, but Bob's family origins were northern, not southern, Italy—the family, which at some point or other had changed its name, was from the Venice-Trieste area and Vesco was only half Italian at that. Straub went on to mention an IOS staffer in Geneva who had "let them down" and been fired. The person hadn't been fired, Lederer later learned to his surprise, but he thought Straub was warning him. Now, leaving Norman's office, it crossed Lederer's mind for the first time that he might, indeed, be dealing with crooks and he decided to quit, though he had "no other job and nowhere to go." His wife was nervous about their safety until they boarded the plane for New York. Willkie Farr's Conwill sent Lederer a reassuring telex, which Lederer didn't receive.

> I very much regret that explanations to you were inadvertently omitted concerning transfers of money to Nassau for FOF and am certain that the reason is that it is in a purely technical rather than substantive area. As perhaps you know, the custodianships of the various funds are being transferred from Bank of New York to American National Bank and Trust of New Jersey. Bank of New York is unhappy about the transfer for what appears to us as economic self-interest reasons and has used every device to delay the transfers. They are now nearly consummated but in the interim to have monies available without having to comply with the Bank of New York manufactured technicalities the transfers have been made. Certainly there was no intention to circumvent any decisional function on your part and I believe it is appropriate for me to convey regrets.

But Conwill claimed he didn't know what the $60 million was for.

Increasingly, things didn't look right to a group of about twenty upper-level administrative folk working out of Ferney and elsewhere who met over drinks to talk about the situation. On Vesco, the consensus at first was that Bernie's boys would "chew him up," one said, but when Vesco survived they had hopes he could rescue the company. Little by little, though, confidence waned. If Bob's boys—LeBlanc, Clay, Straub, Graze, Strickler—were lackeys, why did Vesco need them? Meissner, at least, could be brilliant, but he, like Nasty Norman, was sometimes drunk. Bob, they began to perceive, was childish, to which they attributed his showing off, nor would those of the group responsible agree to pay for the 707 expenses, though LeBlanc in the Bahamas did. With over $300 million left in the funds, IOS could have gotten by on a 1 percent management fee, but Vesco seemed more interested in deal-making than in the serious reconstitution of the company as an operating entity. Disillusion, for some at least, became complete when LeBlanc spoke of "losing" records, which, if he was serious (they weren't sure), would have meant that fundholders couldn't get their money back because their names would have vanished. Still, from self-interest, concern about the sanctity of the files, and uncertainty as to what went on, none of the administrative people quit. They didn't really believe that Bud Meissner, who ran IOS, was a crook, though maybe Vesco was.

According to Meissner, Inter-American was originally intended to be a self-managing regional fund of which IOS had others. Meissner's notion was to reinvest in Latin America the capital IOS had taken out of it, though not necessarily the same amounts in the same places. The first investments were to be in Costa Rica (Inter-American also had an office in Panama)—an office building, for which plans were drawn; a TV station and newspaper; maybe the acquisition of LACSA, Costa Rica's airline; and an oil pipeline across the southern part of the country. The brief prospectus, prepared to satisfy Costa Rican law and backdated to August 1, 1972, listed as chairman and president Dr. Alberto I. Álvarez, a Cuban who had been president of the U.N. Security Council, and prominent Costa Rican businessmen and lawyers as officers. It declared that "developing areas of the world are generally admitted to be attractive investment opportunities in the next decade. . . ." Inter-American was to be the forerunner of other such funds in Latin America, and was tied in to the sale of part of IOS to a Spanish group that seemed to like the notion of bridges to Spain's former colonies.

Negotiations had been under way since early 1972 between IOS and prominent Spaniards and Cubans, including Álvarez; Gonzalo de Bourbon, a pretender to the Spanish throne; his brother, Alphonse de Bourbon y Dampierre, the Duke of Cádiz; Raphael Díaz-Balart, an official under Cuba's Battista, who lived with Castro's ex-wife, Baron de Gotor, the largest private banker in Madrid and an in-law of Generalissimo Francisco Franco. Vesco, who was appointed a Costa Rican trade representative, insisted on being received by Franco, and he was, in top hat and tails—he appeared on Spanish television in the same outfit. One of the group, a tank commander, talked of starting a mutual fund that dealt in arms and offered to give Vesco a tank. "What am I going to do with a goddam *tank?*" Vesco asked. Some of the Cubans seemed to believe that the fund money they were about to acquire—LeBlanc flashed a $2 million cashier's check more or less to prove really big money lay around—could be used to finance an invasion of Castro's Cuba. Díaz-Balart was a founder of the White Rose, which had played a role in the Bay of Pigs invasion. The Spaniards wanted an investment in a near-bankrupt pants factory in southern Spain, of which Franco's wife was an owner. Inter-American obliged with $2 million (out of the $60 million taken from FOF), but just after the SEC complaint the factory closed. The money wasn't recovered.

Willkie Farr's notes from October 1972 disclosed the terms of the Spanish deal. Present were attorneys from WF&G, Hogan & Hartson, and Paul, Weiss, Rifkind, another top law firm which would be Vesco's litigation counsel if and when the SEC filed. Kilmorey sold its interest in IOS for $5.5 million in cash and $5.5 million from a loan by Bahama Commonwealth Bank. IOS, once again, would finance its own dismemberment. The Spanish group was to close-end the funds and go its own way. The Globals would emerge with one-third of the funds' assets—between $100 million and $200 million: the same old "hot," unclaimed money—along with other entities.

Meanwhile, neither Meissner, who resigned as president of IOS when the Spanish deal closed (he would always wonder why he returned) nor Graze knew what was happening to the $60 million that originally belonged to FOF and was now in Inter-American. On paper, the sum was intact (except for the money for the Spanish pants factory), but LeBlanc had been moving money around to give the game players time if the SEC or anyone else attempted to follow it.

A thinking dollar that had been in FOF (strictly speaking, FOF Proprietary) might have found itself in Inter-American. The dollar was owned by FOF, but the voting shares that controlled it lay with two Panamanian companies created by LeBlanc, Phoenix

Financial and Trident. Trident was controlled by another shell, Vector, also controlled by LeBlanc. Part of the dollar (representing $6 million of the $60 million), although deposited first at BCB, went to Bancorp de Costa Rica and was used by Inter-American for "investments" in that country—$1.5 million in land, $3.5 million in Costa Rican cash and bonds, $250,000 in the Costa Rica newspaper *La Nación,* and "odds and ends" as Vesco's lawyers put it. Costa Ricans believed that such investments had been made by Vesco himself, and they helped create the impression that he had enormous personal wealth.

The rest of our thinking dollar—representing $54 million—went to Phoenix and became, Vesco said, $9 million in Costa Rican bonds for the account of Trident in BCB and $8 million in short-term deposits in Costa Rican banks held at BCB for Trident and Phoenix. What remained of it, $37 million, started out as cash at BCB, subject to Trident's control, and was originally lent out by LeBlanc to other banks.

An image comes to mind—a bag of gold sinking deeper and deeper in cloudy water until it falls from sight. Even if Vesco and LeBlanc originally had sound intentions, which was increasingly hard to accept, these activities were more than suspicious.

Our dollar's master, Nasty Norman, had been drinking his head off and dark thoughts throbbed. These were what LeBlanc called the "stupid days," when alcohol plus terror of and truculence toward the SEC before and after its complaint, he claimed, caused him to divert money as far away as Hong Kong. He learned how to incorporate a Panamanian company in an afternoon. He moved money in amounts of $5 million or less to avoid detection in the U.S. where dollar transactions had to clear. (Today, with faster computers, he would have been spotted.) The convoluted accountant suspected that Howard Cerny, a Vesco lawyer and former assistant district attorney for Queens County, New York, had blabbed to the SEC (anyone who was questioned was regarded with suspicion by Vesco) about Phoenix, and, in panic, Norman began to make our dollar do tricks. From Phoenix it went to Numeros (SA), to Worldwide Marketing, to Andromeda, and so on. LeBlanc insisted that despite such maneuvers the dollar always returned to BCB, but this same $37 million would haunt the receivers.

Willkie Farr finally had questions about the mysterious $60 million. Ray Merritt tried to get answers, but Vesco's attention was hard to catch. In the fall, he ran into Bob at Cerny's office; Merritt and Vesco went into a private room and Merritt asked about Inter-American. Vesco, secretive as always, would not provide specific answers, but said the investment would be good for FOF.

"Could you give me some facts that could suggest that to be the case?" Merritt asked.

"I'm not in a position to comment," Vesco told him, because his personal attorneys had advised him not to discuss the matter, which may have been an alibi.

Vesco had already explained that Inter-American hadn't been finished, that the financial mechanics had yet to be fully worked out. Willkie Farr already planned to leave IOS because, when the Spanish transaction was over, IOS, its client, wouldn't exist any more, but, Merritt told Vesco, if Inter-American were completed Willkie Farr would resign immediately.

"Put the goddam money back," Merritt hissed.

"I can't," Vesco said.

But he probably could have and should have.

21

TRIPS

ICC, a small company borne on the wings of its founder's soaring ambitions, had to have *planes,* a sort of he-man fantasy, good business or not, and Fairfield General, an ICC subsidiary, had fifteen or twenty trainers that were rented to students under the G.I. Bill of Rights. It also had a jet helicopter, until Eisenhauer totaled the machine, and a Grand Commander turboprop. Beatty and Larry Richardson, both World War II fliers, wondered why a pilot without big jet experience should have been employed to fly the 707, though Pan Am sent a pilot to teach him.

ICC bought a Grumman Gulfstream from CBS, and, in his acquisitions program, Vesco used the plane relentlessly. The Electronic Specialty takeover, said a former ICC official, could not have been accomplished without the flexibility the plane afforded. After his interests shifted to Europe, Vesco also flew in it continually, but the aircraft had a range of only 2,000 miles and had to be refueled twice en route. Vesco, who never went across the ocean in it, would travel by commercial carrier and expect the red-eyed crew to be waiting. It was not unusual for the corporate gypsy to hit six European cities in one day for three or four days in a row.

The IOS reorganization increased the already hectic pace and a combination of a crew revolt and a near crash by the Gulfstream led Vesco to a larger aircraft. He first wanted a BAC-111, as Cornfeld had had on order, but changed to a standard

Boeing 707. "Once you had made the decision to have a corporate jet in the first place, and I grant you it might not have been necessary," said Beatty, "the 707 was the best choice. It was comparatively cheap, at one-point-two million, and though expensive to operate, represented a huge savings in terms of the next-lowest-priced jet with the needed range." The plane gave Vesco an aerial office, and few, if any, chief executives have flown around with such abandonment. Norman LeBlanc was not the only one who remembered five Atlantic crossings in a single week. First-class tickets would have been cheaper, but the 707 enabled conference-minded Vesco to assemble his people and deliver them en masse and in a condition to work.

Skyways Leasing, a wholly owned subsidiary of Fairfield Aviation, a public company ICC had spun off, purchased the Boeing from Pan American. ICC leased it from Skyways for five years at a descending rate, starting at about $112,000 a month. ICC had the right to make improvements at its own expense, but, though the 707 was owned by Fairfield Aviation, decisions regarding it were made solely by Vesco.

According to Eisenhauer, Vesco named the plane the "Silver Phyllis." (Some understood, given Bob's eccentric sense of humor, *Silver Phyllis* to be a play on the word *syphilis).* For modifications, the plane went first to Israel and then to Qualitron, the last one costing, Beatty said, $300,000. The rest of the $600,000 bill was for normal repairs. The *Silver Phyllis* eventually outstripped, at least in terms of conspicuous consumption, anything with wings, including Air Force One. The seats were reduced from a potential 189 to 22, but not in rows. Entering from the front, the passenger encountered a small table where the crew ate, and beyond that a large lavatory with a sit-down vanity. On the other side was a completely equipped galley and a dining room with separate tables and a divan. Vesco's office had a mahogany desk that could be opened into a conference table and a large chair with "RLV" emblazoned on the headrest cloth. The mini-gym was equipped with the only airborne sauna in existence. Behind a beaded curtain was the discotheque, with a hardwood dance floor, "black" strobe lights, and an expensive sound system. Whores were sometimes aboard for aimless nocturnal flights.

Vesco had a bedroom, and in the air wore velour lounging suits. He was, thought Richardson, a "swinger." To Graze, the 707 was "insane."

Expenses were paid by ICC, which billed IOS, in accordance with the ICC-IOS loan contract, for trips supposedly connected with its business, while Skyways made the mortgage payments to Pan Am. Why didn't the ICC board object to the Roman emperor extravagance? "We did," said Wilbert Snipes. "There were arguments hour after hour in meetings that lasted until after midnight. Vesco would always say, 'Let's talk about it later.' That's what he always said when he didn't want to discuss something. 'Let's talk about it later.' He wore us out." The impression grows that Vesco surrounded himself with pliant people.

Newark, Las Vegas—to which Vesco flew the ICC crowd for gambling—Nassau, New Orleans, Amsterdam, Lisbon, Stuttgart, Kuwait, San José, London, Rabat, Port-au-Prince, around the world with stops at Bangkok, Saigon, Singapore, Hong Kong, Japan—the itinerary ran on, arrogantly, as if Vesco didn't care whose money he spent or how much. Some of these trips concerned the matters most pressing on Vesco's mind—reorganizing IOS, finding a safe place in which to relocate, selling the shell of IOS and doing deals like Paradise Island, which was probably why Vesco flew Resorts International's Crosby to Toronto, and stopped in Rome to meet with two former Bahamas casino managers, the brothers Dino and Eddie Cellini, to discuss gambling projects around the Mediterranean. Vesco flew to Nairobi at the request of IOS president Slater, who asked him to settle a currency problem, but he'd forgotten his crack about ELS executives' African leisure habits: he took Pat on a safari. With IOS paying the $10,000 membership fee, he joined the World Wildlife Fund—its chief, Prince Bernhardt of the Netherlands, was an IOS director—and went in the 707 to Palm Beach for its auction, typically paying the highest price for several paintings. The local paper misspelled his name.

A frequent passenger aboard the *Silver Phyllis* was Donald Nixon, the President's nephew, as Don-Don never tired of reminding people. Young Nixon entered the Vesco picture in 1972. Don-Don was in a hippie group that planned peace demonstrations during the election campaign, which could have been embarrassing to Nixon. Drunk in California, young Nixon decided to telephone Mao Tse-tung to inquire why his uncle's attempts to normalize relations with China weren't proceeding. Unable to get through to China, he attempted to be routed from New York to London to Moscow to Peking, when a voice broke in and said, "Donald, you shouldn't be doing this." (The Chinese learned of the call and were confused, since Henry Kissinger was secretly in Peking at the time.) Robert Haldemann of the White House staff asked Gil Straub, who knew the President's brothers, to take young Nixon out of the country until the election was over, and Don-Don was hired by Straub. Don-Don adored Bob Vesco and refused to leave him even when the Nixons demanded it as scandal brewed. Later, Don-Don decided, without rancor, that Vesco had made him a hostage.

In November and early December, Vesco's use of the plane increased. In five weeks or so it was airborne 93 hours on more than 25 flights, and, including paperwork, the crew put in double that required of airline flight crews, Eisenhauer said. Pressures from Washington built, and the erratic itinerary may have reflected Vesco's worries.

On Sunday, November 26, the 707 was in the Bahamas when Vesco suddenly wanted to fly to Costa Rica even though he had a trip to Spain scheduled. They arrived in Costa Rica at night, and Vesco seemed in good spirits. The next morning before 7 A.M., Vesco telephoned Eisenhauer at his hotel, sounding tense and telling the pilot they would return to Nassau, departing at nine. Eisenhauer reported, "Vesco showed up at the airplane in a wild mood." No wonder. In New York, the SEC had filed the strongest suit in its history.

22

SEE EVERYTHING CROOKED

SEC Files Big Civil Suit Against International Controls, Vesco and 40 Others on Charges of Draining IOS Funds. "Diverting" of $224 Million Is Alleged; Receiver Sought For International Controls.

By Scott R. Schmedel
Staff Reporter of THE WALL STREET JOURNAL

NEW YORK—After two years [18 months, actually] of investigations, the Securities and Exchange Commission dumped a massive, civil-injunction suit on Robert L. Vesco and International Controls Corp. that goes far beyond any anticipated charges of fraud and deceit.

Most significantly, the 53-page complaint accuses them and 40 associates of draining $224 million from the offshore mutual funds of crumbling I.O.S. Ltd. "virtually all of their portfolios of readily marketable securities issued by United States companies."

The "fraudulent" transactions through which this allegedly occurred were "rife with self-dealing" and "detrimental" to the shareholders of the public companies and funds indicated and have enabled the Vesco group to divert the proceeds "to their personal purposes and interest," the SEC asserted.

Founded in 1933 by Franklin D. Roosevelt (the second chairman was William O. Douglas, later of the Supreme Court, who called Vesco a "new buccaneer"), the SEC had received mixed reviews. With the highest reputation of any U.S. government agency for integrity, the SEC through its hard work helped U.S. securities markets become the safest and best-regulated in the world. The SEC was oddly old-fashioned—files were moved in large carts and one defendant solved his SEC "problem" by stealing the cart with his records in it—and could be almost smugly moralistic and judgmental, acting, many in the business community believed, as judge, prosecutor, and jury rolled into one. With a small staff, the agency sometimes focused its efforts on key offenders to make examples of them, utilizing American news organs to spread the word, and to establish case law and its jurisdiction. The commission had long wanted regulatory power over American overseas mutual funds.

A former ranking SEC official said about the commission, "The SEC basically dealt with three groups: first, conservatives who stayed well within the law; second, people who took chances, maybe because lawyers told them, 'Hey, that's okay' or 'You won't be caught.' As it was then, at least, things people might do were honest or on the edges of legality—SEC regulations are complex and constantly changing to stay abreast of new securities practices—and individuals could pass into the danger zone without knowing it or be in the kind of business where you had to engage in certain practices. Third, there was a group really out to fleece people, like altering names on stock certificates."

Vesco, who for some showed signs of instability during the investigation, would admit to being in group two. The SEC believed he was a star of group three—a scoundrel of the worst order.

See Everything Crooked watched the throes of IOS with its cold eye, though secretly amused, perhaps, because of the vitriol Cornfeld had poured on the agency. It could argue that had IOS been compelled to make the kind of disclosures required by American corporations, the overseas monster might have been prevented from falling into the soup, but the commission could make no such claim because it had agreed, for better or worse, to leave IOS alone. By 1970, when Vesco gained command of IOS, the agency hadn't changed its mind about the 1967 order forbidding IOS to have American connections, and the emergence of an American company cocky enough to challenge the rules infuriated it.

Robert Vesco was an almost welcome target for the SEC. ICC's takeover of Electronic Specialty, while not ruled illegal by a judge, had seemed to him evasive and manipulative, and an appeals judge, in a dissenting opinion, had been even harsher about Vesco's behavior. The commission had former IOS sources—Cornfeld among them—who talked about how the IOS takeover had been funded and about Linkink.

Vesco came to the SEC in November 1970 to explain ICC's loan to IOS. He returned in January with his version of the Linkink deal. Stanley Sporkin, then deputy director of enforcement, told Vesco not to proceed. But Bob bristled at "noes" and Hogan & Hartson said the investment wasn't illegal and ICC could put its money where it saw fit. Sporkin, credited with having a powerful impact on U.S. corporate honesty, was a "cop" and felt instinctively that Vesco lied. Because of Linkink, he launched a small investigation that gradually grew. Though he had 150 lawyers working under him, Sporkin took a stronger personal role in the Vesco case than in any other investigation thus far. His attitude was expressed in mid-1971 when he asked Richard Pershing, a former ICC director, "Isn't this [the IOS takeover] the rawest deal you have ever seen?" Sporkin's tone was so conversational that the stenotypist did not take down the question nor did Pershing's lawyer object. Pershing's reply, also not recorded by the stenotypist, was, "No, but it's in the top ten."

William Thomson von Stein, an SEC Enforcement lawyer assigned to the case, didn't like an April 1971 ICC registration statement because he felt certain that Vesco was behind Linkink and the fact wasn't disclosed. Hogan & Hartson and Vesco wrote the IOS sections of ICC filings which failed to reveal that Vesco had arranged Linkink's financing—ICC's board accepted their version because it was from H&H. ICC later filed an updated registration statement in which it admitted to having acquired Cornfeld's shares. That, for the commission, was a tacit confession that the previous statement had been false, and it placed ICC's takeover of IOS under the SEC's jurisdiction, the agency felt, because of the 1967 consent order. From then on, partly because of IOS's notoriety, the drama began to mount.

Subpoenaed on Linkink, Vesco took refuge behind Swiss bank secrecy laws since he was a director of ODB (Geneva), and Hogan & Hartson imported a Swiss lawyer who supported Vesco's position. That didn't matter to the SEC, which wouldn't relent, and Vesco, with H&H behind him, proceeded to sue the commission, a rare step, though IOS had done so before him. A New Jersey federal judge permitted the case to come to trial. Had Vesco triumphed on the basis of Swiss bank secrecy laws, as seemed possible, the agency's long-term objective (shared by the IRS) of preventing Americans from hiding behind foreign financial secrecy laws might have been jeopardized. The trial was brief but nasty. Vesco's lawyer, Sherwin Markman of H&H, brusquely accused Sporkin of conducting a personal feud against Vesco. (Markman later apologized, probably for tactical reasons.) Vesco lost, and the U.S. Supreme Court refused to hear the case.

The SEC didn't like trials because they consumed time, and it lacked experienced litigators with the exception of a few, like Robert Kushner. The agency preferred consent decrees under which the accused, without admitting guilt, agreed not to commit the same acts again—a strange but effective procedure. The SEC was fully capable of tying a defendant in knots, as its subpoena powers could compel people under deposition to testify for days. With court approval, the commission could make repeated requests for documents, and refuse to pass on a company's filings, as it did with ICC's. Nor would the SEC state what it was after in an investigation, imparting an almost eerie quality to its sleuthings, which resembled those of a grand jury, although the agency would have an order of investigation that outlined with some specificity the areas of concern.

Vesco was an unusual antagonist. Proud, arrogant, and supercilious toward those he regarded as lesser lights, he was determined to defy the SEC, which increased the government's antagonism. Had Vesco pulled out of IOS, the fracas would have ended; instead, he escalated hostilities. In 1971, he had Sporkin investigated by a private detective. "You investigate me, I investigate you," he told Sporkin later. (He also arranged for Sporkin to receive a lucrative job offer—the SEC man could not know Vesco pulled the strings—but Sporkin declined.) To Sporkin's associates, only three aspects of the official's personality mattered. He worked too hard, played a poor 10 P.M. game of tennis, and believed not in monetary but in "psychic" satisfaction, which nailing Vesco would have given him. "If we don't stop Vesco now," Sporkin is supposed to have said, "he'll own the world by the time he's forty." According to what Vesco told associates in Costa Rica, he also put a private eye on William J. Casey, the SEC chairman, though Vesco may have been showing off. The late Casey became director of the CIA in 1981, and Sporkin its general counsel until he was appointed a federal judge in 1986.

Vesco's complaint of mistreatment caused an internal SEC review of its procedures, concluding the case should be pursued even harder. The battle simmered during 1972 with the agency taking depositions and requesting documents—the SEC wanted virtually all of ICC's files, and providing them required more than a week. (Vesco moved file cabinets out of ICC to his estate. Shocked, Hogan & Hartson "had no idea Vesco was up to that kind of thing.") Vesco, said ICC president Richardson, had a "long, paranoid list" about the government agency. He was convinced that Thomson von Stein had sent a telegram to the American ambassador in Switzerland at the time of Vesco's arrest in Geneva urging him not to help, which von Stein convincingly denied. The SEC didn't know of the arrest until newspapers reported it. Bradford Cook, SEC General Counsel, and von Stein, did travel to Geneva to ask questions about Linkink, which led to a comic opera attempt by IOS to compromise them with prostitutes.

Months passed without a resolution of the crisis. The Kafkaesque commission would never fully explain what its objectives were, and, in search of answers and influence in Washington, Vesco relied on lawyer Harry Sears, who New Jersey governor William Cahill claimed had more clout in Washington than he did. Sears, whom Vesco had helped with a campaign debt, became an ICC director in late 1971 and was New Jersey finance chairman for the Nixon campaign. (ICC provided two rented helicopters for the effort.) Sears was on excellent terms with John Mitchell, the Attorney General, and Maurice Stans, Secretary of the Interior, both of whom resigned to run CREEP, the Committee to Reelect the President. Sears intervened repeatedly on Vesco's behalf and met with Casey and Cook, who succeeded Casey briefly. He later admitted he had attempted to conceal Vesco's $200,000 campaign contribution, which brought him down. Cook thought the SEC accusation was too broad and badly drafted, but he was also interested in delaying the revelation until after the 1972 elections.

Sears arranged a meeting, on March 21, 1972, with Cook, Sporkin, Kushner, and Vesco, who told them the SEC was burying ICC with demands for documents. The Kilmorey transaction was to close at the end of the month, and Vesco recalled that he said, "You have put us in a position where we have nobody else to sell it to except the management. Do you have any objections to that? We got the standard speech. 'We object to nothing.'" Vesco added, extremely bitterly, "The horse's ass. They led us down the daisy path. I was pissed." Because of the SEC, he had already decided to move from the United States, he claimed.

Angered, too, were the SEC officials. Vesco lost his temper, cursed, called lower-level SEC people "dumb-dumbs," and hinted that he had had Sporkin under surveillance, telling him he had a "lovely house." (Sporkin complained of being followed.) Nonetheless, Vesco composed a letter to Cook on the flight home, in which he said it was "our hope that the divestment of IOS under consideration by ICC will assist in a resolution of the issues with the staff." Fat chance. The SEC disbelieved everything that Vesco said, and particularly his assertion that, with Kilmorey, he was out of IOS. "Negotiating with Vesco was like negotiating with Stalin," an SEC official said.

In addition to 1968 contributions that were known within ICC, Vesco had given $100,000 to the Republicans—Richardson later found it buried in the company books. In 1972, wishing, he told Stans, to be a "front-row contributor," Vesco pledged $200,000 to the Republican presidential campaign—he wanted to donate $500,000 but had been told by Sears that it was too much in view of the SEC investigation. Loyal Ralph Dodd picked up not $200,000 but $250,000, cabled from Nassau, at a New York bank, carried it to ICC headquarters at night with a guard, and, since ICC had no safe, stuffed the $100 bills in the bases of two large lamps in Vesco's office. The extra $50,000 was apparently contributed to the New Jersey Republican campaign. (A mystery was another $250,000 Vesco told columnist Jack Anderson he laundered through a Bahamas casino and gave to a White House courier.) The $200,000 was delivered, by Richardson and Sears, on April 10, one working day beyond the deadline, under a new law, after which contributions had to be reported. A lawyer for the Republicans said that was all right because the money had already been pledged, but nobody expected the contribution to come out. If it did, the Republicans would be over a barrel for accepting the money, not Vesco for giving it, except insofar as he attempted to buy influence, as he clearly wished, over the SEC. For their part, the Republicans didn't appear to regard the deadline with much, if any, seriousness, nor did Sears and Richardson. The money was used, of course, to finance the "plumbers," and led to the Watergate scandal. The SEC complaint made a veiled reference to the contribution: ". . . other large sums of cash have been transferred among and between Vesco and his group, Bahamas Commonwealth Bank, International Controls, and other parties."

The $250,000 came from a Howard Cerny account at BCB, not that the money was his. In mid-July, LeBlanc ordered that the transfer be charged to International Bancorp, back-dated to 1971, but when CREEP returned the entire contribution in January 1973, the money was recouped by a Trident account in the name of Robert Vesco, who, though, claimed he had borrowed the sum in the first place.

"The fool," commented Robert Kushner after he left the SEC and went into lucrative private practice. "If Vesco had only waited six months or a year without doing anything, the SEC would have been out of his way." Kushner had been asked to draft a complaint against Vesco, but in his view, despite everything thus far (except the contribution, of which the agency wasn't as yet aware), the SEC, because of fatigue and pressure, would have dropped the case. Harry Sears was indeed extremely influential and "there had never been a previous case like it where suspicion

Robert and Patricia Vesco with their sons Daniel (left) and Tony in 1960. (New York Post*/Pomerantz)*

Bob and Pat Vesco with Barbara and Ralph Dodd at a New York nightclub in 1962. (Courtesy Barbara & Ralph P. Dodd)

The 1968 Alfred E. Smith Memorial Dinner. Vesco, in white tie, is seated behind Terence Cardinal Cooke and to the left of New York Senator Jacob Javits. Other notables include Vice President Hubert Humphrey, President Lyndon Johnson, James Farley, President-elect Richard Nixon. (AP/Wide World Photos)

The Vesco yacht, Patricia III, *leaves the harbor at Fort Lauderdale, Fla., after being released to the Panamanian Consul General. (AP/Wide World Photos)*

The office aboard Vesco's 707. The plane also had bedrooms and a discothèque. (AP/Wide World Photos)

Bernard Cornfeld, photographed outside his Los Angeles home after his release from a Swiss prison. (AP/Wide World Photos)

Cornfeld's French castle—the Château de Pelly. (Bernard Cornfeld)

The IOS ruling triumvirate: Edward M. Cowett, Allen Cantor, and Bernard Cornfeld. (Bernard Cornfeld)

Vesco at the peak of his power. Being interviewed in 1971 after the takeover of IOS. (AP/Wide World Photos)

Robert Vesco pushes his way through a crowd of reporters on his way to an extradition hearing in Nassau, the Bahamas, November 1973. (The Bettmann Archive)

Vesco is interviewed by Walter Cronkite, CBS News, April 1974. (CBS Photography)

abounded within the agency that the fix was in," Kushner said. The commission, except for Linkink, didn't then have much to go on except personal dislike, nor was it clear the SEC could establish jurisdiction over IOS.

Both H&H and Willkie Farr's Allan Conwill had extensive SEC experience, Conwill having worked for the agency. Reassured by the lawyers that he was on safe ground (privately, commission officials regarded Conwill as "bonkers" and an H&H lawyer as a "whore"), Vesco insistently proceeded with the Venture Fund $20 million "investment" in LeBlanc's Globals, which to the SEC was an improper diversion of funds. The battle lines had been drawn, and Vesco, fearing the SEC might try to put IOS into receivership, began to move large sums beyond its reach, as had not been planned in January 1972, and in complete secrecy. Sporkin couldn't bear to let Vesco get away with it and acted as quickly as he could.

Milton Meissner said he believed the $60 million transfer wasn't legally wrong. For him, the SEC might have criticized the transaction, but, as he had been advised by legal counsel, nothing in the 1967 consent order forbade the movement of funds. If the SEC chose to comment adversely over IOS's choice of banks to put the money in, let it; he, as IOS president, had an obligation he said to save the company and operated under his own business plan. As far as he was concerned, there was, at least at this stage, no reality to charges of "looting."

The SEC believed otherwise. Kushner continued drafting the complaint throughout the Thanksgiving weekend, staying up all Sunday night. As he drove to the airport on Monday morning, November 27, he was thankful for traffic because it kept him from falling asleep in his Japanese car. He brought the documents to Federal court in New York. IOS, ICC, and Vesco's lawyers were notified that same morning.

The commission had two kinds of complaints, "bare bones" with accusations held to a minimum, and what it termed a "speaker's complaint," in which as full a story as could be generated was told. *SEC* v. *Vesco et al.* was a speaker's complaint in full.

The key line in the SEC complaint read:

> . . . from April 1972 [to November 1972], defendant Vesco and his group have caused the Dollar Funds to sell in the United States securities markets a major part of their securities portfolios, consisting of high-grade, readily marketable securities issued by United States companies, in furtherance of a scheme to remove the proceeds from banks located in the United States to entities outside the country and to use these proceeds, which, to date, have exceeded $224,000,000, to further the personal interests and pursuits of defendant Vesco and his group (to the detriment of investors in the Dollar Funds).

Whatever the merits of the SEC action, the statement does not stand rigorous analysis: $224 million or more of these securities were sold—there was no arguing with that—but why wasn't the figure placed at the beginning of the paragraph? Instead it appears just before "to further the personal interests and pursuits. . . ." implying that the entire boodle was misappropriated. This, of course, gave currency to the notion of the largest "wholesale looting" in history. Whatever the sum that was diverted, it didn't approach a quarter-billion dollars.

According to Stanley Graze, the IOS investment adviser, by no means were all the securities blue chip. (Previous fund managers had bought over-the-counter stocks.) The language fell short of "stolen"—"diverted," or "spirited," it said—but the press fell all over the idea that somebody had swiped a quarter of a billion dollars. What the figure mainly represented was the amount of U.S. securities sold and held in IOS fund accounts, mostly in foreign banks; whenever he saw the number in the newspapers, Tom von Stein would shake his head.

The complaint, a prosecutorial instrument, had been constructed with an eye toward news, in no little part because the commission intended to dramatize for foreign banking authorities the urgency it attached to the situation. An enormous amount of money had been placed in an exposed position from which theft could result. Thus far, there was no proof that substantial funds had been misappropriated, only an allegation.

Indeed, later in the complaint the SEC seemed to revise its figures downward, saying that Vesco and his group had converted

$125 million "to their personal pursuits," although adding vaguely that an additional $100 million remained unaccounted for. But a much lesser and more accurate number would not have fetched such headlines.

23

SHOCKWAVES

Hogan & Hartson, according to Allan Conwill of Willkie Farr, had known in depth about the SEC action a week before it was filed but didn't warn its legal brethren in New York. "They didn't want to be tarred in any way," said Conwill, who himself heard rumors that the SEC contemplated suing a New York law firm in the Vesco matter. Though unable to conceive of grounds, he took the precaution of calling Merle Thorpe of H&H, who said he had no information to offer. The two discussed phoning an SEC commissioner, Philip A. Loomis, whom both knew, and Conwill did. Loomis's secretary said he would return the call.

The next day was Thanksgiving, and Conwill, a cripple requiring extensive care since an automobile accident in the late nineteen-sixties, endured the no-news stoically, but, on Friday, he phoned Loomis again and was told to speak with Stanley Sporkin, who asked, "What is the name of the member of the commission staff who leaked this information?" Conwill said he didn't know. "Would you find out for me?" Sporkin asked. Conwill declined, saying it wouldn't be appropriate. Nor, said Sporkin, would it be appropriate for *him* to discuss whether litigation against Willkie Farr was pending. As a former SEC staff person, Conwill was aware of, and had been embarrassed by, the commission's policy neither to confirm nor deny an investigation even when there *wasn't* one, but, he told Sporkin, it might be different with a law firm for which an SEC lawsuit could be devastating, and he cited a case. Fairness, Conwill insisted with mounting concern, required that he be allowed to appear and respond in advance of a lawsuit. Sporkin said he would try to speak to a commissioner.

On Monday, before Conwill arrived at the office, Sporkin phoned and was transferred to Ray Merritt. The suit against Vesco, Sporkin announced, had been filed that morning in the United States District Court for the Southern District of New York. Conwill, Merritt, and D'Alimonte had been named among the defendants.

One of the firm's founders had been Wendell L. Willkie, a popular, liberal Republican and presidential candidate against Roosevelt in 1940. Willkie's portrait hung in a WF&G waiting room. He must have longed to turn his face to the wall.

That same day WF&G issued a press release.

> With respect to an action instituted here today in Federal Court without any notice, by the Securities and Exchange Commission against some 42 defendants, including 2 members and 1 associate of the firm, Willkie Farr & Gallagher stated that the 3 individuals named deny the charges. It is unfortunate that the Commission afforded the individuals no opportunity to be heard prior to the initiation of the action. The firm expresses its complete confidence in the professional and personal integrity of these named individual defendants.

And, on December 4, Conwill wrote Vesco a letter.

> I would be remiss if I failed to express to you my deep regret that the Commission saw fit to bring an action against you which I feel is founded in malice. I particularly regret being unable to participate in your defense because of an assumed conflict in our canons of ethics by reason of my being included among the defendants.
>
> I want you to know that I have enjoyed the relationship and I hope the day will come when it can be restored. I also want you to know that I am confident in your ultimate vindication.

Far more severe than expected, the SEC complaint was like an earthquake to those concerned. The Spanish and Paradise Island deals, under negotiation for months, collapsed along with others, and many individuals experienced anguish. Howard

Cerny, a sometime Vesco lawyer who resigned on being named by the SEC, said that Vesco "felt badly because I felt badly about it, and, you know, I have to be very candid with you, I did feel badly. Here I was, a named defendant in an action. I had worked hard to achieve something in our profession, and then get hit with a lawsuit of this nature, where I felt the only thing that I had done was perform legal services. It just stunned me to think I would be. . . . I thought it was a little below the belt."

Before the SEC complaint, ICC was already a troubled company because of Vesco and the eighteen-month investigation that had exhausted it and its thirty- to forty-person executive staff. All the elements for corporate strife existed and cracks had appeared in the two story headquarters at Fairfield.

Animosity had become pervasive between Vesco and Laurence B. Richardson, Jr., formerly president of All American, a subcontractor for DuPont and manufacturer of aircraft gear, which ICC had acquired in 1970. The son of a U.S. admiral with a distinguished record as an aviation pioneer, Richardson also became a naval officer. He served on a cruiser and then became a fighter pilot. He saw action in the Pacific during World War II. He received a degree in aeronautical engineering at Princeton and became chief test pilot at Chance Vought. He joined Ling-Temco-Vought as vice president for marketing and then All American as CEO. Then about fifty, he succeeded Vesco as ICC's president and chief executive officer. When ICC became "hopelessly involved," as Richardson put it, with the SEC, problems developed on many fronts. For him, the SEC hounded the company. "Almost every financial institution that we visited had been talked to" by the SEC first, Richardson said, and the investigation and its consequences dominated board meetings and even the minutes of board meetings. Always fanatical about every document the company issued, after the investigation commenced Vesco became doubly insistent on rewriting the minutes, and months would pass before he got around to the task. A paranoid style was emerging ever more clearly. He refused to permit conversations about See Everything Crooked to be recorded and a single sentence, "The SEC investigation was discussed," might reflect three hours of unhappy debate. Vesco would permit only Shirley Bailey, the corporate secretary, or Hogan & Hartson to take notes, and Richardson tried to see the H&H ones. He was told by the attorneys "that was privileged, law firm information and that I wasn't supposed to get a copy." By then, Vesco didn't trust Richardson, who didn't trust Vesco either and criticized him for his "typically poorly written" letters.

Nor was Richardson an admirer of Vesco's acquisitions. In 1971 and 1972, as the defense business contracted, the company became low on cash, and that was partly because, in Richardson's view, "at least one-third of the companies that Vesco acquired . . . were worthless." (ICC had twenty-seven operating units by then.) The greatest mistake was the "unwise acquisition of Electronic Specialty in which Vesco paid nearly twice what it was worth, and paid largely in cash. . . ." Richardson wrote several memoranda on the subject, but Vesco either objected to his presentations or the board wouldn't read them, because the SEC topic predominated. Vesco, much as he said on leaving the Swiss prison, told the board, "Since they are accusing me of all those bad things, I may as well do them." Nobody took him seriously, knowing Bobby's penchant for loose talk.

Vesco and Richardson were together on one point, so apprehensive were they over the SEC investigation—the liquidation of ICC by selling off the operating units. But Richardson thought Vesco's plan too beneficial to Vesco, the largest stockholder. Vesco also wanted to sell his shares—strenuous efforts were made—or to put them in a new outfit he formed, Vesco & Co. Architectural plans had been commissioned for a building to house it and land bought; Vesco did not guess the depth of the troubles awaiting him. But Prudential, whose $20 million loan gave it a veto, forbade the transactions.

In September, Vesco resigned as a director and became a consultant at his previous salary of $120,000 a year, plus benefits Richardson found too generous, but Vesco returned to the board ten days later because, he said, a conflict of interest might exist between Hogan & Hartson representing both him and ICC. Richardson felt otherwise. Vesco ". . . came back so he could control the board and handle me. . . . He indicated displeasure with some of the things I had started to do. . . . He didn't want me to think I was running the company. . . . I had started questioning a lot of things that I hadn't paid much attention to before." To Richardson, Vesco had "emasculated" ICC by dominating its board and thus draining the company's strength.

Richardson had considered Vesco honest—in his view, the ABC plan was legitimate—but changed his mind. He and the controller, Gary Benjamin, compiled a "laundry list" of Vesco expenses they didn't believe should be charged to International Controls, including cash advances of about $100,000 to Vesco, who refused to submit an expense account, and the $50,000 to Henry Buhl for his stock in IOS, for which Vesco had various explanations. Vesco did, though, defend himself, saying his $10,000 a month consulting fee was his only source of income, that Richardson had used the "service"—the 707—and that much of the bill represented phone calls for ICC. Richardson—the two bad neighbors had offices on the same floor and used the same ICC letterhead—wrote that Vesco's answers were "unsatisfactory," but some of the items on the laundry list seemed negligible to Frank Beatty—flight tickets and gasoline for Vesco's son Danny, a limousine for Donald Nixon—in view of the major items that were in controversy. The $35,000 lent to Harry Sears (Sears also received $15,000 for helping get Vesco out of jail) after he became an ICC director didn't seem so serious to Beatty, either. Richardson said it was. The feud between Richardson and Vesco degenerated into something like an acrimonious divorce. The suspicion formed in the minds of some of the board members, like Beatty, that Richardson's objective was to discredit Vesco, remove him from the company, and take power once and for all. The leadership was split with Vesco, Beatty, Snipes, Sears, Richard Clay, and Malcolm McAlpin seemingly on one side and, on the other, Richardson, Benjamin, and Leonard Polisar, the general counsel.

In early December, on Vesco's recommendation, the board formed an audit committee with McAlpin, Sears, and Snipes. When the meeting ended, Richardson asked Vesco if the audit committee was an effort to circumvent him, and Vesco said, "Well, what do you think?" "I think it is," Richardson said, and Vesco didn't answer. Bob seemed shocked Richardson had turned on him although after the SEC complaint he had offered Richardson $1 million to leave ICC for IOS and, presumably, a fugitive's life. Again, Vesco seemed to be in a position to dispense IOS money at will.

The main outlay Richardson tried to recoup was about $400,000 in 707 expenses owed to ICC by IOS. One million was in an account at Bahamas Commonwealth Bank, but LeBlanc had blocked it. Learning that Vesco and LeBlanc were in Costa Rica, Richardson dispatched Snipes, a BCB director, to retrieve the money. Snipes did, but he was unable to find another $500,000 the Bahamian bank was supposed to have credited to an ICC account. Beatty, investigating, learned that Benjamin hadn't fulfilled ICC's part of the bargain, to provide its own information on flight expenses. Beatty also believed that Vesco, finding confusion to his advantage, didn't want LeBlanc to settle while Richardson was in charge. Beatty told Vesco, "Get that money paid. You're playing into the hands of Richardson. You're holding out for petty motives." Beatty had begun to lose confidence in Vesco's judgment. "You didn't know what the master plan was. And, as usual, he always added conditions."

By this time, Richardson intended to put ICC in receivership, which some board members saw as a sideways attempt to gain control. Vesco, according to Richardson, "said words to the effect that if I continued to oppose him and pursue the course I was on, I would wind up dead. This was probably in early January. I responded to him that I didn't think he was serious and that he had better hope I didn't meet with any genuine accident because he would be blamed for it."

Events came swiftly to a head. Vesco tried to call a board meeting on Monday, January 22, 1973, and so arranged the timing that the directors received notice by mail only a few hours before. In Polisar's opinion, the notice wasn't adequate and he told Richardson that if he didn't attend, the results wouldn't be binding, so Richardson didn't go. Vesco had two private detectives present whom Richardson forced to sit in the parking lot. They were there, Vesco claimed, because he had evidence of a break-in at his office, but the police weren't called and Richardson thought the reason was to enforce decisions, like a firing. The meeting was rescheduled for the following day. "I guess the feeling was," said Polisar, "that the board of directors of ICC would have cleansed the corporation of Vesco influence at the next meeting and was gathering its forces to do so and would have a majority of at least four to three, and a good possibility of five to two." Their intention was to terminate Vesco's consulting agreement with ICC and cease paying his legal bills, while Vesco's was to dump Richardson and replace him with Elmer Sticco who had come to ICC from ELS. (More than anyone else, Sticco was ultimately credited with saving International Controls.)

The meeting, on January 23, began at 3:30 P.M., recessed briefly at 11:55, and went on for almost two hours more. In addition to seven board members, a number of lawyers were present. The Richardson group believed Snipes was with them, but from the start it became apparent that Snipes, who had arranged Vesco's first loan at American National Bank, would vote the other way, and the three Hogan & Hartson lawyers announced that if Richardson and Polisar, who suddenly seemed to be candidates for firing, were, the firm would resign as litigation counsel.

With one Hogan lawyer, Markman, remaining after the midnight recess, Vesco, who became violently angry, or Snipes, suddenly moved to terminate the controller Gary Benjamin for reasons of economy. Richardson and Polisar were furious. Polisar said that Beatty, who would replace Benjamin, shouldn't be allowed to vote, and Beatty abstained. Beatty had hired Benjamin but believed Richardson used him to create a "cause célèbre." Vesco, not to be trapped, suggested that the two ideas be separated, with the vote to be on Benjamin's termination and not his replacement. Beatty voted, with Snipes, Clay, and Vesco, to get rid of Benjamin, with McAlpin, Sears, and Richardson against. Benjamin was out, a symbol that opposition wouldn't be tolerated.

BY MR. MARTIN MENSCH [attorney for Frank G. Beatty]

Q. (of Mr. Polisar): You can understand that if there is a faction on a board or in a company contending with another faction and if one faction gets the upper hand it would not be unusual for

> them to terminate the employment of as many members of the other faction as they possibly could, isn't that the case?

Polisar, an experienced attorney, conceded that, but disliked the ridiculous justification of economy that masked the naked power play—Benjamin had been given a raise and a commendation only a few months before. But it didn't matter. Benjamin, who took the ax stoically—he was watched to see that he didn't take the wrong papers—was gone, and, very soon after, so were Richardson and Vesco, though Richardson stayed on as a director.

The Vesco drama took on aspects of hysteria. Vesco had asked another Richardson—Thomas, a Los Angeles securities dealer later jailed for fraud—to hire Federal narcotics agents to check his Boonton home and the Fairfield offices for electronic bugs. Vesco paid Richardson with $3,000 in chips at the Paradise Island casino. In early November, Coopers & Lybrand, the ICC accountants, resigned, refusing to give a reason which had to do with accounting. Shirley Bailey had a machine on which she could write checks with two signatures, and Richardson took it away.

Through this dark corporate tapestry lawyers ran like threads. Hogan & Hartson, confused by contradictory statements from the rival factions, announced in November that, except for litigation, the firm would be of limited use to ICC. Rosenman, Goldmark was brought in, but Vesco said that H&H didn't trust the Rosenman firm—to Rosenman's Gerald Walpin, that meant to do Vesco's bidding—and would withdraw if they continued, and he subjected Walpin to abuse for reciting Richardson's laundry list. The Rosenman firm, accused by Vesco of approaching the SEC, was dropped (though Walpin stayed on to represent Richardson personally), to be replaced by McCarter & English, which quit after forty days over the firing of Benjamin. Paul, Weiss, Rifkind, in the shape of Arthur Liman, entered the fray as Vesco's own lawyers. Thus far, only Merle Thorpe, of H&H, had been able to restrain Vesco, but Liman did, too. He told Richardson that Bob would be reasonable and repay $40,000 or so in advances, and, to Richardson's surprise, Vesco agreed although he grumbled.

In November, 1972, as the SEC moved hurriedly toward its $224 million climax, Vesco was subpoenaed, and Kushner, with his sense that money was being stolen even then, wouldn't accept a delay to give Liman time to familiarize himself with the issues. Liman advised his client not to answer questions, and Vesco refused on constitutional grounds, though not entirely for Liman's reasons. He didn't want to disclose the $200,000 campaign gift. ("I hope they're grateful," he said about the Republicans.) Richardson, of course, had delivered the contribution with Harry Sears, and Vesco told him to have a "bad memory" if called to testify. Richardson said he had a good memory, and, again, Vesco warned him about his health.

On December 4, two prominent Democrats, Clark Clifford, Secretary of Defense under Johnson, and Paul Warnke, former Defense Department official and former head of the U.S. Arms Control and Disarmament Agency, were flown to Nassau on the 707 and returned to Washington that same day. Warnke, offered a drink by a "flying Playgirl," was amused by the disco's beaded curtain. Whatever attraction the two lawyers might have found in Vesco, who wanted them primarily as lobbyists with congressional Democrats on his behalf, dissipated when Vesco told them about the Nixon contribution. Clifford said, "Vesco has very difficult and complex problems," but he had "batteries of very able attorneys." Liman and two assistants "debriefed" Vesco and the ICC board assembled at Vesco's Nassau house on Brace Ridge Road. Vesco, who had guards, told his ICC associates, "It's hogwash," and Liman stood up and said, "Yes, I've investigated and Bob will be cleared." The board left the meeting encouraged, but, Beatty said, "We were grasping at straws."

To Richardson, breaking Vesco's control "immediately is the essential element to saving the company." He made serious charges about the independence of the ICC's board, recommending that the company consent to an injunction and the appointment of a receiver to which Beatty was deeply opposed because that would have put ICC out of business, in his view, and the board agreed. On February 6, 1973, Vesco resigned. During the weekend, he went with Don-Don Nixon to Fairfield and packed boxes of papers from his files, also taking some forty gold Patek

Philippe watches with "IOS" engraved on the back. Intended as rewards for the salesmen, Vesco had taken them from Geneva along with other spoils. Vesco gave Nixon a watch that he still wears. The boxes went into Vesco's car and a limousine that almost crashed. Somebody had cut the hydraulic lines, Nixon said. "No Trespassing" signs appeared at the Vescos' Boonton house.

24

THE TRIAL

Judge Charles E. Stewart, Jr., had been appointed to the bench only a few months before without the orientation course Federal judges later received routinely. He was to preside over one of the more bewildering cases of modern times and some of the best litigation talent in the business. Maybe a million pieces of paper would pass before him in the succeeding years. In 1987, the Vesco case had still not ended.

The opening round went to the defense when, in its request for a Temporary Restraining Order, the SEC wheeled into the Federal courtroom on Foley Square, in New York City, a large cart filled with documents. That gave the defense an opportunity to ask for time to study them. To the despair of Robert Kushner, the SEC's lead litigator in the case, Stewart denied the agency's request for a TRO. Though Kushner was certain an appeals court would reverse Stewart, if it came to that, the ruling was a setback because the SEC's Irving Pollack was, at that very moment, abroad, attempting to convince overseas banking authorities to freeze IOS funds. To Kushner, a delay could only lead to more of the "wholesale looting" the SEC charged Vesco with, since the thieves, in Kushner's mind, would try to get the horse out of the barn before it burned down.

But the judge quickly agreed to let the case go to trial (it wasn't really a trial but a hearing about injunctions and the appointment of receivers, as the SEC demanded; an actual SEC-

Vesco trial has never taken place) and set a tentative date of February 20, 1973. The following two months were consumed by seemingly endless arguments over whether the SEC did, or didn't, have a case that merited prosecuting. The courtroom was packed with reporters at the start (the press sat in the jury box, there being no jury), but despite the sometimes dramatic arguments, press and spectator interest turned sporadic.

Vesco's lead lawyer, Arthur Liman, resembled a Roman bust. Tall, arrogant, of piercing gaze and solemn mien, he had graduated magna cum laude from Harvard and magna cum laude from Yale Law School, where he had been the comment editor of the *Law Review* and received an award. He had been a Special U.S. Attorney to prosecute fraud cases, and, in 1971, left Paul, Weiss for a year to become general counsel to the Attica Commission investigating the upstate New York prison riot. He was prominent in the bar association and had large and important clients—the Vesco case would be his most difficult, thus far, at least. (Liman was Chief Senate counsel in the Iran-Contra hearings.)

Kushner had worked with Liman at the U.S. Attorney's office in New York. They were vaguely friends. Kushner had also attended a prestigious law school, Columbia, and worked for a judge. Though he was not an SEC zealot, he claimed, his salary began at $16,000 in 1968 and ended at double that in 1974, when he went into private practice. He was the same age as Liman, who earned considerably more, as did many of the other, differently arrayed defense lawyers. An attorney class struggle lurked somewhere in the picture.

Liman announced that he would have consented to an injunction against violation of securities laws rather than have his client bear the costs of protracted litigation, but on the accusations of bilking the funds he would fight. He would prove, he vowed, that Vesco never asked for or received "kickbacks" or "rebates," "never pocketed a penny"; a restraining order would be a "stigma," exposing Vesco to contempt proceedings if persons not under his control took actions contrary to the order. (One of the SEC's main arguments was that Vesco controlled everybody involved, a half-truth, but in litigation half-truths become whole truths.) Vesco, Liman stated, was ready to appear in court, but the lawyer was in an untenable position if he had to defend civil and criminal proceedings at the same time. Rumors circulated that a Federal grand jury had been sworn in. Liman wanted Vesco to be given immunity from having his testimony used in a criminal trial. "I would like my client to testify in this case," Liman said. "I think it is helpful to him to get his explanations." Liman wanted Vesco to testify behind closed doors. He sounded confident, but Liman always sounded confident, though not to LeBlanc, whose impression had been that Liman expected to lose. Kushner privately doubted that Vesco would show up, no matter what was offered.

Kushner and his colleague Alan Blank were far outnumbered by the defense attorneys—some thirteen law firms participated—but not outdocumented. See Everything Crooked had accumulated 25,000–30,000 pages of testimony and 34 *feet* of documents. Among them, suggested Justin N. Feldman, were documents "spirited" out of IOS improperly, which Kushner hotly denied. Feldman, representing IOS fund management companies, argued that the SEC sought a vehicle to expand its jurisdiction, and, he said, Stewart's court was that vehicle. The action "represents an attempt by the Commission to obtain judicial extension of its jurisdiction to transactions which the Congress has not extended to the Commission. . . . That, in a single sentence, I think, is really what this case is all about. . . ."

Merritt's warning that a disgruntled stockholder might sue over the ABC transaction had been cited by the SEC as proof the plan was fraudulent, and that, Feldman insisted, was taking the Willkie Farr lawyer out of context, because it was only the sort of caution any competent attorney would raise, nor would the deal have been illegal. He said the scheme—the SEC always used "scheme" pejoratively, but a witness who had used "scheme" in planning ABC testified he'd been looking for language between "plan," which was too precise, and "concept" . . . "at the other extreme"; he hadn't meant "scheme to defraud"—called for giving fundholders who didn't demand redemption stock in a closed-end company and that had precedent in U.S. law. Further, the crime that wasn't a crime had only been planned in the United States, didn't involve U.S. investors, and had no substantial effects on U.S. securities markets. After eighteen months of preparation, Feldman claimed, the SEC didn't have a case.

The defense lawyers, more flashily dressed than the prosecution and more flamboyant, met constantly to rehearse strategy, and it was rare when they quit before midnight. Not welcome at such sessions was Simon Nusbaum, who represented some individual IOS shareholders. He was mostly ignored by the opposition and the judge.

Also persona non grata was Walpin, of Rosenman, Goldmark, representing Richardson, who had petitioned to put ICC into receivership and cooperated with the SEC. Walpin felt that the only serious documentation the SEC had was his brief for Richardson asserting that Vesco had bilked ICC, and which displayed New Jersey Bob's high-handed tendency to loot. Others thought Walpin's role was far less crucial. But in a surprise move, Martin Mensch, for Beatty and Richard Clay, asked to have Walpin disqualified because he had been privy to inside information before his client had acted against ICC and, therefore, had a conflict of interest. Exit not gently Walpin, who was quietly delighted because his client, Richardson, would be off the Vesco hook. Shea, Gould replaced Hogan & Hartson, and Milton Gould, the canny old lawyer who, more recently, represented Ariel Sharon in his suit against *Time* magazine, suggested, as the result of Walpin's suggestion, that International Controls be put in the quasi-receivership of a new board to avoid having the company forced out of business, and Stewart agreed, over the strong objections of the SEC, which wanted no whiff of compromise.

Vesco languished at the offices of Paul, Weiss and may have been a spectator in court once. There were conferences with his attorneys to develop his explanations should he appear. But Vesco was in a poor position, especially after the news of his $200,000 cash contribution to the Nixon campaign emerged, shocking Judge Stewart, who gasped, "I just heard of this five minutes ago." Jack Auspitz, a member of Liman's team and in his first big trial, remarked about Vesco, who impressed him, "Bob could figure out twenty-three deals by the time you could figure out one, but the one he picked was guaranteed to get him into trouble." The devil was between a rock and the deep blue sea. If he stayed in the United States, he could have been arrested on a criminal complaint even before a trial—the SEC seemed more than eager to have him incarcerated—placed under prohibitive bail, and kept in jail, which was what he most dreaded. The "deep blue sea" was that if Vesco, angry about the charges against him, failed to appear, he would lose the case by default, no matter how effective his attorneys. They were too effective, perhaps—Liman took his request to have Vesco testify in private to an appeals court, and while he lost, two to one, the judges, especially Judge William Timbers, were critical of Stewart for letting the case drag on. After that Stewart was harder on the defense.

Feldman and others told Vesco repeatedly that he ought to be prepared to settle for the best reality had to offer, a year or two in a country club prison, the deal to be negotiated, but Vesco wouldn't "sit in jail." Nor would he accept a settlement worked out between Sporkin and Irving Pollack on the one hand and Feldman on the other, under which certain assets would have been returned and receivers appointed. As day after day passed without Vesco's appearance, it became increasingly evident that he would default, in court a tacit admission of guilt. Still, the defense struggled on. In the opinion of some observers, the defense ran rings around the tiny SEC team, but the outcome was already decided, as Kushner knew, because of Vesco's absence.

In March, later than expected, the trial entered a new phase, the arrival of witnesses. The proceedings had moved to the "ceremonial" courtroom, a huge, oak-paneled room with bad acoustics. Facing the judge on the left was the SEC table, and, on the right, four or five defense tables with associates behind them. With so many loquacious lawyers eager to be heard and to object —technical matters could occupy days—the trial dragged on and Kushner remarked acidly that, thanks to Liman, they would be there until 1980.

Liman, one of the few people for whom other people would stop talking and listen, argued that the SEC saw Vesco as a figure of pure evil with a grand design. If the SEC couldn't reconcile the facts with its conception, it ignored the facts and adhered to the conception even when the conception was flawed. Kilmorey, for instance. The SEC saw a blatant attempt by Vesco to conceal that he still controlled IOS through his demonic power over LeBlanc, Meissner, Strickler, and Graze; and one of the major controversies in the courtroom was over whether the "Vesco group" (a much argued-about phrase) consisted of Vesco with a criminal intent and yes-men, or whether the others acted on their own. Graze said later that a Vesco "group" never existed, although groupings did—Vesco and LeBlanc, the "employees" Strickler, Straub, Richard Clay, and Ralph Dodd, with Meissner and Graze off on the side.

Feldman argued that the Vesco group was "guilty at most of poor judgment; that they [made] improvident, imprudent investments. Who in this complicated world of ours can conduct business . . ." without mistakes? But the SEC sued for fraud, not mistakes. For it, Kilmorey was not an arm's-length transaction, nor fully disclosed; nor was the adequacy of the money paid (mostly in loans) substantiated. For the defense, Kilmorey was at arm's length (it wasn't), and, if not fully disclosed, then disclosed enough, since Kilmorey was an offshore company, and that, since IOS was losing over $5 million a year, the amount pledged was more than adequate. Kilmorey was not part of the plan to close-end the dollar funds. Its basic purpose had been to remove ICC from the SEC's clutches. But the SEC believed that if it didn't control Vesco, nobody would. To justify that perhaps subjective judgment, the SEC had to prove the Vesco group was guilty of looting in concert.

Much the same dispute occurred about LeBlanc's Globals—whether the transaction was at arm's length, fully disclosed, and designed to get rid of the SEC, or part of a plot to separate IOS and fund investors from their money. "Here, as elsewhere," said Liman, "the SEC has tried to compensate for its failure to demonstrate actual impropriety in a particular transaction by depicting the transaction as part of a larger, more wicked scheme." But the SEC had not backed off from its insistence that Vesco was masterminding Globals as a means of effectuating the ABC deal, the vehicle for skimming off other people's money, all of which led to the specific SEC charges.

EHG was a Puerto Rican real estate development company founded by two brothers who had left Cuba in 1960, Enrique Gutiérrez (whose initials were EHG), an architect, and Ariel, an engineer. (They were nephews of Alberto Álvarez of Inter-American, who received a $290,000 finder's fee for bringing them to Vesco, LeBlanc, and Meissner.) The SEC said, essentially, that EHG, which had built condominiums, office buildings (including the then-largest one in Miami), hotels, and shopping centers, and had become the biggest developer in Puerto Rico and the Virgin Islands and one of the largest in Florida, was crooked. Ariel Gutiérrez testified at the trial that he believed EHG had been a great success. He also said, "The damage that this thing (the SEC complaint) has caused to my company with my lenders—I don't know—I couldn't begin to tell you what damage it will be." (EHG, with over $200 million in financial commitments, lost its credit base and went bankrupt.)

The SEC maintained that Vesco and group had more or less forced EHG to borrow $12 million, from IIT and Venture, $6 million more than the company asked for, and, it said, "Were it not for the Commission's lawsuit, it seems safe to predict that the $6,000,000 reserved for use by the Vesco group would have been fully used for Vesco's interests."

The SEC believed that $6 million of other people's money was "locked up in Bahamas Commonwealth Bank reserved for use by the Vesco group." EHG agreed to buy a $6 million certificate of deposit from LeBlanc, who removed it from Gutiérrez's safe deposit box and put it in his own. (He did, though, lend the money out for EHG to banks that paid higher interest.) Gutiérrez agreed to invest the $6 million "in a real estate company being formed by a customer of your bank." If EHG made the investment, or if one wasn't offered, it would get back the certificate, a loan, of course, from IIT and the Venture Fund. If it didn't accept the investment, though, EHG forfeited the $6 million. Small wonder plaintiff SEC pounced, but there were other ways to look at the arrangement that under less confrontational circumstances might have been explored.

At Vesco's request, Gutiérrez visited properties in Florida, Torremolinos, Spain, and Paradise Island. The idea of investing in a BCB client was no surprise to the Puerto Rican developer, who wanted to be tied to the IOS money tree, and the Vesco crowd for its part wanted to sell the properties because it felt safer in cash, Meissner said. Gutiérrez who, the SEC disbelieved, was outraged at See Everything Crooked: "We have been depicted—and I say this depicted because all my lenders throughout the entire United States—we have been depicted in every allegation that has been made as a front, as a passer of this money, and I can tell you I have never done that, and I am not about to do it for anybody, I don't care how rich that person is or I don't care how strong that person is, and that is the reason I am in this country today [to testify]."

Still, EHG was a perfect instrument for Vesco to have extracted a kickback from.

The SEC charged that IIT's $3 million investment in Vencap (Venture Capital) and FOF's $1 million in Conservative Capital—both formed by Richard Pistell—were inappropriate and improper for the fundholders and represented payoffs to Pistell for having introduced Vesco to Paradise Island and Costa Rica.

The defense made much of Pistell's business background to overcome Kushner's charges that Pistell's companies were "newly formed, thinly capitalized," but Pistell had started a half-dozen companies with very little money and they "were all worth over $100 million today," he said. He had thought the price of gold might rise, and had searched more than two years for a "marginal mine," until he found Chibex, in Canada, and organized a group of investors, including the Duke of Windsor, which put up $500,000. Feasibility studies on Chibex showed that the mine would be marginally profitable if gold sold for $40 an ounce, and Pistell was sure gold would rise much higher than that. "You mean gold will go to one hundred an ounce?" Stewart asked with mild surprise. "You bet," Pistell said. "You'll see it at four hundred." (He underestimated by more than half.)

During the Paradise Island negotiations, Pistell met IOS investment advisor Stanley Graze, who was impressed with Pistell's credentials as a member of the board of a Canadian bank and a director of Amtrak. Graze—Chibex was the only nonstock exchange transaction he engaged in for IOS—and Pistell agreed that the dollar would be devalued and the price of gold would soar. Graze had still another feasibility study done by a retired Anaconda geologist, and, as a result, caused FOF to invest $1 million in the mine, whose shares went up from $.50 to a $1.24. Nonetheless, the SEC said that the transaction amounted to fraud because the "market price of Chibex's common stock, which is thinly traded in the over-the-counter market in Montreal, has not reflected any glowing expectation for the stock." That seemed strange, not only because the stock was traded at far above what Pistell had bought it at, but also because, the SEC seemed to say, the propriety of an investment should be judged by the activity of speculators, not on a company's operations or financial condition. Again, the agency displayed its bias for "high-grade, readily marketable securities issued by United States companies." Even as the SEC delivered its salvos, gold broke $100 an ounce, but as a result of the agency's accusations, Pistell lost the mine. Still, the question of whether the investment violated IOS fund prospectuses remained on the agency's mind.

The Conservative Capital transaction took place in June 1972, to be followed in October by IIT's $3 million investment in Vencap, also attacked by the SEC. Vencap was organized to buy Out Islands Airlines in the Bahamas and didn't seem any more or less appropriate than other IOS-fund investments. Pistell personally borrowed almost $600,000 through Vencap but fully secured the loan. Pistell testified that Vesco never asked for payments, nor shared commissions or kickbacks. "Did Robert Vesco ever get a nickel from you for Vencap?" "No, sir," Pistell told Liman.

And so it went, week after week. "It was winter when we started, now it's spring," lamented a defense lawyer. The SEC received a boost from its surprise witness, Michael R. Bennett, a thirty-year-old former controller of International Bancorp, who resigned only a week before he testified in April 1973, and appeared without counsel. Bennett had gone to Europe for the Christmas vacation in December, 1972, and taken documents with him, uncertain what to do with them, he said. He returned to the Bahamas via New York, checked into a Holiday Inn and phoned the SEC. He thought Vector, another shell owned by LeBlanc (it controlled Trident), to which IBL sold several banks and "junk," as LeBlanc put it, like Commonwealth United securities carried at $1 but worth, late in 1972, some $3 million, was wrong and ought to be shown to "somebody."

The former IBL controller brought a second set of documents to the SEC, encouraged by his roommate, David Warham, controller of Value Capital and Property Resources, who gave Bennett the keys to his office and departed for Miami. Bennett made copies and once again delivered them to the SEC. The defense lawyers swarmed over Bennett for procuring the documents while he was a company officer, and the court seemed to rule that Bennett had taken them without authority and while still on a salary, but Liman, exercised, wanted to summon SEC officials about Bennett's documents. "I am sorry," Kushner said. "I am trying to be calm."

Bennett's effectiveness was reduced when Stewart ruled against his taking of the papers, but Bennett made the point that LeBlanc had threatened him. "You may wake up one morning and . . ." Bennett was being polite. Nasty Norman said he'd have Bennett castrated if he talked. But Bennett didn't like the transfer of funds "to places there was no reason they should go." Bennett's testimony was so riddled with defense objections as to be impossible to follow, but Kushner believed the witness helped establish the interconnections among Vesco-controlled entities, vital to the conspiracy case.

Another SEC "mystery" witness was Martí Figueres, who, unknown to the commission, was furious about See Everything Crooked's undiplomatic assertions that his father, Costa Rica's president, José Figueres, had, in effect, been bribed by Vesco. Martí got into an altercation with Kushner at the courthouse and refused to be interviewed by him before appearing on the stand. That was unacceptable to the SEC litigator who, after tense phone conversations with the staff, decided not to call the witness about whom such fuss had been made. Liman didn't call him, either, because he didn't want to open old courtroom sores again, nor would Figueres, though thoroughly pro-Vesco, be able to add anything new.

After thousands of pages of arguments and testimony, the "trial" wound down, almost of its own weight, leaving the lawyers to present post-trial briefs and Judge Stewart to call occasional hearings as he pondered whether receivers for the IOS entities should be appointed. Meanwhile, lawyer Simon Nusbaum had not been inactive—he had been serving subpoenas in the courtroom, a no-no—and uttered the last words. He referred to the "miserable little fundholders" of which he, anti-Vesco Nusbaum, seemed the only guardian. As the trial ended, Nusbaum told the court, "I will be in touch with you tomorrow."

The SEC, some observers felt, had been less than successful in proving that Vesco hadn't acted within American law, if indeed it applied, although the case may have been too complex, given the elaborate nature of the evidence, to be effectively presented by the commission. Vesco, in fear and petulance, and perhaps poorly advised, had quietly fled long before Judge Stewart's essential agreement with the American government in the late summer of 1973. By then, Vesco had embarked on a new life in the Bahamas and Costa Rica, though not without hope of vindication, and he had already found an important new friend who stood beside him.

Part Three

FUGITIVE FINANCIER

25

THE BENEFACTOR

Odd as it may seem, Vesco's main ally during his nearly six years of exile in Costa Rica was the U.S.'s most durable supporter in Central America, José Figueres Ferrer. He had wide influence in all Latin America, and in his homeland his status approached that of an idol even for those who opposed his policies, and, especially, his enduring support of the fugitive financier.

"Don Pepe," as he was always called ("Don," a term of affectionate respect, "Pepe," the diminutive—as was Figueres—of "José"), was five-foot-three or -four (because he wore elevator shoes he was also known as "Pepe Tacones," for "high heels"), vain (he had a face lift and hair transplant in his mid-seventies), a man who loved women, a convincing orator despite a squeaky voice, an extraordinarily skillful politician, an intellectual, and a fighter. When as president of the country he toured the University of Costa Rica, a demonstration broke out and a student called him *hijo de puta,* "son of a bitch." Figueres, who was proud of his hard "peasant" hands, knocked him down with a backhand swipe. "If you haven't been educated at home, I'll teach you respect," Figueres said. He received congratulatory letters from all over the world. Again in the early 1970s, Sandinistas tried to hijack an airliner at San José's Juan Santamaría Airport. Figueres did not parlay. He raced from his farm, ordered the plane's tires blown out, and had to be prevented by force (one of his people raised the little man from the ground) from entering the aircraft with a machine gun. One of the hijackers came down the ramp carrying a weapon. Figueres, seizing a .45 caliber pistol, shot the man in the stomach from thirty yards away. Once more, Figueres received letters from everywhere in praise of his strong stand, although the shooting has never before been publicly revealed.

Figueres had had a remarkable career. Born in 1906, of Spanish parents who had just immigrated to Costa Rica, he studied hydrological and electrical engineering at New York University and Massachusetts Institute of Technology, supporting himself as a waiter and translator. He didn't graduate and returned to Costa Rica in 1928. Figueres acquired, for a borrowed $8,000, an abandoned hemp farm that he christened La Lucha Sin Fin, "The Struggle Without End." He joked that the struggle concerned paying the bills, but conflict seemed central to his philosophy, as when he referred to his conception of life "that obliges men to fight in bad times and to seek out battle in good times." He spent the next fifteen years or so selling hemp and hemp-processing equipment, becoming the largest rope manufacturer in Costa Rica. Also a welder, he taught rope making, which he regarded as an art. He established a sort of collective farm that tried to provide housing, schools, and medical care to his 2,000 workers. He sent his staff to England for technical studies.

In 1942, Figueres entered public life with a radio broadcast —for individuals to take the air on their own to express their political views was not uncommon in Costa Rica—in which he excoriated the government for irresponsible management and for Communist leanings, a marriage of left and right. The police took him into custody, but, before he was cut off, he delivered his message, "What the government should do is go away." He was expelled to Mexico. In the tangled politics of those days, when the United States and the U.S.S.R. were wartime allies, the U.S. Embassy apparently cabled Washington that Figueres was a fascist. Costa Rica's President, Calderón Guardia, had, even before the United States, declared war on Germany and it followed that since Figueres was against Calderón he must be pro-German. At home, though, Figueres became an instant celebrity; some believed the government had been foolish to arrest him. He characterized Calderón as a "tyrant" and pledged to "mercilessly wipe out the men of the established regime, to combat them to the death if necessary, so that there would remain only the seeds, and to make a new motherland, the new Costa Rica."

Figueres's platform was the critical issue of electoral fraud. After a presidential election in 1948 in which the result—the defeat of the government—was declared invalid, Figueres launched a brief, bloody, but successful revolution early in 1948. Anti-Figueres forces were expelled to Nicaragua, where they attempted to organize a counterrevolution, but the junta head proved forgiving toward his foes. Figueres's house, coffee crop, and rope factory had been burned, and his American wife (he was married twice, to Americans) and their children narrowly escaped with their lives. Still, there were no execution squads, no jailings, largely because of Don Pepe.

Figueres launched many reforms aimed chiefly at the development of a larger middle class. He advocated more advanced technology, a career civil service, and larger foreign investments. An autocrat, he nationalized the banks and vastly increased the bureaucracy, Costa Rican crosses to this very day. He had guaranteed that he would serve for only a year, asked for a six-month extension, was given it, asked for another and was refused by the elected President, Otilio Ulate. But for a dictator to step down voluntarily was almost unknown in Latin America. He took still another unheard-of action: he abolished the military (small as it was). As a student in the United States, Figueres had read H. G. Wells's *Outline of History.* The book advanced the notion of an armyless state, which Figueres never forgot and which, after he took power, appeared eminently practical in preventing a counterrevolution. In his later years, Figueres was nominated for the Nobel Peace Prize for making Costa Rica a demilitarized state and for persuading both sides to lay down their arms after the revolution.

As he put it, "So, in 1948, when I found myself with two armies on my hands—one, my victorious rebel army, the other, the government's defeated army—I decided to abolish them both." Figueres's opponents concede that being spared the expense of a military contributed greatly to the economic growth of

Costa Rica, and a Sandinista-type revolution has not occurred, for which Figueres takes credit.

Figueres was one of the "Four Horsemen" of the Alliance for Progress along with John F. Kennedy, of whom he was deeply admiring, Muñoz Marín of Puerto Rico, and Rómulo Betancourt of Venezuela. He was an active opponent of the Somozas in Nicaragua, Trujillo in the Dominican Republic, Pérez Jiménez in Venezuela, and Batista in Cuba. He helped supply arms and asylum to their foes. As a result, several assassination attempts were made against him, inspired by Trujillo and Somoza.

Figueres was not opposed to the Sandinistas in Nicaragua, believing them, though he preferred democracy, to be their country's best chance, and his youngest son fought with the revolutionaries. He showed the same ideological bent with the Cubans, and an important arms shipment to Castro in the Sierra Maestra was funneled through La Lucha.

Shortly after Castro triumphed, Figueres chose to preach to Fidel before a crowd of 500,000 in Havana on representative democracy, siding with the U.S. in the event of war with the Soviet Union. "I understand your resentment at the United States," Don Pepe recalled himself shouting, "but when it comes to something extrahemispherical I side with them. And Puerto Rico is *not* forced to be a colony." The microphone was snatched from his hands by a Communist party member and some twenty years would pass before Castro and Figueres spoke again, though he generally continued to favor what he regarded as Cuba's legitimate aspirations. But some of Costa Rica's anti-Castroism can be traced to the years that Figueres opposed Fidel. Don Pepe admitted to having worked for the CIA. "At the time I was conspiring against the Latin-American dictatorships and wanted help from the U.S. I was a good friend of Allen Dulles, who, as you know, had a very stupid brother John Foster. Anyway, the CIA helped me finance a magazine and some youth conferences here. But I never participated in espionage. I did beg them not to carry out the Bay of Pigs invasion of Cuba, which was madness, but they ignored me."

From the beginning, Figueres was a strong supporter of Israel, which he visited. Always attracted to the underdogs, he admired Israeli heroism, capability, and productivity and respected the suffering he saw. (Figueres, believing he himself had Jewish roots, as many Costa Ricans also believe they do, attempted to prove it through a lineage study but failed.) His government was among the first to recognize the Jewish state (Costa Rica has consistently voted for Israel in the U.N.) and placed its mission in Jerusalem. Later, Figueres toured the United States to help sell Israeli bonds. Because of him, Costa Rican blacks for the first time won the freedom to move freely around the country, and Figueres supported women's rights. Still, though he denied it, he was a practical politician prepared to deal with his sworn opponents—the Communists and the right wing.

A Spartan who cared little for material possessions, Figueres lived simply—as President of Costa Rica he flew tourist class by preference. A hard worker, he was the author of some dozen books, ranging from planting cypress trees to an exercise in macroeconomics. He was an educator who often wrote in simple language, using peasant vernacular and imagery, so that the people could understand. He was a utopian—an optimist who looked for unusual solutions—and, as such, his perspective gradually elevated and he became impatient with what he saw as petty squabbles, putting values like generosity of spirit and loyalty foremost. In 1970, he was elected to his third term as President by an overwhelming majority. And then arrived the man who, strangely, would prove to be one of the more important individuals in his, until then, charmed life.

When the *Silver Phyllis* touched down in San José on June 29, 1972, those who noticed the heraldry and strange initials on the tail perceived this was no ordinary commercial flight. Pan Am, under contract, wheeled the ramp to the plane, and, breathless with excitement, a slight debonair man in eyeglasses bounded up and inside as soon as the door was opened. Thirty-one-year-old José Martí Figueres, eldest son of the President, was the official welcomer and he was led to the young chief. The tycoon had arrived in Costa Rica.

Vesco and party were awarded special treatment reserved for important diplomatic officials, because José Figueres didn't think a major financier like Vesco should have to stand in line. Customs formalities were speeded up, and a procession of cars picked up passengers at the plane. Vesco had an international reputation because, as head of IOS, he could control investments. Richard Pistell, who had visited Costa Rica, suggested that IOS invest in Figueres's company at La Lucha, San Cristóbal Agrícola y Industrial. The investment was made and Sociedad Agrícola paid Pistell and an associate a finder's fee of $150,000. That, too, was mentioned ominously by the SEC, but finder's fees were hardly shocking.

President Figueres received the not yet fugitive financier at the modest presidential house. Figueres liked Vesco. "He may not have been well dressed but he was audacious and generous, although, after he'd decided to stay, I realized we didn't have much to talk about. I wanted to upgrade him culturally, and Martí and I finally decided that O. Henry was about on his level, so we got him a volume of *The World of O. Henry.* I doubt he ever read the book," Figueres said. (Unknown to Don Pepe, O. Henry had lived in Honduras, a fugitive from American justice as Vesco would become.) The two talked mostly about Costa Rica.

A few days later, following the IOS annual meeting at St. John's, New Brunswick, Milton Meissner phoned Figueres's home from Canada. Rather brusquely, he asked to speak to Vesco, little dreaming that he had the President of Costa Rica on the line. To prevent a repeat of the previous year's turbulent conclave in Toronto, IOS had booked all available hotel rooms to keep out dissidents and reporters. Vesco told Meissner about possible investment in a San Cristóbal housing project, and Meissner came to Costa Rica, bringing with him Ulrich Strickler, of IOS and a Vesco ally, and another man he regarded as an expert. (By law, the President of Costa Rica was not supposed to engage in business while in office, but San Cristóbal was considered more of a national institution, and had never made money.) Meissner decided an IOS Fund (IIT) would invest $2.1 million. There was also another, smaller IOS investment. The enterprise failed—IIT was apparently repaid $600,000. Not lost on Meissner and Vesco was the growing necessity to find a home for IOS-ABC, and Costa Rica, with the aid of the Figueres family, might be able to provide one, but the SEC again doubted that the IOS-related investments in the Figueres companies squared with fund prospectuses and raised the issue of fraud. (In 1986, the Figueres entities were said to be pulling steadily in the black, and hoped to become a $100 million company. Another Figueres son, West Point–educated José María, was largely responsible, but Norman LeBlanc, an unpaid adviser, contributed.) True, Don Pepe would do practically anything to keep La Lucha afloat, but the housing business flopped not because of kickbacks or sinister reasons but out of "incompetence," said a former company official. "Don Pepe Figueres kept changing the designs and we lacked management skills. Vesco, if he had them, was too busy saving his ass to help."

After the SEC November action, Vesco explained the facts from his point of view to Figueres, who concluded Bob was the victim of "persecution," a "myth" fabricated by the American government. "I admire the regulatory work of the North Americans but with Vesco they overdid it. I think he offended their vanity because he was able to stay out."

Doubtlessly, Don Pepe was influenced by the IOS Inter-American's investments in his family companies—in Costa Rica, politics, money, and business were and are so closely related as to be functional parts of each other—but when the Vesco money dried up, Figueres, who always tried to find redeeming characteristics in people, stuck by his protégé even when he endangered his own political standing and that of his party. "Some think I'm guilty of excessive loyalty," Figueres remarked, "but when I make friends I go all the way."

26

"ROBIN HOOD"

The drumbeat of the Costa Rican press began to sound. Before, Vesco, a mysterious figure who came and went in a large jet, had been mentioned only in the context of a "World Financial District," a Figueres-sponsored Costa Rican update of the International Business Zone drafted by Willkie Farr in New York, which because of nationalistic objections didn't pass in the Costa Rican congress. After the SEC complaint, Vesco suddenly emerged as a man who had single-handedly lifted a quarter-billion dollars, an amount roughly equal to the country's annual budget, a feat many Ticos, as Costa Ricans call themselves, rather admired. Vesco did nothing to disabuse anyone of the notion he had untold millions to spread around.

Figueres tried vainly to convince Vesco to stay out of sight and expressed considerable impatience with Vesco's high-profile style of life. The President rode in the front seat of his simple car with a driver, followed by a tiny police car, as a precaution in case Don Pepe's car had mechanical troubles. Vesco traveled in a caravan, two new Range Rovers in front with guards, the financier in his Mercedes with a chauffeur and guard, followed by one or two more Range Rovers. Vesco may have had a reason for the display, to impress the locals with his wealth in hope he would be allowed to remain.

It was the same with the Boeing—only a multi-multimillionaire could afford such a toy. (Even Figueres was unaware that the aircraft belonged to a public company, not Vesco himself.) All fall, the 707 had been back and forth like a shuttlecock from Nassau to Costa Rica, transporting the household goods of the Vescoites who were to set up shop—homes had been rented for them. Their effects went through customs without delay and duty free, causing the press to cry foul. ("We should never have let that plane in more than once," Martí Figueres lamented in retrospect. "It wasn't smart politically.") On one trip in December, Pat brought in $1,000 worth of toys for poor children. "Contraband," thundered *La Nación.* Figueres wrote Nixon that Vesco "would give us the ingredients that we have been lacking in our own plans to create in this half of the hemisphere a window for developing democracy" but felt compelled to appear on national TV to explain Vesco's presence and point out the benefits that could flow from it. Since the SEC case was civil (not that Figueres changed his mind when it became criminal), dealing with the problem was "not our obligation." Privately, Don Pepe sounded somewhat different: "Vesco may have stolen Wall Street blind but all we care about is that he, or we, do nothing illegal in Costa Rica."

Figueres's notions of justice were complex. Those he viewed as setting back slow but steady left-wing progress, terrorists like the M-19 in Colombia, should be dealt with harshly. Those who represented aberrations in the (North American) capitalist system (Vesco) should be given the benefit of the doubt especially since Don Pepe regarded the North American bankers as thieves who manipulated the prices of raw materials and commodities. He shared a Latin-American attitude that the North Americans acted in their own interests, which weren't necessarily those of justice or Latin America.

Small (two million people then) but intensely political, Costa Rica was in its own way a microcosm of the giant to the North, but the strains in its politics, because concentrated, could be seen more readily. The two ruling elites, the Figueres-founded National Liberation Party and what Don Pepe termed the "oligarchs," could never clearly distinguish for the public the issues that divided them, just as the Democrats and Republicans often fail in the United States. The issues had to do with internal economic matters regarding wealth, poverty, progress, political (and personal) power. Lacking, as does the United States, an easily expressible language for such weighty (and concealed) matters, trivia became the substitute for the politicians and journalists. Vesco was surely trivia, but he became an important domestic issue because of the amount of money the SEC seemed to have said he had stolen.

By March 1973, the furor, which Figueres dismissed as "bla-bla," had reached such proportions that Vesco defended himself. He told his staff that he hated the publicity but did practically everything possible to encourage it. He flew from the Bahamas bringing a Cuban-American p.r. man, Raúl Espinoza. Espinoza, who later worked for the Republican National Committee, claimed he had been told to create a "diversion" in Costa Rica for the always grandiose Vesco. Vesco gave what the English-language weekly *Tico Times* described as the "first press conference of his life" as he prepared for a TV-radio appearance. "I believe I am a law-abiding citizen," he said on the air. He claimed the SEC was mad at him because he had bucked Wall Street and invested in developing countries. He said that he "might have to punch somebody [Costa Rican] in the nose," a statement that Espinoza, blamed on "misunderstanding in the translation." "This spectacle has caused tremendous indignation among Costa Ricans," said a congressman, "especially when this man begins to threaten us instead of explaining his activities."

May brought a severe drought, food rationing, a major earthquake in the northern part of the country. A national emergency was declared by President Figueres. None of this was sufficient to drive New Jersey Bob off the front pages. A Costa Rican congressional committee investigating mutual funds gave Vesco a temporary boost, finding no evidence of wrongdoing on his part. "Mr. Vesco and his group [Inter-American] are making substantial investments in Costa Rica, using funds which, according to the SEC, should not have been taken out of the United States (even though originally they had been taken out of underdeveloped countries like ours.)" The report hinted that the United States was in violation of Costa Rica's sovereignty. But in May, a U.S. judge ordered Vesco's arrest because of nonappearance in the Justice Department's criminal action against him, establishing

Vesco for the first time as a fugitive, along with the rest of the "Seven Samurai," LeBlanc, Meissner, Strickler, Straub, Graze, and Clay. Vesco had arrived that weekend in a "flotilla" of three jets, said a paper—the 707, a Sabrejet formerly owned by Allan Butler, and a Gulfstream II LeBlanc had rented from the Teamsters and which had belonged to Frank Sinatra. Among the passengers was a 270-pound bodyguard for Espinoza, whom the talkative p.r. man said he didn't want. Espinoza excoriated the *Tico Times* for claiming that Vesco had fled. He hadn't, said the p.r. man, without producing a body. He denied that the $200,000 Nixon contribution had been "clandestine."

In June ICC received a form letter, addressed to the Vescos, from the Republican Finance Committee.

> As you know the Republican Party is in trouble. *We need your help.*
>
> The deplorable Watergate scandal, in which a few misguided political adventurers exercised extraordinarily bad judgment and performed assorted questionable acts, has cast a pall of suspicion over the activities of the entire Republican party. The Democrats are quite naturally making the most of the situation. They would like to paint *all* Republicans as bad, immoral and unworthy of public office. . . .
>
> P.S. In troubled times it is indeed fortunate to have friends like you. Thanks.

Just as the briefest peace descended, Norman LeBlanc gave a press conference claiming that he and others of the "Magnificent Seven," as Martí Figueres dubbed them, were under harassment by the U.S. Embassy in cahoots with the SEC and CIA. Not to be upstaged by his soulmate, Vesco and guards swept into the Gran Hotel de Costa Rica, in downtown San José, where he chose almost the same moment to grant an interview before the hungry cameras of CBS and NBC. (The two men had been almost besieged by journalists at LeBlanc's house.) Vesco "seemed to be in the position of a professional defendant," he said, and announced that the CIA had endangered his life more than once without specifying when, where, or how. He would return to testify in the Mitchell-Stans case if a special prosecutor were appointed for Watergate, and if immunity was granted him by the SEC, which was out to discredit his benefactor, Figueres. He had, he said, renounced his American citizenship in disgust. A U.S. spokesman said that Vesco couldn't renounce his citizenship without appearing at a U.S. diplomatic office, which Vesco, fearing abduction, would never have done.

Following the broadcast, with high expectations, a covey of newshawks from the New York *Times, Time* magazine, the Associated Press and United Press International, *Newsweek,* the Los Angeles *Times,* Reuters, and two or three others descended on San José, which wasn't accustomed to so much attention, or any at all. The reporters scoured Vesco's favorite haunts, waiting a week, but the fugitive financier didn't appear. "It's a nonevent like the Hughes thing in Managua," said one reporter. (Howard Hughes was then in seclusion in Nicaragua.) "We have to cover it, but we could be here for the rest of our natural lives." Of course, none dared leave in case Vesco showed up and somebody else got the story, but there was little to do in San José except, perhaps, bug phones, as the New York *Times* man said that his was, by persons unknown but probably Vesco's men.

Evidence of Vesco's personal investments hadn't been asked for because he hadn't committed a crime in Costa Rica. Had the reporters wished to know what was happening, they might have tried Alberto Innocente Álvarez, president of Inter-American; Martí Figueres, who succeeded him; or Norman LeBlanc, whose Trident wrote the checks. But "The Man" himself was the focus, and the questions were inevitable. He had to have substantial investments or Figueres wouldn't be protecting him—the gringo was probably buying the country. It was a great game; Vesco stayed mum and enjoyed the fuss.

"Vesco Case Rocks Costa Rica as Principals Seek TV Forums," said a long-winded headline. President Figueres, embroiled in a controversy the likes of which he had never dreamed of in his worst moments, found himself accused by the *Wall Street Journal,* through the SEC, of having $325,000 in his New York bank account, some from Bahamas Commonwealth Bank, meaning, of course, a bribe. Don Pepe (whose skill with money was such that after absentmindedly leaving $10,000 in a hotel room, though he retrieved the sum, never carried any for fear of losing it) retorted, somewhat wearily, on national TV-radio, that the *Journal* was wrong. He said that the real sum in his bank account was $436,000 for his personal and business expenses and it wasn't a bribe. (He also said that $60,000 was for the National Symphony Orchestra, from Pistell and Graze, whose wife was a music lover. Don Pepe appeared to have been thinking on his feet, because Graze and Pistell had made no such contribution.) Figueres did meet with the Symphony's board about what to do with the money, and it was decided to invest in an income-producing property. The result was La Sinfonía, a tree farm that still exists. Don Pepe offered to show all relevant documents to *La Nación,* his principal Costa Rican accuser, and the matter ended. Figueres, though, was just as upset with LeBlanc and Espinoza for their verbal attacks on the American Embassy and publicly chastised them. The President straddled a tight wire between pro-Americanism and pro-Vescoism.

Don Pepe had announced a new newspaper, *Excelsior,* which like La Lucha was an obsession with him. He had managed to survive politically without journalistic support for himself and his party, which was unheard of. He not only held Costa Rican journalism in contempt, but felt the leading papers, *La Nación* and *La República,* printed the antigovernment views of the "oligarchy" owning them. *Excelsior* was to be the finest newspaper the country had ever seen, with eight columns, syndication from American and European news services, and the most modern printing plant in Central America. Rival papers worried, baselessly it turned out, that *Excelsior* would drain their circulation and, being pro-government, serve to perpetuate the Figueres party's power indefinitely, as a similar *Excelsior* had helped achieve for the ruling party in Mexico.

Excelsior's backers were the Presidents of Mexico, Panama, and Venezuela—Venezuela's Betancourt had been harbored at La Lucha. The Figueres family provided part of the land on which stood the large building, prefabricated at La Lucha, plus $750,000 at least. The biggest investor by far, though, was Inter-American, but that was mostly unknown and Vesco received the credit or blame and was marked for even more attention. Figueres called the fuss "bananagate." "I'm tired of it," he complained. "Vesco and Watergate. When will people tire of them?" And, he said in stronger terms, "Everything about Watergate and Robert Vesco is part of [what] we swallow from the *Wall Street Journal,* the Washington *Post* and the New York *Times.* We're like monkeys who imitate the North Americans in everything they do."

But it was too late to forget about Vesco, whose "millions, minions and mystique," as a paper put it, had embedded themselves in Costa Rican consciousness. "Firing" Espinoza (who was "rehired" by Property Resources, which paid his salary), Vesco briefly sought to keep out of sight, and after the American ambassador, on the eve of the U.S.–Costa Rica extradition attempt, asked for Vesco's "preventative detention," the fugitive vanished —he was at La Lucha. He had received chilling news.

In June, Milton Meissner, lured to Luxembourg for a meeting, was thrown in jail by the Luxembourg authorities. Under Luxembourg law, it was forbidden to invest in companies that had debts in a certain proportion to net assets. IIT had had hundreds of millions in debt securities, and Luxembourg hadn't objected before. A Luxembourg judge told him, "You're not guilty, but you're the only one we can get." Meissner had come with what he called a full accounting of IIT and a plan to liquidate the funds. His lawyer, Justin Feldman, had warned him—despite repeated assurances from Luxembourg about Meissner's safety—that perhaps he shouldn't go, but Meissner said he had nothing to hide and the German border was only a few miles away. He was arrested, and the American lawyers protested. The chairman of the Luxembourg banking commission, whose hand Feldman's partner wouldn't shake, smiled and said, "You're naïve." (The lawyers, though, neglected to contact Meissner in prison, Meissner said.) Meissner was convinced the SEC was behind his imprisonment, which the SEC's Irving Pollack denied. Meissner remained in jail for eight months without formal charges brought, and got no help from the American consulate. He was finally released on health grounds—he was losing his sanity—and made his way back to Costa Rica. (By 1986, he had still not received his bail money,

$50,000, much less interest, from Luxembourg, despite written requests that weren't answered. He spoke of $200,000 paid by him in fees.) According to Don-Don Nixon, living with the Vescos in Costa Rica, days were spent on farfetched plans to rescue Meissner. Vesco was ever more fearful for himself.

Don Pepe's successor, President Daniel Oduber Quiros, believed the American extradition attempt in Costa Rica was so badly bungled as to indicate the U.S. didn't really want its quarry. He may not have reckoned on the lack of legal skill and overconfidence of U.S. Justice Department attorneys and their failure to understand Costa Rican law. But Vesco took no chances. With Pat and the kids, he flew to Antigua, where an entity incorporated in Panama had bought a $1.4 million yacht, the *Romántica,* rechristened the *Patricia III* even when the fugitive claimed he didn't own it. Speeding out of the harbor, the yacht cut two anchor lines, and Vesco shouted from the bridge, "Send me the bill! You know where to find me!"*

During the summer of 1973, the United States lost its extradition attempt and two appeals, and Don Roberto, as they had started to call him, felt safe enough to return. (Vesco, who liked the appellation "fugitive financier," thought the "Don" was a reference to Don Corleone in *The Godfather,* and was rather pleased.) In late August, he lunched with his family at Le Grub Pub where a *Nación* reporter spotted him, but, on instruction from the tycoon, the bodyguard wouldn't permit an interview. The reporter was insistent and an arrangement was made. If the paper wouldn't take pictures of Pat and the kids, about whom Vesco was as kidnap shy as he was about himself, the fugitive agreed to be photographed and interviewed in the offices of Bancorp de Costa Rica, where the Vesco gang hung out. In the same September issue the interview appeared, *La Nación* quoted a

* After "Stalking Robert Vesco" by this author appeared in *Fortune* magazine, the editor received the following from Dale Hegstrom: "I was on assignment in Antigua in 1973. . . . A friend of mine with inside information concerning the comings and goings at Nelson's Dockyard called me one day. 'Vesco is in port.' Naïvely, I called the U.S. naval base on the island and told the base commander that America's #1 fugitive was within grasp. He asked me to come out to the base and tell him more. A few hours after that interview, I got a call from the commander at my home. In a rather chilling conversation, he told me, 'We have been in touch with the "highest sources" in Washington, and they suggest that you forget the whole incident.' "

restaurant owner, "From that day (when Vesco first ate here) I have had a fantastic number of clients. They come and ask where Robert Vesco sits; sometimes I say inside and sometimes I say there, outside. Little old ladies have come from San Ramón to see if he is here. . . . Before, I wanted to put an ad on the radio, but since I am being so successful, why do it?"

Vesco told his pulps-to-riches story. "The first thing I did in my life was to sell newspapers . . . then I laid brick." He had belonged to a protest movement (unspecified) but had been too busy trying to earn enough to eat. The plane, is it yours or rented? "It belongs to a company, and the company belongs to my sons." (To the extent that this was true, it meant that Vesco put his shares of the company that owned the plane into a family trust.) Do you need such a big one? "No, but a long time ago, when I traveled . . . to Geneva, I needed such a plane," said he nostalgically, referring to two years before. Do you have others? "Several small ones."

The press, said Vesco, talked a lot of nonsense and the Costa Rican people were being manipulated. Was he afraid of being killed? The "two things" Vesco feared were publicity (as he was presently fomenting) and people "all over the world" who wanted to do something crazy—murder attempts or kidnapping. Vesco was disappointed by the interview, and the others he gave, because he hoped to come across as a plain person and somehow failed.

In September in New York, Judge Stewart decreed that the SEC had established, with the defendants in default, a "reasonable likelihood of success." Vesco, still searching for a permanent haven, visited Argentina and Paraguay twice in the 707, and, in October, an Argentine court ruled that "there is no merit [no basis] to form any criminal case. . . ." against Robert Lee Vesco Sassek (he had taken a second family name, his mother's). He also explored Venezuela, Grenada, Argentina, and Spain as possible refuges. Vesco could have lived safely in Argentina, as he could have in Uruguay. He apparently bought a house in Argentina, but the Argentines decided they didn't want him after all.

In November, a new accusation appeared in testimony before a U.S. Senate subcommittee that Vesco had agreed to provide $300,000 for a heroin-smuggling operation. Vesco responded, "I am the father of four children, two of them teenagers. No one deplores the traffic in heroin and other illicit drugs more than I. And nobody in the world is less involved in this kind of traffic than I." The statement from a U.S. secret agent, who wasn't a U.S. agent at all but a shady character whose story revealed that he had never met Vesco or Norman LeBlanc, whom he accused of gangland connections, was "atrocious and vile." Nor did it seem sensible—at this point, at least—that a man whose position was as precarious as Vesco's would have dared to deal in drugs, the discovery of which would have ended his Costa Rican sojourn. The U.S.–Costa Rica extradition agreement was explicit: an American arrested on drug charges would be sent home.

27

ANOTHER EXTRADITION ATTEMPT

Despite pressure to put him on the Bahamian "Stop-List" of undesirables, Vesco went back to the Bahamas in the fall of 1973, in the teeth of the U.S. extradition attempt there. He needed the Bahamas to do business in, and he believed the Bahamian government would protect him. "Don't worry," he told LeBlanc, but Vesco's confidence was superficial.

Much else existed for Norman to worry about. He sat in his Global office at Bahamas Commonwealth Bank, hands visibly shaking. "Sue the bastard," was his constant refrain. Stanley Sporkin and Irving Pollack of the SEC, he knew, were almost like a road company as they went to Europe and Canada to persuade banking authorities to freeze IOS assets. Sporkin shocked staid, British-trained Bahamian lawyers by pounding on a table. LeBlanc, foolishly Meissner thought, had put $106 million in the Bank of Montreal and it was vulnerable to seizure. Receivers had begun to be appointed, and there was not only an International Association of IOS Shareholders Funds (IASIF) but an International Regulatory Committee of representatives of the governments of five countries. LeBlanc called them vultures. Norman, whose parents read headlines of his thievery in the Canadian press, knew an arrest warrant was out for him. When the court action was quashed, he complained, all he got was a small box in the papers.

Vesco and LeBlanc fought back against the forces arrayed

against them, bringing an action in the Bahamian courts on behalf of IOS Investment Programs. The theory of the case was that LeBlanc's company was entitled to IOS and fund assets that remained outside Vesco and LeBlanc's control. The result was an injunction by a Bahamian court freezing all IOS and fund assets, which put the New York Federal District Court and the Bahamian one in complete opposition. Ultimately, LeBlanc's case was dismissed.

LeBlanc believed he'd prevail in a U.S. court, until his New York lawyers, Skadden, Arps, optimistic at first, spent ten weeks in the Bahamas—LeBlanc would sometimes work with them eight hours a day. They went away convinced that some of the transactions would be difficult to explain and that the conspiracy charges against Vesco would be tied to LeBlanc, too, unless the United States dropped them, which seemed unlikely. Skadden, Arps fees, Norman recalled, exceeded $500,000. Stanley Sporkin telephoned LeBlanc to ask him to testify, but Norman insisted on guarantees that Sporkin wouldn't give, any more than he would relent with Meissner, who offered to appear. Almost as a reminder of American strength, cars parked outside BCB, with their transmitters on, returned to the American Embassy at night, LeBlanc said. His apartment was broken into, the tires of his car blown, and once, as he was driving off, the car went out of control. Paranoid or not, Nasty Norman believed he was being threatened by the CIA.

Vesco and LeBlanc developed a siege mentality. In the "stupid days," Norman said, they spent $780,000 of other people's money building secure office space for themselves on a top floor of Charlotte House. To gain access, you needed a special key. The offices had floor sensors, armed guards, and remote control TV as well. In the center stood an elaborate radio room with the most modern equipment, the only access to which, strangely, was through the closets of the two bedrooms meant to be Vesco's and LeBlanc's. The roof had been strengthened to accommodate a helicopter. The signals from the radio tower were powerful enough to interfere with Bahamian international communications, and the authorities complained. LeBlanc used the new offices only occasionally and Vesco not at all, having by the time the space was finished, in 1974, retreated back to Costa Rica, where it was safer.

Bernie Cornfeld came down to the Bahamas and wanted to see Vesco. He went to James Crosby's office on Paradise Island, but rather than give out the number of the casino's valuable customer—Vesco gambled there almost every night—Crosby said he'd make the call for Bernie. He left the room briefly and Cornfeld found Vesco's number in Crosby's address book, which was on his desk. He phoned and said, "Look, Bob, I've come all the way down here to see you and I would appreciate your cutting out this screwing around and getting together with me," and Vesco agreed to meet him at the casino. Bernie told him, "Bob, I get the impression you're involved in something that's kind of crazy. Do you want to spend the rest of your life as a fugitive?"

"Well, if I'm going to be a fugitive, I'm going to be a rich fugitive," Vesco murmured.

"Doesn't it trouble you that it's other people's money?"

Vesco shrugged.

"What about all those widows and orphans you're robbing?"

"They have their problems and I have mine," said Vesco.

Cornfeld replied: "They'll blow your brains out."

"It's you they are going to get," Vesco said.

"He was right in a way," Cornfeld said later. Arrested in November 1973—Bernie believed that Vesco called the authorities about his presence—Cornfeld spent eleven months in St. Antoine Prison on charges by Swiss IOS employees that he had conned them into buying stock. "I went to prison, not him." Bernie finally managed to raise bail and bravely returned to face trial, despite warnings of Swiss anti-Semitism. He was acquitted—the prosecutor admitted he didn't have a case—and made money on the bail due to the appreciation of the Swiss franc, but he repaid the $10 a share the employees had laid out for IOS stock, at a cost to him of about $1 million. He retired to a Beverly Hills house so large that the girls who answered the phone weren't exactly exaggerating when they said, "The Castle." He still had his castle in France, his houses in Paris and London, a Rolls, and a Mercedes convertible, and three or four servants. Bernie was fortunate but he had fallen a great distance from glory and it hurt.

He stared morosely at the girls in the pool and said, "It's a nice place to live with your memories."

Vesco arrived from his house on Brace Ridge Road on the day he was arrested in LeBlanc's Global office at BCB. Most of the bank employees were unaware of what happened. Vesco didn't display emotion when told that an assistant commissioner of police and a superintendent waited outside, but he did ask to make a few calls. In agitation he phoned Arthur D. Hanna, Deputy Prime Minister (and Finance Minister) of the Bahamas, and complained, "My friends have deserted me." Vesco had contributed, Hanna remembered, in excess of $200,000 to Prime Minister Pindling's Progressive Liberal Party (he gave substantially to the opposition party, the Freedom National Movement, as well) but hadn't been offered protection in return. "Call your friends," Hanna said with a shrug. For him, there was nothing to be done about the U.S. extradition attempt, because it was legal. Vesco claimed he talked to Prime Minister Pindling, who said, "Get yourself a good lawyer." In a white cotton Cuban shirt and red trousers, Vesco surrendered peaceably and was released on $75,000 bail. Vesco had to surrender his Costa Rican passport—his American one had been canceled—and was forbidden to leave the country, although, in one of his airplanes, he could probably have taken off at will and hidden somewhere until he obtained a different passport, which wasn't hard to do. (At one point, Vesco had five or six passports from different countries and complained of the trouble of renewing them.)

They said afterward, as they'd said in Costa Rica, that the U.S. didn't want Vesco returned, because he knew too much about Nixon. Vesco, of course, always hinted that he was a Nixon insider. But a team of seven lawyers, five U.S. attorneys, and two Bahamians worked eighteen hours a day preparing the case. Paul J. Curran, who headed the American team, was convinced the United States would win because a crime was a crime regardless of what label you put on it. Patrick Toothe, one of the Bahamian lawyers, doubted that from the start, although Vesco had antagonized people by calling them stupid and that, Toothe thought, might work against him in court. In a broader, almost subliminal sense, and in somewhat the same way that the SEC had attempted to broaden its jurisdiction in the Vesco case, being tested was whether laws by and for Americans should apply in jurisdictions that didn't have such legislation. In other words, as it had been in Costa Rica, a domestic issue was national sovereignty.

On November 13, two weeks of arguments began in Court Number 1, a two-story white building with the courtroom on the second floor. Although the hearing wasn't expected to start until 2:30 P.M., the press began to assemble at one. Vesco had been expected to walk up the Garden of Remembrance, but a shout from a spectator alerted TV camera crews, photographers, and reporters who scrambled to Shirley Street, on the other side of the small building, and Vesco, flanked by two lawyers, was mobbed by the press. A photographer asked him to smile and the bad man obliged. In a jacket whose sleeves were too long, New Jersey Bob looked healthy and confident although only a few weeks before, in Costa Rica, he'd again undergone surgery for a blocked urethra, and would take a break from the proceedings, which he was required to attend, to have stitches removed.

The outlaw's stubborn defiance of the U.S. government had made him a celebrity and the tiny courtroom was filled. The major American networks were there, as was the international and Bahamian press. There wasn't room for all of them much less the fifty spectators crowded on an upstairs balcony, hoping for a seat inside, and another hundred waiting outside. The courtroom had been locked to keep them from entering.

So many lawyers wanted to attend that, in their packed sections, faces changed every day. Vesco's team consisted of no fewer than eleven attorneys, including two Britons who were flown in, one being Sir Elwyn Jones, former attorney general of the United Kingdom, who would become Lord Chancellor in Harold Wilson's government. Some IOS entity, of course, picked up the legal tab as always. Also at the Vesco table were two prominent black Bahamian lawyers, Orville Turnquest and Sir Étienne DuPuch, considered the sharpest trial lawyer in Nassau. The U.S. table was next to them. In front sat an American stenotypist, brought by the Department of Justice, but the official records would be those of the magistrate, Emmanuel Osadebay, written by hand. The room was hot and only Vesco, it seemed, didn't sweat.

The Americans essentially brought three charges: the misappropriated millions, moved by telexed orders and consisting therefore of wire fraud; the Nixon campaign contribution; and $50,000 transferred by wire from ICC's Bank of America account to a Buhl account in Geneva. It began as a helpful payment to a business Henry tried to start in Geneva—the first payment of a total of $143,000 for Buhl's wife, to whom, long before, he'd given his shares, paying a gift tax to the IRS. He had a contract for his 300,000 shares, at 41 cents a share (Vesco gave higher rates to those on the IOS board who had supported him); and he demanded that Vesco come through.

At Court Number 1, press battles accompanied the legal ones. Vesco, obliged to run the journalists' gauntlet to enter or leave the courtroom, resorted to strategy. At 2:20 one day, two large limousines pulled up outside the courthouse just as they had the day before when Vesco and his lawyers arrived, but Vesco, using the lawyers as a decoy, went into the building through a library on the ground floor. That afternoon at five, the newsmen, with the building surrounded, kept their eyes on the library door, and when it opened and closed a few times the camera people ran to it while Vesco walked rapidly out the front and into a waiting car. With cries of frustration, the newsfolk ran after the prize.

On November 19, Vesco called Pat in Costa Rica to wish her a happy birthday. He chuckled about the fray with the press—not even in Costa Rica had Vesco received so much attention and he reveled in it. He said he was sorry to miss her birthday party—he had his feeble Bahamian public relations firm, Polaris, announce that—but told her that on the legal front all went well, with DuPuch easily outclassing the U.S. lawyers. "What?" Pat kept saying, not entirely, perhaps, because the connection was poor. "What will the future bring?" she wanted to say, in some such words, because, as both knew, if Vesco lost, and lost on appeals, both outcomes possible, Bob would be hustled aboard an airplane and taken to Miami, where U.S. marshals would be waiting eagerly.

Henry Buhl had given, by error he said, misleading testimony to the SEC on the place that he and Vesco had met to discuss Buhl's stock. It was not Geneva, as Buhl had stated in his deposition, but Nassau. Reminded by Vesco by long-distance phone, Buhl changed his story to the SEC. Apparently that had not been communicated to the U.S. legal team and caused it considerable embarrassment. The defense sensed victory when Judge Osadebay ruled that important parts of Laurence Richardson's deposition were inadmissible. DuPuch told the court, with Bahamian rhetorical flourish, shouting and waving his arms, "I would like to say that in my more than a quarter of a century of practice, this is only the third time that the case of the prosecution has been so pitifully and woefully, abysmally without virtue that I [had] the audacity to submit no case to answer. I will not criticize my learned friends, because they have made a valiant effort to breathe life into a case that was stillborn at birth. I can understand now why there are complaints that American prisons are overcrowded, because if a charge like this could bring convictions in any democratic country in the world, then I will come to the conclusion that half the people in American prisons should not be there and indeed would not be there if they had the succor and solace of the blind goddess of justice." The Americans, in short, didn't have a case. Judge Osadebay looked grave.

On December 6, he threw out the case, the main ground being that the prosecution had failed to prove that there were, in the Bahamas, offenses "substantially similar" to the ones in the U.S. law. Wire or mail fraud, for instance, had to cross U.S. state lines and the Bahamas had no such lines. Mail fraud, for that matter, wasn't a crime in the Bahamas and buildings were covered with plaques with the names of companies engaged in activities by mail the United States would have considered fraudulent. In 1984, the British House of Lords decided it didn't matter what the name of a crime was, only the substance of it, and that, in essence, had been the American argument.

The fugitive was free, though displaying secretive traits not so visible before. Wanting to use Stanley Graze's house for a meeting, Vesco obsessively checked the exits. He had a "safe" apartment on the island of New Providence to which he and others of the Seven Samurai had keys. He had money stashed there as well as on the 707, a boat or two, and a truck. He and Norman had something like ten wallets with $5,000 in each. Vesco's life had become dominated by the potential need for a hasty escape. After the trial he always had a briefcase nearby with $100,000 in it—for bail.

28

NASTY EPISODES

In 1971 Vesco pledged to Allan Butler that as a reward for Allan's risks in financing the IOS takeover and the Linkink loan, Butlers Bank would be the center of IOS banking operations. Vesco reneged on the promise because, in Butler's view, he was psychologically unable to relinquish control. For his part, Vesco didn't believe Allan was a strong enough banker to weather the fiscal fury that lay ahead if the reorganization of IOS proceeded, as Vesco was stubbornly determined that it would. For Allan, Vesco's problems with his own company, International Controls, financially shaky, were responsible for Vesco's need for IOS.

Butlers Bank Trust Company founded Bahamas Commonwealth Bank on October 6, 1971, on the instructions of IOS (Vesco). It was to be the lead IOS financial institution and the international banking arm of ABC. It was capitalized at $4 million from Overseas Development Bank (Geneva). BCB's stock was "contributed" to International Bancorp, which gave shares in return, and the result was Vesco's usual chain of command—BCB controlled by IBL controlled by ICC controlled by RLV. Butlers Bank won BCB the right to trade international currencies, vital to LeBlanc for moving money around.

A fully licensed commercial bank with the best banking facilities in Nassau, BCB had spacious quarters in the elegant Charlotte House built by the Butlers. The bank had four or five tellers and a reputation for being a soft touch. Other banks, if they didn't want particular loan customers, would shunt them to BCB, where the pickings were easier. BCB tried to be friendly in order to promote good relations in the Bahamas. The bank's generosity was extensive, if not ruinous.

Outright bribes may or may not have existed, though the receivers listed several missing millions as extortion overhead, without any hard proof. Vesco showed a visitor a yacht belonging to a Bahamian and said, "Where do you think that came from?" But that may have been another example of Bob's convoluted way of showing off. "Favors," though, as Norman called them, were indeed given for political reasons.

According to a local paper, "Even bank officials concede that [BCB] loans show a definite trend toward people closely allied with the ruling Progressive Liberal Party of Lynden Pindling." (The Bahamian Commission of Inquiry said in 1984 that between 1977 and 1983 Pindling received an unexplained $3.5 million more than he was paid in salary.) BCB had promised the Bahamian government to keep Butlers afloat—too many Bahamian banks were failing—and paid $1.8 million for various of the bank's assets. Among them was a $110,000 mortgage for an office building owned by Prime Minister Pindling. Butlers Bank had tried to collect interest and principal but failed and didn't foreclose, though it earned the wrath of Pindling's wife, who accused the Butlers of "hounding" her husband. BCB bought the building for $400,000 to provide Pindling cash for a new home. (Vesco later claimed he was the real owner and held the office building in trust for the Prime Minister, but probably that was not true.) BCB loaned $500,000 to Paradise Bakeries owned by "Ping" Pindling's relatives. It lent three million or so to a pal of Ping's, Garrett "Tiger" Finlayson and his Bahamas Catering, though the money was repaid, with interest. Probably the largest BCB investment went to Pindling's flashy friend Everett E. Bannister, the "Big Cigar" (accused a dozen years later of being Resorts International's Bahamian bagman) for the soon-defunct Bahamas World Airways.

BWA was a financial disaster and, in the opinion of some, was never meant to make money but to be the source of it. A private Learjet was leased in BWA's name for Pindling's use. With two full-time pilots, it may have cost $2 million. Salaries and expense accounts for BWA executives were exorbitant. Despite foreign airlines' rental of its two 707s, it lost almost $11 million. Finlayson, a former tailor whose rags-to-riches career was the envy of black Bahamians, had swapped 25 percent of Bahamas Catering with Bannister for 25 percent of BWA. He was so appalled by the way the airline was run that he returned his stock, he said. LeBlanc said he hadn't intended to pour so much in but Vesco insisted because, he claimed, Bahamian pride was involved; but Bahamian pride meant nothing to IOS investors. It meant much more to Vesco with his secret terror and desire to find an asylum. That Vesco received kickbacks as the price of arranging loans, such as BWA's from BCB, seems likely. Such transactions would help account for the fugitive's always abundant cash.

LeBlanc had become Vesco's psychological accomplice because he still admired Bob, he said. Resigning as IOS financial vice president to run BCB, he occupied a narrow, ground-floor, windowless office guarded by a TV camera. Global rented it from the bank. Norman wore so many hats he sometimes didn't know which one he had on, and his identity problems were compounded by alcoholism. It wasn't unusual for blond, short-nosed, then-pudgy Norman to start pouring gin in his glass at 10 A.M., be zonked by 11, and nearly comatose by noon. The Burble's sodden judgment could be faulty, and his stress level was high—he blamed his drinking on it; previously, he had mostly consumed wine—after he believed he could be jailed. He felt compelled to dispose of money quickly before the SEC and, later, the receivers could wrestle it away, and formed Panamanian dummy corporations into which he stuffed assets. "I have some forty shell companies that I keep putting on top of one another to keep people from finding out what's going on. Of course, they are only good for so long, then I put another on top," said LeBlanc.

The boys lived high—salaries were in the $60,000–$75,000 range, tax free, plus perks that included rents, and they had company planes and yachts to use. LeBlanc financed small businesses for Clay, Straub, and Strickler, loans he wrote off in return for the punishment they (and he) were being subjected to, though Clay claimed he repaid his. Money was passed around with no particular heed for formal bookkeeping. When some $3 million arrived for the Commonwealth United securities, Norman blithely dumped it into Trident (Curaçao) for "expenses."

In his desk, LeBlanc kept stationery, blank but signed by him at various levels of the page so that he could dictate letters from afar. From a Global Holdings account, "[transfer] $94,000 to the personal account of Robert L. Vesco with your goodselves." To Ulrich Strickler $18,000 from Trident, $10,000 for Bob and Pat from BCB. "Kindly let me have $25,000 in $100 dollar bills" charged to the Trident account. "Commencing February 1 [1974], please transfer $8,000 a month from our current account with you to the current account of Mr. R. L. Vesco with you. This standing order is to remain in effect until cancelled or changed by us in writing." In June of that year, Norman wanted a measly $1,000 from Trident transferred to his own account but Trident was overdrawn.

During this period, scams may have occurred. That they may have come after the SEC complaint was not necessarily significant —they might have happened anyway, if they did—but the outright thefts, if they existed, imitated the accusation, just as art imitates life. But the SEC was no longer the only opponent to anger Vesco and LeBlanc. They had to confront the "little" accountant receivers, as Vesco would have called them. Over $200 million had passed through BCB, and, after the SEC complaint, frantic efforts were made to retrieve it and prevent Vesco from capturing more. (Had this been chess, at which Vesco was expert, money might have been compared to territory.) The Luxembourg authorities forced the return of $152 million, and Frank Beatty, once Vesco's loyal ally and who ran Global Natural Resources (the old King Arctic oil properties, plus other assets) because of Bob, quietly removed Global securities from BCB to prevent Vesco from claiming $50 million in a London bank (this same $50 million also belonged to Property Resources). He no longer trusted his increasingly reckless former boss. At the Bank of Montreal lay $106 million Norman had deposited there. The receivers got a court order freezing it, but the money remained on ice, since it was in BCB's name. LeBlanc had begun to crumble. He agreed to release the funds if one of his many companies was paid a $690,000 "management fee" which smacked of a bribe. The receivers refused, partly because they feared the wrath of Stanley Sporkin if they traded with the enemy, which might have been cheaper.

In the summer of 1974, after the Bahamians put BCB out of business, LeBlanc and Vesco fought back, and long and costly litigation followed. The receivers appointed for BCB were themselves inundated with damage claims from other court-appointed receivers. The only substantial asset they had was $25 million from Bank of Montreal, the result of a bargain among receivers to free the rest of the money there. Most of the $25 million eventually went to various dollar funds, but the wars of liquidation had commenced.

Vesco and LeBlanc (the other criminal defendants—Meissner, Graze, Straub, Clay, and Strickler—were out of the action) still claimed to be the rightful heirs of the IOS fortune. They said they had stolen nothing, and that they should distribute the money without the high costs of outside liquidation. The trouble was that because of the SEC and Vesco-LeBlanc's tactics, nobody would have trusted them with coins for the March of Dimes.

In the spring of 1972, Allan Butler reached the end of his high-flying trajectory. After two years of effort and expenses of several million, the deal that would have secured his financial independence from his wife and put him on monetary Mount Olympus in his own right—the takeover of a Canadian conglomerate, Seaways-Multicorporation, collapsed. Vesco had been prepared to inject $2 million from a dollar fund, and he phoned Allan in Toronto, but Butler didn't return the call. Having had enough of Bob's "kaleidoscopic vision" and "bullheadedness," he let the deal fall through rather than be involved with Vesco, whose unpaid $4 million on the Linkink loan was the hole that Butlers Bank couldn't fill.

The Butlers decided to sell rather than hang on, and, oddly, the only place they could turn to, because their association with him had hurt their name, was Vesco. "Bob had given Allan herpes," remarked a Butler associate, "and he couldn't make love with anyone else." Butler was seriously ill with pneumonia for the second time in six months—his efforts to save the business had exhausted him—but with Shirley and their attorney, Harvey Dale, a professor of law at New York University, flew from Nassau to visit the tycoon at Fairfield. Dale said to Vesco, "Don't you think you have an obligation to help? Allan wants to sell but he needs assurances the staff will be kept on. He's turning over ten years of work." Vesco replied, "I'm under investigation by the SEC so I can't do anything, but Norman will." The meeting took half an hour. Butler knew that Vesco knew the only way he could get rid of the Linkink loan was to buy Butlers Bank, which held it.

Dale's estimation of Vesco was far from high. He found him an odd combination of arrogance, low self-esteem, and predator from the steppes. "There are wolves in the civilized world, you know," he told Allan. "You don't recognize them because they hide their true nature, but they exist, believe me." Dale thought he spotted the wolf in Vesco's delight at buying out Shirley Butler, daughter of a *knight*—the title impressed Vesco no end. Dale said, "Normally, Vesco was extremely self-controlled. You couldn't see inside him. But in the instant Vesco decided to take over the Butlers, the wolf came out, jaws practically clicking." Still, Dale gave the wolf credit for a little humor, as few did. He and Dale happened to be on the same commercial flight back to the Bahamas, and Dale, reading *Do You Sincerely Want to Be Rich?*, an exposé of IOS under Cornfeld, asked Bob to autograph it. Vesco wrote, "Wait until you see the next one, Robert L. Vesco." Dale chuckled, but wondered if Vesco meant another IOS exposé, this time about himself.

To Butler, the professor had a colorful imagination. Fairborn (for the LeBlancs' baby, just born and fair) closed in August 1972, over the objections of Dale, who didn't like Vesco's deal—nothing would be in it for the Butlers, he warned. The Butlers' holding company, Lewis-Oakes Ltd., had sixty-odd pieces, and, there being no accurate way to evaluate them, Allan said he would settle for $3 million, which represented Shirley's investment, to be paid off over a three-year period. One requirement, in addition to Butlers ceasing to be a bank, was that the name Butlers Bank be changed, and Norman came up with W.H.O. Holdings, which seemed to the receivers to stand for something like "Who Owns

This?" but Norman claimed he took the initials from Nassau street names.

Fairborn had troubles from the start. LeBlanc wanted Security Capital, in which he, through the Butlers acquisition, had a controlling interest, to buy the $50 million Canadian IOS funds, but, after the SEC complaint, the Canadian government turned him down. Wearing another hat, he tried, he said, to sell the funds, but he was blocked there, too. He discovered, or so he justified himself, that assets of Lewis-Oakes had questionable value, and didn't make his first payment on purpose, although under threats by Shirley Butler he came through with $300,000, but nothing more. LeBlanc seemed to be running out of available money and Dale's warning had taken on the ring of truth.

On February 19, 1973, the Butlers and Dale went to Vesco's guarded home on Brace Ridge Road to ask about the money owed to Shirley, the principal shareholder of what had been Lewis-Oakes. Vesco and LeBlanc were by the swimming pool. "I asked Mr. LeBlanc who held the shares of Fairborn Corporation, and he replied to the effect that he was not sure, but that directly or indirectly he owned the same personally," Shirley said. LeBlanc remarked the shares might be in Antler, and, questioned about what Antler might be, Norman claimed it was one of his forty or fifty shell companies. LeBlanc said something about refinancing the deal and Vesco said, "That's all we can do." Vesco was hard to serve a summons on because of his guards. In one instance, a summons wrapped around a rock was thrown at him. But Dale handed him one (pointedly, not LeBlanc, whom Dale regarded as a stooge) and Vesco was outraged, calling Allan a traitor, and giving him twenty-four hours to change his mind. Butler wouldn't, and Dale put an injunction on the doorhandle of the Sabrejet, notifying the control tower that the aircraft mustn't leave the ground. Within twenty-four hours, it was "planenapped" to Costa Rica.

For Butler, Vesco and LeBlanc's handling of the Lewis-Oakes properties amounted to "criminal mismanagement." He stopped short of "theft." Millions on millions were squandered as when, inexplicably, mortgage payments on the $9 million Charlotte House weren't made and the building was forfeited, or when

LeBlanc sold a 40 percent interest in the Nassau *Guardian,* also worth millions, Butler said, to the employees for $140,000. Partly because of the cancellation of international bank lines for W.H.O. and the withdrawal of deposits from the bank after the sale, a hole of over $30 million (the figure included the ill-fated Linkink loan) appeared. LeBlanc filled it with $37 million from Inter-American but it vanished, too, although LeBlanc claimed that $17 million remained when BCB was put in liquidation. By 1986, the W.H.O. receiver, lost perhaps in the labyrinth, had still not filed a complete report. The enormous loss could be accounted for possibly by overvalued assets, incredible ineptitude, and/or malfeasance.

LeBlanc, the pyramid artist, who to Butler seemed out of touch with reality, made matters even more obscure when, in fear and truculence, he buried W.H.O.'s shares of Security Capital which Allan Butler had given up in the Fairborn deal, in a Panamanian entity, Moropán, early in 1974. He ordered Security Capital to hold a stockholder's meeting so that he, who held the control shares, could oust the management in favor of himself. The management refused, claiming Moropán wasn't the rightful owner of the shares. Norman had outfoxed himself.

Later, in Panama, still drinking heavily, diabetic LeBlanc had a ruptured pancreas, and, for over a minute, his blood pressure dropped to zero. In the hospital for over two months, he meditated with something like clairvoyance, he felt. "Hell," he told himself, "I'm thirty-eight years old. I'm ill. My marriage is on the rocks. I've made no dough. Fuck it. I'm not going back to the Bahamas," where, in any case, BCB had been closed down. He phoned his parents in Toronto and told them he would pursue a new, de-Vescoized career, not that he did entirely.

The Butler assets were returned by a Bahamian court and the couple placed W.H.O. in liquidation. Vesco returned the Security Capital shares from Moropán to the Butlers because he wanted to be able to go back to the Bahamas, and, in 1981, the combined Butler assets were sold for $4.6 million. That year the Butlers broke up, partly because of the strain of the Vesco period, and a nasty divorce followed, though Shirley wanted to reconcile. She refused an offer to drive her home from Lyford Cay. She had put away, according to the club's bartender, Allan Butler said, three or four vodka martinis, wine at dinner, brandy after dinner, then champagne, then more brandy. Someone insisted on following, and, seeing that she had left her purse on top of the car, blinked his lights, a signal she may have interpreted as a suggestion to speed up, though Shirley always drove fast. The car rammed into a telephone pole with such force that her shoes remained inside when she went through the windshield. Shirley remained in a coma until she died in August 1986.

29

BOAT AND AIRPLANE WARS

No letup appeared in the Vesco saga. Event piled on event like scenes in the theater of the absurd. Plot twists were always unexpected, the writer was never at a loss for new material, and the outcome was continually in doubt.

In the midst, and maybe under the cover, of the San José student demonstrations over Vesco in April 1974, Allan Butler's former Sabrejet was snatched at Santamaría Airport, almost hitting two incoming passenger jets as it took off. The pilot, to whom Harvey Dale paid $10,000, claimed he was shot at. Vesco, or LeBlanc, filed suit in the United States, losing, and the outfit that repossessed the plane auctioned it at a remote field in Delaware. With no other bidders, the repossessor bought the aircraft itself for $100,000. Butler sued and was awarded $450,000. For him, it was all in a day's work by then.

Perhaps the Sabrejet was symbolic of the decline of the fugitive's fortunes, because, two months later, sic transit gloria, the 707, Vesco's favorite toy, met the same fate. He had fled the United States in early 1973 while the *Silver Phyllis* was at Qualitron, at Brownsville, Texas, for the final stage of the modification, but Qualitron wouldn't release the craft until paid. Frank Beatty authorized a check for $190,000, but, instead of returning to New Jersey, the plane was flown on Vesco's orders to the Bahamas by Alwyn Eisenhauer. Among his last missions for Vesco was to find an out-of-the-way island to hide the 707 on.

Under its new, court-appointed board, ICC decided to repossess the plane, which had been the source of great contention within the company. David Butowsky, the ICC special counsel appointed by the SEC to retrieve ICC assets, phoned Howard Singer, who had been ICC's general counsel, and Singer enlisted Eisenhauer. Placing dozens of calls, Ike located the plane at Tocumen International Airport at Panama City. Singer couldn't raise enough for the trip, but Eisenhauer was delighted at the chance to show up his former boss. With two other pilots, he descended on hapless Panama.

The 707 had been there almost a month, having been flown in by a Bahamas World Airways crew, landing without permission, and had been impounded for violating Panama's airspace. Eisenhauer, with prior approval from a U.S. judge to seize the plane, since payments hadn't been made, wrote a letter certifying that the 707 was the property of an ICC subsidiary and, becoming friends with a Panamanian aviation official, paid a fine of only $2,500. He tipped the Panamanian guard watching the plane to vanish for the day. While the *Silver Phyllis* was being fueled (for $10,000, out of Ike's pocket) a Learjet that Vesco rented landed with Alberto Álvarez, former president of Inter-American, on board. Álvarez didn't notice the trucks crowded about the Boeing, perhaps because Vesco had changed the tail identification to N99WT and removed the ICC logo. In the middle of the night, Ike took off. The plane landed at Fort Lauderdale, Florida, where Singer had arranged to put a lien on it, and then flew to Newark, where gear was removed so that Vesco couldn't snatch it back. Ike was paid $65,000 for his feat plus expenses of $30,000.

The Panamanian government threatened to cause an international incident and extradite Eisenhauer. Singer coolly told the Panamanian Ambassador to the United Nations that if Panama made a flap it could be certain that unpleasant news stories about Vesco's involvement with Panamanian politicians would appear. Panama said no more.

Vesco heard of the aerial abduction by telephone and pounded the walls of his Costa Rican house. He tried to repurchase the aircraft, but, in New York, Judge Stewart forbade a sale to him. According to Donald Nixon, Vesco had lengthy discussions on re-hijacking the plane from New Jersey. "Wild and crazy plans," reported the President's nephew, "such as putting jets on the lower landing gear for thrust and having another jet pull it up and tow it, with a massive line, so that it would act as a glider." Don-Don was known, like Vesco, to exaggerate.

Pan Am, which held the mortgage, advertised the 707 for $650,000 "as is," although warning that several hundred thousand more would be required to obtain FAA certification. The Rolling Stones' Mick Jagger was interested, as were the government of Venezuela and Elvis Presley, who, through his father, made an offer but backed off when Vesco threatened to sue. (Butowsky sued Presley's estate, because there had been a signed contract, and won $1.1 million.) Later the plane was bought by Imelda Marcos, wife of the then President of the Philippines, and vanished into the Far East.

Vesco did better with the yacht. A transaction was arranged through Columbus Trust, a former arm of BCB, whereby a Panamanian was approached to buy a yacht called the *Romántica* with a mortgage arranged by BCB. The Panamanian company, Andean Credit, bought the vessel for $1.3 million. She was 137 feet long, 121.5 feet at the waterline, powered by two 1,000 hp diesels, and weighed 386 gross tons. One of the largest aluminum pleasure crafts, she could make about 17 knots. She, of course, was financed with other people's money for Vesco's use.

The completely automated *Romántica* sailed to Antigua from Malta, not without mechanical difficulties. One condition was that the seller change the name, and gilt was procured for the new one, the *Patricia III; "I"* and *"II"* had been preempted by the Vescos.

The yacht, which Vesco sailed down Nassau harbor ostentatiously in 1972, was berthed at the Nassau Harbour Yacht Club, and Vesco had it refitted with a hoist that could lift two ocean-racing Cigarette speedsters, 28 feet long, to the sides, and a two-man submarine on top. At its peak strength in 1973, the Vesco Nassau armada had three or four boats, with Tony Vesco, the second-oldest son, and one of his brothers racing the Cigarettes. Tony burned out an engine and Bob complained about the bill. The *Patricia III* put into Miami for $40,000 in repairs, paid for by a check signed by Patricia J. Melzer (Pat Vesco), went to sea, and returned for additional repairs. This time the vessel was seized by U.S. Customs, which claimed that Andean owed $60,000 in duties because Vesco was an American citizen, though Vesco denied he owned the boat, and, in a strictly technical sense, he didn't.

The IRS, which had attached Vesco's U.S. holdings, wanted the yacht, and so did International Controls, which claimed she was an attempt to make Vesco's assets portable. So the vessel sat, the bare-breasted mermaid on the bow meant as a good omen for open ocean, staring at a clump of scrub pines, until in July 1975, a car flying the Panamanian flag appeared, ownership papers were shown by a Panamanian to the Pinkerton guard who phoned the police. They arrived in three police cars with shotguns. Since the U.S. Customs lien had been erased with a check from Andean, the cops did nothing and the yacht, radars whirling, roared out to sea at 6:30 P.M. with a Panamanian crew and an Australian pilot. Vesco had planned the operation from Costa Rica. (Pinkerton agreed to settle for $300,000 to the ICC special counsel.)

The *Patricia III* put in briefly in the Bahamas and Butowsky, alerted, flew down frantically, but he was too late. The yacht underwent a succession of names, the *Joya Oceana, Zodiac*—under that name she was berthed in Nassau on February 1, 1977—*Locust IV,* and was hidden in Panamanian and Venezuelan waters until LeBlanc practically forced Vesco to get rid of her in 1978 or 1979. She was finally sold in Monte Carlo for something like $600,000, which Vesco apparently received, and was used to entertain big rollers at a casino there.

Vesco had other boats at his Pacific Ocean Guanacaste, *finca,* or farm, like a 54-foot Striker aluminum yacht costing $230,000, for which he traded in a smaller Striker. Already extremely fast, and capable with additional fuel tanks of great distances, the *Joya Poco* (a name that makes no sense in Spanish and must have been invented by Vesco) was equipped with a machine gun mounted on a tripod. The captain testified to the U.S. Senate Subcommittee on Investigations that if a vessel followed them, like the Coast Guard, he was to open fire and escape. The captain, whose name was Cook, quit.

30

GOOD ADVICE IGNORED

In 1972, returning from London to Costa Rica, one of José Figueres's main executives at La Lucha, Enrique Carreras, decided to give Don Roberto a lesson in the Florentine politics of his about-to-be-adopted land. With seven hours to kill on the 707, Carreras thought he had plenty of time.

New York and British-educated "Kiki" Carreras, a large, forceful, and articulate man then in his early thirties, with eyelashes long enough to be curled, started with a little history. When Costa Rica had become independent from Spain in 1821, the country didn't have an aristocracy and rich people had been hard-working and development-minded. With the advent of large-scale coffee, banana, and cattle production in the late 1800s, an aristocracy had emerged that ceased to function for the general welfare or to display initiative, partisan-minded Carreras said. Figueres, the first President not from the half dozen or so families that had ruled Costa Rica since independence, and the son of immigrants at that, had sought to develop a left-of-center middle class, which the aristocracy resisted. Vesco could become an issue in a politically charged atmosphere fanned by the press, Carreras pointed out. The foreign investments Figueres promoted could be interpreted by the landed gentry as threatening its position. Costa Rican society, despite its emphasis on democracy and free elections—strongly supported by conservatives, too, and perhaps the country's only real distinction in Central

America—was more fragile than appeared and hard to comprehend by outsiders, said Carreras. Vesco shifted in his seat.

Kiki plunged on, speaking faster. In many ways, Costa Rica wasn't prepared for the ways of its model and essential protector, the United States. (By 1986, Costa Rica, receiving $700 million a year, was, on a per capita basis, the second largest recipient of U.S. aid, after Israel.) Without U.S. support, Costa Rica might collapse into chaos overnight. Vesco had to be careful not to upset the political balance, to handle himself and his investments with caution so as not to become the focus of a dispute between Figueres and his adversaries. Costa Rica needed Vesco's IOS money but not turmoil.

Vesco rudely interrupted to order pizza from the female flight attendant and began to explain, at length, how the perfect pizza was prepared. He baked excellent pizza indeed, Carreras would learn. When Carreras got home, he told a friend that Bob would settle in Costa Rica. The friend was delighted that a personage as powerful as Vesco had chosen their country. "You wait," Kiki said prophetically. "He'll be thrown out within five years."

After his extradition victories, Vesco felt secure enough about his Costa Rican presence to buy, from an American Del Monte executive, a $500,000 house in the exclusive Lomas de Ayarco section of San José. He subsequently purchased adjacent acreage and two small houses in the rear for an office and a guest house. (Today, the former Vesco establishment is featured in guided tours.) The place had a metal fence in front to which Vesco added, on the sides, 10-foot walls. Though North American reporters made much of the walls, they were not uncommon in San José to prevent thievery, but five advance-model TV cameras mounted in the front and back that could be trained to follow cars and pedestrians in a sinister, Big Brother fashion, were. (Almost next door was the large, also walled-in Soviet Embassy compound. It later had outside TV cameras, too, but not so visibly.) Inside the Vesco arena, where some dozen guards, in shifts, stood twenty-four-hour watch, a 35-foot radio tower was erected. It transmitted to another tower atop Irazú volcano to the east, which, because of the height, could broadcast as far as Nicaragua and Panama, each several hundred miles away. The Vesco forces had six authorized radio bands, and a foreigner claimed to have overheard on one of them, the press reported, plans for twenty radio towers and sixty transmitters around the country, which caused still another flap. Minister of Public Security Mario Charpantier investigated and said the story wasn't true. Still, Vesco, whose bodyguards hefted Motorola walkie-talkies, had intense, real or imagined, needs for security—two of his cars had submachine guns in carrying cases in their trunks—that made an inconspicuous life impossible, especially in a country where rumors flourished like tropical plants, and most of all during an election season.

No fewer than eight political parties were in contention in 1974. The favorite, a lawyer, Daniel Oduber of Figueres's National Liberation Party, took a comparatively soft view toward Vesco, but in Congress another controversy erupted. A revised extradition law known as the "Vesco law," backed by still-President Figueres, was approved over loud cries that the legislation would block the extradition of Vesco, as was Don Pepe's intention, because it offered the right of political asylum, which in any case was a generally accepted though unwritten law in Latin America. The legislation was rushed through and passed despite opposition from the majority of Figueres's own party. Students interrupted debates carrying signs that read "Vesco Law No!" and "How Much $!" A large demonstration was scheduled.

Figueres lashed out at what he called "pseudomoralists who are talking of moral standards without having the necessary credentials" while a congressman charged that the demonstrations were being organized in foreign embassies, accounting for the anti-Yanqui signs and pamphlets against the United Fruit Company. It looked as though Vesco was provoking, or being used to provoke, a major incident. Thousands of students took to the streets, mostly before TV and radio stations, for the publicity, but expanding the demonstration to include the U.S. embassy. It became violent when rocks were thrown at the National Assembly building where Congress sat. Police broke up the demonstration with tear gas.

In his most furtive periods, Vesco could be hard to reach.

(One reporter spent three months, he said, of round-the-clock calls to mystery numbers using code names, as instructed, while Vesco's security apparatchiks checked him out. He got his interview.) During the furor over the Vesco law, though, Don Roberto granted an interview, with color photographs, to the *Tico Times* at his walled-in home. The richly decorated bar looked out on a swimming pool. The large living room had a tiger-skin rug on a thick blue carpet, and pictures of African wildlife hung on the walls. Vesco protested that the demonstrations weren't really against him, despite the anti-Vesco signs, and told of how, at a bank, a pregnant woman had welcomed him to Costa Rica and started to cry. He made, for him, a major though self-serving concession, since he never admitted to responsibility, legal or otherwise, for what had gone wrong. Maybe half of what led to his present plight had been under his control, and, if he could live life over again, he wouldn't have made the contribution that caused Nixon so much trouble. He said he could adjust to being without money, since he'd been poor before, and found being a celebrity of sorts a "strain." If the Costa Rican newspapers never mentioned him again, he'd be happy. He thought that "things would calm down."

That was wishful thinking. The interview only evoked further cries for expulsion. And still another scandal brewed. President-elect Daniel Oduber, two days preceding his inauguration, May 10, 1974, met with Vesco at a private residence for a secret noon meeting that lasted an hour and twenty minutes, Vesco arriving in his Mercedes without license plates. (In Costa Rica, instead of giving parking tickets, the police removed license plates.) Oduber brought a letter he had carefully composed to Vesco, who, as both knew, though few others did, had lent Oduber at least $200,000 for his campaign. (Vesco also contributed, in lesser amounts, to the other parties. As with his other contributions, they came from a company he or LeBlanc controlled, like Inter-American.) The money had actually arrived via Figueres, who, Oduber thought, rather jealously shielded his protégé; when Oduber repaid, it was at LeBlanc's request and the money went to him. Don Roberto read the letter in the President-elect's presence, nodding now and then.

Oduber, who said he would not permit Vesco to be extradited, and believed Vesco had brought $25–$30 million of his own money to Costa Rica, displayed a contradictory attitude toward the North American. During his presidency, he said, he talked many times with the U.S. Justice Department, hoping it would follow through on the extradition, and wanted modernization of Costa Rican legislation to include contemporary crime that might include Vesco. But Vesco was a "shareholder" in Figueres's companies and "his problems become yours." (Later, Oduber and Vesco both invested in a Cessna Citation, with the financing arranged by Martí Figueres who got a cut but in the end lost, for him, a fortune.) Vesco would receive the same treatment as any other immigrant and should no longer expect special favors at the airport. Make your investments visible, Oduber warned; put your money in agriculture, cattle, and tourism so Costa Ricans could appreciate them. Don't, the President-elect specified, make media investments or employ any member of the Costa Rica government or expulsion would result. Vesco must not become a "permanent scandal." Keep your nose clean, Oduber warned sternly in so many words, and "all will return to normality. Then it can be shown whether you are telling the truth or whether those who are pursuing you are acting in bad faith," an allusion to the SEC.

About this time, Julio Suñol, a former Communist congressman who had "reformed," came out with a best-seller, *Robert Vesco Buys a Republic.* Suñol, chief of the editorial page of *La Nación* and former publisher of the defunct *El Diario de Costa Rica,* had claimed Figueres had offered him $600,000 for *El Diario* and Suñol's becoming editor of *Excelsior,* so that he'd lay off Vesco, assertions that Figueres hotly disputed. In his book, Suñol wrote, "President Figueres has merits that history shall recognize, but on the other hand, he sinfully implanted for the first time in 150 years of independence and political autonomy a cynical school of corruption and disrespect for the good traditions, and that was the price everybody paid." Despite such outbursts, Suñol lacked documentation of what, exactly, "Don Dinero," as *La Nación* called Vesco, personally owned in Costa Rica.

Unknown to Suñol, severe doubts had developed within the

Figueres inner circle about Vesco's ability to provide financing. The fugitive had begun to complain about telephone and legal bills that seemed to indicate nervousness about money. Ralph Dodd, in Costa Rica on a visit, noted that his former boss's hard-work habits had turned to comparative idleness. He still talked dreamily about projects, such as buying the *Queen Elizabeth II* and bringing it to a Central American fiefdom he proposed to form on a Panamanian island where you could launder cash and gamble. But when legitimate deals were presented Vesco always found a reason to decline. Enrique Carreras pointed to signed contracts to deliver polypropylene bags for fertilizer and to the lack of enough equipment to produce them. Vesco had pledged another million, from whatever IOS related entity, but failed to come through. Vesco was not, Kiki told them, "the goose that laid the golden egg." Yes he was, answered Don Pepe, only, "We have overestimated his capacity for laying them." (A local political joke of the time was "Do you know who made Vesco a millionaire? Don Pepe Figueres. Vesco was a multimillionaire when he came.")

Robert Hutchison's *Vesco,* which appeared in 1974, seemed to confirm that Don Dinero was insanely rich. The former IOSer left no stone unturned trying to prove that the runaway seven were the greatest thieves in the history of finance. (Vesco said that the CIA had paid for *Vesco.*) Asserting that Vesco et al. had looted IOS not of the SEC's $224 million but of $500 million, Hutchison reinforced Suñol's view that Vesco was a whale in a small pond, but what mattered to him was not so much Vesco's immorality, as the American government saw it, as that a man with a fortune on a par with Howard Hughes or the Shah of Iran might be too potent for the local economy and, being a fugitive, would give Costa Rica a bad name. Partly because of Vesco, the North American press said Costa Rica was losing its luster for American investors and retirees.

So the battle centered on the "image" Vesco gave the country and its institutions. Oduber's letter, released by him to the press, brought accusations that the new President had demeaned himself before "The Man," who hadn't even bothered to reply. A little embarrassed, Oduber responded that he didn't need an answer because he had discussed matters in person with Vesco. (A wag suggested the country's name be changed to Costa Roberto.) Oduber had weighty matters to be concerned about—poverty, a banana workers' strike, a meat surplus, and while Vesco, whom Oduber said he'd "inherited" from Don Pepe, was obviously secondary, the issue wouldn't go away. In August, Vesco was accused of hiring non-Costa Rican guards, and he responded from his sanctuary that the guards were Ticos and had been hired by a Costa Rican security company. He neglected to add that the company, Securitas, was his. And, as usual, Vesco went too far when he said that it was common to have guards in Costa Rica. That brought an immediate response from Urbina Pinto, of the right-wing Costa Rica Libre movement, that guards were *not* needed in that country. "I don't think," said Urbina, "that you are the person most indicated to show us the best path." By now, Vesco had succeeded in uniting all shades of political opinion in Costa Rica against him except for the pro-Figueres left-of-center with its international outlook, impatience with what it considered Costa Rican provincialism, and loyalty to Don Pepe, who remained on the fugitive's side.

Urbina also referred to a U.S. Customs seizure in Miami of arms for Vesco's bodyguards—another front had opened in the Vesco war. The question quickly became major as the U.S. Senate Permanent Subcommittee on Investigations, headed by Senator Henry M. Jackson, who intended to run for President and may have perceived Vesco as a potential issue, heard testimony that Vesco, along with Martí Figueres, had been involved in a negotiation to import 2,000 submachine guns into Costa Rica and to start a machine-gun factory there. To some extent it was true, though the question became entangled with U.S. Customs seizure, in San Antonio, of arms aboard a Learjet owned by a Vesco friend, Los Angeles securities dealer Thomas Richardson. These arms, in a small quantity, did appear destined for Vesco's use, and Richardson, in another bizarre twist, was supposed to have flown in one Elizabeth Adams, aka Alix Flemming, with prostitutes for New Jersey Bob, or so the Jackson subcommittee heard, not that Costa Rica was short of whores.

The machine guns were a different story. Enter another character of characters, Mitchell Livingston WerBell. A millionaire arms dealer from Georgia, inventor of a silencer, and co-designer of the Ingram miniaturized submachine gun, WerBell, in his sixties, was the founder and guiding spirit of the Abaco Independence Movement. He wanted to secede from the Bahamas on New Year's Day, 1975, and set up an independent state offering a tax refuge to investors. The plan failed, but Vesco, said the Bahamian press, was involved in training mercenaries in case the Bahamian Government tried to intervene. WerBell visited the Costa Rica potentate with a notion of making machine guns there, but Vesco, though he seemed interested, had been told by Martí Figueres that, in the present political climate, there was no hope that necessary legislation would be passed.

Public Security Minister Charpantier had said Vesco would be thrown out if he engaged in illegal arms traffic, and Vesco met with him for three hours. He had no guards, and Alberto Abreu, in charge of Vesco's security, and José María Pla, one of Vesco's lawyers, sat behind him as protection in case anyone tried to take a potshot through the window. While the talks were under way reporters leaped onto the balcony of the minister's office and burst in, snapping pictures. A reasonable deal was struck. The reporters could cover not the first but the second half of the meeting, during which Vesco, discussing the arms proposal, remarked, "This is not the kind of deal I'd finance," whereupon the journalists broke out laughing, thinking that guns were exactly the sort of deal Vesco would be in.

The documents Vesco produced satisfied Charpantier, who saw "no evil whatsoever." Most of the weapons Richardson was supposed to import were still on order. Nor was it at all unusual for men in Costa Rica to own and carry weapons—Vesco packed a pistol in his waistband, along his spine. He characterized the arms hoopla in the U.S. Senate as a "campaign to discredit me directed from the United States."

But there was no letup within Costa Rica. Democratic Renovation Party members asked Oduber to throw out "El Hombre" as an undesirable alien "harmful to the country" and to invoke the 1884 Expulsion of Foreigners Act, a motion that had been simmering for months. They called also on the judiciary for the repeal of the hurriedly passed "Vesco law" and/or to reinstate the former law. "This is open war," a Costa Rican congressman said, with a touch of glee, "and Vesco knows it." Two hundred sixteen national leaders "from all walks of life" signed a "Call to Conscience," read on national TV and radio, that referred to the "massive buying up of land, the domination of vast enterprises already established, and the absorption of communications in order to condition public opinion—which are typical forms of foreign intervention." The Vesco affair was "affecting the present national crisis." (Left unspecified, once more, was what Vesco personally owned there.) In the cold—for Costa Rica, 61.5° F.—winter rain, 5,000 people, in a line that blocked traffic, signed the manifesto. Costa Rica, diagnosed a newspaper, had "Vesco fever."

Again, Vesco used the air to defend himself. At a cost of far less than $5,000, he bought a half hour of TV and radio time, and, with newspaper ads in advance, the "Bobby Vesco" show went on December 4, 1974, the host's thirty-ninth birthday. The professional quality of the speech was accounted for when it turned out Figueres had written some of it. "Better I write his speeches than he writes mine," Don Pepe quipped, after a newspaper had apparently swiped a draft and seen Figueres's handwriting. Don Pepe also said, "Before, United Fruit always wrote the speeches of Costa Rican presidents. Now, we write the speeches for the foreign investors." With Pat Vesco seated demurely in an executive chair by her husband's desk, her little feet not quite touching the floor, smiling from time to time and gazing at her hands—it was her virgin TV appearance—Vesco, who had a new hairstyle and whose safari jacket matched his wife's simple suit, spoke in a wooden voice that gradually relaxed. "Dear Costa Rican friends: I never thought that I would find myself before a network of television and radio, addressing a whole nation," he began, simultaneously translated. He had refrained, he said, from answering the attacks against him, "endured patiently so many lies and offenses, thrown against me WITHOUT ANY PROOF . . ." The caps were in the script. ". . . a great false scandal for the purpose of justifying my expulsion, serving internal political interests . . . equivalent of delivering me to the politicians in the United States, who do not forgive me, either, because in two political campaigns I was a strong supporter of Nixon . . ."

New allegations had surfaced that Vesco had Mafia connections, and he denied them, observing they were "a sad cross only persons of Italian origin such as myself must bear through life." Elizabeth Adams, aka Flemming, having testified before the Jackson subcommittee about bringing prostitutes for Vesco to Costa Rica, had recanted, claiming she had been pressured, Vesco said, and waved an affidavit to prove it. Ms. Adams's affidavit, sworn to in a Los Angeles court and dated October 7, 1974, made the following statements: she did not know Robert Vesco, had not spoken to him in person or on the telephone or ever seen him, nor had she traveled to Costa Rica. She had never "sent, solicited, procured, pimped or pandered any women for prostitution for Mr. Vesco or any of his associates." Vesco didn't say so on the air, but the Adams affidavit went on, "I have been harassed, embarrassed and great mental pressure has been put on me by certain people unknown, which, I firmly believe, has been initiated by Bernard Cornfeld on behalf of the U.S. Government for reasons of Mr. Cornfeld's personal gain and to try to embarrass Mr. Vesco. I have been hospitalized as a result of physical attack and beating by two negro males who entered my home illegally, by force, and proceeded to do me bodily harm, after which they left with nothing taken from my home or my person from them. Their purpose was evidently not for any financial gain but only to do me physical harm." Nonetheless, whatever the truth, Ms. Adams apparently was jailed briefly and paid a fine.

Vesco went to the SEC charges.

> The mysterious $224 million is simply the SEC's inaccurate approximation of the value realized by the IOS mutual funds by liquidating the Wall Street investments. The SEC's obvious concern is that money be invested in the United States, and not in other countries which is where the money originally came from.
>
> . . there has been no looting, no loss of $224 million, but the investment decision to which the SEC objects will result [because of the timely decision to sell out of U.S. Securities] in savings of millions of dollars for fundholders.

He had made mistakes, Vesco admitted, such as misunderstanding how to phrase statements to the local people or press. Also, "we may have protected our persons and families excessively, not knowing the mutual respect and the peace under which you live." But ". . . Costa Rican people are not fully informed of the extremes which some political groups will go in pursuing me, and which represent the same forces that took care of first eliminating President Kennedy because of his internal politics . . . and President Nixon because of his external politics and independence of judgment. They . . . will dare anything. It is obvious to many how they have interfered in Costa Rica, how they finance certain groups and use certain persons to distort the whole pacific life of this country and its exemplary democracy." (This last was pure Figueres.)

Was Vesco too big for Costa Rica? How big was too big? "Do we really want economic development? Do we really wish that the savings of other countries' capital be brought here to strengthen our own? Do we really need a stronger balance of international payments? Even more fundamental, are we really anxious to bring poverty to an end?"

Vesco continued his rite of self-justification. Following Oduber's advice, he had taken himself out of sensitive investment areas like communications and transport and put himself into helping the Costa Rican government in its fiscal situation, in "projects of living and drinking water" (he had bought government bonds), in hospitals, and development. Many investments alleged to have been made by him were by companies in which he had no interest and did not direct, such as Inter-American. "True, some of the owners and managers of those companies may be acquaintances or friends of mine, but so are many financial leaders around the world."

A Vesco-like mixture of fact, fantasy, and showing off, the speech was surprisingly well received, better than the appearances of newspaper publishers who, rejecting the fugitive financier's offer to join him on the broadcast, took time of their own to respond a few nights later. The *Tico Times,* by no means a Vesco supporter, described him as having "poise, dignity, humility and a cool *simpatismo.*" Its critic, an American, finally realized what the broadcast reminded him of, the famous Nixon "Checkers" speech, in the 1950s, only without the cocker spaniel. Vesco had tried to embrace the spectrum of Costa Rican opinion and even touched the sore spot of exploitation by big American companies, in making himself Costa Rican, too. "We? Our country?" the critic wondered. "There was something funny there. An appeal. I am not a rich gringo. I am one of you. I've only been here two years and I can't speak Spanish. But I am you."

Vesco was promptly accused of meddling in Costa Rica's internal affairs, but the man on the street, in various interviews, didn't generally seem to think so. A farmer said, "If he's guilty, then let's throw him out. If he's innocent, then let him stay." "Yes, let's get rid of him." "We have to expel him." "I personally don't think he's doing anything illegal here." "Aren't you afraid to stand here and answer questions?" asked one bystander. "He's a very powerful man and has a lot of people around the city. They could be watching you now. I'd be careful if I were you." Relieved by "Seeing him in person, defending himself, and not relying on hired hands to do it. I think he's a good person and I believe everything he said. I had my doubts before, but you could see in his eyes that he wasn't lying . . ." "He's put a lot of money into the country and he's stimulating the economy." "Many students here lack information and they act impulsively. It's mostly older people that are obsessed with throwing him out, and they get the students fired up." "I think he told the absolute truth. I didn't want him to stay before, but now I'm convinced he's helping the country."

Thus ended, for Vesco, a trying year, but not without promise of achieving the main goal, to stay in Costa Rica. One reason was medical—periodically, his doctor, Jaime Gutiérrez, would "Roto-Rooter," as Vesco put it, his penis to remove the chronic blockage.

31

THE VESCOS AT HOME IN COSTA RICA

Settling in behind the walls of the Lomas de Ayarco compound, Mr. and Mrs. Fugitive Financier—the "Famous Fuge" the family called him—tried to have as normal a life as possible, as plain folks will. The big house could accommodate live-in servants, and they had three of them—a cook, an assistant cook, and a maid, plus a gardener, a handyman who came during the day, and a maid for the office. Pat cooked breakfast—you couldn't expect the Costa Ricans to fix American-style pancakes—and the children went to school except for Daniel, who was in college in New Jersey. Tony, in his teens, went to Country Day; Dawn, also a teenager, attended St. Claire, a Catholic girls' school; and Bobby Jr., Country Day, to which, because of his coordination problems, Vesco contributed special equipment as he had to the school in Mountain Lake in New Jersey. (A newspaper claimed Vesco bought Country Day, but the staff denied it.) Except for the guards, who took the younger kids to school and picked them up, or that Pat's armed chauffeur drove her to the supermarket, it was, on the surface, pretty much the way rich people lived in the tropics, where help was cheap.

Bob rose early—before 6 A.M., and since he was often on the telephone half the night, Pat complained he didn't sleep enough—and jumped in the heated pool. He joined the family for breakfast and, at seven-thirty or eight, wandered down, past the tennis courts he rarely used, to the offices at the rear of the property.

Already there was his secretary, María Ermida Ulate, daughter of former President Otilio Ulate. María Ermida worked fourteen-hour days and not because she was forced. She loved the Vescos and especially Bob. For María Ermida, except for her father and second husband, "Mr. Vesco was the most wonderful person in the world. People weren't fair to him."

Vesco's workday began with coffee and verbal translations by Ulate of articles about him in the newspapers, mostly unflattering, but Vesco remained impassive. He was, generally, both secretive and emotionless, on the surface, but Ulate felt sure Vesco was hurt by the newspaper accounts and maybe responded with headaches. He kept a bottle of aspirin on his desk and she watched it decline. It was her idea that Vesco meet the publishers of the leading newspapers. The elegant Rodrigo Madrigal of *La República*—to become Foreign Minister—wouldn't see him, but *La Nación*'s Guido Fernández—to become Secretary of the Interior—said, "I thought you were a devil," not that it did any good editorially for Don Dinero.

News of Vesco's whereabouts in San José had been printed, of course, and, if a pilgrim to the holy shrine required further directions, he or she had only to guide themselves by the radio tower. The line in front of the office would start to form before 8 A.M., and, in a short time, twenty-five or so Costa Ricans stood there. (If it rained, good-hearted María Ermida would bring them inside.) These people, too, were reacting to Vesco's bruited wealth. A woman with a child in her arms might want milk and Ulate would fetch it from the fridge. They might need clothes, and Pat Vesco, who always seemed to have old garments around, would be summoned from the main house if she wasn't on hand already. If small amounts of money were asked for, Ulate might give some, reimbursing herself from petty cash. Few if any of the more simple requests were turned down in the four years of charity at Lomas de Ayarco. In more complicated cases, María Ermida requested notes that, translated, went to Vesco. He rarely gave cash, and then in amounts of no more than $1,000, although he did fly a man to the States for a cancer operation.

Letters seeking assistance also poured in, as many as a thousand a month, claimed Ulate—two rooms with file cabinets stored them. Out of such requests might come uniforms for church or orphanage soccer teams. (Balls and trophies were on hand at the office and freely passed out.) The town of Matapalo, not far from Vesco's *finca* in the province of Guanacaste, was a special recipient of Vesco favors. He bought paint for the houses which, several months later, were all spruced up, and carried in tomato seeds, teaching the inhabitants how to plant them. The press seemed ignorant of such benefactions, but in 1976 or 1977, when Vesco was named honorary citizen of the town of Santa Cruz, it was reported, to everyone's surprise, that the Vescos had given a substantial sum to provide the school with desks, chairs, uniforms, and so on. "This may be contrary to the prefabricated image of Mr. Vesco, but that's how it is," his spokesman said. Vesco hadn't sought publicity "because whenever we disclose something like this, we end up by having national dignity invoked against us. It's a personal thing with the Vesco family, that's all." Some of Vesco's civic contributions coincided with the political campaign against him, as if to soften the attack.

Vesco had earned $2.5 million in transactions while at ICC, and, he told Meissner, truthfully or not, another $5 million in a deal. The interest alone on such amounts would have been plenty to make him wealthy, especially in Latin America, but the fugitive typically didn't put money in safe investments—he didn't have a bank account in his own name, not surprisingly—and went through large sums, whether his own, IOS's, or both. Pat would visit relatives and a health clinic in California once a year. Fearful she'd be kidnapped, her husband provided a private jet. He bought her two emeralds in Argentina for $85,000. The couple had the latest in electronic gadgetry. They flew in loads of toys for Costa Rican children. A round trip on a small, rented jet to Miami, with waiting time, cost $5,000, and flights happened frequently. (For a wedding present, Vesco gave Enrique Carreras a round trip to New York in a private jet, plus a weekend in a penthouse at the Pierre.) Black Angus steaks, crab, mozzarella cheese, and, above all, pepperoni sausage were flown in, and, once, when the kids wanted Bazooka bubble gum, which made larger bubbles, Vesco airlifted some from Florida. The boxes said "Bazooka" and Costa Rica customs went berserk.

Vesco's secrecy about money was virtually complete, but he did complain it cost him $500,000 a year to live during the Costa Rica years. He paid off journalists to soften them up, it was said, and gave large "tips" to low-level government officials, including customs. He made loans to prominent merchants and agriculturalists to curry favor, and purchased from an important Costa Rica politician cattle that arrived more dead than alive. From this same politician's wife, the Vescos paid handsomely for jewelry that turned out to be junk. Though in no position to object, Vesco was bitter in private. Pat bore it all stoically, and not without humor. At a social function, she overheard someone remark about her husband, "He's the man who stole one hundred million dollars." "Excuse me," she said, "it was more than two hundred million." Before, Pat had been modest about money but she had changed. She said, "I'm one of the richest women in the world and I can do what I want." That may have been bravado.

Vesco's security system, including a full-time, $1,000-a-month American radio operator, cost about $100,000 a year. His phone bills were prodigious. Until 1974, when Bahamas Commonwealth Bank was placed in receivership, IOS-related companies paid Vesco's legal bills, but after that he was on his own, according to LeBlanc. Litigation against the fugitive was continuous, as were his efforts to avoid extradition. He spent at least $4,000 a month on Costa Rican lawyers and a one-shot fee of $80,000 for a comparatively simple service. There were probably steep bills, paid or unpaid, from Edward Bennett Williams's office in Washington, one of whose members came to San José to meet with Vesco.

Don Dinero must have dipped into somebody's capital for the $500,000 house. He also bought a $200,000 dairy farm at which he spent a few weekends and which he ultimately traded for a Florida house in which Dawn Vesco lived. (Vesco claimed he owned Florida properties in Panama City, Homestead, and Miami —apartments, then.) He put some $850,000, according to José Figueres, into Costa Rica water bonds but disappointed the authority by selling them because he needed the money, he told Don Pepe. These, plus the *finca,* appeared to have been Vesco's only substantial personal investments in Costa Rica.

In the fall of 1974, Vesco—for security, he was always listed in the passenger manifest as "Mr. Lee"—made eighteen trips to Guanacaste, in a Navajo aircraft he bought but someone fronted for, to supervise the renovation of the *finca,* purchased earlier in the year, which faced on the Pacific Ocean. Owned in Pat's name, though Vesco said he wanted to be buried there, the magnificent 1,000-some-acre property received extensive improvements. Vesco built a six-bedroom, two-section house with two swimming pools, but it was hardly lavish. More costly were paved roads, reforestation (250,000 teak seedlings were planted, worth millions when grown), a lake stocked with fish, and the paving of a dirt runway, which Vesco enlarged to 4,000 feet to accommodate small jets. Don Pepe referred to the place as a "runway with a farm." Vesco put, all told, more than a million dollars into the Guanacaste *finca,* employing more than a hundred people. As usual there were payoffs of one kind or another. The Figueres company lent Vesco two tractors in hopes he would follow through on his promise to bail out *Excelsior.* He didn't. In the same spirit, the Figueres group paid Vesco's Costa Rican attorney's fees of $5,000 to $10,000 per month for a time.

At the ranch by the sea the security mania remained. When Vesco paid a call, he arrived in the usual procession, a Jeep with men carrying machine guns in front, the Mercedes, another Jeep, with more machine guns in the rear. In his house, the basement had a spiral staircase lined with steel bars that could be locked at the top. A metal door below led to the yard. Inside was a strange collection of gadgetry—four old-fashioned teleprinters, expensive radio equipment, several phones with scrambling and recording equipment (none hooked up), and a number of fine bowling balls. Vesco planned to build a "Great Gatsby" home on the property, which may have included a bowling alley.

At Guanacaste, Vesco's squadrons were soon fleshed out. The air wing consisted of two small C-10s, an Aerocommander, and the Cessna Citation he and Oduber were partners in. Vesco had some idea of forming a transportation company and may have put $1 million into it. The sea-going wing consisted of three Cigarette boats brought from the Bahamas, the Strickler yacht, and the *Patricia III,* which must have made it through the Panama Canal.

One cost the Vescos avoided was entertainment. Bob and Pat had few guests at the *finca* and it was the same in San José. Pat did have some Costa Rican friends, but Bob was detached from Costa Rican society. The couple applied for membership in the Union Club, which turned them down, perhaps because they weren't children of members, but so did the exclusive Costa Rican Country Club, despite the loans Vesco had made to members, and the Costa Rica Yacht Club. José Figueres phoned, or was called by Vesco, almost every day but wasn't around much, and Martí appeared usually for meetings. Vesco mostly saw the old guard, one of his New York lawyers, Robert Foglia, who had moved to Costa Rica for the moment; LeBlanc, recovering from the near-miss with death in Panama; Meissner, out of prison but frail and developing skin cancer and eye problems; Gilbert Straub, who had started a successful restaurant, Piccola Roma, but whose new wife bitched at the Costa Rican surroundings, as did he; Ulrich Strickler, over six feet tall, Swiss, and uncommunicative, who always wore the same pants (or identical ones) and shoes; bearded Richard Clay, who amused them by appearing in a ten-gallon hat ("Here comes the cowboy," Pat would giggle), trying to bring some amusement to the grim circle, but whose wife absolutely forbade them living in an out-of-the-way place like Costa Rica. In the evening, the Vescos watched American movies, and on several occasions, Vesco flew secretly to New Orleans for pleasure. Though the Vescos liked Costa Rican life, there was a constant strain.

Stanley Graze, whose wife had died from cancer, didn't often laugh. He became incensed at Vesco's anti-Semitic remarks, and said that he was Jewish, which Vesco didn't seem to have known. Graze felt that Vesco never trusted him after that, and, for his part, Graze had begun to regard Bob as an "s.o.b. who hurt, denigrated, or corrupted everyone he had contact with."

Bob may have enjoyed toying with receivers from the various IOS entities who visited him from time to time, hoping to be pointed to the missing millions. (He had one for dinner at his security chief's house—the place was completely bugged.) He would be hostile at first, then bantering, hauling out a battered briefcase with cracks in the sides. He seemed to know where every single piece of paper was, finding them at will, but when it came to hard information Vesco had none to offer. He retained, though, an air of command. He was quick at learning games like "Boggle," played poker once a week, was a member of a gun club, and still tried to pretend his existential situation was some sort of sport at which he excelled.

Vesco experimented with wandering around downtown San José on foot, followed by his guards, but he was always spotted and touched, and, when passing a radio station, a reporter would run out on the street with a microphone, with other reporters soon following. The couple tried nightclubs, but, as usual, people approached them. Not that Vesco didn't enjoy the attention—in a Range Rover, he would salute passersby as though he were Mussolini. At night, prowling the mansion, Vesco would always visit the guardroom where the TV monitored for anything stirring outside. He had an alarm system, but in the years at Lomas de Ayarco, it sounded only when the equipment was tested. A gun did go off once inside the compound when a guard shot one of the Vescos' dogs by mistake.

The kids weren't easy, either. The second oldest son, Anthony, was rebellious. He was a serious problem for the Vescos. Bobby Jr. was thought to have released a German shepherd, knowing that the dog took a dislike to a particular guard, and it attacked him. Dawn, insisting on driving back from Guanacaste, got into an accident and put a guard in the hospital. In 1976, the Vescos gave her fifteenth birthday party at a discotheque, importing Hollywood's Steve Major. While the event was a success, it was downhill from then on, as far as her parents were concerned. She married very young and had a baby. The Vescos, who disapproved of the marriage, didn't see her for several years. After Dawn divorced, she and her parents reunited.

Pat had problems of her own. Pregnant in 1975—she was nearly forty—she spent most of her time in bed in the later months. When born, her son Patrick required a rare blood transfusion, and Vesco put ads in the papers, using the family name. María Ermida, realizing that she herself had the requisite blood type, raced to the hospital, but there were already twenty or so people in line. As before, Vesco was a dutiful father, changing the baby at night, and would wander over rocks at Guanacaste to find Patrick a starfish.

Yet hatred, at least political hatred, of Vesco was profound. Daniel Vesco fell in love with a beautiful Costa Rican woman, Ileana Pinto, with whom he had two children before they divorced. Her father, a sugarcane producer, was a prominent Costa Rican and an ally of by then President Rodrigo Carazo. Carlos Pinto was in a difficult position, since his daughter's future father-in-law had been Carazo's prime target in the election. Nonetheless, intensely loyal to his daughter, he stuck by her, and, against the wishes of some of the family, the couple was married—first, in November 1978, in the Bahamas, with some guests from New Jersey, and then at a fancy wedding given by her parents at the Costa Rica Country Club. The officiating priest expelled the reporters and news photographers there because Danny was Bob's son. José Figueres was Vesco's stand-in to give away the bride, and he chuckled about photographs with the beautifully dressed ladies from high society, which had never accepted him. Pat's designer gown came from New York, though she ordinarily dressed plainly.

Vesco's children and Danny's new wife all seemed to believe that Vesco was innocent of wrongdoing, a victim of circumstances. Not surprisingly, perhaps, there were few or no questions from them about how the Vescos managed to live so high and on what. Vesco continued to display a calm front, but Figueres, aware that the Vescos' Costa Rican life bordered on being sad, urged Bob to turn himself over to the American authorities and submit to a few years in a low-security prison—such a deal could be arranged, Don Pepe believed. Jaime Darenblum and Gonzalo Facio, then Costa Rican Secretary for Foreign Affairs, both Vesco lawyers, researched at Don Pepe's suggestion whether Vesco, if he surrendered, could get such a sentence and concluded that he could, Facio having traveled to the United States. Figueres told Vesco to accept because the situation was untenable for everyone, but Vesco, burying his face in his hands, murmured, "It's too late."

32

VESCO'S ALMOST FINAL CHAPTER IN COSTA RICA

Late in April 1974, Vesco had some good news, the first since winning the extradition fight in Nassau. In New York, a Federal jury acquitted John Mitchell and Maurice Stans of conspiracy, obstruction of justice, and influence peddling on Vesco's behalf, charges that had struck some as overkill, although there was little doubt then that, given the political climate, all three would have been convicted had Vesco appeared. Through his Nassau p.r. outfit, Polaris, Vesco issued a statement. The verdict was "sound and reasonable," he said. "There was no conspiracy between Mr. Mitchell, Mr. Stans, and myself, for the straightforward reason there was never any need for one. The civil action by the Securities and Exchange Commission against myself and others is a matter which I am completely confident will be resolved satisfactorily without resort to any so-called conspiratorial methods. My motivation in contributing to the President's re-election campaign was no different than of any other contributor—I simply and sincerely hoped to see Mr. Nixon re-elected to the Presidency of my former homeland. . . . If there has been any conspiracy it all has been on the part of those individuals and groups who seek to undermine the public's confidence in the President by any means, and I, for one, decline to be part of such an insidiously dangerous undertaking."

The acquittal of Mitchell and Stans blunted one of the major charges against Vesco, but he was confronted with still another action, by the IRS, on his expense accounts, and he showed no sign of wavering in his determination to stay away. Nor did the U.S. Government intend to compromise with Satan. U.S. Attorney Curran, denying that Vesco had offered to return under certain conditions (although Vesco had made the offer on Costa Rican TV), said that New Jersey Bob was "not off the hook. He is a fugitive from justice and certainly will be prosecuted if he sets foot in the United States or moves to a country from which he can be extradited." The new American ambassador in Costa Rica, Terence Todman, held a press conference at the embassy, and the first question, of course, was about the fugitive financier. "I'm surprised you should ask about Vesco," said Todman with a laugh. The United States, he insisted, would continue to seek extradition, but Vesco should return home to prove his innocence. Vesco responded in a letter the newspapers printed, "I must admit I got quite a chuckle as a result of reading your politically motivated statement that I should voluntarily return to the U.S. to prove my innocence." Perhaps he was still chuckling when a self-made Costa Rican millionaire complained, "In the United States we are known more for Vesco than anything else." Vesco was not chuckling when, in double-page newspaper ads, he charged See Everything Crooked with "persecution, infamy, libel and (causing) indescribable suffering for me and my family."

The *Tico Times* apologized to its readers, some of whom, it knew, were tiring of the Vesco story (as was he, Vesco said) but felt obliged to continue the coverage. One strange episode the newspapers didn't have in full. A local lawyer, Gerardo Fernández, sued and obtained a judgment on behalf of ICC against Vesco and LeBlanc for $2,188,354 and interest. Fernández had no known offspring. Shortly thereafter, the daughter of Fernández's brother Roberto received a call from an unidentified man saying that she had a child who could be kidnapped or killed and should tell her uncle Gerardo. According to him, Roberto rushed over and gave his daughter a pistol. He phoned Vesco and left a message on the answering machine to the effect that, while he didn't know if Vesco was behind the threat, if anything happened to his daughter's child, the matter would be between Roberto and Robert alone. He was sending Vesco a telegram and copies to the papers.

Roberto Fernández quickly had a call from the man in charge of Vesco's security force, Alberto Abreu, who said that Mr. Vesco had planned to come to Fernández's home to deny involvement but would not because Fernández had contacted the newspapers. Then a friend phoned Roberto. At a café, he had overheard somebody making a call that sounded threatening. Could it have been the same man who contacted Roberto's daughter? Fernández was close to a detective and asked him to find out who the caller had been. The detective was able to identify a Cuban member of Vesco's bodyguard, and the friend, when the bodyguard was pointed out to him, confirmed that this was the fellow who had made the call. Fernández rounded up four large men. He went to the ballet that night, making sure that he was seen, while the toughs followed the Cuban, broke his jaw, and put him in the hospital. He was given twenty-four hours to leave the country, and did. If the Cuban ever came back, Roberto Fernández swore, he would kill the man. An unsolved mystery of the Vesco case was that Don Dinero didn't have a Cuban bodyguard, nor did any of the guards go to the hospital except the one in the crash with Dawn, but the episode, if nothing else, showed how high tempers ran.

In the press, Vesco was compared to the devil in *The Exorcist,* and the body he was said to occupy was Costa Rica. Thus far, though, protests had been mostly verbal, with cries for Vesco's ouster by important groups like the National Development Association, but a new element appeared. Calling itself the Civilist Revolutionary Movement, its pamphlets claimed "combat units will enter into action of a radical and perhaps destructive form" if the government didn't meet its demands for confiscation of all Vesco's Costa Rican properties and investments, and, in addition, an investigation of José Figueres's business deals since 1948, and of charges that the Communists had received $8 billion from the U.S.S.R. between 1962 and 1972. It insisted on 100 percent salary increases for the Civil Guard, the rural guard, and national detectives. Beleaguered Mario Charpantier, the Security Minister, maintained the Movement didn't exist, but just the same, a caller announced a "Vesco protest" bomb at the airport restaurant. A device was found, of a "firecracker type," unlit.

In 1976, the CIA, FBI, Drug Enforcement Authority, and SEC dispatched one James W. ("Skip") Wilson, age twenty-seven, to Costa Rica. He had a criminal record: altering a Florida motor vehicle title (a felony), grand larceny, aggravated assault and battery, violation of probation, and false checks. He had served a year at Six Mile Creek in Tampa and had become a CI, cop-ese for confidential informer. This was the hound the United States sicced on Vesco.

Wilson had a high estimation of his physical powers, as he revealed in sworn testimony in July 1976.

> THE WITNESS: I understood that they would be happy if it was possible that I could, you know, by any means place any of these gentlemen [the Seven Samurai] in their hands. They would appreciate it.
>
> Q. When you say "by any means," did you include the use of force?
>
> A. I didn't think they were going to walk with me to the airport and get on the plane.
>
> Q. Do you think that if you were alone with Mr. Vesco you would be physically able to overpower Mr. Vesco?
>
> A. It would have to be something that would have to be tested, I guess. I don't know the man's capabilities. All I know is my own.
>
> Q. Did you consider yourself as a physically capable person?
>
> A. If you look at my record, it speaks for itself. As an example, three gentlemen jumped on me in prison and I wound up being charged with aggravated assault and battery, and they wound up in the hospital.
>
> Q. Were you charged with that?
>
> A. No. I was charged with assault to commit battery.
> I had five different charges in one fight. Two guys jumped me with broken-off cue sticks, and I took the cue sticks away from them and put them in the hospital.
>
> Q. Was Mr. [U.S. Attorney Eliot] Sagor aware of these items from your records, which you have stated to us?
>
> A. Mr. Sagor was aware of my complete record.

* * *

Q. Was getting Vesco into the trunk of your car something that you understood to be within your discretion in the context of your mission?
A. I understood it to be something that was possible, would take place, or could take place.

Wilson, who had relatives in Costa Rica, broke parole by traveling there. He had a Costa Rican tourist card. An article on him had earlier appeared in the *Tico Times* about rock concerts he had promoted in Costa Rica, and he used it to apply for a job with Vesco. Nothing happened, and when he returned to Tampa, he served a short jail sentence. When Wilson mentioned his Vesco approach to a U.S. law enforcement official with whom he'd had frequent contact, his "friend" politely asked if he could notify the Department of Justice. Wilson said fine.

He soon found himself in New York with the U.S. Government paying the plane fare (it balked, though, at recompensing Wilson for thirty dollars a cab driver had gypped him out of for a ride from LaGuardia to Foley Square, headquarters of the Southern District of New York. He should have taken the bus, he was told.) He met with U.S. attorneys and the DEA.

Q. In the conversation to which you just referred, was there any discussion of your acting as an assassin of Mr. Vesco or anyone else?
A. I was only asked if I knew of anyone with the capabilities to commit this act.
Q. Did [U.S. Attorney] Ross ask you whether you would be willing to do it, to commit an act of assassination against Mr. Vesco?
A. He may have. I'm not sure.
Q. Do you recall, Mr. Wilson, the conversation on June 17th?
A. I recall the fact that we had a conversation.
Q. Do you recall mentioning during that conversation you were asked whether you would be willing to assassinate Mr. Vesco by persons in the U.S. Attorney's office in New York?
A. This is very possible that I did state this.
Q. Could you tell us, to the best of your present recollection, as to whether Mr. Ross or others did make such a proposal to you concerning your services in that regard?

* * *

> A. And I believe that he [Ross] before I could even answer him, I believe he asked me, "In fact, would you consider it, doing anything of this nature? . . ." I do know that I was asked by Mr. Ross if I knew anyone with the capability of committing an assassination attempt, and I do know that I was asked how much do I think it would cost, and I believe that I was asked would I consider it.

The "group" as Wilson termed them (Eliot Sagor, he said, called Vesco an s.o.b. and a con man) agreed to finance, on the part of the U.S. government, Wilson's ill-fated Costa Rican incursion. He or others invented code names for what he was supposed to investigate: "whiskey" for guns; "bananas" for drugs; "records" for money; "cattle" for stocks, bonds, and documents. Vesco was "Vickie"; LeBlanc, "Linda"; Meissner, "Mary Ann"; Graze, "Alice"; Clay, "Clara"; Straub, "Sharon"; Strickler, "Stacy."

After several trips to New York, Skip arrived in San José. He was to use his own discretion but check back. Under a false name, he telephoned María Ermida Ulate, Vesco's secretary, and said he had information on someone sent by the United States to spy on Vesco. A date was made for Wilson to receive a call at 10:30 A.M. at a restaurant, and Skip, panting with excitement, arrived three and a half hours early. Evidently, he intended to play a double game.

A short, fat man drifted in pretending to photograph some teenagers, but Wilson noted the camera pointed at him. At 10:30 sharp, Vesco called and said he'd phone back in twenty minutes. He did and told Skip he'd be collected that evening by a fat man Wilson thought he'd recognize. The man—his Toyota had a two-way radio—drove Wilson to a "secret" location; they crossed a bridge, went down a dark road—Wilson worried about being bumped off—and came out on a main road near a disco. A Volkswagen slid in behind the Toyota followed by a Land-Rover. Men with handguns in their belts asked Skip to step out. A silver-gray Mercedes pulled to a halt in the center of the street, and Wilson was instructed to get in the car.

I look in the back and Mr. Vesco is sitting in the back. And I turned around and shake Mr. Vesco's hand and I make apologies for my, you know, knowledge of etiquette and protocol and that, say that, "I have never had the honor of being in anyone's company of such stature as you, and he says to me, "Well, I am sure that you have."

And I said, "Well, anyway, can I sit around sideways," and I turned to my left and I put my arm over the back of the seat and faced him.

I said, "Is it all right if I turn and face you where I can talk more freely?"

Mr. Vesco says, "No, I think for the moment you should turn and just look forward."

So that's exactly what I did. I turned around and I was looking forward.

* * *

"Well, that's what you say. They seem to have a little more on you in New York than that, from what they told me."

And he says, "Well, my word, I have got someone that can back my word up pretty good. I have got an ex-President of the United States that can back my word up."

I never told Mr. Vesco this, but I was thinking, "Mr. Vesco, who in the world would believe him?"

Q. By "him," you mean whom?

A. Nixon, because I'm sure that's who he was referring to. And I said, "Well, I'll tell you, Mr. Vesco. What can I say? All I can say is that now I'm in San José. You know, you pretty well have control of me, and what do I do?"
And Mr. Vesco said, "Well, as far as that goes, I have had pretty much control of you all along from the beginning."
That kind of shook me up a little bit.

The Mercedes was driven around the city. As Wilson nervously put his hand into his pocket for a pack of cigarettes, a guard, who sported a Magnum revolver, put a "wristlock" on his hand. Skip seemed to have told the truth, that he was a confidential informant, on the theory that Vesco would hire him away. He was forced to telephone a U.S. Attorney in New York, but something he said—as usual, Vesco recorded the conversation with a suction-cup mike—made Vesco doubtful about him.

Vesco told Wilson to wait in his hotel room and before long a Costa Rican immigration officer and a policeman appeared. Skip was accused of trying to find work, against the law for an alien, and the American was promptly delivered to San José Penitentiary, where he was placed in an underground cell, six-by-six-feet across.

> My cell was kept shut with a concrete bolt that slid into the wall and a latch that was like a padlock. And they didn't have a padlock, so they used a pair of handcuffs that they ran through the ringer to keep it closed.
>
> And, like I say, there was indications of human manure in places, and there was human urine standing in places an inch thick on the floor. It was just a terrible place to be. You can hardly breathe in the place.
>
> Q. Were you fed?
>
> A. The first three or four days I wasn't fed anything, and I was lucky to get water occasionally.
> I was allowed cigarettes, but no matches. I got one cigarette lit from a guard and I went through four or five packs of cigarettes on a chain, lighting one off the other. Some I didn't smoke. Just to have a light.

It took Wilson ten or so days to contact the U.S. embassy and an equal time passed before he was released. He developed, he said, boils and dysentery and tried to commit suicide by hanging. Instead, he was booted out of Costa Rica.

U.S. Attorney Robert B. Fiske admitted that the American government paid for Wilson's trip but "once he was there he was on his own." Although Skip blamed Vesco for landing him in jail, he was even more bitter at the United States for failing to pay his out-of-pocket expenses. Vesco phoned him and proposed a deal. If Skip would agree to be questioned, Vesco would have a joint TV-news conference with him. Wilson already had a local Tampa TV contract and had been paid $2,500. The Vesco-Wilson show never came off, but Wilson gave a deposition before lawyers for Vesco and Graze, who hoped the charges against them would be dropped because of the Department of Justice's misconduct in the Wilson matter. But the judge who presided over the criminal case, begun in 1973, against the Magnificent Seven, refused to read the document unless the two fugitives appeared. Vesco refused and so did Graze, who couldn't afford the bail money he was certain would be imposed, much less the million or so he anticipated in legal fees. There the story ended.

In Costa Rica, Vesco appeared on Jack Anderson's TV show "The Truth." Asked by the columnist whether he'd gotten to Nixon, Vesco said that Nixon had "full knowledge" of the contribution and that Vesco's name was on a list of thirty-seven people to be pardoned by the former President. (Apparently, for the fugitive, Watergate intervened.) Vesco's investments in Costa Rica were "insignificant" to the economy; he had no links to the Mafia—"if anything, they'd be a wholly owned subsidiary of mine." If "they" allowed the full story to come out and dismissed the charges, he would return to the United States. Vesco took a lie detector test for Anderson and passed when he denied having stolen $224 million. However, he refused to answer the question of whether he might have taken less.

Vesco contributed to a fiesta at Heredia, a town not far from San José, and was made honorary president of the fiesta committee. He watched a bullfight and crowned the fiesta queen, but *La Nación* and *La República,* spoiling the fun, demanded the money be returned. Staunch Vesco defenders wanted to hang his portrait in the school assembly hall, but the Minister of Education prohibited "any homages to Vesco in this school or any other school because he doesn't deserve them." Vesco replied, predictably, "The campaign of persecution against me stains the civic fiesta in Heredia with politics because of my presence." He might have moved to another country, but the question, increasingly urgent, was where. In 1977, Vesco began collecting his loans at a discount and selling assets like the Navajo plane.

"It was a week of sour news for beleaguered financier Robert Vesco," reported the *Tico Times,* "with foreign accusations and local revelations teamed up to produce a good case of monetary indigestion." Vesco was supposed to have lent $770,000 to the Figueres Sociedad Agrícola, by then the Unión de Compañías de

Centroamérica (he had taught the company a few things about changing names, spinning off assets, and leaving liabilities behind), but the money had come from Bahamas Commonwealth Bank a few years before, and the BCB receivers, wanting to retrieve it, sued Sociedad Agrícola and UCC. Vesco was accused in Congress of controlling two newspapers, a TV station, and three radio stations, which he again denied. Proposed anti-Vesco legislation, fuming statements, and lawsuits swirled in the spring breeze. One of the suits may not have sounded like much to Don Dinero at first, but it dogged him from Costa Rica.

A seventy-seven-year-old architect, Carlos Rechnitzer—"the mouse that roared," the press called him—sued Vesco for $236,000 lost in IOS investments. As the case wore on, Rechnitzer began to carry a lead pipe wrapped in architectural renderings. It was the first time he had been sued by a Costa Rican in a Costa Rican court, and Don Roberto "welcomed" the chance to prove his innocence. U.S. Attorney Sagor offered to come to Costa Rica with a "ton of documents," and Rechnitzer, acting as his own attorney, flew to New York several times for information. In October, a judge decided that the case could be brought to trial. Rechnitzer, announcing he would also sue important Costa Ricans, billed it as the "trial of the century." Smiling, "El Hombre" arrived in a blue pinstripe suit and a gray silk tie, striding through the open door and patting a child as he passed. The architect looked frail and very white. Everyone carried his own chair as they went into the judge's office. While the court pondered, though the architect couldn't understand "how they could be so stupid," Vesco sued Rechnitzer for libel, promising to donate the proceeds to charity. The judge prohibited Vesco from leaving the country.

Meantime, it was anything but quiet on the political front. José Figueres expressed impatience with Costa Rican politics. The Congress, he said, was "one of the most backward," and he recommended a strong man or group to carry out a national housecleaning that would require a year. Costa Rica was "scandal prone" (a new accusation had emerged, in all seriousness, that Vesco earlier had used the 707 to smuggle in pepperoni sausage). "We end up falling like toads into yellow journalism," said Don

Pepe. He sounded like 1948 and seemed to be running for President again, with Vesco rumored as his backer, as Figueres recommended a change in the law that prevented Presidents from serving more than two nonconsecutive terms. If Figueres ran, his opponent would be Rodrigo Carazo, for whom Vesco would be the main campaign issue, although Carazo had been Don Pepe's pupil.

If the Costa Rican congress was a harbinger, the autumn of 1977 did not bode well for the fugitive. President Oduber revealed that he had previously urged his party to vote for the "Vesco law" because of anger at American reprisal threats if it wasn't shelved. Oduber now favored the law's overturn, and Congress, in a surprisingly fast 48–1 vote, repealed it. The courts would have the right to provide a two-month preventative (from escape) detention in jail for anyone whose extradition was called for. The noose around Vesco's neck tightened.

The court waltzes continued. Whether Costa Rica had an extradition law after the changes came into question—the U.S. embassy professed itself bewildered—and a judge ruled that the new law "died before it was born." Vesco's scrappy right-wing lawyer, José María Pla, claimed that Rechnitzer had been "unpatriotic" to put his IOS $236,000 outside Costa Rica, whereupon the architect said he had made the money in Nicaragua; his suit was then disqualified because the alleged crime hadn't happened in Costa Rica and, anyway, Rechnitzer couldn't prove ownership of the IOS-related shares. Jubilation reigned briefly at the Lomas de Ayarco compound. Vesco said he had had no doubt of the Rechnitzer outcome, but—1977 being the year he fulfilled the residency requirement—he would not apply for Costa Rican citizenship until his legal troubles had been solved. In fact, he didn't dare.

In the middle of all this, Vesco's San José house was attacked, sort of. Gerardo Villalobos, an unsuccessful 1974 presidential candidate who went to rallies on horseback to demonstrate the need to economize on gasoline and whom many Costa Ricans regarded as a kook, was a candidate for the 1978 elections. Alerting reporters and the Vesco compound (which did not take him seriously) as to his arrival, Villalobos came wrapped in a Costa

Rican flag and armed with two pistols. Out to prove that Costa Ricans weren't cowards, as Don Pepe had accused them of being, Villalobos shouted, "Vesco! You're a thief who has corrupted us! You're the reason there are not tourists here, why our hotels are empty. It's your fault!" He proceeded to riddle the building, and shoot out a tire on the Mercedes before the police arrested him.

"As far as I know," President Oduber said, "Vesco can leave or enter the country whenever he wants." Oduber was in a perpetual tizzy about Don Pepe's protégé. "At no time have I talked about throwing out anyone," the President said in June 1977, but in July he said Vesco had to leave. (Oduber had changed his stance for political reasons, but Don Pepe assured the fugitive Oduber's new position was cosmetic.) Vesco had previously said he hoped to stay, but if not, he had plenty of places to go, he claimed, without specifying where. Then Vesco said he planned to remain at least two more years and grow pineapples. Oh no, he wouldn't, according to the Women's Civic League, which demonstrated and wrote a letter to Rosalyn Carter, who was due to arrive in San José, asking for "aid in our fight to prevent our democracy from being overshadowed by evil alien influences, out of all proportion to our environment." (The First Lady refused to comment on the Vesco case.) Vesco and his son Danny's Costa Rican passports were stolen from the glove compartment of Danny's car. Danny's was returned but not Bob's, which might have been construed as a hint.

Rechnitzer lost the case after Vesco had left, and, despite rumors that he was tied in with Meyer Lansky and Somoza, Vesco might have stayed in Costa Rica to this very day had he remained inactive. But his purported backing of *Excelsior* (it closed from lack of funds), his contribution to leading politicians, considered immoral, and his behavior did him in.

To Juan José Echeverría, a congressman who became Minister for Public Security and the Interior under Carazo, Vesco behaved "like he owned the world. He was arrogant and insulting. He pointed his finger at people." Echeverría was infuriated when, at a bar, Vesco's guard inspected the men's room and stood outside while the master peed, allowing no one else to enter. Carazo, running hard on a unity ticket that saw Vesco as the "symbol of corruption in official circles in Costa Rica"—decided he'd made his point and campaigned on other issues, winning easily.

After the election, a large public meeting took place at a town called El Tobogán with all parties represented, petitions were signed, bumper stickers issued saying "Vesco Fuera" ("Vesco Go Home"), and that, for New Jersey Bob, was that.

He hastily applied for citizenship, which stirred another protest and thousands of signatures. Figueres, loyal to the end, went on TV and radio in early April to defend Vesco and testified on his behalf. But the handwriting was on the wall, and Pat left with the children for the United States on April 21, 1978. That same day, Vesco asked the court for permission to take a ninety-day trip, and had to put up a $120,000 pledge to cover bail for himself and Norman LeBlanc in the still-pending Rechnitzer case. The two departed on April 30. Shortly after, a letter from Vesco was released in which he said he wanted a chance to return and defend himself, but on July 12, the borders were closed to him, though Pat and the kids could come and go as they liked. Thus, rather anticlimactically, Vesco left Costa Rica, not for the last time.

Afterward, high school students polled thirty Costa Ricans of different ages and backgrounds, and the results, while not scientific, were surprising: 77 percent thought that Vesco had done no harm and 60 percent believed he should be granted citizenship; 73 percent believed he should be allowed to stay. Even today, while many Costa Ricans aren't quite clear anymore about Don Roberto, his name still makes headlines. After he left, rumors had him in Guanacaste. As the result of one, police rushed to the Vesco *finca* and blocked the runway with felled trees, but, except for caretakers, the place was empty.

Late in 1978, Public Security Minister Echeverría received word that Vesco was aboard a plane from the Bahamas that would refuel in Costa Rica. Echeverría did not inform the Costa Rican police, but he called the American ambassador, Marvin Weissman, and said, "We have information Vesco's on the plane. I have a fully fueled Costa Rican jet at the airport. Please inform Miami my plane may be coming with Vesco." "What about legal proceedings?" Weissman said. "You want him, don't you?" Echeverría snapped. The minister went to the airport himself and boarded the plane, but Vesco wasn't there.

33

SIDESHOWS

Perhaps only Vesco could have cooked up situations that involved an alleged $10 million bribe of the Carter administration, Libyan petroleum and planes, a Bahamian oil refinery, and much else. By then, the SEC and the news had enshrined the fugitive in the Con Man Hall of Fame, and, just as decades earlier every small-time hood wanted to be associated with gangster Al Capone, so minor-league wheeler-dealers yearned to do business with "The Man." Vesco had become a magnet.

Within weeks of Jimmy Carter's election as President of the United States in 1976, Vesco was approached by three Georgians —the fugitive called them the "peanuts Mafia"—who flew to Costa Rica in a private plane one of the group owned. Among them was Robert L. Herring, thirty-seven or so, who that same year had been convicted of fraud in his home state. They would use their President-elect contacts to secure settlements for American fugitives *for a price.*

The gray Mercedes picked them up at their San José hotel, and drove them to a farmhouse (probably LeBlanc's) where Vesco and Nasty Norman waited. Vesco wanted the United States to revoke his citizenship so that no further extradition attempts would be launched. His idea was to exert his influence in Central America, pervasive, he claimed, to gain approval there for the proposed Panama Canal Treaty. "The primary thrust of it was that something had to be done about Mr. Vesco's problems, that he was a strong man down there; otherwise, the United States would not get a Panama Canal Treaty. Revolutions could be bought for fifty cents a head, and Mr. Vesco was in a position to do that. Just basically the fact he was a strong person," one Georgian recalled. (Hearing Vesco brag, LeBlanc smirked, knowing how Bobby liked to shoot his mouth off.) In exchange, the State Department was to put in a good word for Vesco with the Justice Department.

One of the Georgians, Fred E. Bartlett, Jr., had a law partner, Harry Wingate, who had worked on a committee with Cyrus Vance, Carter's nominee for Secretary of State. Bartlett and Wingate met with Vance in New York "to see if there would be some way that they could put in a word to please try to go get the Vesco matters settled up," Bartlett said. But Vance replied that "he did not see any way that they could deal in any way with Mr. Vesco."

Vesco would produce letters from the presidents of six nations in the Central American area, one from Costa Rican President Daniel Oduber, and former President José Figueres was eager to help, if only to get Vesco out of Costa Rica. Robert Herring had contacted William Spencer Lee IV, a lawyer from Albany, Ga., who was close friends with Hamilton Jordan, Carter's chief of staff designate. Vesco sent from Costa Rica a small jet—the Cessna Citation he had a piece of—with Oduber's letter to Carter. Lee explained, "The letter was delivered to the airport in Albany, Georgia, the day before Christmas, 1976. I, along with R. L. Herring, met the airplane at the airport and picked up a manila envelope that was folded over, and I don't remember what was on the front of it." Lee delivered the letter to Americus, where Carter campaign headquarters had been, and then met with Charles Kirbo, Atlanta lawyer and Carter confidant, about the Vesco matter, but Kirbo didn't want to play.

The Georgians had mentioned a fee for their services of $10 million, which Vesco wouldn't have paid, but LeBlanc knew of an item that had escaped the receivers' attention. In Panama, shares of Property Resources Ltd., owned by Value Capital Ltd. (the spinoff of IOS banking assets), but pledged to Emir—one of Norman's countless shells—were coming up for judicial auction. In 1974, Vesco caused VCL to borrow $30,000 from Emir as a means of hiding about 3,000,000 Class A shares and some 10,000 common, virtually all the PRL stock originally issued to VCL. The PRL shares had value, and the VCL receivers might pay as much as $11 million (one half of their worth), the fugitives told the Georgians. For Vesco, who saw them as bit players, it was a no-lose situation. If they could bag the Carter administration and solve his legal problems, it cost him nothing, and, if they failed, he was no further behind than before.

Herring, who sold heavy equipment, paid Lee a $10,000 legal fee and promised him a cut of $1 or $1.5 million of the Panama swag—as an attorney Lee earned $40 or $50 an hour. In 1980, a Senate subcommittee on improvements in judicial machinery, dissatisfied with previous investigations of improper contacts among Vesco and U.S. government figures, launched still another one (grand juries in Washington and New York were also investigating). Senators Orrin Hatch (Utah) and Dennis DeConcini (Arizona) grilled Lee relentlessly. His only job, Lee testified, was to learn whether the White House would be favorably or unfavorably disposed to hearing Vesco's side of the story. Lee was not stupid. He showed insight into Vesco's constant use of a tape recorder, for instance. "He is a very mysterious person. He says something and lets some time expire. And he says something else like he's taping it. I don't have any problem if he's got tapes. I would imagine the man does have tapes. If I had to guess, he's taped everything because he likes to involve people in things. His only means of survival is to get somebody in a compromising position." Still, Lee didn't question Vesco's theft of an immense amount of money which, for him, seemed to increase Vesco's credibility even when the fugitive claimed he could stop the Panama Canal Treaty.

For the senators, Lee's proposed fee was extremely high, considering how little was asked of him.

> SENATOR HATCH: Could I interrupt you for a second? In other words, for an answer to the question: Would you be willing to sit down and discuss this with Mr. Vesco, either yes or no, you were going to get $1 million?
>
> MR. LEE: That is what I understood.

> SENATOR HATCH: Mr. Vesco must have been a real stupid businessman.
>
> MR. LEE: You know, Senator, I can't understand how that is stupid. If you happen to have $225 million and you are a hunted person or, from what I understand, the CIA was trying to assassinate him or whatever and you wanted to be left alone, it might not be too high a price to pay to be left alone if something is done with it. You know, I can understand—
>
> SENATOR HATCH: Is that what Mr. Vesco wanted? He wanted to be left alone?
>
> MR. LEE: That is what he initially said to me. He just wanted to be left alone.
>
> SENATOR HATCH: What did that mean to you?
>
> MR. LEE: It meant to me that he wanted the CIA to quit trying to kill him, from what he said they were trying to do.
>
> SENATOR HATCH: I thought what you just testified to, there was no quid pro quo at that time.
>
> MR. LEE: Well, you see, it was not anything that I was going to do. My role was to go to the Carter administration and make them aware of the fact that it would be very difficult to negotiate a favorable Panama Canal Treaty unless somebody was willing to sit down and listen to him. Now, that's fine. Whatever happened as a result of that, I don't care.

Lee was frequently challenged for giving deceptive answers in a lie detector test.

> SENATOR HATCH: Let me go back to the polygraph examination. The polygraph operator states: Based on the polygraph examination and interview, it is concluded that Lee was deceptive in denying that he personally discussed the Vesco matter with Hamilton Jordan prior to May 1978.
>
> MR. LEE: Well, I don't care what it says. I never discussed the matter with Hamilton Jordan.

In Lee's version, instead of Jordan, he met in the White House with another old friend, Richard Harden, on February 8, 1977. Lee revealed the $1 million offer, but Harden advised him not to approach Jordan. Lee said he agreed. (Again, the polygraph operator disputed Lee's veracity.)

Harden testified he didn't tell Jordan about the Lee meeting, but the next day Harden met with Jordan, and Carter's phone log showed a call to Oduber that same day. On the fifteenth, Harden met with Carter and discussed the conversation with Lee, and Carter wrote a note to Attorney General Griffin Bell: "Please see Spencer Lee from Albany when he requests an appointment." Bell denied receiving the note.

In August 1977, the Georgians flew to Panama, and, in the absence of other bidders, bought the PRL stock for $39,000, transferring it to Corma, a dummy corporation the Georgians owned. In the Bahamas, Lee and Bartlett set up Southern Ventures for Herring, the purpose being to launder the proceeds from the sale to VCL. By then, Vesco had upped the possible take to $50 million. The receivers not only turned the Georgians down but notified the SEC, which interrogated Herring and others and forbade them to sell the shares. Much against the wishes of the SEC, Beatty's Global Natural Resources got the Corma shares from Vesco to free up other assets for $150,000 toward the fugitive's legal bills.

In Lee's view, "R. L. Herring was in a con job to bilk Mr. Vesco. . . ." Lee described Herring as a "habitual liar" even though the lie detector accused Lee of deception. Vesco triumphed in the battle of polygraphs.

> Mr. Lee was deceptive in denying any knowledge of Ham Jordan ever speaking with Robert Vesco.

* * *

> No. 2: During January 1977, did you [Vesco] have a telephone conversation with Spencer Lee IV, who was at a Washington, D.C. hotel, during which it was represented to you that Hamilton Jordan was present?
>
> [Vesco] answered yes to that. . . .

The lie detector said that Vesco told the truth. Lee conceded that Herring might have represented himself as Jordan when Lee was out of the room.

In September 1978, Jack Anderson, the columnist, using Herring and Vesco as sources, ran columns claiming a Vesco-connected "$10-million political fix" involving Jordan and Kirbo.

Anderson said Herring had copies of letters from Lee to Jordan and Kirbo detailing the $10 million offer from Vesco. Anderson began to backpedal, admitting that Herring didn't have authentic letters—Herring's wife had "reconstructed" them and long after the alleged dates. In Lee's opinion, the reason was that Herring had been indicted for embezzlement. "He figures that, if he could get a congressional investigation started, that he would be given immunity with the things he had jimmied up." Kirbo flew to Georgia to see Herring's wife, who had a tape recorder in her purse, and, according to it, Kirbo said, "I'm just an ordinary Georgia cracker. . . . It's a mistake to be too open with the FBI." Anderson reported the conversation without revealing that he had the tape, until Kirbo denied the statement.

Vesco had a meeting on July 4, 1980, in Nassau, with Senators Hatch and DeConcini, in lieu of an appearance before the Senate Permanent Subcommittee on Investigations, which couldn't provide immunity. Two days before, a polygraph expert, Warren Holmes, came from Florida to administer a lie detector test to Vesco but refused because the fugitive insisted on writing the questions. One of them, Vesco said, were he to pass it, would "cast doubt on truthfulness of testimony made by Spencer Lee, Harden and President Carter" (who had appeared on videotape before the Washington Grand Jury).

To the evident frustration of the two senators, the trail ran out, and it was never fully clear whether the White House didn't have a greater involvement than anyone admitted. DeConcini, at any rate, tried hard to have Vesco testify in the United States. In September, he wrote the then Attorney General, Benjamin R. Civiletti, about finding conditions under which the fugitive could appear, but Civiletti responded that Justice couldn't authorize negotiations with Vesco, as it had before. DeConcini said: ". . . it is my understanding that the Department offered him a plea bargain in 1973. A memorandum from his attorneys [Edward Bennett Williams] confirms this offer." DeConcini went on, "I am astounded that the Department of Justice would seek to force a United States Senate Subcommittee to conduct its investigation on foreign soil because of the Department's unwillingness to cooperate." He hoped the department would "reconsider," but it would not.

In 1981, Robert Herring was convicted of first-degree murder and received a twenty-year sentence. Spencer Lee IV became County Attorney of Dougherty County, Georgia.

The next drama starring Robert L. Vesco had a new supporting cast, though the Georgians appeared on stage briefly. Libya was the "Big Sand Box," Chairman of the Democratic National Committee John C. White, "Blanco," and Vesco the "Vicar." The FBI remained the FBI.

The Vicar tried to rescue Libyan planes. The Libyans had bought eleven Boeing 727s for $30 million in 1970, all but two of them having been delivered by 1978; three Boeing 747s for $65 million, none delivered; sixteen Lockheed C-130 Hercules for about $130 million, eight of which were delivered. In 1976, the State Department blocked the export of the remaining planes because of Libyan terrorism, and the other eight C-130s, which the Libyans especially wanted, sat warehoused at Lockheed's plant in, of all places, Georgia.

What followed might have been a comic opera except that it was a serious, carefully calculated attempt to subvert U.S. policy regarding Libya. It involved the FBI and the U.S. Department of Justice's Southern District of New York and their informants, about whose status each was ignorant. Vesco wrote at least part of the plot.

In 1978, James W. Brewer was indicted for mail fraud and agreed to become a "confidential source" for the FBI, which put him to work on an Abscam-related project known as the Gold-Con Operation. It used the Abscam boat and FBI agents dressed up as Arabs. Brewer, who created Inter Alia Finance for the FBI, said, "I knew enough people to start with and one thing led to another. We would find a person and get introduced to another person. We had a party on the Abscam boat and invited several people who were in the insurance business, and so forth, one day, the same way the Abscam thing started. That was kind of the way ours worked out, too. Cases developed in various parts of the country. We were working such things as these boiler rooms selling phony gold, oil, commodities, in addition to the banking thing."

Brewer was to offer "targets" the chance to commit crimes, and one was James ("Jimmy") Day, a former Texas legislator who had become a lobbyist for a rich Texas family named Moody that Brewer had also worked for. According to Brewer, Day said that Hamilton Jordan and John White had said they "were not too confident Carter was going to make it again and they were interested in deals to make money." (Day's statement was the only evidence of such a remark.) Only Day said it was Brewer's idea to contact Vesco, meaning the FBI's, but Brewer claimed it was the other way around and Day was after money.

Brewer, a professional sleuth, required four months to contact Vesco, because the fugitive was still waiting for results from Spencer Lee. Finally, Danny Vesco called, and on September 4, 1978, Brewer brought Day and another Moody aide, James Wohlenhaus, whom Day considered his administrative assistant, to the Bahamas to visit. Vesco told them he had fed Jack Anderson "only so much as to get it [newspaper coverage] started." The result, he hoped, would be a Grand Jury investigation and public pressure. Spencer Lee IV had failed to get Vesco off with a "slap on the wrist," but were he allowed to return to the United States to testify he could "clear all the names of the people in the Carter administration" (names that had been implicated only because of Vesco). In exchange, he wanted the United States to revoke his citizenship and would say, as U.S. marshals booted him out, "I've paid the supreme cost." That was the kind of convoluted logic Vesco specialized in and which had helped land him in exile. The other plotters deliberately encouraged his fantasies.

Vesco II (as the Senate Judiciary Subcommittee called the events to distinguish them from "Vesco I," the Herring matter) was the fugitive's notion of obtaining the release of the two embargoed 727s and the three 747s—the C-130s weren't mentioned yet, apparently. Vesco said he had a partner, the deputy of Colonel Muammar el-Qaddafi, the Libyan leader, and, if the State Department would free the planes, unidentified people in Washington could rake in $7.5 million and Vesco an equal amount for his services, whatever they were supposed to be. (The $15 million represented the increased value of the aircraft since they had been bought.)

In November 1978, the State Department released the 727s after written assurances from Libya that it wouldn't use them for military purposes. Whether Day had anything to do with freeing the planes wasn't clear, but he asked to see Vesco about money. The fugitive said he was leaving for Libya. Norman had visited Tripoli four or five times in 1977 and 1978, he said, but this time he and Vesco used a very circuitous route, and Vesco tried to change his appearance with different eyeglass frames—the frames, he insisted, altered the appearance of a face. According to LeBlanc, the Libyans—Vesco had never been there before although he described them as "old friends"—treated the two as ordinary businessmen and they received no special favors, not even free hotel rooms. Nor did Vesco, to his irritation, meet Qaddafi. Another deal besides the planes was discussed—oil.

Vesco returned, claiming the Libyans wouldn't pay him for the 727s without a "nod" from an American official confirming that Vesco and his group were responsible. Day hadn't been paid except for $8,000 given by the fugitive, who didn't intend to lay out more money. Day said, "At this point in time, when the plane situation was not a reality, and the (Libyan) Ambassador had told me this, I conveyed to Mr. James Brewer that I was washing my hands of the whole damned thing, that I had spent all the money I had intended to spend out of my pocket."

Brewer was upset, meaning the FBI was. It had been watching the plane situation closely. Brewer said, "Oh, I don't want you to. We can't do this. We've gone too far. Would you take in a partner if I got somebody to put up the money?"

"If somebody puts up the money, then I'll continue to run with this thing," Day said.

Brewer checked his contact list and came up with one James Feeney, who belonged to the same London club and with whom he'd had "business dealings." For $50,000, Feeney could become Day's partner. Feeney was interested because Day had been talking of his group's share of the $7.5 million from the Libyans, which would amount to $2 million out of the money earmarked for Washington to be divided by Day, Brewer, and Wohlenhaus. Feeney would get a slice of the pie. Brewer didn't tell Feeney that he worked for the FBI. He introduced Feeney and Day in January 1979, and Day laid out his contacts as he had for Vesco: White, Democratic National Committee chairman and former Texas Secretary of Agriculture whom Day had known for twenty years, Hamilton Jordan, Charles Kirbo. Feeney insisted on meeting the famous fugitive and Day agreed, provided Feeney gave him $10,000 up front. Feeney wrote a check drawn on the First National Bank of Teheran.

Vesco arranged for Day to meet the Libyan representative to the United Nations, Mansur Kikhia. The ambassador told Day that there had been no "payoff" and "no money for airplanes." In the Bahamas, where Day took Feeney, Vesco said, "Ignore him (Kikhia)"; Vesco would get the money from his Libyan partner, Major Abdul Salam Jalloud, Qaddafi's deputy. Vesco reviewed his agenda, avoiding extradition, the release of the planes, and an oil deal that involved a Bahamian refinery. To Feeney, the fugitive wanted "total control."

Feeney's check to Day bounced, and small wonder. His business lay in "briefcase banks" existing only in his attaché case, like the First National Bank of Teheran, based in St. Vincent, in the Caribbean. The banks advertised for loan customers, promising easy credit and low interest rates. The applicant had only to pay a fee. In addition, Feeney and his group palmed off worthless checks. By December 1978, more than $4 million in phony checks had been issued in the name of Feeney's offshore "banks." He had pleaded guilty to such charges in the Eastern District of New York and awaited sentencing; he believed he was under investigation by the U.S. Attorney for the Southern District of New York, which had previously indicted him. Feeney thought his information on Vesco might be worth consideration if not immunity from further prosecution. Ironically, perhaps, the FBI informant's introduction of Feeney to Vesco gave Feeney a chance to bargain with the Southern District, which might have been his intention all along. Thereafter, Feeney informed on Brewer, who had made it possible for Feeney to cooperate with the Southern District.

Feeney, who had previously bagged another fugitive, said he

would produce Vesco at his own expense, the price for which was immunity. The Southern District was skeptical until Feeney presented a cup he said Vesco had handled. The U.S. Attorney sent the cup to the FBI, which, agreeing the fingerprints belonged to Vesco, asked how the Southern District had obtained them, but the Southern District, to protect its informant, wouldn't reveal Feeney's identity.

In March 1979, the State Department rescinded the ban on the three 747s for Libya. After Libya flew 1,500 Libyan troops, in 727s and C-130s, to Uganda to help Idi Amin against anti-Amin rebels and Tanzanian regulars, the ban on the 747s was reimposed. That same month, the coffee cup caused the Justice Department to summon the FBI and the Southern District for a meeting. Philip Heymann, assistant attorney general for Justice's Criminal Division, learned that Feeney informed for the U.S. Attorney's office, which discovered that Brewer informed for the FBI. It was agreed that the two investigations would be continued separately, and neither informant would be told of the other. But Brewer indiscreetly had told a friend who his employer was and the friend told Day, who said, "Are you kidding me?" Day did not divorce himself from Brewer, because he thought he could outsmart him and the payoff seemed close. But Day didn't suspect Feeney.

Feeney still owed Day several thousand dollars, and Day came to New York to collect. Feeney wore a concealed tape recorder to keep the Southern District abreast of developments. Day said that because of the 747 release everything was still "on course" and he expected a call from Ambassador Kikhia that week. Feeney warned that there might be a leak because Brewer talked too much. James Wohlenhaus, also at the lunch, said that Vesco was not a big problem because "they want to get rid of him as bad as he wants them to let go of him." Day said, "They don't want him back in this country. Never. We don't tell him that."

On April 11, the FBI and the Southern District both taped the same meeting, although the FBI agents didn't know who Feeney was. The Southern District had a recorder on Feeney while the FBI concealed one in Brewer's briefcase. Feeney, Day, Wohlenhaus, and Brewer met in Brewer's room at the Waldorf-

Astoria. "Blanco," said Day of John White, was "having Hamilton [Jordan] and [Charles] Kirbo to do this thing [regarding the planes]." Wohlenhaus said that the Libyans planned to release $250,000 a day for eleven days, totaling $2.75 million, and Blanco would receive $1 million. In Brewer's view, "Mr. Day would appear, if you were trying to cast a movie, as a typical crooked Southern politician. It's very difficult to tell at times . . . what is fact and what isn't. . . . He's almost to the point of being a pathological liar. . . ."

FBI agents followed Day from the Waldorf-Astoria to LaGuardia Airport, where he caught the shuttle to Washington. At National Airport, Day met Alex Phillips, assistant to John White (whom Brewer had told he was an FBI informant), and they went to the Washington Hotel to meet a Vesco representative. Phillips posed as White on a dry run to learn if anyone was trying to set up his boss. The meeting was monitored by the FBI, Vesco's gumshoes, and, perhaps, the Southern District of New York.

A week later, Day met with White at the Democratic National Committee headquarters, and, the next day, White called at least three State Department officials, one being Warren Christopher, deputy secretary, to ask about the planes and the feasibility of a meeting between President Carter and Ambassador Kikhia. Vesco had become suspicious when the pseudo White didn't know who Edward Bennett Williams was, and, on April 23, he asked Day what was happening. Vesco recorded the conversation and gave the tape to the Senate Judiciary Subcommittee, then investigating Vesco's attempt to reverse the ban on the Libyan planes. After Day had given Vesco his customary assurances about the fugitive's "problem," Vesco asked if the "Kirbo-Jordan [meeting] was the starting point of President Carter's knowledge of White's contact with me [Vesco]." Day said that White reported to Carter and Hamilton Jordan that the release of the planes was a "gesture of good faith in these places." Vesco asked if Carter "knew of White's [financial] interests" in the release of the Libyan planes, and Day said, "Yes."

Day, Wohlenhaus, and Feeney flew to the Bahamas in late April and again in early May, accompanied by an FBI agent. The agency knew that Feeney was cooperating and that he needed more money to cover his $50,000 obligation to Day. Nonetheless, the FBI began an investigation of Feeney. Kikhia, dissatisfied with Vesco, met with Day alone on May 20, in Houston, and Day proposed $15 million for the 747s, whose release the State department was reconsidering because of the Libyan activities in Uganda. Day proposed $7.5 million for each 747 the United States let go, but Kikhia countered with a $10 million offer for the planes, which Day rejected. He did, however, offer to be Libya's lobbyist for three years.

Kikhia, Day, Feeney, Brewer, Wohlenhaus, and "Wise" (an FBI agent named Witowsky) dined that evening at a Houston country club. The New York, Houston, and Miami FBI had the meeting under surveillance, as did the Southern District, but no recording was made of the gathering, perhaps because the FBI and the Southern District each believed the other was doing the job. It was the gang who couldn't tape straight, even though the meeting was a presumably critical turn away from Vesco. The Libyan ambassador told all present that he had met with Vesco but wanted no further dealings with him, because the fugitive spoke too freely on the phone with no other purpose than embarrassing the Democratic party. Kikhia believed his own phone was tapped, which wouldn't have been surprising.

Kikhia forwarded Day's proposal to Libya and met with Day, Wohlenhaus, and Feeney in Kikhia's office in United Nations Plaza. The ambassador said to Day, "You are not taping this conversation," and Day assured him, "Oh no, I have no tape." Feeney, who sported a recorder for the Southern District, stayed silent. A meeting with John White was discussed, and Kikhia agreed to the "agricultural modification" of the troop-carrying C-130s to make their release more palatable to the United States.

White, on June 20, finally met Kikhia at the Washington Hotel's Skytop Restaurant. Wohlenhaus, Brewer, and Feeney watched from a nearby table. Vesco's operatives were probably present, and so was an investigator from the U.S. Attorney, Southern District, seated at still another table. An FBI camera ground away. Day and Kikhia arrived, but the chairman of the Democratic National Committee was almost an hour late. While the Brewer group waited, Wohlenhaus remembered how it all started.

"We hadn't the slightest idea (how to contact Vesco) and Day says let me tell you something, if there's one man I know that knows how to contact Vesco, he said, it's Jim Brewer. And I'll be damned [Brewer did it]."

Feeney said, "Is that right?" and Brewer said, "Yep." Wohlenhaus said, "So he set up the meeting [which] couldn't have been better." Brewer put in, "I probably know somebody to get almost anybody if . . . yeah it may take me a little while but I mean, ah. . . ." Wohlenhaus offered, "I've always wanted to meet the man [Vesco] and when I walked in, I don't think I've been more impressed in my life. Cause I'm like, you know . . . I've seen his pictures in all the magazines, books, and when I saw him I said you know that's him. I recognized him. That's him. And he had on this ragged [unintelligible] little shirt. And he was sitting there in his house. And there was Norman [LeBlanc] standing right behind him. And I said just like a picture out of a book I have [an] exact picture. I was impressed. I was really impressed." Wohlenhaus laughed.

The Kikhia-White meeting lasted only twenty minutes and must have been something of an anticlimax, although the ambassador was smiling as White left, seemed to Brewer "very happy," and went at once to phone the Libyan embassy. He now felt he could approach White directly. According to Day, White had said, "Ah, here is my private phone number. He said you and I are on a direct communication that at any time you need to talk to me through [Jimmy] Day or you can talk to me direct." Day's credibility as a Libyan lobbyist had been established.

After the June 20 meeting, Day told Feeney that the monies going to White would be divided among White, Jordan, and President Carter. White's share would be "washed through a Caribbean bank in amounts of about $100,000 a year."

On it went. The Libyan chargé d'affaires told Day, Wohlenhaus, and Feeney that his country would pay $150 million to have the C-130s released and "Mr. Vesco knows that." No less than $1.5 million would be advanced for the three schemers to represent the Libyan government, one-third of the budget in cash for bribing congressmen, the chargé said; in his letter to the Libyan, Day referred to "direct public relations expenditure."

Despite the big numbers, Feeney still owed Day $23,000 out of the original $50,000 agreed to, and at a meeting in the Bahamas that summer Vesco pressed Feeney to pay "or step out of the deal" from which Vesco was being eased out. Feeney, if he coughed up, would represent Vesco in future Libyan dealings, the fugitive said. The Southern District asked the FBI for the money, but the FBI balked, insisting that Feeney become an FBI informant, which Feeney rejected, and, finally, the Southern District refused to fund him, despite the U.S. Attorney's insistence that Feeney needed the funds in order to continue his participation in the Libyan deal. Within days of denying the Southern District's request for $23,000, the FBI authorized spending $25,000 in an unsuccessful attempt to bribe John White.

"This is very obviously an investigation that should never have begun," concluded the staff of the Senate Judiciary Committee. "The time and money that the FBI spent to join two demonstrably cunning manipulators (Vesco and Day) directly contravenes Congress' intent in enacting a criminal conspiracy statute to deter, not to promote, criminal combines. The FBI's job is to detect conspiracy, not create it."

The results? James Brewer was still an informant as of 1982. James Day became an informant himself, pleaded guilty of lying about his influence with White—the U.S. Attorney in New York charged that Day took $8,000 from Vesco by falsely representing he had persuaded Jordan and John White to assist Vesco—and went to jail for a four-year term, later reduced to two, for defrauding Vesco and overstating his influence with high officials in the United States Government. The Department of Justice refused to appoint a Special Prosecutor and the charges against White were dropped. James Feeney, despite his cooperation, was convicted, and jailed on earlier charges; James Wohlenhaus, a Brewer target, remained under investigation. The Libyans received the two 727s they wanted. Vesco, then in Nicaragua, was still a fugitive.

In the Bahamas, Vesco had attempted still another deal. In 1978, he approached Raymond Mason, president of Charter Oil, which once had been interested in acquiring part of IOS, with the idea of selling IOS remnants that had cash and marketable real estate, but Charter concluded it couldn't do business with Vesco until he settled his legal problems with the United States.

Vesco also talked oil. His notion was that Charter, negotiating to buy a refinery in the Bahamas, in which Libya had a stake, would process Libyan oil for resale in South Africa. At 50 cents a barrel, Vesco would have earned, he said, up to $50 million. But, testified a Charter official, "Mr. Vesco did claim he had some influence with the Libyans [but] never interceded with the Libyans on behalf of Charter. . . ." Still, Vesco phoned Mason that he was entitled to a $5 million finder's fee. Mason rejected his claim.

In July 1979, as his Bahamian haven was becoming unstuck, Vesco made frequent telephone calls, late at night and early in the morning, to the Charter official about the finder's fee, in the course of which he reduced his demands to $500,000 and then $250,000. Vesco's lawyer also phoned, but, eventually, the calls stopped, though in 1980 Vesco called to say he hadn't intended derogatory statements about Charter.

Once again, Vesco had failed to achieve his dwindling dream —safety for himself and his family. According to LeBlanc, Bob was "dry" financially, but as much as ever determined to stay out of prison. He told many people, "If I went in, I'd be killed within thirty days."

34

RETURN TO THE BAHAMAS

In a chartered turbojet, loaded, a bystander noted, from a "pick-up truck filled with documents," a somber Vesco and LeBlanc flew to Panama, or so the flight plan stated. They didn't set down there, though, but changed the route several times during the trip to avoid detection, landing after a nonstop flight probably at Great Harbour Cay in the Bahamas, staying four or five days to fish. The Bahamian government, confused perhaps, denied Vesco's presence, and a report that the fugitive was in Grenada sent journalists scurrying there, but he and LeBlanc came in quietly to Paradise Island by boat, avoiding Nassau airport.

In July 1978, Vesco's Costa Rica citizenship application was rejected because of his involvement in local politics and because, since he had declared himself a pauper there, he lacked sufficient economic reserves—the whale had become a legal minnow, not that anyone in Costa Rica believed he was broke. The Bahamian visit looked as if it might last years, though Vesco couldn't predict. A major disadvantage of his position was that he could not make long-range plans. Too much depended on the mood of his hosts and the disposition of his foe, the United States. In Antigua, he later told Jeffrey Harley that his "toll" in the Bahamas amounted to $3 million, though the fugitive invariably exaggerated or lied.

As in Costa Rica, Vesco obtained important backing. A prominent member of the opposition party who also happened to be a Vesco lawyer, Orville A. Turnquest, wrote in 1978, in support of

Vesco's application for permanent residency, that "Mr. Vesco is a man of exceptional business insight and financial ability, and extremely interested in the development of small countries such as the Bahamas. . . . He has demonstrated the type of investor confidence and interest in civic development which today would essentially enhance a new developing Nation. He is a man of strong personal conviction and a devoted family man, given to clean personal habits, all of which have impressed me as desirable qualities."

Pat, Robert Jr., little Patrick, and Dawn flew in, and the Vescos rented a rather run-down house called Melteme, on Eastern Road in Nassau. Curiously, in view of Vesco's terror with being captured, the house was on the sea, from which a surprise landing could be made but which also offered a means of quick escape. The rent was $2,000 a month, and the landlord, learning of his tenant's identity only after the lease was signed, was furious that he hadn't charged more. The bills were paid by a Bahamian accountant, Fred Murray, to whom a messenger delivered $5,000 in cash each month, Murray said. The sum didn't include the telephone bills.

A man who had known Vesco in the old days, when he had been jauntily flying back and forth between the Bahamas and Costa Rica—confident, superficially at least, that he could make a deal with the United States, or, if not, live out his days splendiferously—saw him at a school watching little Patrick play baseball and found him changed—"more withdrawn and subdued, with some of the fight leached out of him." And Vesco worried increasingly. Costa Rica wouldn't let him return, and the Bahamas wouldn't give him a commitment that he could remain, though a Bahamian lawyer told him, "The Bahamian bar association should have a statue of you for putting so many of our kids through college."

Nor was he doing well on the U.S. legal front as the years dragged on. In October 1978, Judge Stewart held Vesco and LeBlanc in contempt of court for failing to turn over the Property Resources shares that had been dangled like bait before the Georgians, and, soon after, an arrest order for Vesco was issued. The SEC moved to have him fined $5,000 a day for the succeeding thirty days, and $10,000 a day for every day he remained outside of the United States, which, Vesco said, would be forever. "I'll get homesick when I'm in the grave."

Privately, though, he was eager to reach an accommodation with the SEC. He wrote to Stanley Sporkin in 1976 and talked to him subsequently on the telephone. Sporkin, adamant that the fugitive return and stand trial, had announced on TV that Vesco offered to return 80 percent of the missing money if he could keep 20 percent, which seemed to contradict a letter Vesco wrote Sporkin on September 1, 1977. "Dear Stanley, I repeat my offer . . . to have a conference in Costa Rica with you or your representatives to demonstrate I never received a penny of the '224 million' and further to use my best efforts to assist in obtaining the maximum benefit for I.O.S. Ltd. and the Dollar Fund shareholders in the liquidation process . . . I look forward to hearing from you." He didn't. The SEC would only communicate with him in what Vesco referred to as a "third party response," his lawyers.

The SEC opposed an arrangement worked out by Shea, Gould, ICC's lawyers, and accepted by Judge Stewart, whereby Vesco's 25 percent of the company he founded—he had been blocked from selling the shares—was canceled. In exchange, Vesco was released from paying ICC $5.3 million that had been awarded it. ICC would pay $840,000 to the IRS, which had ruled that, since the 707 had been exclusively for Vesco's use, its expense had to be viewed as income. International Controls paid $160,000 to the Vesco kids, except Patrick, to dispose of their claims on the company, and Pat was to be paid $255,000 for the Boonton house, later sold at judicial auction by ICC for about $500,000. ICC also received Vesco's 75,000 shares in a Massachusetts pharmaceutical distribution company, worth $1.35 million. Vesco glumly signed the agreement that seemed to sever most, if not all, of his financial ties to the United States. (Related to the settlement, special ICC counsel David Butowsky came to the Bahamas to depose Vesco. At the casino, he taught Butowsky how to play baccarat, and when Butowsky won, Vesco rewarded him with a kiss on the cheek. Sporkin, hearing of the buss, was furious. There must be no intercourse with the enemy.)

Vesco's increasingly vain hope was to find a permanent refuge, though nobody really wanted him because of the American government. He asked the Bahamian government to give him a year or so to reach an accommodation with the receivers, a crowd of whom joined those already there. More than $300 million in cash and real estate had been recovered but plenty still seemed to be missing. The situation for the accountants was bizarre. After all this time, they still couldn't trace the vanished money. It was as though they'd been booby-trapped by two mordant characters who pretended to try to be of help.

LeBlanc, who remained in the Bahamas for a year with Vesco while he explored his own Costa Rica status, gave the Global receiver, Roger Hendrickson, $373,000 in missing notes—that is, obligations, not cash—as though to encourage him, but Hendrickson pointed to an unaccounted-for $11 million. Norman said he couldn't investigate without the records of Bahama Commonwealth Bank, and *its* receiver, under Bahamian bank secrecy laws, had denied him access, as the receiver had to Hendrickson. The stalemate was almost complete. The Trident records would have helped, but LeBlanc didn't reveal that they could have been found at his Nassau lawyers, DuPuch and Turnquest. LeBlanc did deliver the records of Trident's parent, Vector, wrapped in a red ribbon, but Vector's cupboard was bare.

At one point the receivers were so irritated with LeBlanc that they spoke of having him arrested but didn't know where he lived. Leaving their hotel, they saw Norman MacDonald, as he called himself, using his mother's last name, washing his car down the street.

Another claim against Vesco was that of a German woman who filed a paternity suit based on alleged events in Hamburg in 1968, but the German Bahamian who tried to serve the fugitive couldn't penetrate the guards. Probably, the woman had read that Vesco had stolen the legendary $224 million and hoped to part him from some of it.

The liquidation of BCB would have continued almost indefinitely because remnants of IOS still controlled by Vesco and/or LeBlanc had claims on the bank for the same monies that the receivers did. Not only that, but there were ordinary Bahamian depositors who wanted their money from the closed bank and would have to be paid first as a practical political matter. John Orr, receiver for Fund of Funds, proposed a solution that Vesco accepted. Vesco and LeBlanc would assign their claims to FOF, and FOF would pay the Bahamian depositors in full. Despite an understanding with Arthur Hanna, then Minister of Finance of the Bahamas, Vesco took credit and got a headline VESCO STEPS IN. Orr wanted to see VESCO STEPS OUT.

During the negotiations with Orr, Vesco, guarded less obtrusively, could be seen eating ice cream at Howard Johnson's in downtown Nassau. He still believed his extensive difficulties with the United States could be solved, and, important to his ego, he still had money. (There was a capitalistic existentialism in Vesco's mentality, not "I exist, therefore I am" but "I exist rich, therefore I am.") The Vescos had received about $500,000 from the sale of the Costa Rican compound, and he bought an old yacht about sixty feet long, which he named the *Salude.* Vesco completely renovated it. The finishing touches were done at Melteme, which had a dock, by Vesco and his captain, Ulis Brown. The *Salude* ferried Vesco, Pat, and the kids in attendance to their secret hideaway, a lovely 195-acre island called Cistern Cay, fifty-five miles south of Nassau, and Vesco paid Ken Cartwright, a Nassau car and boat dealer, $180,000 cash plus fees for most of Cistern Cay and an attractive house on a high bluff. (The property wasn't owned by Vesco directly, of course.) Vesco was a genius at concealing his movements and it wasn't until 1981 that the reporters knew that he lived there.

Vesco would drop in at the Nassau *Tribune,* sometimes bringing his own handwritten articles on his case, bits of which the paper occasionally printed as parts of other stories. Vesco's journalistic attempts were not editorials—although, in one, he did insert the word "infamous" before "SEC complaint"—but naïve efforts to dramatize his plight. Jack Anderson, Vesco wrote, "went on to report that, evidently fearful of spooking their quarry into flight, U.S. officials didn't even let the Bahamian government in on the situation," that the United States explored other means than extradition to capture Vesco. He was obsessed, and rightly so if only in the sense that, after years of pursuit, the American government had by no means given up.

He was obsessed as well with $850,000 he believed was owed to him from a deal with Everett E. Bannister, Prime Minister Pindling's man, and Tiger Finlayson, whose restaurant, Mona Lisa, Vesco thought BCB money had financed. Finlayson said he hadn't gotten any and showed Vesco his mortgage. "Ask Bannister," Tiger advised, and Vesco muttered that Bannister had outsmarted him again. Vesco had evidently been promised shares in Finlayson's Bahamas Catering, but Bannister said, "They're all gone."

Vesco was increasingly powerless and subject to what others did or said. In 1984, a convicted drug dealer, Timothy Irwin Minnig, testified before the Bahamian Commission of Inquiry, investigating government corruption because of the drug trade, that in 1978 Vesco told him he paid $100,000 a month to Lynden Pindling to avoid being deported. Vesco, Minnig said, offered the drug dealer safety for a million dollars, and, since Minnig's drug operation had encountered difficulties, he agreed. After he had given Vesco about $400,000, Minnig wondered what the money had bought him, and would pay no more until he saw results.

According to Minnig, Vesco said he would prove where the money went by letting the drug dealer observe the next payment to the Prime Minister. Minnig went to a branch of the Bank of Nova Scotia, he claimed, emerging twenty minutes later with $100,000 in a manila envelope. He and Vesco drove to Pindling's house. The Prime Minister had just said good-bye to his luncheon guests. Vesco approached him and the two men went inside for about ten minutes—Minnig recalled "trying to be polite" about the new Bahamian television service as he talked with a minister responsible for it. Vesco came out and they drove away. Minnig's difficulties subsequently eased, he said.

In his testimony, though, Minnig had trouble describing the route he and Vesco had taken, and the commission became skeptical, and more skeptical still when Minnig described the Prime Minister's house inaccurately. F. Lee Bailey, Pindling's lawyer, suggested that Minnig had been "scammed" by Vesco with a bogus Prime Minister, but that, the commission believed, was unlikely because a phony Prime Minister wouldn't have had guests. Most telling for the commission was Minnig's story that he had withdrawn $100,000 in twenty minutes, and the manager of the bank testified that such large sums were not kept at the branch. Minnig's accusations were thrown out, nor did the "protection money" he paid do Minnig any good since he was eventually expelled.

On December 29, 1980, Vesco, in chin whiskers, held a press conference at Big Al's Restaurant in Nassau announcing he had filed for political asylum. He feared persecution and being clandestinely captured and taken away. He was a refugee, he said, and for the first time, admitted he had nowhere to go. He virtually begged to be allowed to stay.

A divided picture of Vesco emerges during the second Bahamas period. On the one hand, according to the car/boat-dealer Cartwright, he helped the poor. On the other, he exhibited stinginess toward those who worked for him loyally and under trying conditions.

Late in 1979, ever more frightened of being apprehended, Vesco chartered Cartwright's 58-foot Hatteras and embarked on a cruise that lasted sixty days, putting in at Great Exuma, Stocking Island, Samson Cay, Little Cat Island, Andros, Chubb Cay, Freeport (Grand Bahama), Great Abaco, Spanish Wells, Harbour Island, Cape Eleuthera, Morgan Bluff, Little Walker Cay—thirty or forty islands rattled off in no particular order by Cartwright's charter captain, John Pratt, who remembered:

"It was a strange trip. I had a funny feeling—I couldn't figure out what Vesco would say or do. I had to be ready at all times because he'd give me only a half-hour's notice about our departure time and destination. I had to tell him sometimes, 'You don't know where it is or how long the trip will take.'

"Before we left, Vesco told me I wouldn't need a mate because all of them would help and they knew what to do. On board, besides Bob, were Pat, Patrick, their son, Dawn and her kid, and an American nanny for it. Nobody lifted a finger. Vesco went to bed at one or two and was up early. So was I. I took care of the boat, did the laundry, cooked. Just before dinner, Bob would go to the freezer and pull out what he wanted and throw it in the sink. If they went out to dinner on one of the islands I had to wait up to get them back on board at maybe 2 A.M. He even asked me to help take care of Dawn's baby—maybe a year old; she was a teenager—but I drew the line there. I was supposed to have time off. I had one night in two months.

"They were the worst set of people I ever had on a boat—I told him that. Nobody ever smiled. Vesco stayed by himself reading and doing book work. Dawnie pouted. Pat walked on the beach gathering shells. The nanny was grumpy—she stayed out all night whenever she could. I put in twelve-hour days, at least, and when it was over he gave me a lousy $1,300 tip on a charter that cost him more than sixty grand for the boat alone."

Captain Pratt had in tow a 17-foot whaler for the indolent family to ride to the beach in, and side-by-side with the yacht was still another boat, Vesco's speedy 27-foot Seacraft captained by Ulis Brown. The vessel was meant ostensibly for fishing, and, while Vesco occasionally bottom-fished at night, he never strayed far from the Hatteras. He was not alone in being nervous. He'd given Pat a strobe light to signal with, and once he'd been out for no more than half an hour when she started flashing—for no particular reason. The Seacraft was rarely used, and its purpose, as seems evident, was for a quick escape in an emergency.

35

ESCAPE FROM THE BAHAMAS

The Kingfish had become the most publicized criminal of contemporary times, and U.S. law enforcement authorities were humiliated by the failure to apprehend him. In their minds, not only had "The Man" successfully stolen hundreds of millions of dollars but stories of Vesco's drug involvement were rife, even though the Bahamian Drug Enforcement Authority had not found evidence of Vesco's involvement in the narcotics trade. But Vesco's island, Cistern Cay, was only a few miles from Norman's Cay, the largest drug-smuggling center in the Bahamas and under intense surveillance. At the least, Vesco was guilty of proximity.

The FBI's concern about, and anger at, Vesco had increased with newspaper accounts of the Herring bribe story and the Libyan plane operation. Said FBI informant Brewer, "I think Nehrbass [Arthur Nehrbass, acting head of the FBI Miami office] and I think the FBI's opinion is that it's kind of an embarrassment to the country because he [Vesco] is constantly . . . causing all those things to happen. It seems like we're helpless to do anything about it. He causes embarrassment to everybody. Every effort should be made to stop this, which means to bring him back to this country so that this sort of thing could be [stopped]. He's sitting a few miles off on an island manipulating all these sorts of things." Brewer said about Nehrbass, "I heard him make a statement that before he retires, which he is thinking of doing momentarily, he would like to bring Vesco back. It would be kind of like his last trophy sort of thing. It's personal in a way. It's a challenge . . . something he'd like to do."

The American government was out to catch the Kingfish by almost any means, and the Bahamian government was fully informed but helpless to intervene even if it wished; it may not have known about a Bahamian pilot who, arrested in 1981 for flying "illegal" Colombians to Florida, and who had worked in a peripheral capacity for Vesco, was brought to an FBI office and promised a year's probation if he would lure Vesco on board an airplane and fly him to the United States. The pilot said he agreed, but Vesco was in hiding by then.

In 1979, the first visible evidence of Operation Kingfish appeared in the shape of the *Rampage,* a 55-foot Hatteras—it may have been the Abscam boat—with perhaps five men, some in wet suits, aboard, including Nehrbass. They were spotted in Nassau harbor, and anchored off Athol Island, a mile or so from Vesco's house on Eastern Road, with what an observer described as a "huge telescopic lens." Vesco had assembled a group of defenders—maybe romantically, they told of arms dropped from the *Rampage* in plastic bags, with pennants to locate them, to be used in an assault—and Vesco's defenders were prepared to handle them if anyone tried to abduct him. (Such things could happen in Nassau. Another U.S. fugitive opened his hotel door there, was jabbed by a needle, and woke on his way to a Texas jail.)

The FBI recruited a reporter, Bob Collins, of the Camden, N.J., *Courier-Post.* Collins's reward was to be similar to that offered other reporters,* an exclusive on the Vesco capture story. Collins was to take pictures, ingratiate himself with Vesco, and, if possible, gain access to the Vesco house—lightly protected because the Bahamian government objected to too many guards—in order to scout it. Collins was chosen because he had done previous work for the FBI and because he wouldn't attract attention. As it was, Collins had difficulty in learning where Vesco lived—people, he said, were protective, and he couldn't ask the authorities.

Vesco installed a Sperry-Rand automatic pilot on the *Salude,* and the FBI reached the mechanic who repaired it and asked him

* Including this one.

to install a homing device on the vessel. The man became upset and told his boss, who forbade him to do so. Vesco learned of that; loose talk by the FBI at the Green Shutters Restaurant in Nassau was overheard and reported to Vesco who had pictures taken, just as the FBI photographed him.

According to Collins, one FBI idea was to abduct Vesco by boat, another to entice him aboard an aircraft, drug him and his guard, land at a U.S. Bahamian base, arrest the fugitive, and return him to the United States. (Collins, accurately or not, claimed he spoke with Prime Minister Pindling, who warned him against becoming party to a kidnapping.) Collins would write his story aboard the plane, pictures would be taken of Vesco being brought off, and Collins would have a scoop. But the pilot was to have been a man already held on a narcotics charge, and, if Vesco were overdosed, Collins feared he might be blamed because the FBI would deny responsibility. Concerned, Collins, who had talked to Vesco by then, sent word that he should phone him in Camden. Collins tipped him off. Vesco thanked him and asked what he could do in return. Collins mentioned an interview down the line. Collins was certain the United States tried to convince the Bahamian government that Vesco was in the drug business. Nehrbass denied some of Collins's rendition but not all.

Vesco was to have been thrown out of the Bahamas in January 1981, and his disappearance to Cistern Cay after the Big Al's press conference meant to some that he had already fled, but he had appealed. Still, the CIA planned around his January expulsion date. A document, on CIA letterhead, with the signature of the sendee and the recipient removed, stated, "Attached is the latest situation report on the Vesco operation. Please see that it is updated." The report said nothing unusual went on at the Vesco house. Telephone calls and mail were "normal," nor was Vesco radioing anything. He didn't seem to be about to bolt for, say, Colombia, which Collins claimed was the fugitive's next destination. "An apparent spurious radiation in the 15-meter radio band on Dec. 19. The spectral analysis revealed nothing of significance. . . . Photomicrographs were unremarkable in every aspect. . . . Unit was informed . . . former investigator Senate Perm Committee on Invest. . . . Special diplomatic activity continues with respect to site A. . . . Travel arrangements complete all parties can assemble within 16 hours. . . . NOAA [satellite] material accurate. . . . Their [sic] has been no family action of significant mention. . . . 10 aspects to project. . . ."

Around this time, the Bahamian police put Vesco under surveillance. They had their hands full since the Shah of Iran and Anastasio Somoza of Nicaragua, were also in the Bahamas. The Bahamians had begun to act in the same indecisive manner as had Oduber in Costa Rica, never being clear whether Vesco could stay or go, although Clement Maynard, Minister of Home Affairs, clearly wanted the fugitive banished. Vesco's lawyers tried to prove he had no authority to deport him. The American Embassy, according to Arthur D. Hanna, then the Deputy Prime Minister, didn't approach the Bahamian government directly, but it did make unpleasant consequences of concessions to Vesco known. The U.S. Customs operating on Bahamian soil to facilitate American travelers could be withdrawn, and the American news media could be fed stories about the Bahamian crime rate, among the highest in the world. Such reprisals would directly affect tourism.

Vesco told Hanna that Maynard's brother was wanted in the United States on drug charges and that the Minister of Home Affairs tried to swap the fugitive for him, but there wasn't any proof of that. Indeed, in all probability the Bahamian government would have sent Vesco to some other place than the United States on the grounds that it was up to the United States to extradite him. At one point, Vesco was told to depart and did, apparently for the British Turks and Caicos Islands to the south, but, however it was done, the fugitive was readmitted on Eleuthera, and was once more officially in the country. The Bahamian cabinet then voted, seemingly with reluctance on the part of some, to declare Vesco undesirable—the cabinet wouldn't reveal the reason except that the action was "in the public interest"—and Vesco was placed on the "Stop-List," meaning an arrest order if he remained.

Vesco was said to have bought the Prime Minister, but either the allegation was false or his handwritten letter to Pindling and Pindling's reference to it were masterpieces of duplicity. "This," noted the P.M., "was delivered to my house last night by a man who identified himself as Robert Vesco."

> Although non-authoritative persons have stated that the government intends to allow me to stay permanently in the Bahamas, I have received no communication of any kind (pro or con) from the Minister of Home Affairs for months.
>
> Therefore, I am forced again to ask you if you intend to let me stay or if not then how much time will be given to leave so that I can realistically begin to seek a location. Under the circumstances it has been impossible to plan, or make any arrangements, particularly when my movements in and out of the Bahamas are restricted.
>
> I would also hope that you will consider a meeting as requested in my last note.

It would seem that Pindling not only didn't know Vesco well, although the Libyan oil deal may have been discussed with him, but, if only for political reasons, also went out of his way to reject Vesco's requests for meetings.

Vesco's tone was one of controlled panic, and, indeed, he acted like a desperate man. He paced his living room, constantly peering out to sea. Although the Bahamian police thought he was at his house—two police cars were parked in front and a police boat guarded the rear—Vesco had left and was moving frantically around the islands. He had started to wear theatrical makeup like an actor. In 1973, Norman LeBlanc had hired a Bahamian golfer, Donald "Nine" Rolle, who had won a Caribbean championship, for publicity tours for Bahamas Commonwealth Bank. Rolle, who would become president of a Citizens' Committee for Human Rights, credited BCB with making it possible for black people to borrow money in the Bahamas. "Before," Rolle said, "black people couldn't borrow a nickel but BCB changed all that." Maybe. Rolle had lunch with LeBlanc almost every day, he said, but only in 1978 did he become friends with Vesco. The golfer had helped arrange a Nassau fight for Muhammad Ali whom he found awfully smart. "I knew Martin Luther King, who was superbright. But Robert Vesco was the smartest man I ever met."

For Ken Cartwright, the car and boat dealer, Vesco had become too "paranoid" to tolerate, but not so Nine Rolle (the nickname derived from dice). For months the strange pair darted furtively around the islands, except for one or two occasions when Vesco got an extension to stay and returned to Nassau. Rolle remembered sleeping in bushes with his hat as a pillow or fishing off rocks with Bob "like two niggers, eating sardines from cans." Nine owned a house or two, and they lived in one of them. He rented apartments for them in his name—at one, on Grand Bahama, after the tenants had left, the landlord found a driver's license bearing a photo of a dour-faced man in glasses—Vesco—and the signature "Dennis Richardson." Richardson was the name Vesco used in Antigua. They stayed on Chubb Cay, the Berry Islands, and others with, Rolle claimed, the Bahamian Central Intelligence Department (CID) on their trail, so that, if Rolle had to go to the store, he changed cars because the police would have recognized his.

In return for his assistance, Vesco appeared to have offered Rolle his share of Bahamas Catering, on the basis of what Bannister was supposed to owe, but, if so, the offer was specious because the fugitive had nothing on paper. Rolle showed no resentment. He felt an almost fanatic altruism toward Vesco, and was not alone. A group of four or five Bahamian blacks took the fugitive's welfare as almost a personal matter and met with him as far away as Turks and Caicos. The rescuers, headed by a seventy-or-so-year-old tile maker named George Haestie, known as the "Bishop," tried to find Vesco a place to go. Vesco claimed that Haiti or Guyana would accept him, but a Guyanese official denied such a discussion had occurred, although he said, "We would have been happy to have him. Dollar-poor countries don't give a damn about U.S. white-collar crimes." Clandestine conferences took place at two, three, or even four in the morning among the agitated Vesco, Rolle, Haestie, Orville Turnquest, and, perhaps, Dione Hanna, another Vesco lawyer. Hanna's father, Arthur, the Deputy Prime Minister, was Haestie's nephew.

Haestie suggested Antigua as a refuge, apparently with Pindling's blessing, and a new recruit was added, Thomas Robinson, for whom the Nassau stadium was named. A sprinter, Robinson had been a finalist in four Olympic games. Tommy Robinson was not a Vescophile like Rolle. He thought he would be paid (he wasn't) and he wanted to help the government of Antigua.

Haestie had already determined that Antigua might be receptive, and Robinson was picked as intermediary because he had been a classmate of Lester Bird, an All-American broad jumper at the University of Michigan in 1961. Bird was the Deputy Prime Minister of Antigua and the son of Vere Bird, Antigua's long-time Prime Minister. Robinson, at Vesco's expense, went to Antigua on several occasions. Lester asked his father about admitting Vesco, but Vere said no. Robinson then said that Vesco was prepared to invest in Antigua and a negotiation took place, the result of which was that Antigua, with cabinet approval, would give Vesco residence status, as the Bahamas would not. As far as Antigua was concerned, Vesco hadn't committed a crime and there wasn't an extraditable offense.

Captain Ulis Brown was dispatched on the *Salude* with Bill Schacter, an experienced Miami boat man Vesco met in the Bahamas. Three police boats followed them from Nassau Harbour, searching the vessel for Vesco and contraband but finding neither. Schacter and Brown were bound on a circuitous route for Antigua. On or about September 15, 1981, the wanted man came to Nassau airport, in plain view of immigration authorities but disguised, boarded a twin-engine, prop-driven Aztec, while Haestie and Robinson took an Eastern flight to Miami and on to Antigua. Vesco may have traveled to Eleuthera, where another plane picked him up. Once more, the fugitive had taken wing.

36

VESCO IN ANTIGUA

Vesco, in a straw hat and carrying fishing rods, arrived at Antigua a week before the government expected him. He insisted on passing customs without formalities that might identify him, and, arrangements not having been made, a forty-year-old white Antiguan named Jeff Harley rushed to the airport to get him through. Harley, Vesco's unofficial contact, would see the fugitive almost daily until his tumultuous departure eight months later.

Harley was delighted to meet the "greatest swindler of all times." He saw the "golden apple in the sky" but didn't get much of a bite.

Temporarily, at least, Vesco felt safe in Antigua, as safe as a hunted and haunted man could. As before, Pat and young Patrick flew in, and they rented, for several hundred dollars a day, Antigua Village #2, a two-bedroom, two-story condominium. All the older kids came down, using the name Richardson as Bob had called himself since the last hectic days in the Bahamas. When they arrived, Vesco rented the next-door villa. From a previous visit, Vesco knew the landlord, Tony Velardi, who owned Castle Harbour (now the Flamingo), one of Antigua's three casinos.

On the surface, the Vescos seemed to live a normal life and were accepted as normal people. Pat, who wore her hair long and did needlepoint, cooked unless they ate out. Every weekday, Vesco drove to work in a rented used green Toyota, which he later bought, returning home for lunch, which Pat prepared, and then he napped. An abductor would have found the Kingfish stretched out in the bedroom in full view, nor were the outside doors locked. Then back to the office for a few more hours. After that, in shorts and a T-shirt, the enigmatic man would walk on the beach with Patrick, who had a tutor, throwing a Frisbee ahead for the boy.

To Antiguans who worked for Vesco at odd jobs, he appeared cheerful, relaxed, patient (unlike the tourists), chatty, and generous. They liked him, and after Vesco had left, and they realized who "Richardson" had been, they were thoroughly surprised. Stedman Scotland, driver and handyman—three years after the fugitive departed, he still remembered the Toyota's license plate: AG 3801—said, "I felt sad when I heard. He showed an interest in me. I hope I can see him before he dies. I'd like to be at his bedside and have him tell me all he's done." (The United States shared Scotty's desire.) Once, Scotty asked Richardson-Vesco if he believed in God, and Vesco said, "Yes. You think I'm a heathen or something? I'll prove it by going to church with you," a Baptist church, as it turned out. On Sunday, Vesco was dressed in a suit—the first time Scotty had seen him so attired—but it rained too hard to go.

A young woman who drank an occasional beer with Richardson at Shorty's on the beach considered him scruffy, but Vesco constantly changed his facial hair as part of his disguise and was growing a beard. Later, she was flabbergasted to learn her drinking companion was the notorious fugitive. For once, Vesco had no guards and wandered the streets. On Independence Day, November 1, 1981, when Antigua became officially free of British rule, the dignitaries poured in and the Vescos moved to a hotel across the island so that Bob wouldn't be spotted. The Antiguan government believed, wrongly, it seems, that Vesco was in touch with members of the American delegation, and that the United States, though knowing where he was, didn't bother him. Both notions were counted in Vesco's favor.

Vesco passed himself off as an investor looking for opportunities. His office, on Redcliffe Street, was made available by the law firm of Bird & Bird, the dominant political family on the island. Vesco paid $200 a month for four rooms. He had two secretaries, Norman LeBlanc's daughter, Debbie, and Pauline Rayne, who could never decide what the boss occupied himself with, aside from endless overseas phone calls. She, too, believed Richardson was simply an American investor, though investments failed to materialize. One of her tasks was to pick up money wired from Barclays Bank in Nassau, and she nervously carried, in canvas bags, sums of $10,000, $25,000, $30,000, and $70,000 from the bank to the office, though Vesco may have had other sources of money. How Vesco used the money is unknown, but expenses on the *Salude,* brought from Nassau and fully crewed, must have been high. And, again, he had to pass through the "toll gate"—payoffs to Antiguan officials running as high as $10,000 a month.

Richardson talked blandly of at least two deals—a banking facility at the airport, probably to process "hot money"—and some sort of independent banking kingdom on the neighboring Antigua island of Barbuda. Nothing happened. Nothing happened with the basic arrangement, either. It had been negotiated, partly by the Bahamian runner Tommy Robinson, with Vere C. Bird, Antigua Prime Minister for over twenty years. The fugitive agreed to invest $15 million for a 500-unit housing project. Vere's son Lester, Deputy Prime Minister, six foot six, 270 pounds, announced the investment on the radio about the time of Independence Day without revealing the source of the money. V.C., also physically huge, had much to consider in real world terms. U.S. pressure—Vesco appeared to be a thorn in the side of Uncle Sam—could be intense. On two Antiguan military installations alone, the United States paid an annual rent of $4.1 million, which could always be withdrawn especially as the Americans insisted they were obsolete. But maybe the Americans could be persuaded to relent on the question of Vesco especially if he were a useful member of the Antiguan community—nearly ten years had passed since the SEC complaint, and, for the moment at least, the United States was quiet, like a dormant volcano. Besides, there was the future to keep in mind.

Even antigovernment radicals like Tim Hector, publisher of the scathing *Outlet,* admired Vere Bird. "When I grew up—a good friend of Lester's by the way—all of us suffered from some form of malnutrition, though we didn't know it. Vere wiped out disease and poverty, and I'll always be grateful to him." Vere wanted either Lester or his brother, Vere Jr., to succeed him—there was intense rivalry between the two—and the $15 million housing project would be a major accomplishment for the Bird boys, who needed something that could be compared with their father's accomplishments. Besides, the houses would be built in different areas and help get votes (not, as it turned out, that the Bird party needed them. In the 1984 elections it won all seventeen seats in Parliament. The opposition claimed the election was rigged).

The Birds assumed that Vesco had the funds to invest. Robin Hood had stolen $224 million, hadn't he? The American news media said so, and even if the figure was somewhat inflated for sensationalistic purposes, Vesco had to have a bundle. Still, having reached an understanding and arrived, Vesco backed off, to the Birds' bewilderment, annoyance, and, finally, fury. He started to make excuses. Dealing as he always insisted "one-on-one" with Lester Bird (meaning only the two of them) Vesco would say, "This isn't the time to proceed. Let's wait a bit." Chain-smoking Kools as usual, he talked about his plans for Barbuda. But he wanted to change the rules, asking to be classified, as he had in the Bahamas, as a "political refugee," which didn't appear to have much to do with investments. The Birds believed Vesco was stalling, and wondered if he really was willing to invest $15 million. According to LeBlanc, Vesco didn't have it. Again, he bluffed, betting that luck would suffice.

Hector, whose *Outlet* taunted Lester Bird about the housing project, saw in a restaurant the profile of the man seated with Jeff Harley. Harley, who had a degree from Cambridge University, had settled in Australia, where his parents lived. He had killed a person in a car accident, been put on probation, and eventually returned to Antigua. He had been to school with the Bird brothers and become a sort of unofficial wheeler-dealer who took overseas investors around to sell them real estate and such. For Hector that was a clue. "I know that face," he thought, and asked a woman acquaintance who had IOS stock whether she'd gotten her money back. "Some," she said. Had she ever seen the man who had run IOS? No, but she had a book that had photographs. "That's him!" Hector said with excitement.

Nobody had ever accused the *Outlet* of over-research, but Hector worked hard on the story and Vesco learned of it. He sent word he would buy Hector a printing press—Hector's was ailing —if he didn't run the article, but Hector refused. Word of Vesco's presence also reached other ears. Lester Bird was livid about Vesco's noninvesting and told Harley to apply pressure. Harley called a man in Atlanta. There was talk about threatening Vesco, and, if that didn't work, of kidnapping one of his children until he came through. The man taped the conversation, which was heard by a reporter with the Atlanta *Constitution.* The reporter went to Antigua where he met with the American chargé d'affaires, Paul Byrnes, who made an inquiry, though didn't seem to think the information was significant. The Birds denied Vesco's presence but the reporter confirmed it by different means. He learned of a plot by individuals in the narcotics trade to drug Vesco with a dart gun and spirit him off the island, presumably for a U.S. reward. (Some Florida law enforcement types in Broward County also heard of the dart plan and, in the absence of U.S. action, were prepared to implement it themselves but were forbidden by their superior.) The reporter, frightened that he might somehow be dragged in, alerted the FBI.

On Saturday, March 6, 1982, Robert Coram of the *Constitution* broke the Vesco-in-Antigua story in his newspaper and events moved swiftly. Vesco had already displayed signs of anxiety. Pat and Patrick left, and he moved onto the *Salude,* anchored in English Harbour. He pestered his secretary about another Bahamian bank transfer, which failed to arrive, but a pilot flew in with a shopping bag containing money. The fugitive's phone bill seemed to have increased. Running at about $1,200 a month previously, the last one, which Vesco never paid, came to $10,000. The *Constitution* story finally triggered an American response. The U.S. chargé d'affaires told an Antiguan minister that the "shit had hit the fan"—the U.S. State Department wanted Vesco out. The cabinet met hurriedly, deciding Vesco wasn't worth a confrontation, especially as he hadn't lived up to his $15 million commitment. The U.S. government requested permission to send the FBI to establish his presence, at least. (The North Americans, a cab driver said, carried guns and handcuffs.) The Antiguans agreed but began to act in a contradictory fashion.

On the morning of March 10, a Wednesday, Harley was aboard a commercial flight to Miami, but, as it reached the end of the runway, the plane was recalled and Harley was asked to disembark. The FBI, he was told by an Antiguan official, had come from Haiti and the Dominican Republic, where, as in other places, agents were attached to the embassies. The lawmen, who searched for the fugitive's nonexistent plane, appear to have been purposefully misdirected. An assistant commissioner of police assigned to Vesco sent them to nearby Barbuda to give Vesco time to escape. He seems to have been paid $10,000 by the fugitive. Harley raced to Redcliffe Street with the warning, and he and Vesco walked out. To Pauline, Vesco's secretary, Mr. Richardson, who in any case never smiled or laughed, displayed anxiety for the first time.

Panic would have been more like it. For the rest of the day, Vesco hid at Castle Harbour, going that evening to Harley's house, along with Pat and Patrick, who had returned to the island. An official car with a policeman arrived with an invitation for Harley to a governmental function, but Vesco, believing he was sought, ran off into the night and Harley didn't find him until 2 A.M., down the beach, huddled under a bush in pouring rain. The next day, Harley moved the fugitive with Pat and Patrick to the home of a new recruit, a Jamaican named Winston Gray, owner of an ice plant. Harley chose Gray partly because of his cool. Vesco stayed in Gray's spare bedroom for two nights, constantly smoking Kools and drinking coffee to stay awake. (Even earlier, he had summoned Harley in the middle of the night because he was jumpy.)

Moored alongside the *Salude* (which left port on Friday to commence a month-long odyssey) at Nelson's Boatyard, in English Harbour, was the *Realitie,* a 29-foot Phoenix diesel that Vesco had previously chartered for fishing. The *Realitie* was dispatched to Crabbs Marina to have her bottom cleaned in preparation for a trip. At 6 A.M., on March 13, 1982, the *Realitie* departed with Vesco, Harley, Gray, and the captain, Johnny Potter, on board. The weather had been bad for a month, and a gale, almost a hurricane—Antiguans still remember the storm—was running. The others didn't want to leave, but Vesco insisted, and the vessel sailed in screaming winds and roaring seas.

Vesco had left Antigua, and the government issued a statement that, while he might have been a tourist there, it had had no dealings with him. That was a lie—but an understandable one, perhaps.

37

THE ROAD TO CUBA

The destination was St. Martin, normally about a three-hour trip, but which, because of the storm, took most of the day. Instead of following the island chain, as usually done, the *Realitie,* equipped with Satnav (satellite guidance) and compass, went directly across in twenty-foot waves. The craft was built for rough weather, but as it lurched into troughs with sickening speed, Vesco's helpers were keenly aware that they could drown, ending the fugitive's dreams as well as their own.

Vesco remained below, afraid of being spotted, though there were no other vessels in the vicinity, peering through portholes for search planes, though there were none. As they neared St. Martin, Vesco came topside and had an altercation with Gray, the mustached ice man, about what course Potter should follow. Gray won that and the subsequent battles.

The *Realitie* docked at Philipsburg—there was no customs check in the duty-free port, though they were required—but Vesco, who had shaved his beard, became agitated at the sight of cruise ships, convinced he'd be recognized. Harley rented a car, for cash—nothing must be on paper—and surreptitiously picked up Bob at the quay. All four went first to Little Bay, as Harley remembers, to another hotel and then to Mullet Bay, where Vesco burned papers he'd brought, flushing them down the toilet. They all lived and ate in the same suites. Vesco would let no one out of his sight, perhaps in fear he'd be turned in. At night he would nod fitfully, rise, pace, peer through the windows—always on guard against the FBI, which he saw everywhere.

The fugitive spoke of people who would come from the States to aid him, but only one did, a young man who left almost immediately. Vesco phoned Don Pepe Figueres for help once more, without results. But on the evening of the second day on St. Martin, a Mexican Gulfstream jet, whose pilot had some sort of diplomatic status, arrived to fetch him. It has been supposed that the plane was arranged for by Carlos Lehder-Rivas, the Colombian drug king. The next morning, Vesco refused to fly on it. He was convinced that the FBI would interdict him at the airport. He wanted to reboard the *Realitie,* but Gray asked the raving man, "Where would you go?" At last, Vesco gave in and Harley drove them to the airport. Vesco wanted to board at the end of the runway, but the Mexican captain wouldn't—he taxied to the terminal—and Gray and the fugitive, pretending to have been on board already, slipped through customs. Jumping into the plane with the sack of money brought from Antigua, Vesco hid on his hands and knees in the aisle to avoid being seen until the plane was ready for takeoff. "His spirit," said Gray, "was broken."

Vesco had his fall-backs as usual. The *Salude* was off nearby St. Barthélemy, and a colleague flew in after the fugitive had departed to make sure he escaped. Vesco always managed to muster loyalty because people felt sorry for him, because he appealed to their sense of adventure, and because they expected the supermillionaire to pay them well. He badly disappointed the Antigua group as he had others. Harley, who expected $100,000 for his services, received $3,000, and Gray only got the used Toyota, parked on an Antigua street as a ruse, which he was somehow supposed to divide with the *Realitie*'s owner. But everybody was glad to have the famous fugitive off their hands.

Vesco's position was unenviable by any standards. He had no safe place to go. He pinned his hopes on Costa Rica because of José Figueres and the hospital in San José. Exacerbated perhaps by stress, his urinary problem had returned. But whether the Ticos would accept him was unknown. The jet probably flew him to Mexico from Colombia, and from there he employed two aircraft to confuse the control tower at Llano Grande International Airport in the northern part of Costa Rica, not too far from the Guanacaste *finca.* One plane landed briefly at an airstrip, and Vesco was picked up by a car whose driver may not have known who he was. After, perhaps, a short stay at the ranch, he was taken to San José in early April. Vesco called Don Pepe, who summoned Enrique Carreras. "Do you know who's here?" he asked. Carreras said, "Don't tell me. Vesco." Figueres nodded silently, and Enrique groaned.

"Vesco was beside himself," Carreras recalled. "He complained of being ripped off wherever he went. He needed a sanctuary for himself and Pat and a place where Patrick would be in school. And his health was terrible." For the moment, the question for the Costa Ricans was where to shelter Vesco. The Figuereses had La Lucha, but everyone knew that Don Pepe hid people there—not just political refugees, as frequently in the past, but those who had fallen into trouble in the United States and other countries for white-collar crimes. Vesco was lodged in safe houses, and, at one, was robbed of $25,000 but had no legal recourse since, in theory, he wasn't in the country.

Vesco stayed in Costa Rica until April 30, 1982, undergoing medical treatment for the urinary blockage. The best time to bring him to the hospital was during the rush hour, nine in the morning. He was treated as an outpatient.

The President-elect of Costa Rica, Luis Alberto Monge, had to be informed, and Carreras went to his house. "I have news," Carreras said, in Monge's bedroom, where Monge was dressing. "You don't mean. . . ." "I'm afraid so. He's here," Carreras said. Monge fell back on the bed and gasped, "I felt like a cathedral ceiling just dropped on me. What am I to *do* with Don Pepe? Tell him I beg him to get Vesco out. The country is broke. The economic problems are the worst in our history. The corruption is incredible. I can't handle Vesco, too. Promise me Vesco will leave before the inauguration." Enrique promised Vesco would be gone within seventy-two hours.

Figueres telephoned Tomás Borge, one of the nine Nicaraguan *comandantes* who ran the government and Minister of the

Interior, with whom he was acquainted. Figueres explained Bob's background briefly. Borge said, "We're not exactly sure who this Vesco is, but we'll oblige as a favor to you." To avoid detection, Vesco and Carreras flew from a soccer field—leaves clogged the landing gear and the Cessna had trouble taking off—and landed safely in Managua, where they were lodged in a government guest house. Vesco stayed there about two weeks, during which time Pat and some of the kids came from Miami. Carreras brought his own family to make the Vescos, jittery in still another environment, feel safer. A Costa Rican doctor came, and so did two physicians from Cuba, a neurologist and a neurosurgeon. They determined that Nicaragua lacked the necessary medical facilities or even a proper urologist. Vesco by then suffered from uremic poisoning and ran a high fever. He would have to visit Moscow, Budapest, or Havana—places safe from the U.S. authorities—"or he dies," Borge said. Vesco demurred, claiming he was certain he could remain in Costa Rica. "It was an empty hope," Carreras said, "the hope of a desperate man." But Vesco insisted on returning. "The FBI will catch you," the *comandante* warned Vesco, and Enrique said, "You'll get Don Pepe in trouble. I want nothing to do with it." At the last moment, Carreras agreed to be a passenger, though dreading the trip. "Don't worry," he told a Nicaraguan official who accompanied them to the airport. "We'll be right back."

On May 12, the Cessna landed at Llano Grande airport at Liberia, Costa Rica. The Vesco attorney, José María Pla was alerted by Don Pepe, and rushed to the airport. Vesco's plane landed at 9:30 A.M. Vesco descended, his arms, the lawyer noted, "like those of a concentration camp victim. He was very pale." He wasn't recognized immediately by customs and Pla felt obliged to identify him.

A woman at immigration phoned her boss, the Minister of Security who, unfortunately for Vesco, was attending the first cabinet meeting of the Monge government. He whispered to the President who said, "Ministers, I have Robert Vesco coming for an operation. What do you decide?" The answer, accompanied by thumbs down, was "No! No! No!"

Pla told Vesco, "The answer is no. You have twenty minutes."

(The American Embassy was also notified and demanded Vesco's arrest. "There are lots of doctors in the U.S.," someone there said. But Costa Rica replied the fugitive hadn't passed through immigration and wasn't technically in the country.) Vesco lay on his side on a bench and raved, "I'm sick. My wife is waiting. My son's Costa Rican. I'm an Italian—I have an Italian passport. I'm a Costa Rican income resident."

Pla said gently, "They've given you twenty minutes."

"Not twenty," Vesco snapped. "Five." On the plane, as it overflew his *finca,* Vesco looked down and wailed dramatically at what was past, passing, and to come. He may have been delirious, or crazy, or both. He returned to Nicaragua.

Carreras recommended Budapest—an aspiring politician, he may have wanted Bob as far away as possible—but Vesco chose Cuba, and on Saturday, June 12, Borge having made the slow arrangements, Vesco and a companion left for Havana on an Air Cubana Ilyushin. There were no formalities like visas. On the way, the companion tried to soothe Vesco, telling him that although Cuba lacked fancy supermarkets he'd find life tranquil and safe for himself and his family if he decided to move there. "Look," Vesco said, "I'm nervous. I'm jumping over the wall and there's no way I can come back to the other side of the wall."

The companion muttered something about dealing with both the Greeks and the Trojans, as he called the United States and Cuba.

"No," said Vesco. "I have an enemy on the other side, and the enemy of my friend is my enemy. This is a serious step."

Vesco was given a day to relax and a driver to tour Havana. On the next, he was admitted to a military hospital, CIMEQ.

His body made his poor psychological condition apparent. His feet had thick calluses from having gone shoeless so long on the boat in the Bahamas and Antigua. His eyes were inflamed because he had been afraid to see an ophthalmologist, his teeth rotten because of his terror of what a dentist might stick into him. He refused to take more than a local anesthetic, and, as an instrument was inserted into his penis, had to be strapped down. His screams could be heard down the hall.

Vesco was released after a few days and returned to Nicaragua, though he shuttled back and forth to Cuba. How bewildering the number of countries must have seemed to Pat, who would have given practically anything to be in Detroit: the Bahamas, almost completely North Americanized despite tough black faces and a harsh political style; Costa Rica, striving to become the Athens of Central America and a virtual U.S. dependent; tiny Antigua, American-green to its soul; Nicaragua, wood-burning cookstoves in backyards, buses only miracles prevented from collapsing under the weight of passengers crowded even onto their roofs, masses of soldiers, shortages of everything, even water. For the first time in Nicaragua, the Vescos saw real poverty almost everywhere. It was inescapable.

Still, though isolated, the Vescos lived in their usual upper-class style with the apparent blessing of the revolutionary Sandinista government. The first residence was a provisional one that had belonged to a general during the Somoza regime in a government compound located in the Planetarium district outside Managua. They then moved to the luxurious Los Robles neighborhood within the city. The house had been confiscated from a pro-Somoza sugarcane grower, and Vesco bought it for about $60,000 from the hoard he always carried. The residence was guarded by soldiers.

The fugitive's on-and-off presence in Nicaragua—he was there until the fall of 1983—was unknown to the newspaper *La Prensa,* which had run stories on the fugitive while he was in Costa Rica. The Ministry of the Interior, in charge of domestic security among other things, was aware of his presence, however. José Figueres, highly skeptical about Bob's assets, nonetheless hoped he could attract investments, or so he told the Nicaraguans. They gave Vesco the benefit of the doubt and a run-down DC-3 in which he toured the country for several weeks with Enrique Carreras to inspect possible tourist sites. Vesco prepared a plan, with charts and maps, for two hotels, one at a Pacific beach site, Pone Loya, and the other in the mountain district at Matagalpa, the site of fighting later between government forces and the Contras. His proposal included gambling—in 1986, Nicaragua announced that a casino would be built—but, as usual, nothing came of Vesco's schemes.

Fear was a constant feature of Vesco's life even if he had to interpret reality to justify it. When the United States invaded Grenada in October 1983, he was convinced that the objective was himself because his yacht was supposed to have been there—it was in Cuba by then, as was he. He believed the Contras would capture Managua and turn him over to the Americans. Although he'd expected to live in Nicaragua, he sold the Los Robles house to the government for $9,000, and sought asylum in Cuba.

38

OF COKE AND CHICANERY

Don Pepe Figueres retained a caustic affection for Robert Vesco whom he regarded as a victim of an overly strong case against him by U.S. authorities plus personality defects that may have been a result. But one day the old man, knowing I had researched the fugitive exhaustively, frowned and asked me, "Do you think Bob has been involved in the drug trade? If so, I'd be happy if he were shot."

I was aware, of course, of the narcotics allegations but doubted them as did Vesco's former associates in the United States. For them, Vesco, the family man, thief or not, would never sink to drugs. That would have seemed out of character, as they recollected him. But the person they remember may have no longer existed.

One reason I didn't give credence to the drug talk was that I believed U.S. law enforcement officers deliberately spread unverified information to advance their careers. For instance, in the early seventies, Frank Peroff told a Senate committee that Vesco would provide $300,000 for heroin smuggling. Stories appeared in the press even though investigators could find no proof—a code-marked "secret" U.S. telex strongly disputed the Peroff story. "I realize," said a straightforward DEA official at the time, "that any attempt to connect the name of Robert Vesco to an international drug investigation would make news." Said another, "I can't find anything indicating this guy is involved with junk."

"Who needs drugs?" Vesco told Ken Cartwright, the Nassau car dealer, as he expressed concern about his children. Vesco obtained a letter under the Freedom of Information Act from the Drug Enforcement Authority that seemed to clear him of narcotics charges. He sent a handwritten letter to the Bahamian Commission of Inquiry on the drug trade there denying he was ever involved.

Still, Vesco was capable of believing his own stories—even if false. And his anger toward the United States was profound, disaffection deepening over the years as he sought safety. Seldom would Vesco admit that he brooded about his homeland—though he missed, he once confessed, stuffed turkey at Thanksgiving—but just as spurned love can turn to hatred, Vesco may have wanted to inflict harm on what he considered his former country, and his love of money coupled with adventurism could have led him into uncharted seas. He was increasingly cynical, and, considering the wildness of the past decade of his life, nothing seemed impossible. Above all, he was reckless, as his history with IOS amply illustrated.

In his letter to the Commission, Vesco said he had met only once with Carlos Enrique Lehder-Rivas whose Bahamas drug-center island, Norman's Cay, was only a few miles away from Vesco's hideaway, Cistern Cay. The Commission concluded that Vesco had known Lehder better than that. Still, the evidence, the Commission decided, was "insufficient to support a finding that Vesco was involved with Lehder in the smuggling operation on Norman's Cay."

"Joe" Lehder was the son of a German engineer who had moved to Colombia and married a Colombian. Macho, swarthy, and attractive to women, Lehder went to New York at eighteen and was arrested for selling marijuana. He served time in a state prison. He moved to Detroit, was arrested again, for involvement in interstate auto theft, and served nearly two years at Danbury (Connecticut) Correctional Institution. In 1975, he returned to Colombia to become the reputed "*narcotraficante número uno.*" In 1981, leaving the Bahamas, he moved his operations back to

Colombia, buying a farm outside the town of Armenia, where he was born in 1947, and publishing a newspaper in which he attacked U.S. and Colombian officials. He had political ambitions, advocating the expulsion of the DEA. He called Adolf Hitler "the greatest warrior in history" and insisted that Jews in Europe in World War II died only working in fields and factories. He formed a nationalist party and funded a right-wing paramilitary party, Death of Kidnappers, charged with killing "dozens of leftists and labor organizers; it is also said to number former police and military officials in its ranks," reported *Newsweek* magazine, but Lehder was supposed to have dealt with the Cubans. At his private resort, he allegedly built a discotheque dedicated to John Lennon, with a statue of the rock star, nude except for a helmet and guitar, with a bullet hole through the heart.

In 1978, Lehder set up shop in the Bahamas on Norman's Cay, the island being within nonstop flying distance of Colombian loading areas and a convenient refuelling point for trips to the United States, although trips could be made directly. Lehder seemed to have had a staff of thirty to fifty, including seven or eight pilots. According to one of them, Edward Ward, a self-confessed drug smuggler, Lehder, from about January 1979 to January 1980, flew to the United States cocaine that cost in the neighborhood of $40 million in Colombia and wholesaled for $150 million in the United States. (Federal agents "estimated" his take at between $160 and $320 million—quite a spread).

Norman's Cay had been a favorite anchorage for yachtsmen, but, after Lehder arrived, two large prefabricated hangars were erected and work was begun to extend the runway. Lehder bought part of the island and treated it as a private citadel. Residents were frightened into leaving, with no help from Bahamian police. Visitors were discouraged by guards, Dobermans, and threats. A professor who rented a diving business there found equipment and luggage had been vandalized and fuel drained from his plane. Lehder's men forced him to take off and he barely succeeded in making a forced landing on a beach at a nearby island.

According to Willard Rose, mate on Lehder's yacht, the *Fire Fall,* on one occasion Lehder and Vesco spent four hours together. To Lehder, whose hatred of the United States was said to verge on the pathological, Vesco was as a god because he had successfully defied Uncle Sam. (Vesco, no doubt, pushed the fugitive image for all it was worth, gripped by his own peculiar pathology.) The most famous of fugitives and the king of coke were both about to be placed on the Bahamas "Stop-List," were being or about to be pursued by police from several countries, and would shortly vanish—Vesco to Antigua, Lehder to Colombia, following several ineffectual raids on Norman's Cay and a 1981 U.S. grand jury indictment, making Lehder a fugitive from U.S. justice, too. Lehder was extradited from Colombia and brought on a DEA plane to Florida in February 1987.

Vesco was repeatedly linked with Lehder in the narcotics trade, and *Fortune* magazine, which refused to disclose its informant, declared in 1986 that he helped Lehder get permission to use Cuban air space for drug overflights. That Vesco was in a position, psychologically or politically, to help Lehder in Cuba seems unlikely. Earlier, though, Vesco does appear to have been active in the narcotics trade. The Drug Enforcement Administration denied it has a warrant out for him and stated that he would not be arrested on drug charges in the United States. Its NADDIS (Narcotics and Dangerous Drugs Information Service) computer does, however, tie Vesco and Lehder together in at least one transaction, in the Bahamas.

I managed to find my own informant, who had participated in events about to be described and has never been tapped by the United States. According to him, Vesco's idea wasn't to engage in the drug trade but to manage the traffickers' money, narcotics folks often being poor investors. No doubt, Vesco engaged in hard sell about his proficiency with investments.

There is little or no doubt that at least one of Nicaragua's ruling *comandantes* was aware of cocaine traffic there. Although Nicaragua dismissed the allegations as "*tonterías*"—nonsense—in 1984 Federico Vaughm, associated with the Nicaraguan procurement agency SEBIMEC and an aide to Interior Minister Tomás Borge, was indicted by a Miami Federal grand jury. That year, a Cessna Titan with 1,452 pounds of cocaine aboard had been hit by Nicaraguan antiaircraft fire and had to make an emergency landing at an airfield outside Managua. The pilot, Barry Adler Seal, was allowed to return to the United States and came back in a C-123 to retrieve the drugs, which Vaughm personally helped load, receiving a fee of $1.5 million for providing "secure facilities" in Nicaragua, according to the U.S. case. The United States had photographs to back the allegations. Vaughm's face is visible and he was identified to me by someone who knew him. The picture was taken by a camera concealed by U.S. officials—Seal had become an informant and was murdered in February 1986.

Another version of the Managua event came from Álvaro José Baldizón, formerly Chief Investigator of the Special Investigations Commission of Borge's Ministry of the Interior (MINT). Baldizón defected to the United States and provided extensive information and documents on the activities of the Nicaragua government. Given the unavailability of U.S. sources and the use of propaganda against government opponents, the absolute truth is impossible to determine, but in terms of drugs, Baldizón's facts seem consistent with those of others.

In 1984, Baldizón's office received a report that linked Borge with cocaine smuggling from Colombia to the United States. Borge's office told Baldizón to investigate the report as a compromise of a state secret, which shocked the informant, especially when he was told by his superior that the information was known in the ministry only by Borge, his assistant Captain Charolotte Boltodano, and a few others, plus members of the Sandinista National Liberation Front's National Directorate, the heads of the government. Boltodano told Baldizón that Borge had made contact with the Colombian dealers through Captain Paul Atha, director of H&M Investments, which handled business activities, as part of MINT, at home and abroad to obtain U.S. dollars. Boltodano also said that MINT used the drug money for clandestine operations outside Nicaragua. Baldizón was instructed to pass information on cocaine trafficking to Borge and not to investigate.

Several months later, Baldizón watched a plane being fired on by antiaircraft guns. He went to Borge's office on another matter, but the minister left for Los Brasiles Airport. Boltodano later told Baldizón that Borge had ordered everyone away from the plane, placed it under custody until he arrived, and personally removed several bags of cocaine, which seems doubtful.

According to other testimony, Vesco had been associated the previous year with Atha, Vaughm, and James Herring, Jr., who said, "Although I have been previously engaged in narcotics smuggling and trafficking, I voluntarily, with no charges or threat of prosecution, came forward to work as a government operative." So incredible seemed the information Herring filtered to U.S. officials that at first they refused to believe it, but he had documents, photos, and the results of lie detector tests to back him up. Most impressive, perhaps, in terms of veracity was Herring's command of details.

Bearded, dark haired, 5 foot 9, James Alexandre Herring, Jr., is from Tallahassee, Florida. He was decorated for bravery for military service in Vietnam. He managed a jewelry store and was vice president of an insurance agency. He was an auxiliary deputy sheriff with the Leon County (Tallahassee) Sheriff's Office—a plaque hangs on his office wall. None of this, it would seem, was good enough, and, Herring succumbed to the lure of adventure and supposedly easy money.

In 1979, when Herring was in his early thirties, he went into the restaurant-bar business, and what he called a "gradual descent" began. He met marijuana smugglers, and, a boat expert, did odd jobs for them like procuring radio equipment and a generator. He was arrested in Florida and put in solitary confinement for a month to persuade him to cooperate. He wouldn't, and the charges against him were dropped.

Wishing to "straighten out my life and drop the underworld connections," Herring, in 1980, started Everything Goes, Inc., which would locate hard-to-find items—gun collections, antique furniture, carousel horses, prehistoric shark teeth, whatever. His brochure bent over backward to explain Everything Goes wouldn't be stopped by legal or ethical niceties.

On his honeymoon in the Bahamas, Herring showed a local jewelry store owner rubies he had as a loan collateral. He believed them fake and they were, though high-class ones that had value. The jeweler, having perhaps read the brochure, said he might have need of Herring and, a few months later, asked him to come to Miami. There, the jeweler announced he had a wealthy friend needing a British passport and an American green card. He was a fugitive but he was not, as Herring suspected, Robert Vesco.

With ease, Herring found an Englishman who bore a good resemblance to photos the jeweler provided and who, for $1,000, was persuaded to apply for a new passport, his own having expired. Herring took the passport to the Nassau jeweler who insisted on introducing him to the fugitive. He would pay $50,000 for it, the Bahamian candidly admitted, of which Herring's share would be $15,000. Herring didn't object. On the way to the fugitive's house, they passed a car containing the islands' other leading fugitive. Vesco had been there to discuss the sale of his Costa Rican ranch but there hadn't been a deal.

The man Herring was about to meet was the reputed hashish king of Europe and much wanted by Interpol. If Herring, or anyone else, gave thought to benefits the narcotics trade conferred, the man's then house was the utmost confirmation. It sits atop a hill on Paradise Island facing the eastern part of Nassau across the channel. Painted white, broken by two wide, bronze-embellished metal gateways, behind one of which lurks a four-car garage, the concrete wall is fully two blocks long. Ostentatious statuary covers a bright green lawn. The house seems to ramble on, with covered walkways joining various sections. The hashish king had a palace that made Jim Herring's eyes pop.

Tall, with reddish-blond hair, in his late forties or early fifties, Dutch, with a thick accent though he spoke several languages, Jitze Kooistra, nicknamed Joeb, had arrived in the Bahamas with $6 million—Herring was led to believe—and a common-law wife, Catherina Maria Dekker. Though Bahamian pressure was making him desperate, the Dutchman wasn't pleased with what Herring delivered; the jeweler had misunderstood; not an English—the Brits were after him, too—but an American passport was what he desired. (The United States had not yet indicted him, though it would.) Herring, the professional finder, complied. He proceeded to get Kooistra a U.S. passport in the name of one Walker, having paid Walker, who didn't have one, $1,000 or so to apply. The likeness between Kooistra's photos and Walker's face were good enough to work. Herring also obtained a new passport for himself—his having been confiscated when he'd been arrested—in the name of Clint Hill, having paid Hill a similar sum.

But Kooistra-Walker's American passport lacked a Bahamian entrance stamp. Herring had a pilot friend fly from Florida and park at the edge of the airstrip. He took a set of Kooistra's clothes to the plane, had Kooistra go to it, change, and march through Bahamian customs, where his passport was stamped. The Dutchman was then flown to the United States.

For Herring, Kooistra had "class," and he went to work for him on a per-job basis—picking up a tape in Mexico, moving the family to Europe, looking at boarding schools for Catherina's child from her marriage, bringing cash provided by Wallace Whitfield, Kooistra's lawyer and a prominent member of the government opposition. He also supplied the Dutchman, who had an insatiable sexual appetite, with prostitutes. He became Kooistra's right-hand man.

Herring and his wife cruised with Kooistra on his 85-foot, steel-hulled yacht. About January 1982, Kooistra said, "I met Vesco again—in my last meeting in the Bahamas I was introduced to Mr. Angelo by Mr. Vesco, who was his personal assistant. [That is, Angelo was Vesco's assistant.] We exchanged telephone numbers. I lost sight of both gentlemen for a while, till, in 1982, in Antigua, accidentally I met Mr. Vesco again. He had the police department raid my boat with my wife and child in jail—and while I was in Paris at that time, he told me to call a number, and I called the commissioner of police. . . . For a small donation and a promise to leave the island, I could leave." Vesco regarded Antigua as his "private preserve," and "I shouldn't be there." Kooistra may have held a grudge toward Vesco but money mattered more, and some months later Kooistra met with Angelo at the Omni Hotel in Miami.

Angelo's real name was Adolph Loia—an American whose father was of Italian extraction and whose mother was Costa Rican. A former jockey who had worked in casinos, Adolph-Angelo was about fifty years old, short, fat, and married to a Taiwanese woman they called the Dragon Lady. Angelo had run a computer-games parlor in San José and worked for "Swifty," as

Vesco was also known then. (Loia was undoubtedly the man who took photographs of Skip Wilson, who had come to Costa Rica at the behest of the United States to try to nab Vesco, and delivered him to the fugitive.) In Miami, Loia had Vesco's "shopping list" and the Dutchman, expecting to share in the profits, brought in his man, Herring.

Angelo didn't quite specify where the goods on the typewritten, pages-long list—which included computers, Caterpillar parts, medical supplies, and toilet tissue—were supposed to go, but one item, a valve used in a sugar cane distillery, convinced Herring that Cuba was the destination.

Trying to arrange such deals cost Kooistra, who, "kind of irritated," had Angelo call Swifty to tell him, "Look, I'm out a hundred thousand already, please, what do you want? We want a contract and we want to see some money." Typically, Vesco failed to deliver.

Nonetheless, Angelo met with Federico Vaughm and both traveled to Europe to see Kooistra. A trading company that would handle both Nicaraguan and Cuban activity was to be formed in Brussels. They asked Kooistra if he could move cocaine in Europe: "I said yes, simply, and we made arrangements to start this business."

The Dutchman, fast running through this fortune, felt eager to return to the narcotics trade, and Herring, through his previous drug contacts, said he established a tie, in Bolivia, with representatives of the Suárez family, well known in cocaine circles, and made a buy there, as a test, amounting to some 20 kilos, for which Vesco and Kooistra put up roughly $50,000 each. The cocaine, with street value of $1,200,000 in the United States, uncut, was shipped by Herring to the Bahamas, hidden in a TV set, along with other "family goods," mothballed to hide the coke odor. Angelo collected the shipment and arranged for the drug's transportation to Florida, apparently by air.

Shenanigans commenced at once. Vesco's man Angelo told Kooistra's man that the Dutchman took him for a ride (Herring secretly agreed), and that Kooistra and Herring-Hill would be cut out altogether unless Herring told Kooistra that the shipment had been damaged and less than half could be salvaged. Reluctantly, Herring agreed, he said, and Angelo gave him two keys (kilograms) of cocaine to seal the deal. Herring sold Kooistra's portion, plus his secret shares, giving some of his own take to Kooistra, because he felt guilty. Angelo handled Vesco's coke on his own, moving it in California. Vesco and Angelo probably got a return of ten times their investment.

In late '82–early '83, Herring went back to Bolivia by the route he had used before—via the Bahamas and Panama—with Kooistra's second stake. Angelo met him there with Vesco's $100,000 share. They compressed the cocaine into the walls of a food freezer in place of insulation, and Angelo (Herring with his lack of Spanish had had too much trouble before) shipped it to the Bahamas, where, he claimed, Bahamian customs "popped" (confiscated) the freezer. Herring, who received all of $5,000 for his efforts, was dubious—to him, Angelo-Adolph was "stiffing" Vesco and the Dutchman, but there was nothing to be done and Angelo dropped from sight for a month or two as if the heat were on. (Herring was later convinced the cocaine had never reached the Bahamas.)

But Angelo emerged with another intriguing proposition, Herring was to procure cocaine-processing materials and be presented in Nicaragua, whose officials would participate in a transaction, as an expert on suitable landing fields and sites for a cocaine refinery. With money from Angelo, Herring went to New York City, where he obtained a hundred pounds of inositol (powdered Vitamin B), Manatol (baby laxative), benzocaine, and procaine (which numb the nose, as does cocaine), plus assorted stainless steel mixers, sealing machines, grinders—the tools for preparing uncut cocaine for market. In Tallahassee, he packed them in a large trunk, adding a machine gun, pistols, cigarettes, and Scotch—"toys for the boys." He awaited instructions which soon came.

He and Angelo traveled from Miami on Aeronica, the Nicaraguan national airline, to Managua where they were greeted by Federico Vaughm and Captain Paul Atha. He also met, he said, Minister of the Interior Tomás Borge. "He shook my hand and said thank you, we appreciate your help." Herring's "Clint Hill" passport wasn't stamped and soldiers unloaded the trunk. He was taken to inspect possible sites, like an old Somoza rice plantation with an airstrip. It was decided that for the initial small batches of cocaine a Managua location would be cheaper and easier.

Having returned after a few days, Herring was on his boat at Fort Lauderdale when a panicky Angelo phoned him. He had been about to ship a Vesco-ordered load of equipment from Islamorada, in the Florida Keys, but the captain chickened out and Angelo didn't know where to find another. Did Clint? On impulse, Herring volunteered.

A 44-foot Albine trawler, packed with equipment—electronics, batteries, and various stuff—was docked at a small marina. The "ethical outlaw," as Herring described himself, steered the trawler in high seas, without radar and with faulty loran, to Varadero Beach for a rendezvous with a Cuban gunboat. The trawler flew a diver's flag for identification. On the gunboat's bridge, like commanders, were two men named Junco and Jesús, both of Cuban internal security, or "DGI," Herring would learn, and Vesco who radioed, "Want us to shoot a few rounds across your bow like we're stopping you?" Swifty seemed in complete charge.

The boat was unloaded by what seemed to Herring "people from the intelligence circles of Cuba and also some uniformed people who seemed to be something like sailors or recruits of a sort—they wore blue uniforms. And we were always escorted to government housing in the Varadero Beach area where we were comfortably wined and dined and openly discussed the operation and any future needs of the Cuban government." In a Greek fisherman's hat, Vesco, described by Herring as graying, "weathered," and wearing a beard like Castro's, took the trawler's contents to Havana and, returning with his son Tony, whom Herring described as a "little slow," spoke of his contact with the "Bearded One," who might have been Fidel Castro, his brother Raul, or anybody else.

Herring (known to Vesco only as Clint Hill) sailed to Marathon Key, went to his own boat, the *Charisma,* at Fort Lauderdale, and then to Miami where he telephoned a friend to meet him at Tallahassee. This fateful friend, but for whom Herring's activities might never have become known, had been selling Herring's cocaine and was to deliver a small amount of cash. At the Tallahassee airport, Herring, trained in such matters, was suspicious so the two men drove in separate cars to a deserted spot. They had no sooner parked than county deputies surrounded them.

They strip-searched both of them and all but undressed the cars looking for coke. The friend, who had unwittingly sold cocaine to the Feds, was arrested on federal and state charges. Nothing against Herring could be proved, and he was let go. Out on bail, the friend insisted he wouldn't reveal Herring's complicity but needed help. Herring agreed to supply information to him.

The owners of a northern Florida flying service, one an airline pilot, had an arrangement to lease a Jet Star and asked Herring to steal it, the notion being to collect on the insurance. (The airline pilot was later convicted on a similar charge.) Herring had only to arrange payment of $150,000—a third would be his—and a plane worth $3–$5 million could be lifted under an elaborate plan. The plane would be leased by a fictitious company called Trufuflex by Angelo posing as a Miami businessman who wanted to look at land in Costa Rica and Nicaragua. One member of the crew would be ignorant of the plot, to add legitimacy. The Jet Star would land in Nicaragua, where payment by Angelo would be made, proceed to Costa Rica, where arms or drugs would be placed on board, and go back to Nicaragua, which would seize the craft because of the contraband. Nicaragua would detain the pilots briefly and then expel them to the United States. The plane would be flown to Cuba, which would refuse to release it.

A cashier's check, apparently for a two-day charter of the Jet Star, was duly paid. Angelo and Herring joined Vesco's Bahamas accountant, Fred Murray, in Nassau (the flight would not be as well monitored from there) and the four flew to Cuba via Cozumel or Cancún in a Hawker Siddeley, a small British jet Angelo had chartered. Meetings were held at Vesco's two-story house on a canal at the Hemingway Marina at Barlovento, outside Havana. A plan to deliver 1,000 riot shotguns to Honduran guerrillas was discussed. (Later, Herring, through his friend, notified U.S. authorities that Vesco, in transit, would be in Tegucigalpa, the Honduran capital, but they failed to act.) Murray went over money matters with Vesco, and Herring says he saw, on the plane, ledgers with multimillion-dollar entries. Herring presented the Jet Star scam for the fugitive's approval. "Vesco got up and shouted, 'Goddam! Me and the Beard [Castro] could stand up in that.' Vesco was pretty fuzzy, but he did have great knowledge of boats and planes. He referred to headroom," Herring said.

The Jet Star, it would seem, was actually flown to Managua, but Angelo was late with the money and the pilots returned to Florida, where the aircraft was seized by a bank for nonpayment on the lease.

Herring's next mission to Nicaragua occurred in April 1983, where he learned from Vaughm that Colombian dealers, in cooperation with the M-19 Colombian insurgents, were to participate in a drug deal. "We help them, they help us," Vaughm said. Herring, the only one among the plotters who knew how, was to be the official cocaine cutter.

Back in Florida, waiting for the shipment to arrive, Herring made several trips to Cuba, this time in the *Charisma.* He brought supplies like toilet bowls for a house Vesco was building on Cayo Largo. One of the Cubans, a DGI man who went by the name of Nelson, attempted to persuade him to accept cocaine instead of cash, but Herring declined. Nelson also suggested that Herring deal with the Cubans directly, cutting out Vesco. Herring was paid $8,000 per round trip in $100 bills which Junco, Vesco's DGI bodyguard, kept in a canvas bag.

Herring considered the pay "bargain basement," but the purpose "wasn't to make money so much as it was to gather intelligence," which Herring continued to pass to his beleaguered pal whom the Feds wouldn't take seriously. They wanted his source to appear in person. Herring furtively shot pictures with an Instamatic camera of a Cuban gunboat and microwave communications equipment. He seems to have been more concerned with "U.S. national security" than with narcotics, and he would hold back certain items from shipments so that merchandise couldn't actually be used by the Cubans.

With Colombian coke delivery imminent, Herring met with a Kooistra associate, Core A. Cahuzak of International Marine Services in Amsterdam. Kooistra had devised a scheme (Herring claimed he'd put the notion in the Dutchman's head) to ship the cocaine to Europe inside a marine salvage winch. The front was to be a salvage operation in Lake Managua. The winch, weighing four or five tons, would arrive on Iberia Airlines. Herring and Cahuzak went from Miami to the Bahamas, where Herring picked up Kooistra's $100,000 portion of the investment—Vesco's was already in Managua—and continued to Nicaragua, again on a private jet.

Herring checked into the Hotel Intercontinental in Managua. The winch was taken by army truck to a government house controlled by Captain Atha, who, like Vaughm, was associated with the Ministry of the Interior. The house had a wall around it and uniformed troops were stationed at the front door and at the gates. Herring's chemicals had been brought and the coke was already there, along with two Colombians. (Later, in the United States, Herring, shown photographs, identified them as Ricardo Ochoa and Pablo Escobar, both indicted in Florida on drug charges.)

While Cahuzak removed the winch cover, Herring went to work in a rear bedroom. The cocaine, in plastic garbage cans, weighed 25–27 kilos and was 95–97 percent pure. It was to be cut to 85 percent pure, about 33 kilos in weight. With coke bringing $80,000 a kilo in Europe, the difference in price before and after cutting was perhaps a half-million dollars. The whole shipment had a street value of about $2.8 million. Actually, because of a glut on the market, the coke brought only $30,000 a kilo, or about $1 million. Herring's pay was supposed to be $50,000 but he received only $8,000.

Herring skillfully separated the "rock," formed in the baking process, from the "shake" or powder. His plastic gloves were coated with snow. He poured each kilo into Seal-A-Meal bags. Needing scissors to cut the bags, he went to Atha's office to look for a pair and found Robert Vesco.

Vesco was on the phone, and he sounded upset. "Why did they hold it?" he cried. "Where is it now? Brownsville?" Herring eavesdropped momentarily outside the door and heard mention of several arrests at Brownsville, Texas.

Herring labored late to complete the cutting and in the

morning, in drizzling rain, he and Cahuzak, assisted by armed Nicaraguan soldiers, put the thirty-three bags inside the winch. The winch was shipped to Belgium, where Kooistra took possession.

On the plane to the Bahamas, Herring mentioned Brownsville to Angelo. "Yeah, it's equipment made by Rand. [Actually, a subsidiary of Ingersoll-Rand.] A big deal with the Cubans. The stuff will be released," Angelo said confidently. As soon as he could, Herring gave the information to his friend to be passed on to the Feds in his struggle for leniency.

Kooistra's sales seemed unexpectedly slow and worry grew among the Nicaraguans that the Dutchman was cheating them. Vaughm was dispatched to Brussels, checking into the Hotel Metropole. According to Kooistra, Vaughm was given $100,000 and Dutch guilders worth $750,000. The bulk of the money was said by "Dekker" to have been sent to Nicaragua by diplomatic pouch. ("Dekker" was the name used by Kooistra, then in prison in Tallahassee, Florida, to conceal his identity when he testified before a U.S. Senate subcommittee.)

Herring was scheduled to make still another run to Cuba. Equipment was stored on a warehouse on 78 Street in Miami controlled by a family of Greek origin named Yamanis, friends of Vesco, two of whom had gone to jail for long sentences on marijuana charges. The goods were hauled to Cayo Largo. Included in the cargo were North Star computers and a red Doberman for Junco. The U.S. Customs had the *Charisma* under surveillance, and, perhaps tipped off by someone at the marina and ignoring Herring's unlikely claim to be going fishing, seized it. There were no criminal indictments but Herring talked to an alert U.S. Attorney who assigned him to a special U.S. Customs agent. Herring had become an official informant.

Herring had intended another trip to New York for more processing materials, but Angelo wanted him in Nicaragua for the next job—50 keys of coke, he said, and sufficient Manatol, benzocaine, and procaine were on hand for cutting it. Herring suspected something was wrong, but he complied. Angelo told him a ticket waited at the Aeronica desk at Miami Airport but none was there. He had Angelo's Managua number, most likely at Vesco's house in Los Robles, and Angelo said he'd forgotten that the ticket—one-way, it turned out—was in another name, Edwin P. Wilson. (Edwin Wilson: the man subsequently sentenced to sixty years in prison for selling arms to the Libyans.) Herring later figured Vesco or Angelo had chosen a false name to hide his departure but had no idea why that particular one was chosen.

Herring was collected in Managua not by Angelo or Vaughm but by guards who'd escorted him to a government safe house used for dignitaries. He was greeted by a Nicaraguan female official who kept an eye on him. His passport had been taken, and he remained there for ten days in growing anxiety, having concluded, learning Angelo had left, that he was a hostage to force Kooistra to pay up. Vaughm finally appeared, having satisfied his superiors about the money, and, when Herring demanded to leave the country his unstamped passport was returned. He was able to leave on the next flight to Mexico, but his passport had no Nicaraguan stamp. He contrived to slip through Mexican customs undetected. At the Continental Airlines desk he learned that the next flight to the United States was likely to be the last before a strike. But he had no Mexican entry stamp. Herring spotted a Mexican customs official on the phone, with his back turned. He crept up, stamped his own passport, initialed it, and departed for Houston, a shaken man.

Herring received "use immunity"—meaning that anything he told wouldn't be used against him; anything the government turned up on its own could be—from the U.S. Attorney for the Northern District of Florida, David McGee. Information he provided led to the arrest, guilty pleas, and convictions of numerous individuals charged with everything from airplane theft to passport fraud to contract murders. He was obliged to report those who contacted him with illegal deals, and among those he turned in was Jitze Kooistra who foolishly entered the United States to see a girl friend in Pompano Beach.

Meanwhile the fugitive still had business to complete in Managua. He presented a number of ideas to listeners, including Russians. He argued that the Swiss were considering the disclosure of secret bank accounts after years of negotiations with the

United States. The U.S. government was concerned that 20 percent of its currency was "hot" and outside its control and thought seriously about changing the design and color of its currency to foil counterfeiters and stop the laundering of cash. It would require an exchange of the old money to force it into the open. (The Swiss, in a 1984 referendum, voted against opening bank records to tax authorities. In 1986, the United States announced a new type of dollar bill.)

Vesco's solution was the Delta Triangle. The three Caribbean nations of the left—Cuba, Nicaragua, and Grenada—would organize what would be, in effect, a new trading bloc. It would accept the "hot" money and issue new currency in exchange, which would be backed by Russian gold and freely convertible. Vesco believed other nations would accept the Delta currency, which could be used for commerce and tourism in Communist countries and accepted in Western Europe as well. It wasn't clear what would happen to the pool of old flight dollars in Delta—Vesco spoke of forcing a devaluation of the dollar and said they could pose the threat of economic warfare with the United States. Cuba rejected the proposal as impractical and the Russians followed. Another brainstorm had failed to materialize, and Vesco repaired to Havana.

39

VESCO IN CUBA

> SENATOR HAWKINS: Vesco told you he is living in Havana as the guest of the Cuban government?
> MR. DEKKER: His egomania—he told me once that he runs the central bank.
> SENATOR HAWKINS: He has a big ego, doesn't he.
> MR. DEKKER: Yes.
> SENATOR HAWKINS: What was Vesco's relationship to the Cuban government, in your opinion?
> MR. DEKKER: At that moment, very strong. If it is still that way after the disasters, I do not know.*

For Cuba, Vesco would be quite as difficult as he had been for Costa Rica, only in a different way. Though Fidel Castro said that Cuba harbored the then-ailing fugitive for humanitarian reasons —as it undoubtedly did with a quirky, ideological, anti-Yanqui twist—the Cubans entrusted him with hard-found dollars, supported him financially, and handed him a bill for $880,000, according to the fugitive. What happened well illustrated Cuba's plight, partly the result of antagonism between it and the United States.

In the mid-1950s, Cuba's per capita income had been one of the highest in Latin America. Twenty-five years later it was far from that. Cuba does not provide extensive statistics, but its economists declare that comparisons are meaningless because

* "Role of Nicaragua in Drug Trafficking," p. 39. Hearing before the Subcommittee on Children, Drugs and Alcoholism of the Committee on Labor and Human Resources, United States Senate, 1985. Dekker is Jitze Kooistra.

they don't take into account that, under Batista, wealth was concentrated in a few hands, nor would economic statistics reflect great advances in education, medical care, support for the elderly and so on. Nonetheless, Cuba—just as Costa Rica needs U.S. support—requires the $4 billion in annual aid it receives from the Soviet Union. The Cubans, while faulting their own bureaucracy, corruption, and inefficiencies, also blame the country's condition on the U.S. embargo and military expenses forced on it by the United States. Cuba was prepared to employ unusual means, and one was Robert Vesco.

If the fugitive had ceased to pretend he was a major investor, he did rave about his high-level contacts, and a friend, listening, said, "Don't bullshit these guys." Vesco snapped, "How do you think I've gotten by all these years?" Because he sounded knowledgeable about real estate, the Cubans involved him in a plan to develop Cayo Largo, off the southern Cuban coast, as a tourist resort. Customs formalities would be waived, private ownership permitted, hotels and condos built, and investments encouraged. There might have been a banking setup of some kind. It was the sort of enclave that had attracted Vesco before.

It was reported that the eighty-eight pairs of $6,000 classified infrared night-vision binoculars confiscated at a Florida dockside were a Vesco-arranged shipment for Cuba. A much larger Vesco importation attempt was established by the U.S. Attorney in a Brownsville, Texas, trial in November 1983. The spring before, a subsidiary of Ingersoll-Rand, California Pellet Mill Company, with offices in San Francisco, received an inquiry from what appeared to be a Costa Rican outfit called Cominsa, later changed to Imbagua, an acronym in Spanish for water-pumping equipment. A man representing both companies, José MacCourtney, negotiated the purchase of ten of California Pellet's mills plus extra equipment. In payment for the first shipment, a check from Barclays Bank in Nassau for $712,337.50 was deposited in California Pellet's account at the Bank of America. Another apparent Costa Rican named Luhr was also involved. Luhr was Meissner's mother's name and appeared on his Costa Rican passport. Meissner denied any knowledge of the deal but said Vesco well knew his second last name.

The company produced machinery that compacted fine substances into dense solids—ranging from animal food to municipal waste conversion into fuel. Still another application was treating the residue from sugar-cane processing, bagasse. Bagasse can be converted into briquettes for fuel for a refinery's boilers. A refinery could thus be made self-sufficient in energy and perhaps have fuel pellets to sell. The equipment Imbagua bought was a recent model and probably the best of its kind.

At about the same time MacCourtney came to San Francisco, a car dealer from West Columbia, Texas, Richard S. Bettini, received a phone call from an old acquaintance. On instructions, Bettini always referred to the man as a "friend," so as not to prejudice the jury. The friend was Vesco, who, the prosecutor reminded the judge, "absconded from the United States with 300 million dollars." Vesco wanted to talk about old times in Detroit. Soon after, Pat Vesco called from Houston and Bettini said he would like to visit. Vesco phoned again, suggesting that Bettini fly to Cancún, Mexico. He was met there by a pilot to take him to Cozumel. Airborne about ten minutes, Bettini heard the pilot request permission to enter Cuban air space, and cried, "Turn around! Go back!" but the plane landed in Havana. The Cubans wanted his passport, and Bettini, who hadn't brought it, begged to be flown out but the pilot refused. The terrified Bettini was placed in a small room. His surprise at all this seemed a little feigned—Mr. or Mrs. Fugitive must have given him some destination—but Vesco's whereabouts in early 1983 were still unknown.

"Then this friend came, whom I hadn't seen since 1967, and put his arms around me and kissed me and I felt like hitting him," Bettini said. Vesco drove Bettini to a modest, white stucco house at the Hemingway Marina at Barlovento, about fifteen minutes from Havana. Pat was there and they talked about old times in Detroit, like playing pinochle. Bettini spent the night on Vesco's yacht, chock-full of equipment, he noted. The next day the fugitive came to the point. He asked Bettini do him a favor by renting a warehouse in Houston to store food-processing equipment for a company called Imbagua in Costa Rica, where the equipment would be sent.

With two other car dealers, Bettini arranged a $10,000, one-year lease on a warehouse near the Houston ship canal and sublet it to Imbagua for $18,000, the difference being expenses and commissions, according to Bettini, who believed the check came from Barclays Bank. The lease was signed on June 10, 1983.

Vesco called about the warehouse and told Bettini to wait until he was contacted. Bettini then heard from a man who identified himself as French Canadian. He said a truck would arrive soon at the warehouse. There evidently would be other shipments in the next two or three months. But the truck, a trailer instead of a flatbed, wouldn't fit inside, and Bettini was told to send it on to Harlingen International Airport near Brownsville.

Meantime, the main actors, Albert Anthony Volpe, thought to be a Canadian organized crime figure, Alejo Quintera Peralta, a Mexican businessman believed to be from Cuban intelligence, and Salvador Ramírez Preciado, a Mexican air cargo expert, had not been idle. Ramírez tried to convince one air freight outfit to file a flight plan for Costa Rica, fake engine trouble, and land in Mérida, Mexico, where the pelletizing equipment would be unloaded. (It would then be forwarded to Cuba, perhaps through Nicaragua.) When the airline refused, Ramírez found another—Global International Airways of Kansas City. Just before the Fourth of July, two heavily laden flatbed trucks left Sparks, Nevada, bound for, the drivers learned en route, San Antonio, where they met still a third truck, from Crawfordsville, Indiana, also carrying pelletizing equipment. The conspirators contacted the drivers at a motel and told them to proceed to Brownsville. The trucks were assembled at the airport and unloaded as a Global 707 freighter took off from Baltimore.

The U.S. Customs had been tipped off that industrial equipment was to be exported illegally, and agents watched the equipment being loaded on the 707. However, one of the large pieces wouldn't fit so the plane still hadn't been loaded by evening. Volpe and Ramírez had planned to fly separately to Mexico on a chartered aircraft, but, becoming suspicious, tried to take off. Customs alerted the control tower, which ordered the plane to return. Ramírez denied a connection with the 707, but the agents searched his briefcase and established it. U.S. Customs seized the equipment at Harlingen and more at a Chicago warehouse. None was ever returned to California Pellet Mill, which took a small loss because it was building the other mills that had been ordered by Imbagua.

Some two days after Ramírez, Volpe, and Quintera had been arrested, Vesco phoned Bettini and said, "Things are all screwed up. Things are messed up. There are all kinds of problems. I want you to call Bob Foglia in New York or New Jersey." Bettini did, and Foglia, one of Vesco's lawyers, flew to Houston and then to Cancún where a plane from Cuba brought him $240,000, with which he posted bail for the three jailed men—$25,000 for Quintera (someone else put up another $25,000), who fled to Mexico, $50,000 for Volpe, who, said *Forbes* magazine, skipped to Canada and then Yugoslavia, and for Ramírez, who was the only one who stood trial. He received a five-year prison term but perhaps he was lucky.

Bettini, whose family described him as bitter at Vesco for having deceived him in not admitting the machinery was destined for Cuba, died in an ambulance the day before his forty-eighth birthday of a massive heart attack, though he had had no previous coronary difficulties. Quintera was reported shot to death two weeks before the trial commenced. His brother had died shortly before in a Mexico City helicopter crash. Volpe's brother Paul was found dead in the trunk of his wife's car at the Toronto airport. He was supposed to have just returned from observing the Brownsville trial.

In Cuba, the Vescos lived well but not lavishly, although they had two Mercedes with drivers. They had a house in the Siboney district, not far from a compound where Castro and other high officials live, and another, more spacious one at the Hemingway Marina at Barlovento. The house faced a canal and Vesco berthed one of his yachts at his own wharf. After the U.S. Customs seizure at Harlingen, the Vescos moved to a smaller place, on Havana's wide Fifth Avenue and then back to Siboney where Vesco did his own carpentry.

Castro said that Vesco was simply one more foreign resident, but it wasn't true. Vesco's access to Cuba had been the result of a call by Tomás Borge to his Cuban counterpart, Minister of the

Interior Ramiro Valdez. Vesco was assigned to the Compañía Importadora-Exportadora, or CIMEX, one of whose people, Junco, had fought with Castro in the Sierra Maestre and had been with Cuban intelligence, the DGI. He was Vesco's gofer and watchdog and he seems to have reported to Tony de La Guardia, a State Security Colonel. In 1983, after the pelletizing deal was stopped, Vesco's relations with the Cuban government turned sour, and the Cubans gave him a bill Vesco variously claimed was for $880,000 or $800,000, though LeBlanc believed $400,000 was a more reasonable figure.

Vesco had charged personal bills to CIMEX—the costly telephone, rents, cars, airline tickets to Nicaragua, flights for other people to various places, and, it was said, a $150,000 advance commission. (He played around with another commission, for Cuban Monte Cristo cigars to be sold in a one-shot shipment to a Las Vegas casino that would give them to big-rollers, but the deal fell through.) Cuba was prepared to write off its investment in the sugar equipment, plus the bail it appeared to have provided, but wanted the rest of its money. When Vesco couldn't or wouldn't pay, his boats—in which, the FBI knew, he had cruised off the coast of Florida, landing at least once at Key West—were embargoed and his long-distance telephone rights restricted. His boats were seized by the Cubans as collateral but returned in a settlement.

Vesco claimed he didn't pay the Cuban bill because he feared that if he admitted he had ready sources his hosts would demand even more. But he also told people he was broke. Despite his consistent fabrications, it doesn't seem likely that Vesco, if he had the money he is supposed to have clipped, would deliberately have chosen impoverished, difficult Cuba when more pleasant refuges could have been found. For LeBlanc, Vesco was down to his last half-million or so, though Pat still had her jewels. He may have received, in kickbacks and commissions, many millions, but the costs of fugitivehood were enormous and Bob always squandered money. Within a year, Norman predicted in 1986, Bob would be virtually penniless.

In 1985 occurred another strange episode that put some light on Vesco finances. Midyear, the Vescos sold the Guanacaste *finca* to a group of rich Americans that included Manfred De-Rewal, owner of a Guanacaste hotel. The price was $1.2 million, and Norman and Pat went to Panama City to pick up the first payment, $600,000, of which $240,000 was in cash. Prompted by American officials who thought the money might be narcotics related, the Panamanians, who fully cooperate with the United States on any matter related to drug trafficking, arrested the two, who spent the night in jail. On their release, they discovered the $240,000, of which $60,000 was intended for LeBlanc for his services over the years, was missing. Vesco had phoned Reggie Donawa, an Antiguan who with Ulis Brown had sailed the *Salude* from Haiti to Cuba, and asked him to come from Antigua to Panama City. Reggie's job was to bring some of the proceeds from the *finca* sale to Cuba. He picked up the money, he says, from a Panama bank and placed it in the hotel safe deposit box. He realized he was under surveillance and was arrested that night on suspicion of drugs. He protested his innocence and indeed, hardly understood the sort of trouble his courier role might put him in. The authorities—Donawa wasn't quite certain who they were—took the safe deposit key away from him and put him on a 2 A.M. plane for Miami. Whoever had the key must certainly have removed the money. Word of this event reached many ears, especially after Pat, at Vesco's insistence, filed a report on the episode in Costa Rica.

The Cubans were furious at Vesco for the report because of the publicity potential. They seemed to believe that Pat took the money. LeBlanc thought the Panamanians had done so, while the Panamanians blamed the American drug officials or Pat and Norman or Norman and Bob in tandem. Vesco said it had been LeBlanc, and telephoned him in Costa Rica to announce he had a contract out on Nasty Norman's life. LeBlanc shrugged.

In the fall of 1985, a small unofficial Costa Rican diplomatic party, headed by José Figueres, visited Havana on the Central American peace issue. While there, Figueres saw Vesco, who said that his "problem" with the Cubans had been solved. He had made an arrangement to pay the bill with the *finca* money. But, sitting on the rug with bare feet at Don Pepe's Cuban government guest house, he repeated the threat against LeBlanc. What agitated him more, though, was his son Tony.

One of the final ironies in the Vesco tale is the family that is supposed to have been sacred to him. Dawn and her son, Robert, Jr., seemed all right and came down from Florida to visit, but Danny, the eldest, broke with his father and did not speak to him for several years—in 1985, after calls from Bob, Danny relented for a while. Still, he evidently detested the onus attached to his name, and in 1986 changed it to Daniel Williams. Bobby Jr., who tried to hit Vesco with a coat rack in Cuba, served in the U.S. Army but only for a year. Tony's temper was a problem, and Bob sent him out of Cuba, but only briefly. ("Tony's problem," Meissner believed, "was that Bob was always on his back.") Stiff-upper-lip Pat was often depressed and had to leave Cuba for U.S. visits to preserve her sanity.

Vesco's relations with the Cubans soured not only because of money. In October 1983, a mob of reporters descended on Cuba after the U.S. Grenada invasion, and Vesco, with his love of publicity, made a furtive attempt to be interviewed, which the Cubans forbade. To them, Vesco had become an embarrassment, and they virtually begged Figueres to make unofficial arrangements to place New Jersey Bob in Rumania with whose President, Nicolae Ceausescu, Don Pepe was close. Figueres declined because, he said, Vesco had come to Cuba through the Nicaraguans and was no longer his responsibility.

Castro claimed that Vesco was not under house arrest or anything like it, seeming to imply that would have been illegal in Cuba, but Bob was tightly supervised, and Meissner had to obtain permission to see him. Vesco was not allowed to visit hotels, because he might meet reporters there, and sometimes couldn't even go shopping. Junco kept an eye on Bob, stateless, everywhere unwanted, everywhere regarded with suspicion, without real rights and privileges, subject to Cuban dictates. Vesco could hardly have been said to be free.

The Cubans didn't wish Vesco to talk about the activities he had engaged in on their behalf and, besides, felt an obligation to ensure his safety—the North American authorities had by no means lost interest in the fugitive whose seizure would have been as humiliating to Cuban security as his avoidance of arrest had embarrassed the United States. In fact, U.S. efforts were still under way. Ernest R. Keiser, a man in his early sixties, had successfully lured former CIA agent Edwin P. Wilson, the Libyan arms supplier, to the Dominican Republic, where he was refused entry and put on a plane to New York City. Keiser either approached, or was approached by, U.S. Attorneys and the U.S. marshals to capture other important fugitives and Vesco headed the list. Keiser, a U.S. marshal, and a government informant flew to Mexico City, where Keiser talked to Vesco on the phone, trying to convince him with details provided by the informant that the two had met before. He wanted to entice Vesco to the Bahamas, on the pretext of arranging another pelletizing deal, but, suspicious, Vesco shied off.

In 1985, Keiser, accused of larceny, was shot in the back the day before his fraud trial opened, forcing a postponement. Keiser vanished to become a fugitive himself. Keiser said that Vesco, or Wilson from his prison cell, might have arranged the shooting and the theft of his briefcase, but it seemed likely that the shot, which missed vital organs, had been arranged by Keiser himself.

In August, 1985, Cuba held a five-day conference on Third World debt, attended by more than one thousand Latin American politicians (though not the key ones to Castro's dismay), in which the Cuban leader urged cancellation of Latin debts to the U.S. as part of the liberation struggle. An NBC TV crew wanted a shot of Vesco. The stakeout, across the street from his house, began at dawn. Among the crew was Nicole Szulc, daughter of Tad Szulc, even then interviewing Castro for his book *Fidel,* which may have contributed to Fidel's anger over the incident. The photo shows a gaunt man in casual clothes with a lined and somber face, hardly the ebullient chief of International Controls. During the press conference after the closing session, Castro's voice rose as he cited complete details of the NBC caper. He conceded it was "probable" that Vesco lived in Cuba. He told the reporters, "I know you've become interested in Robert Vesco, more even than with the debt dialogue here . . . to divert attention . . . and this is taking place through the actions of the U.S. intelligence services." Castro denied that he had had "business dealings or economic interests" with Vesco who, he said, was "hunted like a deer through the world. . . . They're persecuting a man that's living with his wife and [family]. What do they want to do, take his eyes out, or turn him into ground meat?"

After the conference Fidel went into a tantrum associates described as similar to those of the early Cuban revolutionary period and which lasted several days. A psychologist friend was brought to calm him. "*Puta coño,*" Castro profanely kept calling Vesco, whom he had never met but whose presence had upstaged his meeting. "*Puta coño.*" Washington might have said something similar.

40

SOMETHING HAPPENED, BUT WHAT?

Like a vein of pure gold, riches glitter deep in the American dream. But dreams aren't meant to be interpreted literally—you must poke around in them to learn what they have to say, be it unconscious wishes or buried warnings about the future. The American dream isn't to be carried to extremes, even by those who attempt to claw their way to the top as the dream seems to urge. Restraints exist on those who would overstep; powerful prohibitions govern economic behavior, not merely against cheating and lying but excessiveness—too much ambition and greed.

Through smarts and luck, Vesco achieved the financial objectives of the American dream. When he gained control of Bernard Cornfeld's undisciplined IOS, he set his sights on becoming a world-class capitalist. What he lacked in education (a sore point with him), experience, and maturity, he tried to make up for by ingenuity, determination, and trickiness. In a circle that held the possibilities for good and evil, Vesco could make the full swing without trouble until he reached the last twenty degrees, and there ran into a blindspot. With IOS he had, as they say, the world by the tail, but he began to overreach.

Oddly perhaps, considering the emphasis he placed on his own mental abilities, a basic charge against Vesco was poor judgment. He erred in assessing how far rules could be bent without others perceiving them as broken, and "if everything that's right doesn't always look right," as Vesco said, a case can be made that everything ought to look right as well as be right—a disparity between the two being cause for caution, of which Vesco had little. Instead, in his hubris he defied the governmental gods and fell. There is an Italian word for this, probably the longest in the Italian language, *precipitevolissimevolmente,* meaning, roughly, "If you climb too high, you fall suddenly to the same spot you started from."

Vesco and his cohorts, for example, tried to set themselves up as venture capitalists, which was in the entrepreneurial spirit, all right, except that they used other people's money, not what they raised themselves, treating the IOS entities as a private preserve. ("We were trying to give the guys"—Meissner, LeBlanc, Graze, and Strickler—"a chance to do their thing.") The risks they took with other people's money increased as the SEC isolated them. And the human price was high. One German wrote the receivers that he was not only unemployable he was broke. He was a multiple amputee and had invested all his money in Venture Fund.

Vesco suffered from a shortcoming common enough in his native land—bravado. A more seasoned individual would probably have "walked away" from his overseas acquisition after SEC hostility toward it became apparent. Instead, convinced by top-flight legal talent, itself victim of hubris, a liking for high fees, and, as a result, a poor analysis of consequences, Vesco proceeded according to plan, thus challenging the mighty and self-righteous SEC. Vesco became a business rebel, but it wasn't as though he had a noble cause, only money and pride.

After the SEC accused him and others of looting, Vesco stumbled into a trap from which, given stubbornness and a certain romantic bravery—Vesco always maintained the United States persecuted him unjustly—there was no escape, especially after his campaign contribution to Nixon was revealed. Terrified of prison and convinced he would never get a fair trial, he made himself into a new sort of financial adventurer, a con man who persuaded several small nations that he was something like a private World Bank. Essentially a right-winger, he turned to Communist Cuba, where he inevitably ran into trouble again because of his manipulativeness and pathology.

Having concluded that Vesco had crook potential, the SEC intervened and a fiscal Greek tragedy was in the works. Over comparatively trivial (considering the consequences: the destruction of IOS) machinations—Vesco's takeover, which might have been viewed as a clever and distant ploy, and his misstatements about the ownership of Cornfeld's IOS shares—the SEC subjected Vesco's company, International Controls, to the toughest investigation it had ever launched, having as the objective the enforcement of a consent order with IOS (the SEC had agreed to leave the company alone provided it did no business in the United States) to which it attached an almost religious fervor. Vesco and the Commission became obsessed with each other. The agency deeply wanted to bring an alleged criminal to justice.

Vesco's movement of money out of an IOS fund—$20 million from Venture to LeBlanc's Globals—was designed, in part, to eliminate the SEC from the picture but achieved the opposite. The Commission bore down even harder, not only because it searched for any opportunity to prove the theft it fully expected, but because the transfer occurred in the teeth of its investigation, which the agency viewed as an affront. Still worse judgment on the Vesco group's part was to take $60 million from the Bank of New York for Inter-American.

Buried in the SEC complaint against Vesco et al. was the presumption of guilt. Given its negative reading of Vesco's character, the Commission acted as though the money *would* be stolen if the agency remained idle. That the boodle belonged to foreigners really didn't count; the alleged misappropriation did, even if the SEC had to apply its standards overseas. It was determined to pursue the "white whale," as it called "Moby Dick" Vesco, to the death.

The SEC hurled two types of harpoons—the investments that had been made and the diverted money. Always, the Commission maintained the investments were improper, designed to advance Vesco's "scheme," but the defense lawyers defended them transaction by transaction. That they were often not conducted at "arm's length" seemed indisputable, and you had to ask, even if you accepted Vesco's claim that he was trying to save IOS, whether that was any excuse to risk other people's money.

There *was* a choice—to put the swag in interest-bearing accounts and thus protect the fund shareholders—but Vesco followed a more aggressive if not fraudulent financial policy. Of the $224 misappropriated millions—a figure the SEC knew was vastly inflated as the press interpreted it; the number, as Vesco said, mainly referred to securities sales by the dollar funds—$60 million to Inter-American from Fund of Funds was the major piece of change, and Vesco controlled it. After serendipitous journeys arranged by LeBlanc, $37 million vanished into the maw of Bahamas Commonwealth Bank, which left $23 million that was, at best, squandered in Costa Rica and Spain, on the newspaper *Excelsior,* in land, prefab housing, the Spanish pants factory, twenty-five small investments, travel, offices, and so on. Every one of Inter-American's "investments" failed, a sad commentary and bound to provoke questions. How could investment folk presumably as sophisticated as the Vescoites—after all, they pared off IOS funds because they supposedly could handle them better—have made so many mistakes? They blamed SEC pressure, but what about Inter-American's distinguished board of directors who were supposed to pass on the outlays? Were they paid off? Why weren't business records preserved? (Vesco had a set on his boat but never turned them over. LeBlanc, Inter-American's banker, who wrote the checks, burned his records after the statute of limitations expired, he said). Why were memories so fallible? If money was purloined, the easiest place would have been from Inter-American, which never provided a report to Fund of Funds, as it was supposed to each month.

"Bob aside, from what I can tell, some of the so-called Vesco group," Meissner remarked, excluding himself, "through fees, loans they didn't repay, expense accounts, bonuses, perks, and so on, one way or another they *may* have dealt themselves a grand total of several million from Inter-American. But, don't forget, they felt unjustly accused, bitter, and entitled to something."

Some of the same questions dog Bahamas Commonwealth Bank. True, LeBlanc, who ran it, was heavily involved with his lawyers in a possible defense. True, he was often drunk. Still, a capable man who did all right for himself when he wasn't handling other people's money, LeBlanc, despite an investment committee at BCB, did so poorly as a banker as to raise doubts. For him, "We may have walked on a gray line—there was nothing wrong with that—but pressure pushed us into a black zone where we didn't want to be. We would have benefited from management fees but that's all. A combination of events forced us to be less than orthodox."

The unaccounted-for money at BCB remained another major mystery. The bank went bust because of uncollectible loans to W.H.O. Holdings, Bahamas World Airways, and so on, for a total of $60 million, about what was missing from other accounts. Eleven years on the job by 1986, the BCB receiver, Tony Jones, of Peat, Marwick, Mitchell concluded, "There is no clear evidence of money taken from the bank and put into Vesco's pocket. You can speculate that some of the transactions entered into may have been for his or LeBlanc's benefit, but proof is absent. Still, a deep hole exists—between $30 and $35 million—that could mean imprudent investments or misappropriated funds. I don't know."

Out of BCB went $8 million from Property Resources to Banco de Panama, and, lacking cooperation from Panamanian authorities, the receivers never found it. Two men, names known to the author, bragged openly to a third about pilfering the money from Panama—one more proof that funds were placed in exposed positions and could have been dipped into. Another loss was $20 million from IIT and perhaps $15 million belonging to Gulfstream. But a grand total of what was missing can't be arrived at because of the deliberate confusion, and lack of records, caused by Vesco and LeBlanc's games.

Was Vesco, abetted by LeBlanc, a thief and nothing but a thief as the SEC still contends? The facts don't always confirm the accusation, but Vesco was larcenous enough to look after his own interests first. Before the SEC complaint, IOS monies were used to benefit ICC stockholders, of which Vesco was the largest. After he fell into disgrace, Vesco's huge expenditures as a fugitive had to come from somewhere; the only logical somewhere was IOS or monies, like kickbacks, related to IOS. Vesco found ways to divert funds that weren't his. (His earlier gains must have been long spent.)

Milton Meissner's plan had been for IOS to liquidate itself, as a single receiver, but the SEC wouldn't hear of letting Vesco et al. anywhere near the boodle, and receivers were appointed in various jurisdictions, virtually a new industry. The sprawling nature of IOS, with a jungle of companies created by Cornfeld and Cowett, required that approach, but the enterprise was marked by conflict over what money "belonged" to whom. The receivers spoke of "my" money, meaning what each tried to collect for their respective shareholders. Every year the receivers convened, with perhaps a hundred people in attendance, and while they tried to thrash out their differences, lack of communication and disputes among the claimants was rife. The receivers were always curious how Vesco and LeBlanc seemed to know the results of their proceedings almost as quickly as they happened. After such gatherings, lawyers in attendance would phone other lawyers to tell what occurred, sometimes with incredulity, and word got back. Otherwise, the IOS liquidators had to file reports where the company was registered, St. John, New Brunswick, and the fugitives would send their own legal beagle to inspect them.

As of the time of the appointment of its receivers, Venture Fund financial statements showed each share of Venture to be worth $8.43. Despite the $20 million loss incurred by LeBlanc and Vesco, as of 1986 the Venture Fund receivers had paid $9.00 per share, with more to come. When the IIT liquidators were appointed, the IIT financial statements said that each IIT share was worth $7.50, but that included the $15 million lost in Gulfstream. As of 1986, the IIT liquidators had paid dividends of $7.50 a share, with more to come. Property Resources recovered nearly $150 million with $25 million to come. BCB, paying about 65 cents on the dollar, returned $75–80 million, with $45–50 million to come.

When the FOF liquidator was appointed, the FOF records (prepared by LeBlanc) said that the FOF assets were worth $98,674,000. That figure was illusory since the $98 million included the $60 million that had been sent to Inter-American. Accordingly, the realistic value of the FOF assets as of the appointment of the FOF liquidator was under $40 million. However, as of 1986, the FOF liquidator had sent the shareholders

$134 million, with more to come. That result was due, in large measure, to the active litigation conducted by FOF, in which more than $100 million was recovered from Willkie Farr & Gallagher, Bank of New York, Arthur Andersen, former IOS accountants, ICC, BCB, American National Bank and Trust Company, and so on.

How much the liquidations cost was unknown because the court-appointed receivers had no obligation to report them to a central source, and didn't. A reasonable estimate was between $50 and $100 million. The receivers justified the amount as being from interest, but the money came indirectly from the shareholders who, waiting years, were paid in post-inflation dollars, without interest. At least, the receivers said, they had salvaged something, for otherwise the vulturous Vesco et al. would have picked the IOS carcass clean. Torrents of "What If?" questions follow. What if the SEC had ignored IOS? Would Vesco, as with the potentially profitable Resorts International transaction, have been able to pull it off? Or would his character defects—manipulation and the inbred habit of dissimulation—have prevailed against the interests of IOS?

Ironically, the pool of "black" or "hot" money on which Vesco, the lawyers, and the rest had relied on not to be reclaimed and, thus, to provide $200 million or so for a new offshore corporation proved to be a myth. Though it took four mailings and several years, the dogged FOF receivers using the IOS record center at Nyon, at considerable cost, reached 95 percent of FOF investors representing 95 percent of the assets. Other receivers had similar results. Vesco, though he told LeBlanc he planned to retire, was still short of his thirty-seventh birthday when the SEC acted in 1972. His ego demands were immense, all the more so because by the tenets of the American dream he had triumphed, and early. He had boasted about his wealth and congratulated himself on his shrewdness. He developed the sort of pride that can't take rebuffs, and the SEC accusations against him, fair or not, and whether he admitted it or not, were a devastating blow to his sense of superiority.

Though Vesco pretended his troubles with the U.S. government would be resolved, and put great effort into a solution, with each passing year his situation deteriorated, and lost was any rationale that he had acted in the best interests of IOS; he had made a mess of it instead. He'd tried to play with the system, but all he got was a bum check made out to bearer. Carried on the psychopathology that must have always lurked unseen, Vesco began to descend, with a strong assist from law enforcement, into eccentricity.

None of the seven criminal defendants lives rich, with the exception of Gilbert Straub. By SEC accounting *each* owed, as of 1983, $640 million, the $224 million said to be purloined, plus compound interest, and the figure rises every year. (Occasionally, they receive bills.) How were the Seven Samurai to pay?

Milton Meissner, who might have saved IOS had he been strong enough to withstand Vesco, lives with a lovely woman in a rented house in Costa Rica. He has severe medical problems, including cancer and poor eyesight. In his early seventies, his U.S. assets, including his life insurance policy, having been attached, he survives on Social Security and on the interest of his principal, $120,000, he claims. As interest rates descended, his financial situation became grimmer. Rationally, he believed, he contemplated suicide.

Meissner, who answers the phone with "Bueno," was easily approachable after being assured I intended to be objective. He spoke with candor, and I found Bud's crookedness was impossible to believe.

The same with Stanley Graze. He, too, has had medical problems and, in his late sixties, has survived them. Like Meissner, Graze, the former IOS investment advisor, had a modest income partly from Social Security. He has a young wife and four children, the oldest being six. He says he is happy and has no desire to return to the United States.

The rest of the criminal defendants were about fifty years of age in 1986. Gilbert Straub inherited considerable money, partly from his father, who had substantial holdings in Green Stamps. Straub and his wife live in Germany, London, Panama City, and the Bahamas.

Richard Clay became a born-again Christian and lives modestly in Nassau, working in real estate. He speaks of the anguish of being a fugitive.

Ulrich Strickler bought a dairy farm in Costa Rica, succeeded, and sold it for much more than he paid. He worked for a Swiss firm in South America and then returned to Switzerland, learning the authorities there had no arrest warrant out for him, as they did for most of the others.

Norman LeBlanc spent years, he said, pulling himself out of a psychological slump. His cheerful wife, his former secretary, raises horses at their *finca* outside San José, and Norman works hard as an investment adviser, earning the respect of his Costa Rican clients.

Martyrs, as they consider themselves, they have paid a heavy price in exile. In his own way, each has contrived to patch together some sort of life, though not without anger and defensiveness, and has found some measure of tranquillity. Perhaps they changed, but their leader still had ambitions about being a master financier long after reality had decreed otherwise, and, of the Seven Samurai, he, the boldest, suffered most, along with his family. There was no internal accounting and no peace.

Epilogue

Vesco Visited

I had been tracking Robert Vesco for over a year and had all but abandoned hope, although, in Cuba, he was tantalizingly close to the United States. The fascination he exerted on me concerned a theory I hit on during my research. To me, Vesco had a secret nobody else seemed to have guessed, but I had to see him myself to be certain.

I had been in Havana in 1985, but Cuban officials, learning of my presence and purpose, had told me rather abruptly to leave. I had lost my visa but they could have issued another. "The time isn't right," they said, without explaining. "Go out. Come back. Then we'll cooperate with your project." But subsequent visa requests were ignored. The Cuban government didn't say no, but it didn't say yes, either, and I began to think it was the fugitive himself who didn't want to talk to me. Still, José Figueres, three times President of Costa Rica, who had shielded Vesco during his nearly six years there, spoke to Bob, urging him to clear up, once and for all, the question that had dogged Vesco since 1972: had he misappropriated, or swiped, the kingly sum of $224 million? Figueres, approaching eighty, wanted Vesco off his conscience, one way or another. His impression was that Vesco agreed to be interviewed, although, given the convoluted nature of the fugitive's responses, it was hard to be sure.

In July 1986, I was invited as a writer to attend a ceremony in Nicaragua and went, out of curiosity, not partisanship. While there, to prove I had exhausted every avenue, but with little anticipation of success, I applied once more for a Cuban visa, this time as a tourist, not Vesco analyst, and for $10 the slip of paper was mine. No attempt was made that I could discern to run a check on me.

I had been warned in the United States that I would be foolish to visit Vesco because my personal safety might be at risk, and I felt somewhat apprehensive. So did Enrique Carreras, José Figueres's right-hand man, who was to accompany me because he knew Vesco and his way around Havana. Our worry wasn't the fugitive but the Cubans. Suppose the Cuban consulate in Managua had made a mistake in letting me in? Suppose, since we planned to approach Vesco without official permission, they arrested me. "You might spend a few days in jail," Kiki Carreras told me. He added reassuringly, "But only a few."

On Wednesday, July 30, Carreras, Leslie Mandel, an American friend, and I flew from Managua, Nicaragua, to Havana on Air Cubana. I passed through customs without incident. Our first step was to rent a car, a Fiat, and drive to the house where the Vesco family had last lived as far as Kiki knew. He recognized it by an oddly shaped TV antenna Vesco himself had made. The house was white, two stories, with a fence and a hedge. I parked around the corner because a man stood outside who might have been with Cuban security, Carreras thought. He approached quietly. Both the man, and a woman who emerged, affirmed that whoever had lived there had left the month before. As I drove away, the man eyed us suspiciously.

At two in the morning on the day that Carreras left Costa Rica, Figueres suddenly remembered that Vesco had called several weeks before with a new phone number, for use only in an emergency. We checked into the Hotel Riviera in Havana and phoned the number Figueres had provided—Carreras hadn't wanted to announce our arrival because he feared the fugitive might shy off. Now, Kiki asked for "Tom." "Who's Tom?" I said after he'd hung up, and he said, "Tom is the name Bob uses." "Any last name?" "Just Tom, but there isn't any Tom there or Patricia, either." I was depressed—we had no other leads.

We had the inspiration to use Figueres's name, and Kiki

phoned again to announce that he had a note for Tom from José Figueres of Central America. (In it, Don Pepe Figueres once more urged Vesco to see me.) This time the response was equivocal: Carreras should call back at ten in the morning as if whoever answered the phone would decide by then whether Tom was there or not. Hope flickered, though I remained dubious, and Kiki, too. At 4 A.M., loud knocking sounded at my door and I half expected to find the Cuban police, but it was Carreras demanding the keys to the Fiat. At six he called. He had a second Vesco number.

Unable to sleep, the Costa Rican had gone in search of another night owl, a prominent member of Cuban internal security whom he found at an outdoor party filled with happy Cubans. The security man and he went somewhere for a drink, and Kiki mentioned the note he wanted to deliver. The security guy called his office and returned with another number for "Tom." We knew for certain now that Cuban security kept track of Vesco.

Leslie had spent a good part of the night flipping through the latest Havana telephone book we could find. Dated 1979, it had 800 pages and contained about 190,000 names. Our notion was that while people move in such countries, phone numbers don't, and with an astonishing diligence she discovered the number on page 618, and the address to go with it.

Carreras told us in the morning that the location was not too far from the hotel, or so he thought. She commenced looking for the second number, finding that, too, in what appeared the same neighborhood. If worse came to worst, we would try a frontal assault, although for the moment caution seemed the better tactic.

At 8 A.M., Kiki, who still couldn't sleep, called phone number two and got Dawn Vesco, Bob's daughter. Carreras knew her and they exchanged salutations. Dawn said she'd come to live in Cuba with her young son. Her mother, Patricia, was on "vacation," a rather illuminating term that probably meant the United States. Her father would be back in a few minutes, Dawn told Kiki, who woke me with the good news. At eleven, Carreras called phone number one, learning that Tom was expected in a few hours. He called Dawn again and was told the same.

The day before I had almost convinced myself I would not find Vesco and today I was sure I would, but the afternoon passed without word. I sat restlessly by the Riviera's magnificent saltwater pool. I went to my room on the sixteenth floor. Just before six, Carreras burst in, ran to the window, and pointed down. "See the lamppost by the pool? No, that one, with a little table beneath it. That's the spot Vesco wants. He'll be here in ten minutes."

On Carreras's instructions, I placed myself near, but not too near, the appointed table underneath the outdoor light. An hour passed, dusk fell, and Kiki grew even more anxious, rising, pacing, peering, sitting, rising, pacing . . . his prestige as Vesco-finder was on the line. At last he made thumbs up, and a bearded figure in a sheer cotton shirt, shorts, sandals, and a white sunhat, a little over six feet tall, appeared from nowhere. Vesco! He took a chair with his back to me. At the same moment, three Cuban men in street clothes slid into the table between Vesco and me like a wall. Though they ordered beer and chatted, they sat forward alertly and I had to conclude they were bodyguards, which surprised me. I'd assumed that on this Communist island Vesco would feel safe from any threat by U.S. authorities.

Unable to resist, I took quick steps to Carreras's side. Vesco's head swiveled toward me—I didn't imagine a deeply startled mouth—and Kiki said brusquely, "Leave." I returned to my table. Kiki, then, hadn't broken the news, didn't want to spook the prey who, as I'd seen, was nervous enough. More minute-hours passed and it was I who was nervous, because I feared Carreras would overdo the preliminaries and "Tom" would escape. I marched over, sat at Vesco's side, put out my hand and said, "Hello, Bob. It's time we met." And he said, "I just heard you were here."

The smile displayed small teeth. The nose between the dark glasses was slightly pocked. The face behind the long, black, and grayless, probably dyed, beard was hard to fathom. He bore no resemblance to the overweight man I'd seen in photos, being thin but not gaunt, and handsomer than I'd expected. He looked to be in good health. He spoke well and carefully. He exudes, I thought as we went on, a sense of self-possession bordering on arrogance, though of a type I wasn't familiar with. Whom did Vesco remind me of? I toyed with Darth Vader of "Star Wars"—because of the beard and sunglasses, I suppose. No, Tom made me think for whatever reason of Bernard Cornfeld whose company, IOS, Vesco was supposed to have looted. Still, I strongly doubted that Vesco's apparent confidence was real.

On my earlier trip to Cuba, I had brought pepperoni sausage that Vesco was supposed to be fond of, his brand of cigarettes, Kools, and fine chocolate for Pat on the mistaken assumption the items wouldn't be available in Havana. Before my ouster I'd requested a Cuban official to deliver them. Had he? Yes, Vesco had received the presents, he said without interest or thanks. I mentioned some of his old associates I'd talked to, but he put me off with an extended palm. What he intensely wanted to know was how I'd gotten a visa to Cuba.

"I applied," I said. "Where?" "In Managua," though Carreras must have told him. Tom had further questions about the visa, all of which pointed to a conclusion Kiki had attempted, he later told me, to disabuse Vesco of, that I was from the Central Intelligence Agency. Me? The CIA? The notion was preposterous. "Well, you had trouble with your visa, didn't you? Don't you think if I'd wanted to see you, you would have gotten a visa a lot quicker?" "I thought you wanted to see me," I said, irritated. "You told Don Pepe Figueres so." "Well," Tom said, "words are words. Maybe I didn't really want to." But I knew, behind the CIA suspicion, dwindling in his mind, and the verbal fencing, Vesco wished to talk with me. The question was how much and on what terms.

I decided to provoke him. Against Vesco were seven counts for obstruction of justice, conspiracy to defraud the United States, defrauding ICC (the $50,000 that went to Henry Buhl), etc., each carrying a fine of $10,000 and five years in jail. I said, "Why don't you give yourself up? I've spoken with lawyers; they believe—given how long ago it happened, the lack of witnesses now, the shaky nature of the government's case—that you wouldn't get much more than six months." Tom laughed at the notion of turning himself in, and I wondered if fugitivehood hadn't become suitable to him in a way, as an ego prop, because it provided him with identity. But he changed the subject.

Did I, as Carreras had hinted, have the manuscript of my book on him with me? I nodded. He insisted on reading it before we proceeded, and I, who wanted as much contact with the subject as possible, said I'd be happy to comply but wanted to speak with him first, if only to explain the tentative nature of some of what I'd written. We rapidly reached an impasse, and the world's most famous fugitive said he had an "engagement" and would like to confer with Carreras alone before he departed. We shook hands and I left.

"What did you think of him?" Carreras asked.

"He's sort of impressive. I liked him."

"People do. He liked you, too."

"He's a paranoid first-class, of course," I went on. "Gets up in the morning, puts on his paranoia suit and doesn't take it off until bedtime."

"He's not that bad."

"Oh yes he is. You'll see."

At three in the morning, Vesco arrived at the hotel nightclub with Junco, his Cuban government nursemaid and liaison. Dracula, it seemed, would only come out after dark. Carreras, still up, asked about the "engagement," and Junco, out of Vesco-Tom's earshot, said he'd wanted to return home to his young son Patrick, Dawn and her son, and Tony, Bob's second eldest son, to be sure everything was all right in Pat's absence.

"He's very protective toward his family," Kiki said. "That's the key to understanding him."

"Maybe the family is his way of explaining to himself why he's in jail," I offered.

"He's not in jail."

"Sure he's in jail. Cuba for him is a jail."

The deadlock continued on Friday. Vesco would meet with me only after he read my manuscript, and I would give it to him only after we spoke again. Vesco dispatched a messenger, or guard, to the hotel to fetch it and phoned Carreras four times—he would not call me directly—but I wouldn't budge, though he sent me a message: "Tell him if he won't give me the book he might as well get the next plane out of Cuba."

On Saturday I capitulated—I'd let him have the manuscript, unflattering parts and all, though not the chapters on Cuba and drugs, which I'd left behind. It seemed the only way. Carreras mentioned that when a writer had let Howard Hughes, Vesco's idol read his manuscript on him, Hughes had torn it up. That led to a scramble for a copying machine—I had another manuscript in New York but this dogeared one had been heavily worked on. The hotel copier was broken, as I somehow anticipated, and this being an alternative workless Cuban Saturday, no copier in Havana seemed available.

While we discussed what to do, including the idea of retyping the sections handwritten during the trip, another Vesco messenger-guard came for the manuscript and departed without it leaving a note with still a third phone number. Carreras called; Vesco was at another house, an hour's drive outside Havana, which he seemed to rent for weekends, though nothing, I felt sure, was a certainty in the shadowy world "Tom" had created for himself.

I made a suggestion: Carreras, in the rented car, could carry the manuscript, catch up on badly needed sleep while Vesco read it, and then bring it back. I also sent Leslie Mandel's camera for Kiki to photograph Vesco. Carreras departed after another conversation with Vesco, who warned him about being followed.

"By whom?" I said contemptuously.

"By you," Kiki said.

Kiki returned late that evening. "He got a kick out of reading about his old days. He's really flattered that you should have researched his life so carefully."

"How far did he get?"

"About a quarter of the way. He's a slow reader."

"I told you he would be. Quick with figures yes, but words no. Words aren't his element. Where's the manuscript?"

"He's still reading. He'll have it back in twenty-four hours."

"And the camera?"

"He kept that too."

In the package for Bob was a letter from *Fortune* magazine assigning me a piece on Vesco in Cuba, and I wondered if I'd thrown too much at the man I'd labeled paranoid. How would he react? Would he indeed tear up the manuscript? Sunday passed without word and neither the manuscript nor the camera came back. We drove to Barlovento for lunch and saw another previous Vesco house, on the yacht canal, pleasant but modest. When we returned to the Riviera, Carreras and I had a drink, and I asked, "What's Vesco up to here? You've spent time with him."

"He says he's sort of retired. He has a small office in a suburb —don't ask me where—works part-time. He does deals. . . ."

"According to him."

"Small ones, two or three a year. He tries to triangularize merchandise—chemicals, fertilizers, oil; he still has other contacts—but he couldn't be very successful since he can't travel or operate normally, and he hasn't been able to do a deal for the Cubans. He's having to cut back and he sold his boat or boats," said Kiki in his excellent English.

"He can't be happy, can he?"

"The Cuban people and he have something in common, he says, though he's not a believer in ideologies. They have to survive as best they can, as does he. He stays out of trouble. He's not watched by the Cuban government but he is escorted. He's pleased that his son Patrick does well in school, and Tony's in guidance. He pretends he's happy to Pat, and she pretends to believe him, but he'd like to get out and live in Costa Rica or Panama, if they would have him."

"Any chance of that?"

"I doubt it. But he'd also like to set up a meeting with you after tomorrow night in a different country, if he can arrange it. He suggests Budapest or Peking." I laughed.

Early Sunday evening there was the most violent electrical storm I'd ever experienced. Scissors of lightning cut the sky. The wind rose. Leslie Mandel and I took refuge by the pool from which, through a glass wall, the Malecon, the road along the sea, could be observed and the ocean behind it. Carreras appeared in the gloom, agitated, and said in a hoarse whisper, "It's you or him. Either you go or he goes."

"He?"

"Vesco. He's over there. Who do you think the waiter is for?"

In a corner sat bearded Tom. I learned afterward that Vesco's

CIA suspicion had changed—found a different target—not me but my companion.

Leaving, I nodded sardonically at him. He remained expressionless. After all, as I knew by then, he had agreed to meet me the following day, and his security concerns seemed ever more symptomatic. He said to Carreras, during the storm, "See that guy in the car? If he's hit by lightning, they'll claim I blew him away with a flame thrower." According to Carreras, the van was of a type used by the U.S. Special Interest Section—there is, of course, no American Embassy in Havana. Leslie and I watched from the hotel window as two automobiles drew up. Vesco climbed into one. He had that evening not three but four bodyguards apparently. And he hadn't really left, just created a "diversion."

In the morning, Carreras returned the camera that Vesco had given him, but not the manuscript. He also gave me a letter, written by Vesco, that I was to rewrite in my own hand and sign.

August 4, 1986

Mr. Robert Vesco
Havana, Cuba

Dear Bob,

I wish to express my thanks and gratitude for the interview you gave me last Friday, August the first, here in Havana.

By having sent the manuscript on the book I've written on you through Enrique Carreras, I hope you appreciate the trust I have in you. Please return the manuscript today, Monday, to me personally when we meet again this evening.

Sincerely,

Arthur Herzog

A new reason for anxiety had appeared: our cover had been blown. The Cubans knew why I was there. Might they prevent Vesco from appearing? "What's the purpose of the letter?" I asked.

"Public relations with the Cubans. He says three journalists a month, on a slow one, try to see him. He's afraid of putting too much pressure on his hosts."

I rewrote and signed the letter. "When is this famous meeting to take place?"

"Between six and six-thirty."

Six, six-thirty, eight, eight-thirty came and went. I was more and more convinced Vesco wouldn't show, and decided to end the book with "Robert Vesco also stole my manuscript." I went down to Carreras's room. Beads of sweat on his upper lip, he tried to call phone number two, the one Dawn had answered, but, because of the storm, the line was dead, and number one didn't answer. On the sixteenth floor again, in desperation I worked on the Vesco paranoid angle, the one I'd brought to Cuba and was more and more convinced was correct.

After I returned to the United States, I checked with an eminent psychiatrist, Dr. Arnold Cooper, Professor of Psychiatry at Cornell University Medical College, in New York, and former president of the American Psychoanalytic Association, as to what paranoia's most important symptoms were. I meant "pure" paranoia, not that touched by delusionary schizophrenia. True paranoids, I'd learned, were comparatively rare, though statistics were lacking.

Cooper said, without first-hand knowledge of my subject, "Hypervigilance is one. The paranoid is always alert to danger. He or she deeply believes in elaborate notions of self-defense. In their minds, they have to scheme because others scheme against them. They can be likable, clever, intelligent, seem reasonable and calm on the surface, but if you look beneath you find unrealistic and irrational ideas hidden away to which they respond. They have highly grandiose visions about being kings of the universe. To them no limit exists on their ability to bring about what they want."

"Would gambling fit in?" I said, recalling Vesco's casino habits.

"It might. The paranoid can beat the odds, beat the system, beat the universe." Cooper continued: "They don't have close relationships—the wife of a paranoid man is never really told what he's up to mentally, and becomes an appendage. Truth to the paranoid has no meaning, one way or another. He can do illegal things and justify them to himself. And, if you believe everyone's an enemy, and has to be dealt with unscrupulously, people will treat you as an enemy, too, and deal with you unscrupulously. I don't know when the symptoms begin to show—the research on paranoia isn't all in—but I'd think although it's a middle–old-age disease, some of them, like grandiosity, would appear pretty early."

In my Havana hotel room, thinking along the same lines, I pondered the many pieces of Vesco's story—the iron-hard determination to succeed displayed by the adolescent who I doubted had time for recreation; appearing in a homburg and suit on a hot summer day; the "first call" to Europe from a car; the "grandiosity syndrome" Payn talked about; "Would you believe the U.S. government the next IOS acquisition?"; the fear of losing control and the inspection of every piece of paper that left ICC; the lie about how much ELS stock was owned and untruths about Bernie's shares; the lawyers' suspicions about Bob's veracity; Pat Vesco's seeming naïveté; the single-minded quest of an offshore empire; the what-must-have-been-traumatic effect of a night in jail and abhorrence of it; the threats to steal; the uneasiness Vesco generated, especially with the SEC; the decision to defy it; the unrewarded Nixon contribution; the tremendous sums Vesco spent; the hiding of money by Vesco and LeBlanc (I would read that paranoia *à deux* was possible); the complex machinations with Property Resources stock and the Libyan planes and oil; the inability to stay out of the limelight in Costa Rica; disguises and the frantic flights around the Caribbean; even the drug trade, if that aspect reflected Vesco's belief he could do and get away with anything. . . . The items, singly, might not have meant much, but together they added up to a case. The symptoms may have strongly affected Vesco's life and career even before he became a fugitive (itself a probable paranoid act); if I was right, afterward it became full-blown. Of course, I could have been wrong. Bob might say that night, "Come on over to the house and meet the kids. I'm sorry Pat isn't here. Let me explain how I got where I am. Shit, was that stupid. Maybe, if I tell the U.S. government I'm turning myself in, and I let them in on my secrets—I have some, believe me—they'll give me a break. I'm not really so bad."

At 10 P.M., the phone sounded. "Contact," Carreras cried. "He wants me to come downstairs."

"You! What about me?"

"He wants to talk to me first."

"Again! He's talked to you I don't know how many times."

"That's the way he wishes it."

I had utterly given up. "Tell him if I don't get that manuscript back I'll kill him."

"You sound like him," Kiki said blandly.

A few whiskies later, at midnight, I answered the phone and heard Carreras say, "The lobby." We walked outside and down the Malecon. After a few steps Kiki stopped and glanced back to be sure we weren't followed—he had passed, I thought, into Vesco's secret world. We turned the corner and went a little further until, standing before me in the dark, was a man in shorts and a short-sleeved shirt.

"Here's your manuscript," Vesco said, handing me the same shopping bag in which it had departed. "Let's talk over there."

We entered a small, dimly lit park before what seemed to be a housing project. I could almost smell the security guards, but Carreras had wandered elsewhere. The fugitive sat calmly on a bench, as did I.

He sounded clear and rational. He wasn't wearing sunglasses, and the eyes, as best I could make them out, looked alert and focused. I asked a question or two:

"What do you live on?"

"I work like everyone else."

"Why do you need guards?"

"I've always had guards."

"I'd like to meet Pat and the kids."

"You won't," he said. But with a hint of "until." "I've read your book."

The only objection he seemed to have was remarks about his son Tony which on legal grounds I subsequently omitted. "Not true." He felt compelled to protect Tony but not himself. I didn't, but soon did, understand.

Vesco rose and sat impatiently like a busy corporate executive walking around, when all he had was time. We talked idly some more.

"I'd like to see you in daylight."

"You will, if . . ."

"What about the assignment from *Fortune?*" (I almost added, "You always wanted to be on the cover of *Fortune* and here's your chance, although under different circumstances.")

"Oh, plenty of people have come down with *Fortune* assignments. I don't think I'll oblige, at least not yet."

His need for control was nearly palpable. It was almost as if our positions were reversed, with me as supplicant and he as ruler who dispensed his favors, instead of the truth: I could leave Cuba at will and he, terrified of the United States, could not. His central fears tethered him with bonds of psychological steel. He came to the point.

"Your book is incomplete."

"What about my accounts of your breathtaking departures from all those places?"

The faint smile told me what I suspected—he'd enjoyed his hair-raising escapades, which must have confirmed the fears that already gripped him. But they weren't games. They were his reality at the deepest level. "You have most but not all of it." That, I thought, was undoubtedly true, especially the shadowy part of his existence over the past thirteen years.

"What about the rest?"

"It's my story. Talk to my lawyer. The kids have trusts that include literary rights."

He bargained, as I'd assumed he would. "We'll see," I said, feeling almost sympathetic, though the SEC would laugh at me for failing to understand the nature of pure evil. But I wasn't a gnostic who believed in the sharp split between good and bad. I was firmly in the psychoanalytic camp.

He would make arrangements for our next meeting. As he walked away from me, I called, "Bob, was it all worth it?"

Vesco didn't reply. He climbed into one of the two East European cars, his security men around him like a flock of birds.

INDEX